SUPERMAN
RETURNS

THE MOVIE AND OTHER TALES
OF THE MAN OF STEEL

SUPERMAN RETURNS: THE MOVIE AND
OTHER TALES OF THE MAN OF STEEL
Published by Titan Books. Cover and compilation
copyright © 2006 DC Comics. All Rights Reserved.

Originally published in single magazine form in SUPERMAN RETURNS:
THE MOVIE ADAPTATION, THE AMAZING WORLD OF SUPERMAN
(METROPOLIS EDITION) #1, THE ADVENTURES OF SUPERMAN #575,
SUPERMAN #185, ACTION COMICS #810, and SUPERMAN SECRET
FILES AND ORIGINS 2005. Copyright © 1973, 2000, 2002, 2004, 2006
DC Comics. All Rights Reserved. All characters, their distinctive
likenesses and related elements featured in this publication
are trademarks of DC Comics. The stories, characters and
incidents featured in this publication are entirely fictional.
DC Comics does not read or accept unsolicited
submissions of ideas, stories or artwork.

Titan Books, a division of Titan Publishing Group Ltd.
144 Southwark Street, London SE1 0UP.
Printed in Canada. This edition first published: June 2006.
ISBN: 1 84576 282 7. ISBN-13: 9781845762827.
A CIP catalogue record for this title is available from the British Library.
Publication design by Peter Hamboussi.

1 2 3 4 5 6 7 8 9 10

SUPERMAN CREATED BY JERRY SIEGEL AND JOE SHUSTER

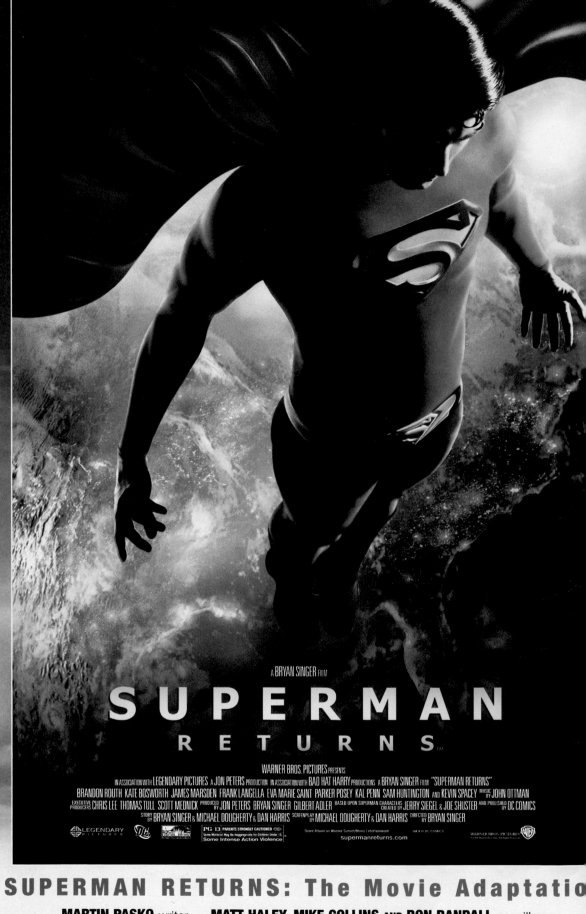

A BRYAN SINGER FILM

S U P E R M A N
R E T U R N S ™

WARNER BROS. PICTURES PRESENTS

IN ASSOCIATION WITH LEGENDARY PICTURES A JON PETERS PRODUCTION IN ASSOCIATION WITH BAD HAT HARRY PRODUCTIONS A BRYAN SINGER FILM "SUPERMAN RETURNS"
BRANDON ROUTH KATE BOSWORTH JAMES MARSDEN FRANK LANGELLA EVA MARIE SAINT PARKER POSEY KAL PENN SAM HUNTINGTON AND KEVIN SPACEY MUSIC BY JOHN OTTMAN
EXECUTIVE PRODUCERS CHRIS LEE THOMAS TULL SCOTT MEDNICK PRODUCED BY JON PETERS BRYAN SINGER GILBERT ADLER BASED UPON SUPERMAN CHARACTERS CREATED BY JERRY SIEGEL & JOE SHUSTER AND PUBLISHED BY DC COMICS
STORY BY BRYAN SINGER & MICHAEL DOUGHERTY & DAN HARRIS SCREENPLAY BY MICHAEL DOUGHERTY & DAN HARRIS DIRECTED BY BRYAN SINGER

LEGENDARY PICTURES   DC   PG-13 PARENTS STRONGLY CAUTIONED Some Material May Be Inappropriate for Children Under 13. Some Intense Action Violence   Score Album on Warner Sunset/Rhino Entertainment   TM & © DC COMICS   WARNER BROS. PICTURES
supermanreturns.com

SUPERMAN RETURNS: The Movie Adaptatio

MARTIN PASKO writer   **MATT HALEY, MIKE COLLINS** AND **RON RANDALL** pencillers

NATHAN EYRING   LARRY MOLINAR colorists   **KEN LOPEZ** letterer

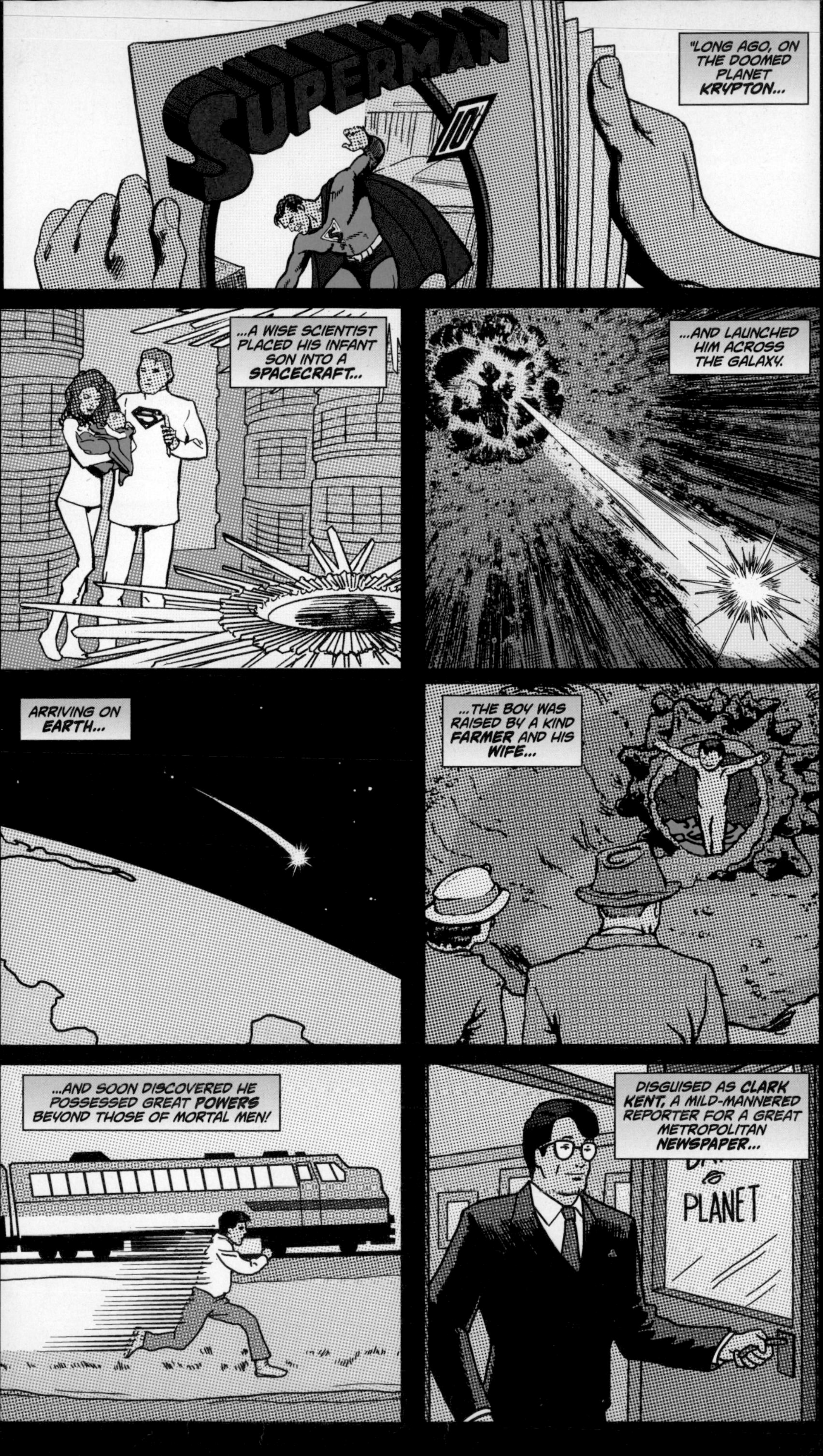
SUPERMAN
10¢
"LONG AGO, ON THE DOOMED PLANET KRYPTON...
...A WISE SCIENTIST PLACED HIS INFANT SON INTO A SPACECRAFT...
...AND LAUNCHED HIM ACROSS THE GALAXY.
ARRIVING ON EARTH...
...THE BOY WAS RAISED BY A KIND FARMER AND HIS WIFE...
...AND SOON DISCOVERED HE POSSESSED GREAT POWERS BEYOND THOSE OF MORTAL MEN!
DISGUISED AS CLARK KENT, A MILD-MANNERED REPORTER FOR A GREAT METROPOLITAN NEWSPAPER...
PLANET

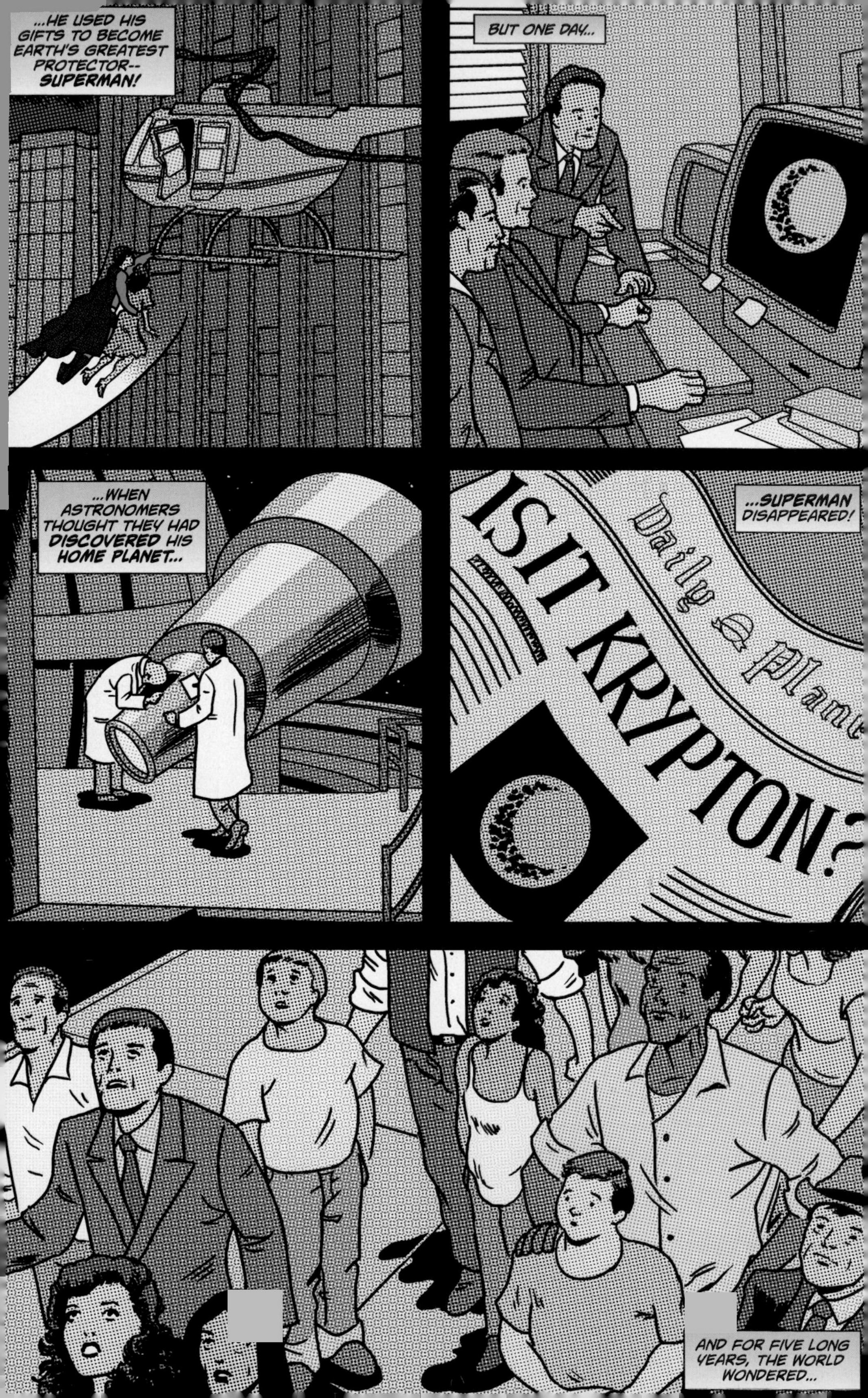

...HE USED HIS GIFTS TO BECOME EARTH'S GREATEST PROTECTOR-- SUPERMAN!
BUT ONE DAY...
...WHEN ASTRONOMERS THOUGHT THEY HAD DISCOVERED HIS HOME PLANET...
IS IT KRYPTON?
...SUPERMAN DISAPPEARED!
AND FOR FIVE LONG YEARS, THE WORLD WONDERED...

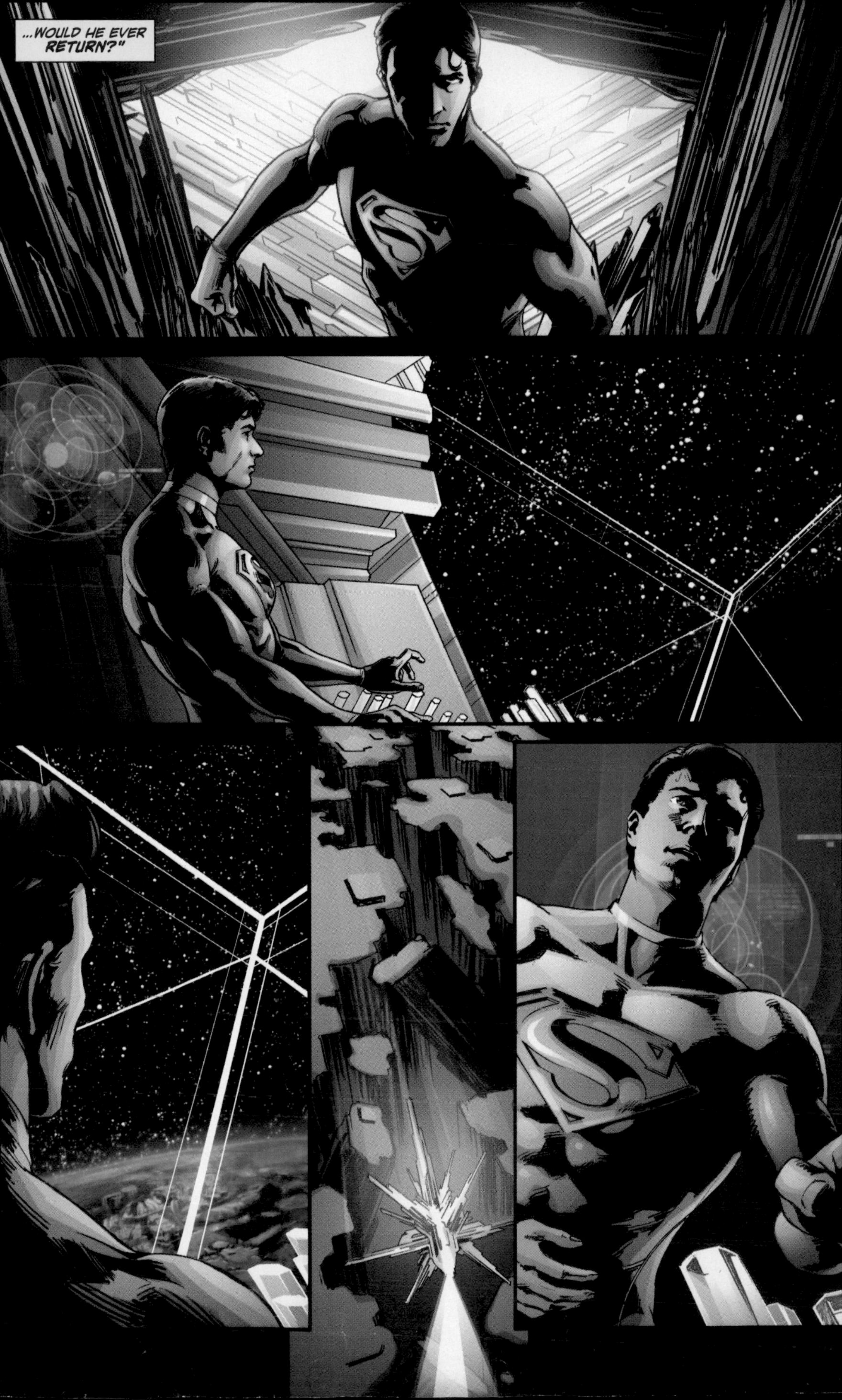
...WOULD HE EVER RETURN?"

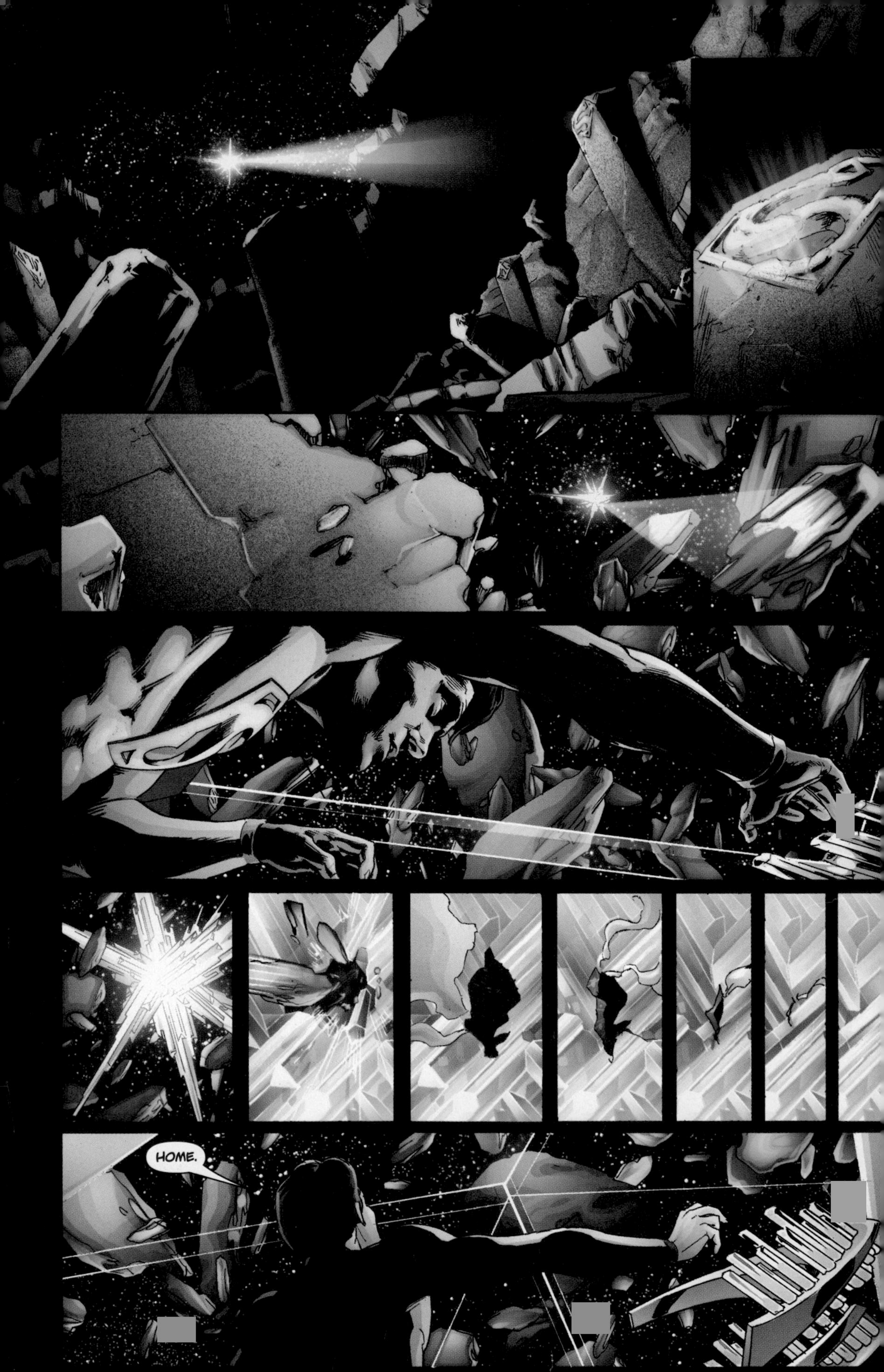
HOME.

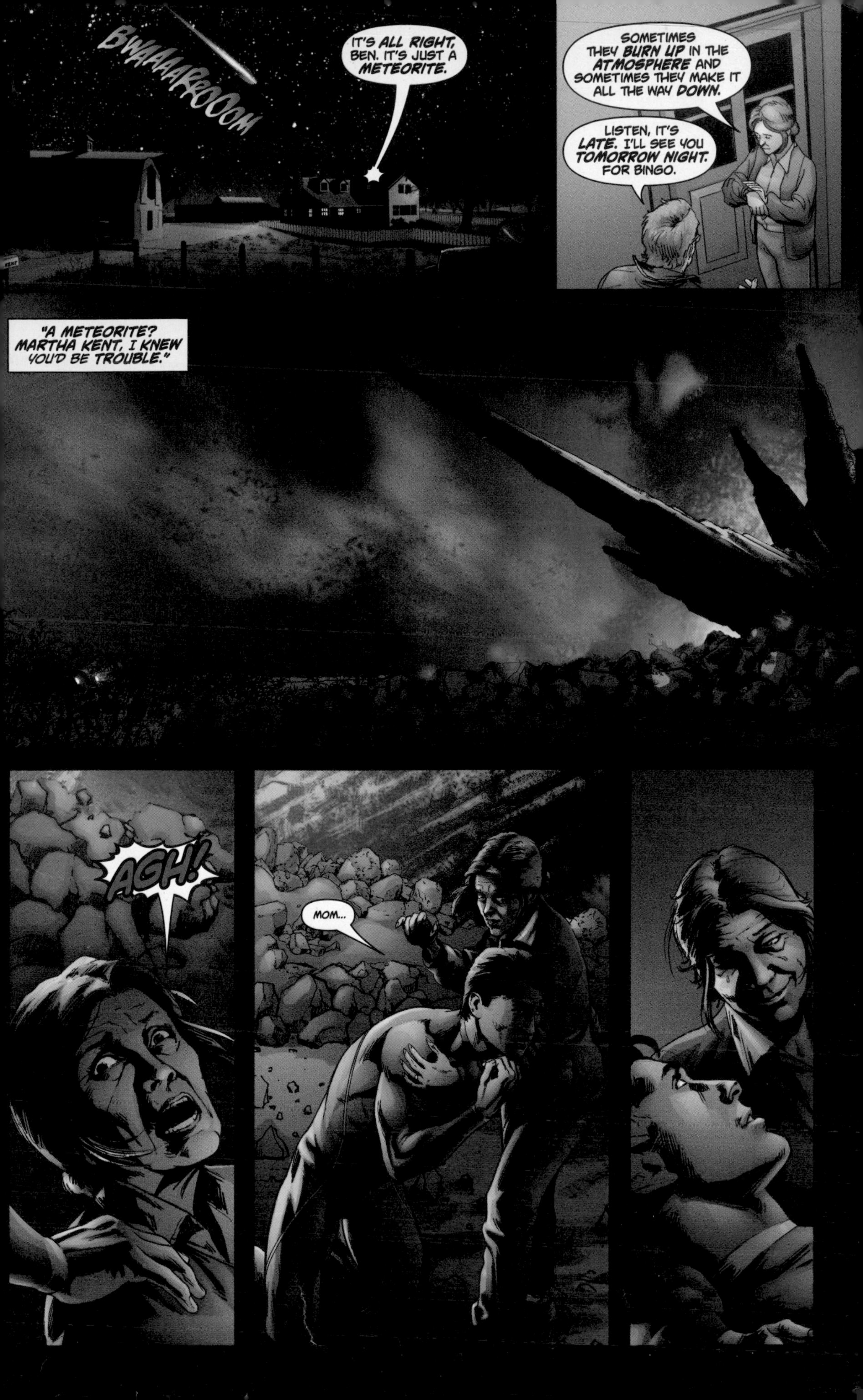
BWAAAARROOOM
IT'S ALL RIGHT, BEN. IT'S JUST A METEORITE.
SOMETIMES THEY BURN UP IN THE ATMOSPHERE AND SOMETIMES THEY MAKE IT ALL THE WAY DOWN.
LISTEN, IT'S LATE. I'LL SEE YOU TOMORROW NIGHT. FOR BINGO.
"A METEORITE? MARTHA KENT, I KNEW YOU'D BE TROUBLE."
AGH!
MOM...

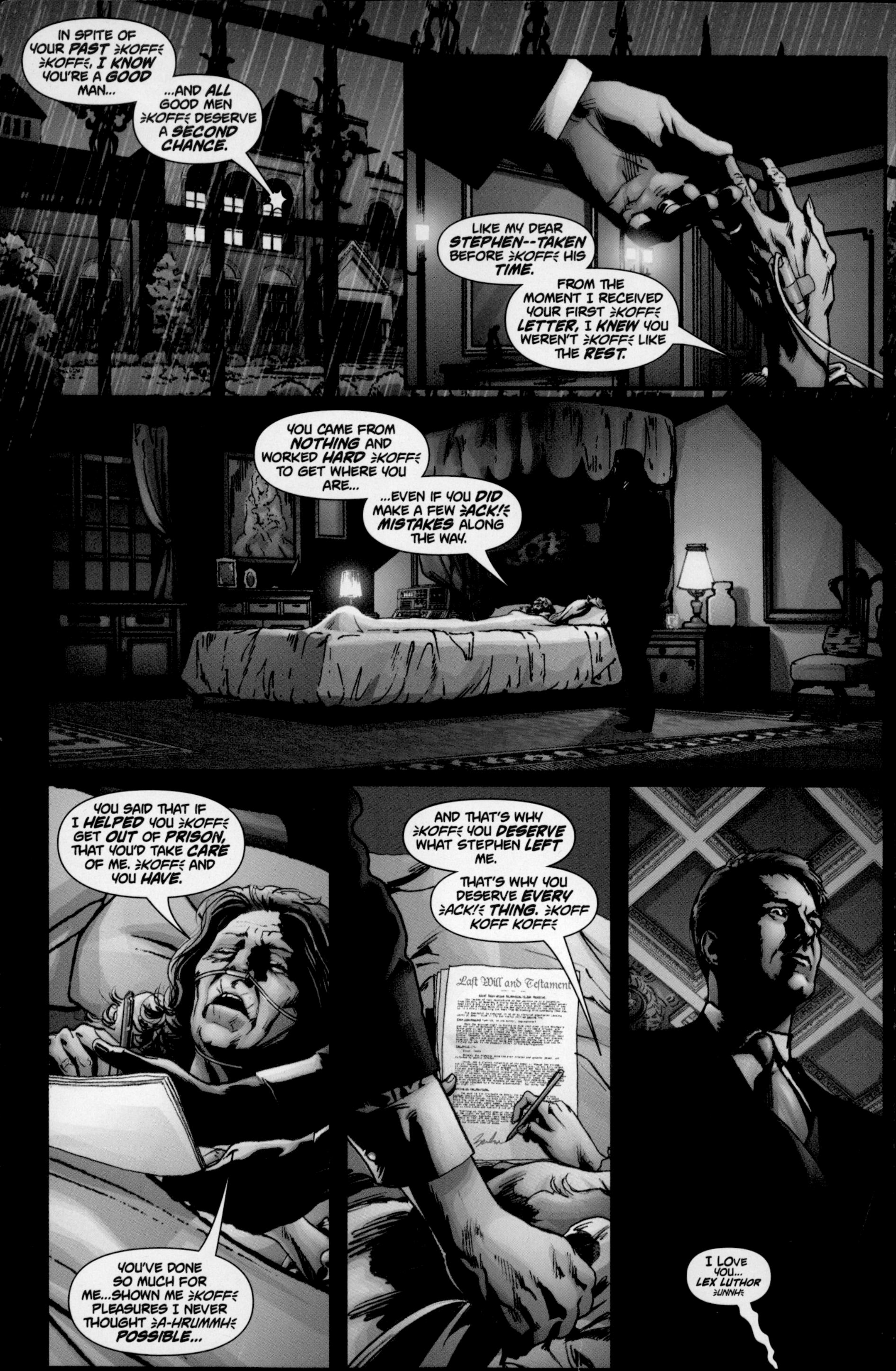

IN SPITE OF YOUR PAST ≷KOFF≶ ≷KOFF≶, I KNOW YOU'RE A GOOD MAN...
...AND ALL GOOD MEN ≷KOFF≶ DESERVE A SECOND CHANCE.
LIKE MY DEAR STEPHEN--TAKEN BEFORE ≷KOFF≶ HIS TIME.
FROM THE MOMENT I RECEIVED YOUR FIRST ≷KOFF≶ LETTER, I KNEW YOU WEREN'T ≷KOFF≶ LIKE THE REST.
YOU CAME FROM NOTHING AND WORKED HARD ≷KOFF≶ TO GET WHERE YOU ARE...
...EVEN IF YOU DID MAKE A FEW ≷ACK!≶ MISTAKES ALONG THE WAY.
YOU SAID THAT IF I HELPED YOU ≷KOFF≶ GET OUT OF PRISON, THAT YOU'D TAKE CARE OF ME. ≷KOFF≶ AND YOU HAVE.
YOU'VE DONE SO MUCH FOR ME...SHOWN ME ≷KOFF≶ PLEASURES I NEVER THOUGHT ≷A-HRUMMH≶ POSSIBLE...
AND THAT'S WHY ≷KOFF≶ YOU DESERVE WHAT STEPHEN LEFT ME.
THAT'S WHY YOU DESERVE EVERY ≷ACK!≶ THING. ≷KOFF KOFF KOFF≶
Last Will and Testament
I LOVE YOU... LEX LUTHOR ≷UNNH≶

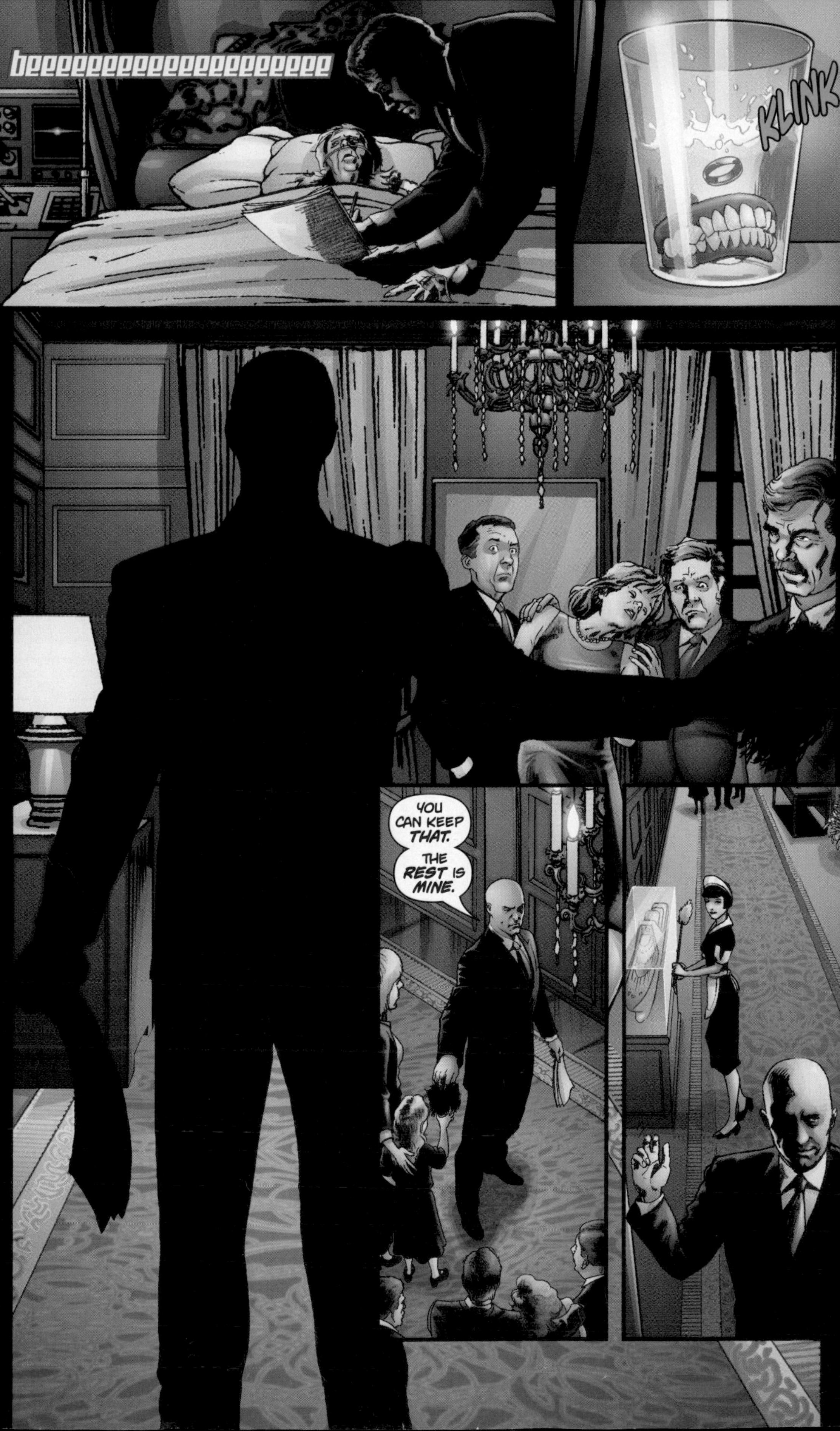
beeeeeeeeeeeeeeeeeeeeee
KLINK
YOU CAN KEEP THAT.
THE REST IS MINE.

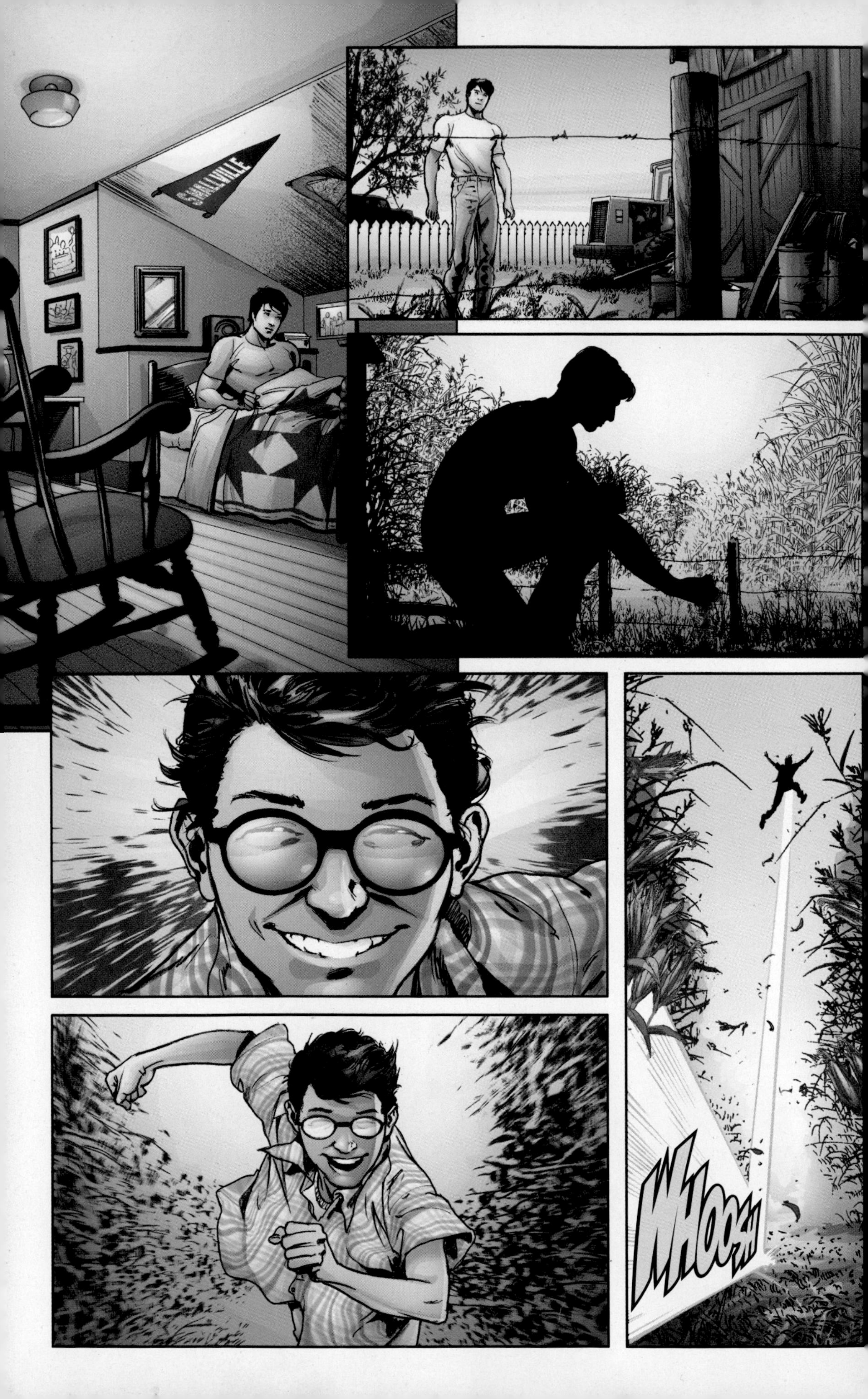
SMALLVILLE
WHOOSH

WOW.

"PEOPLE HAVE ALWAYS LONGED FOR GODS, MESSIAHS, AND SAVIORS TO SWOOP DOWN FROM THE SKY AND DELIVER THEM FROM THEIR TROUBLES.

EXTRA

CAPED WONDER STUNS CITY

WHY THE WORLD DOESN'T NEED SUPERMAN

"BUT THE SAVIORS ALWAYS LEAVE, AND INSTEAD OF FACING OUR TROUBLES OURSELVES...

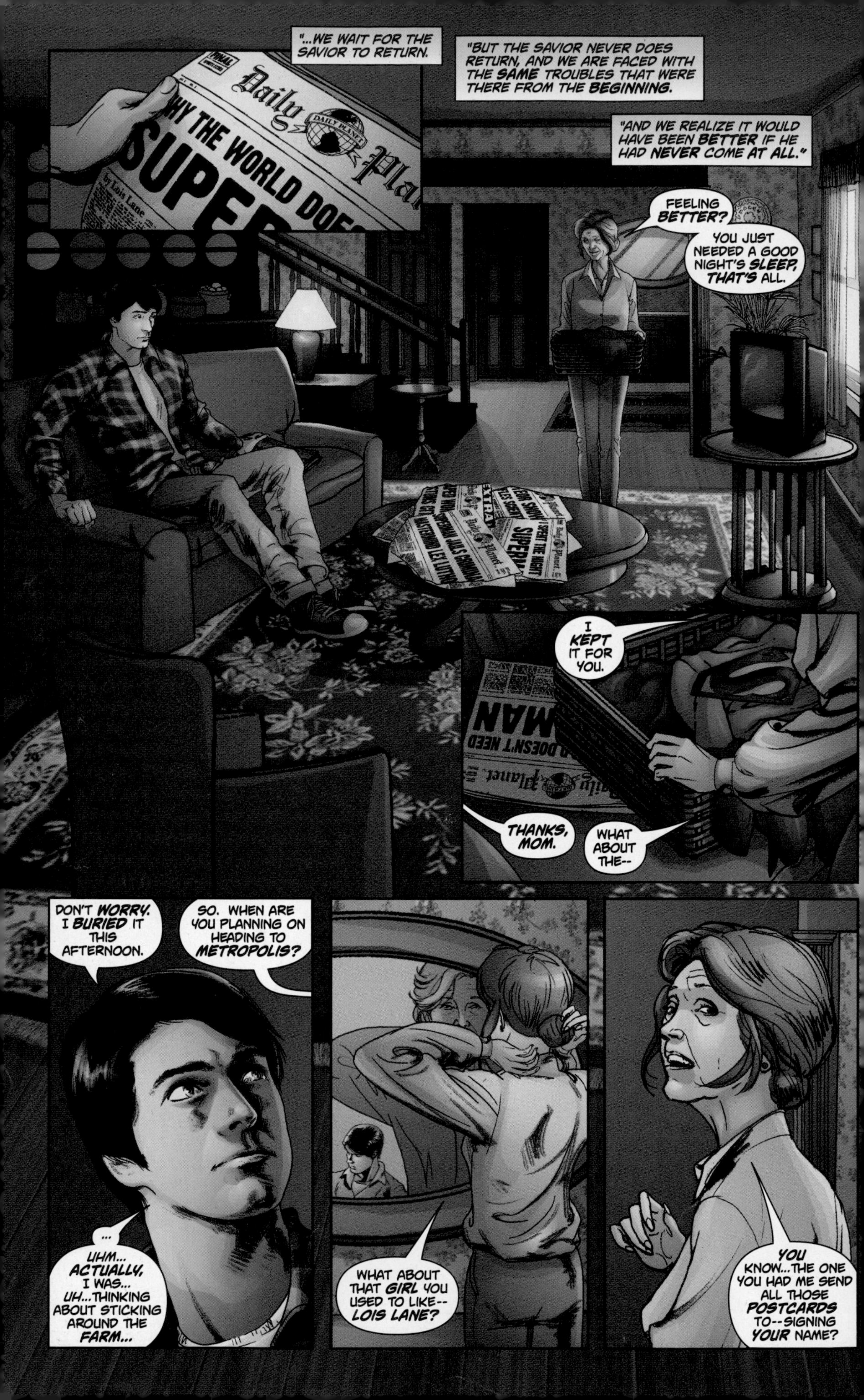
"...WE WAIT FOR THE SAVIOR TO RETURN.
"BUT THE SAVIOR NEVER DOES RETURN, AND WE ARE FACED WITH THE SAME TROUBLES THAT WERE THERE FROM THE BEGINNING.
"AND WE REALIZE IT WOULD HAVE BEEN BETTER IF HE HAD NEVER COME AT ALL."
Daily Planet
WHY THE WORLD DOES
SUPER
by Lois Lane
FEELING BETTER?
YOU JUST NEEDED A GOOD NIGHT'S SLEEP, THAT'S ALL.
I KEPT IT FOR YOU.
D DOESN'T NEED
MAN
THANKS, MOM.
WHAT ABOUT THE--
DON'T WORRY. I BURIED IT THIS AFTERNOON.
SO. WHEN ARE YOU PLANNING ON HEADING TO METROPOLIS?
... UHM... ACTUALLY, I WAS... UH...THINKING ABOUT STICKING AROUND THE FARM...
WHAT ABOUT THAT GIRL YOU USED TO LIKE-- LOIS LANE?
YOU KNOW...THE ONE YOU HAD ME SEND ALL THOSE POSTCARDS TO--SIGNING YOUR NAME?

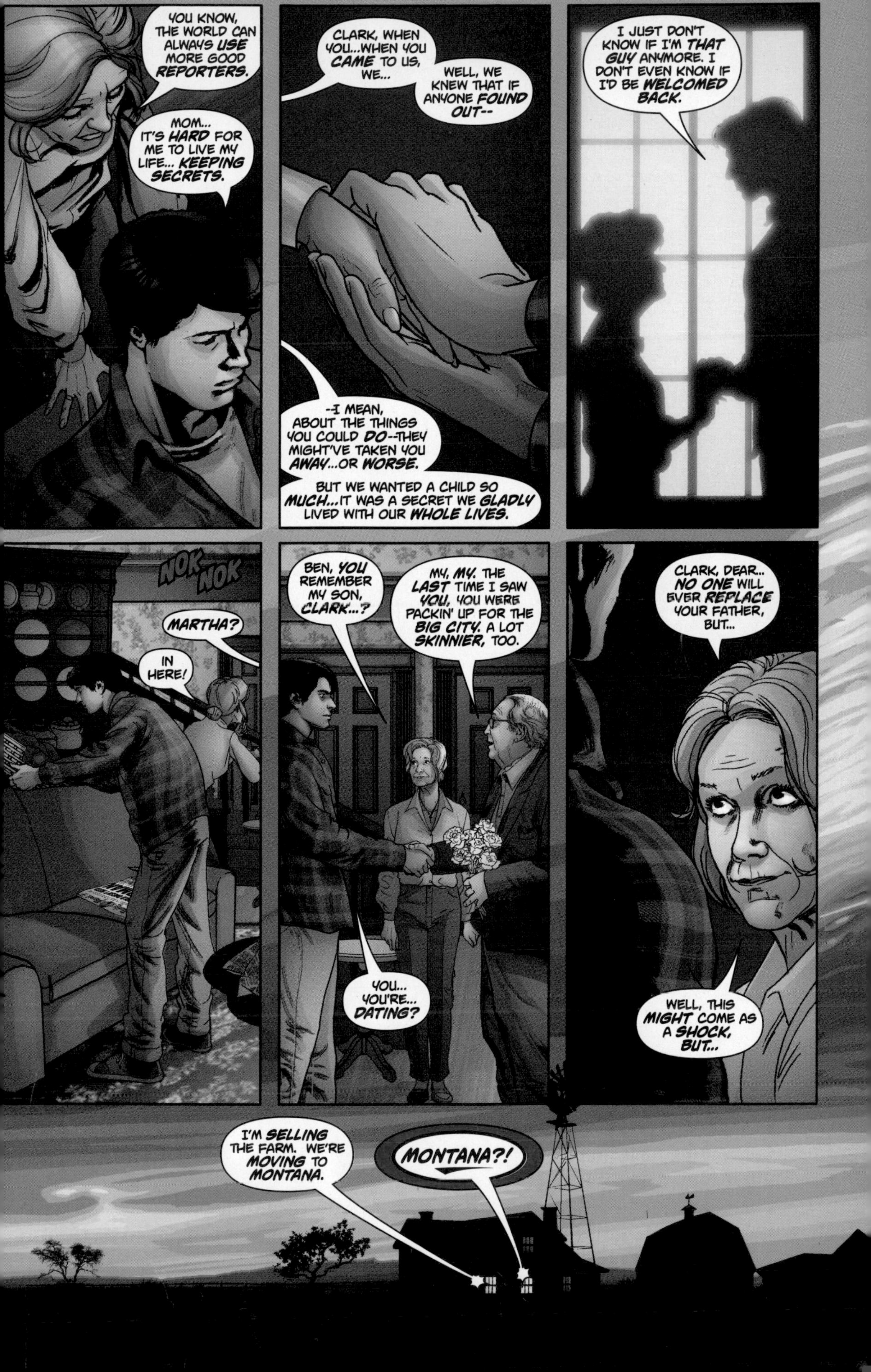

YOU KNOW, THE WORLD CAN ALWAYS USE MORE GOOD REPORTERS.
MOM... IT'S HARD FOR ME TO LIVE MY LIFE... KEEPING SECRETS.
CLARK, WHEN YOU...WHEN YOU CAME TO US, WE...
WELL, WE KNEW THAT IF ANYONE FOUND OUT--
--I MEAN, ABOUT THE THINGS YOU COULD DO--THEY MIGHT'VE TAKEN YOU AWAY...OR WORSE.
BUT WE WANTED A CHILD SO MUCH...IT WAS A SECRET WE GLADLY LIVED WITH OUR WHOLE LIVES.
I JUST DON'T KNOW IF I'M THAT GUY ANYMORE. I DON'T EVEN KNOW IF I'D BE WELCOMED BACK.
NOK NOK
MARTHA?
IN HERE!
BEN, YOU REMEMBER MY SON, CLARK...?
MY, MY. THE LAST TIME I SAW YOU, YOU WERE PACKIN' UP FOR THE BIG CITY. A LOT SKINNIER, TOO.
YOU... YOU'RE... DATING?
CLARK, DEAR... NO ONE WILL EVER REPLACE YOUR FATHER, BUT...
WELL, THIS MIGHT COME AS A SHOCK, BUT...
I'M SELLING THE FARM. WE'RE MOVING TO MONTANA.
MONTANA?!

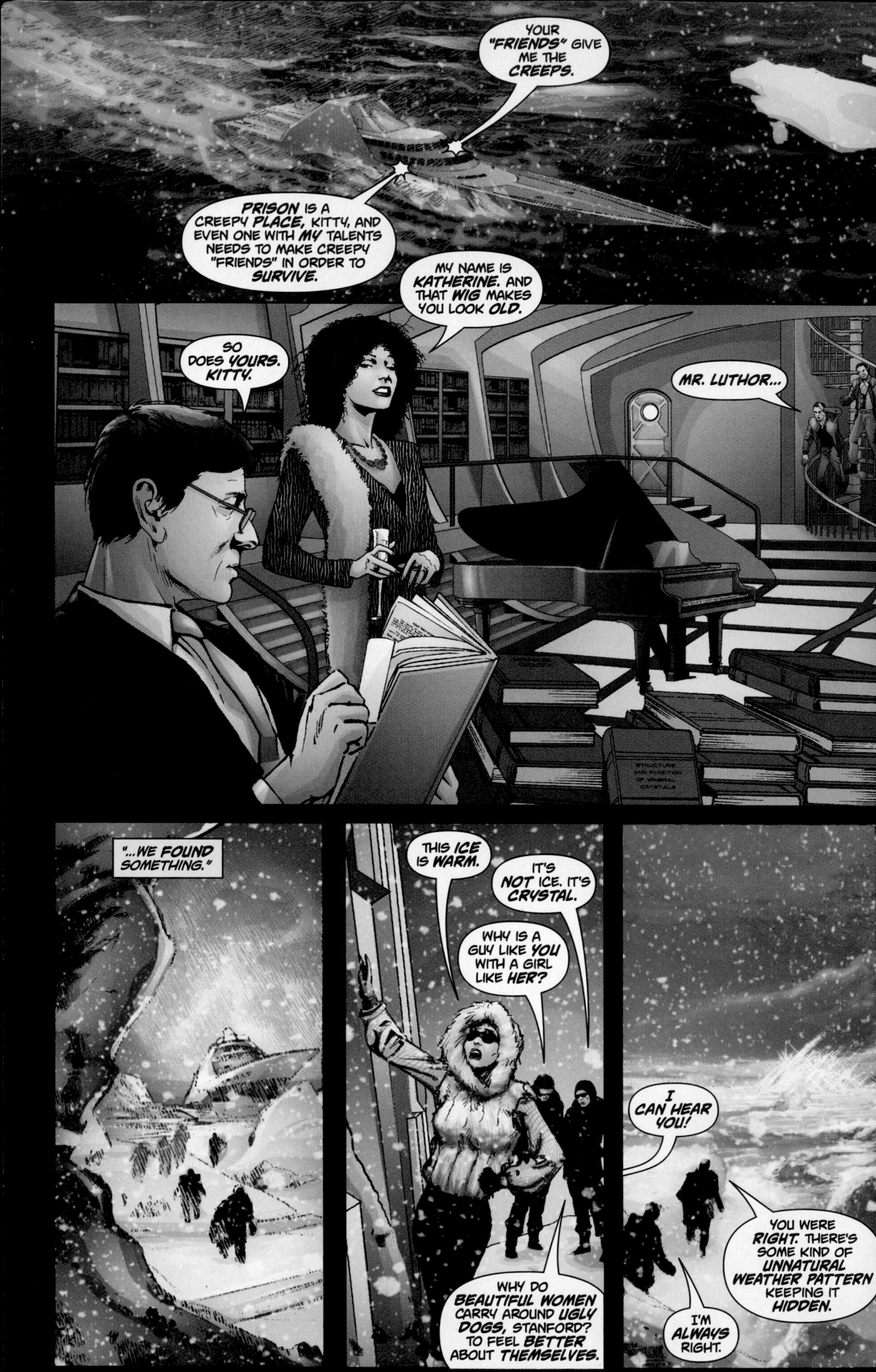
YOUR "FRIENDS" GIVE ME THE CREEPS.
PRISON IS A CREEPY PLACE, KITTY, AND EVEN ONE WITH MY TALENTS NEEDS TO MAKE CREEPY "FRIENDS" IN ORDER TO SURVIVE.
MY NAME IS KATHERINE. AND THAT WIG MAKES YOU LOOK OLD.
SO DOES YOURS. KITTY.
MR. LUTHOR...
STRUCTURE AND FUNCTION OF MINERAL CRYSTALS
"...WE FOUND SOMETHING."
THIS ICE IS WARM.
IT'S NOT ICE. IT'S CRYSTAL.
WHY IS A GUY LIKE YOU WITH A GIRL LIKE HER?
WHY DO BEAUTIFUL WOMEN CARRY AROUND UGLY DOGS, STANFORD? TO FEEL BETTER ABOUT THEMSELVES.
I CAN HEAR YOU!
YOU WERE RIGHT. THERE'S SOME KIND OF UNNATURAL WEATHER PATTERN KEEPING IT HIDDEN.
I'M ALWAYS RIGHT.

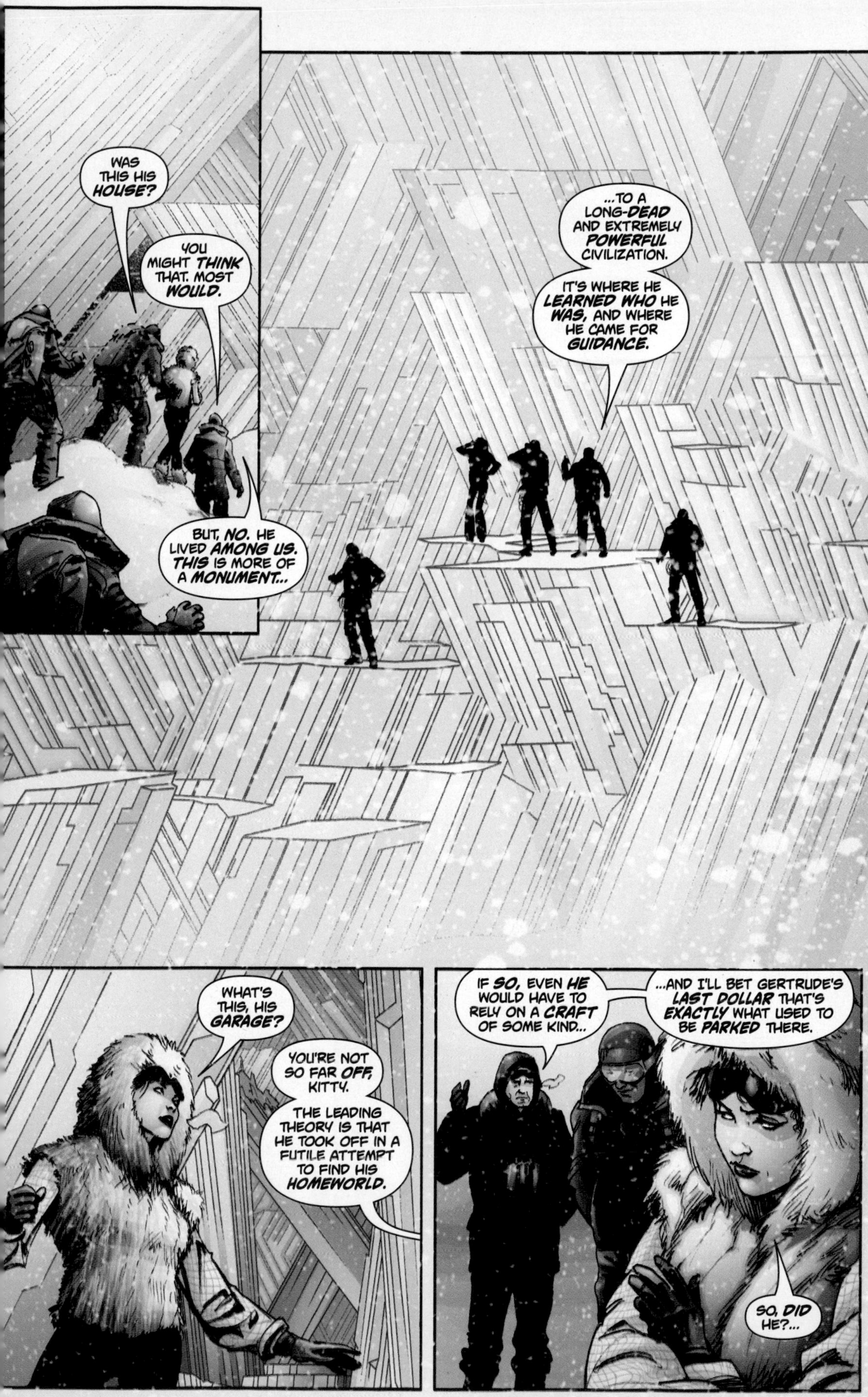
WAS THIS HIS HOUSE?
YOU MIGHT THINK THAT. MOST WOULD.
BUT, NO. HE LIVED AMONG US. THIS IS MORE OF A MONUMENT...
...TO A LONG-DEAD AND EXTREMELY POWERFUL CIVILIZATION.
IT'S WHERE HE LEARNED WHO HE WAS, AND WHERE HE CAME FOR GUIDANCE.
WHAT'S THIS, HIS GARAGE?
YOU'RE NOT SO FAR OFF, KITTY.
THE LEADING THEORY IS THAT HE TOOK OFF IN A FUTILE ATTEMPT TO FIND HIS HOMEWORLD.
IF SO, EVEN HE WOULD HAVE TO RELY ON A CRAFT OF SOME KIND...
...AND I'LL BET GERTRUDE'S LAST DOLLAR THAT'S EXACTLY WHAT USED TO BE PARKED THERE.
SO, DID HE?...

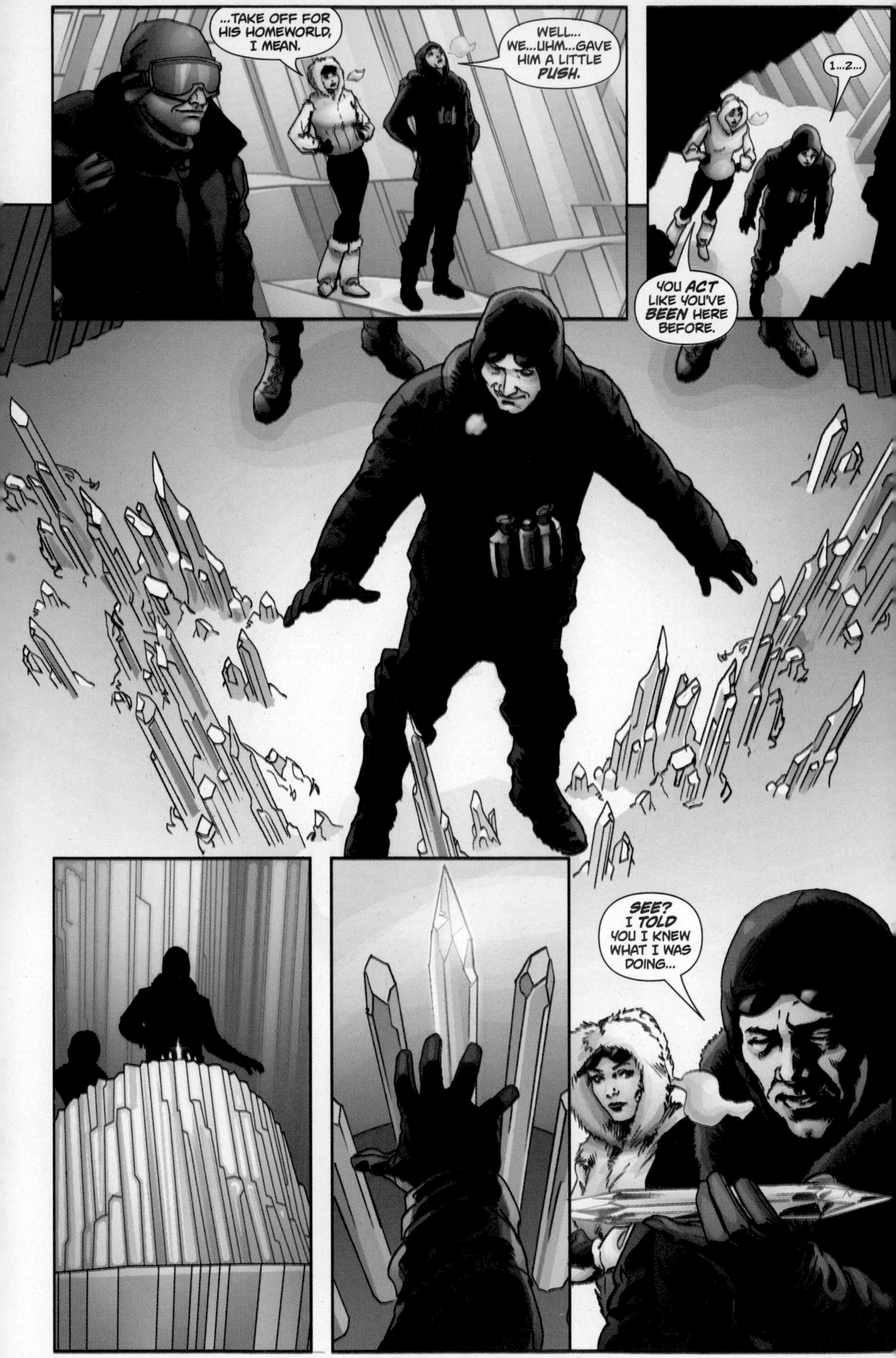
...TAKE OFF FOR HIS HOMEWORLD, I MEAN.
WELL... WE...UHM...GAVE HIM A LITTLE PUSH.
1...2...
YOU ACT LIKE YOU'VE BEEN HERE BEFORE.
SEE? I TOLD YOU I KNEW WHAT I WAS DOING...

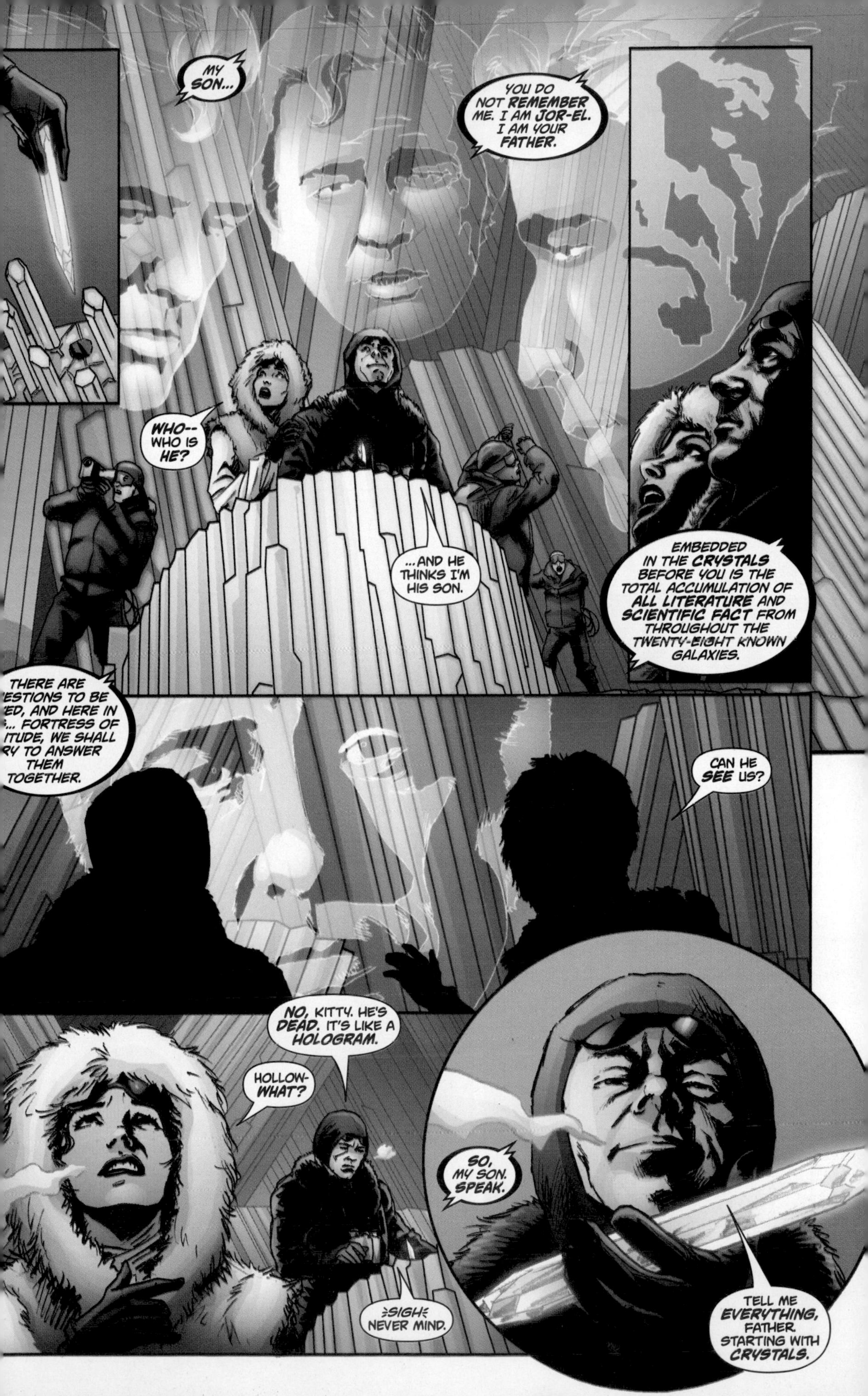
MY SON...
YOU DO NOT REMEMBER ME. I AM JOR-EL. I AM YOUR FATHER.
WHO-- WHO IS HE?
...AND HE THINKS I'M HIS SON.
EMBEDDED IN THE CRYSTALS BEFORE YOU IS THE TOTAL ACCUMULATION OF ALL LITERATURE AND SCIENTIFIC FACT FROM THROUGHOUT THE TWENTY-EIGHT KNOWN GALAXIES.
THERE ARE ESTIONS TO BE ED, AND HERE IN ... FORTRESS OF ITUDE, WE SHALL RY TO ANSWER THEM TOGETHER.
CAN HE SEE US?
NO, KITTY. HE'S DEAD. IT'S LIKE A HOLOGRAM.
HOLLOW-WHAT?
SO, MY SON. SPEAK.
SIGH NEVER MIND.
TELL ME EVERYTHING, FATHER STARTING WITH CRYSTALS.

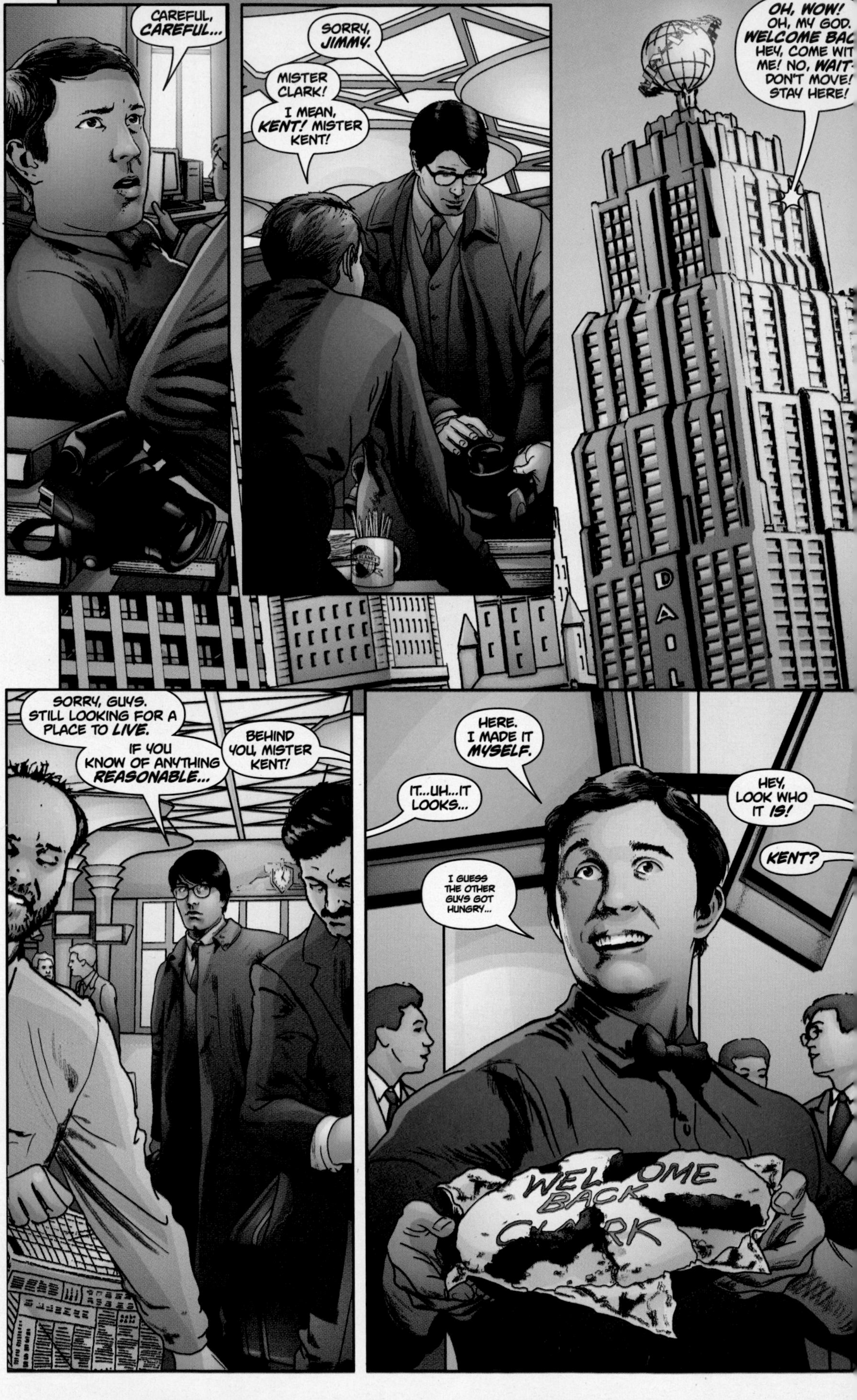
CAREFUL, CAREFUL...
SORRY, JIMMY.
MISTER CLARK!
I MEAN, KENT! MISTER KENT!
OH, WOW! OH, MY GOD. WELCOME BAC HEY, COME WIT ME! NO, WAIT- DON'T MOVE! STAY HERE!
SORRY, GUYS. STILL LOOKING FOR A PLACE TO LIVE.
IF YOU KNOW OF ANYTHING REASONABLE...
BEHIND YOU, MISTER KENT!
HEY, LOOK WHO IT IS!
KENT?
HERE. I MADE IT MYSELF.
IT...UH...IT LOOKS...
I GUESS THE OTHER GUYS GOT HUNGRY...

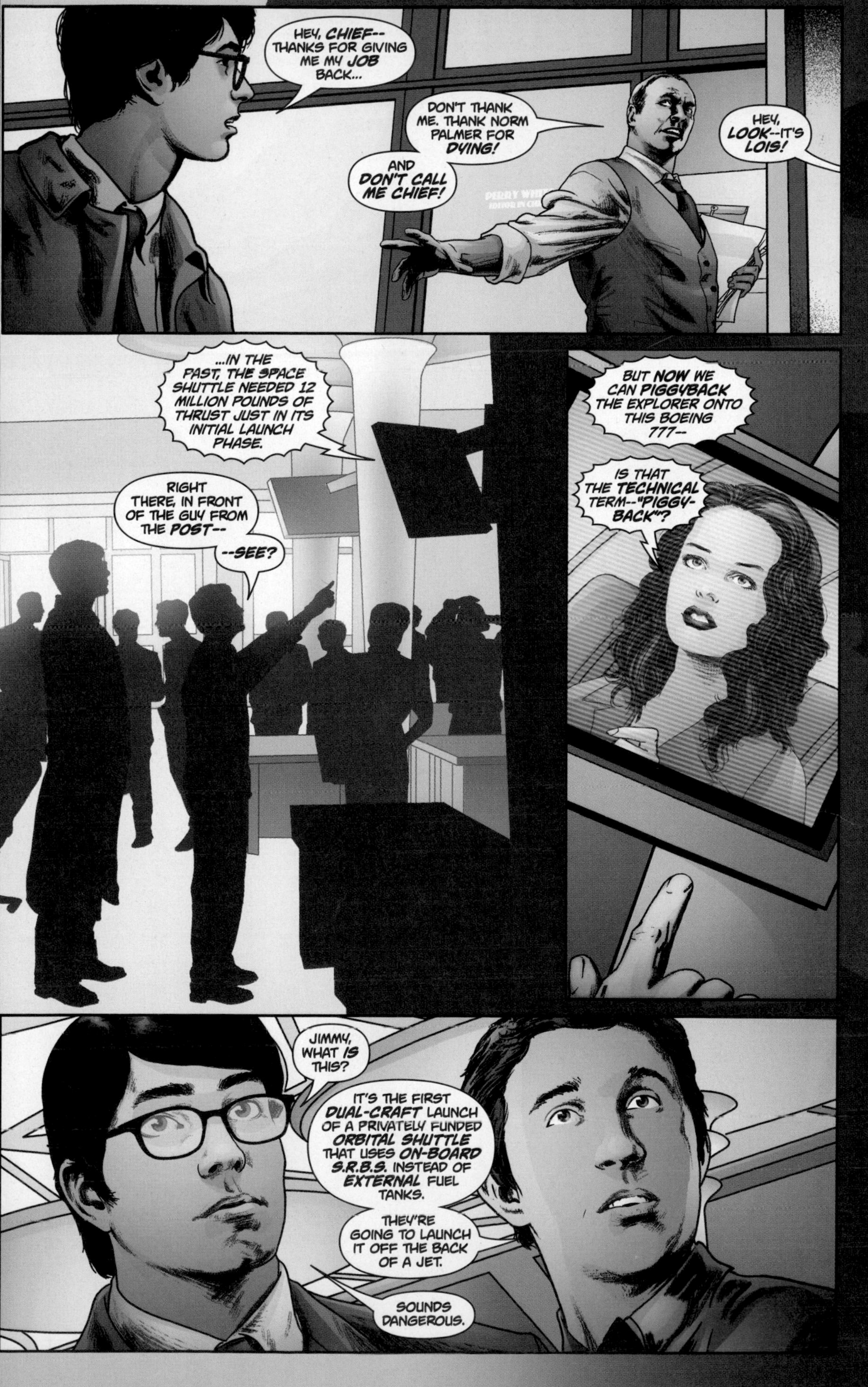
HEY, CHIEF-- THANKS FOR GIVING ME MY JOB BACK...
DON'T THANK ME. THANK NORM PALMER FOR DYING!
AND DON'T CALL ME CHIEF!
HEY, LOOK--IT'S LOIS!
...IN THE PAST, THE SPACE SHUTTLE NEEDED 12 MILLION POUNDS OF THRUST JUST IN ITS INITIAL LAUNCH PHASE.
RIGHT THERE, IN FRONT OF THE GUY FROM THE POST--
--SEE?
BUT NOW WE CAN PIGGYBACK THE EXPLORER ONTO THIS BOEING 777--
IS THAT THE TECHNICAL TERM--"PIGGY-BACK"?
JIMMY, WHAT IS THIS?
IT'S THE FIRST DUAL-CRAFT LAUNCH OF A PRIVATELY FUNDED ORBITAL SHUTTLE THAT USES ON-BOARD S.R.B.S. INSTEAD OF EXTERNAL FUEL TANKS.
THEY'RE GOING TO LAUNCH IT OFF THE BACK OF A JET.
SOUNDS DANGEROUS.

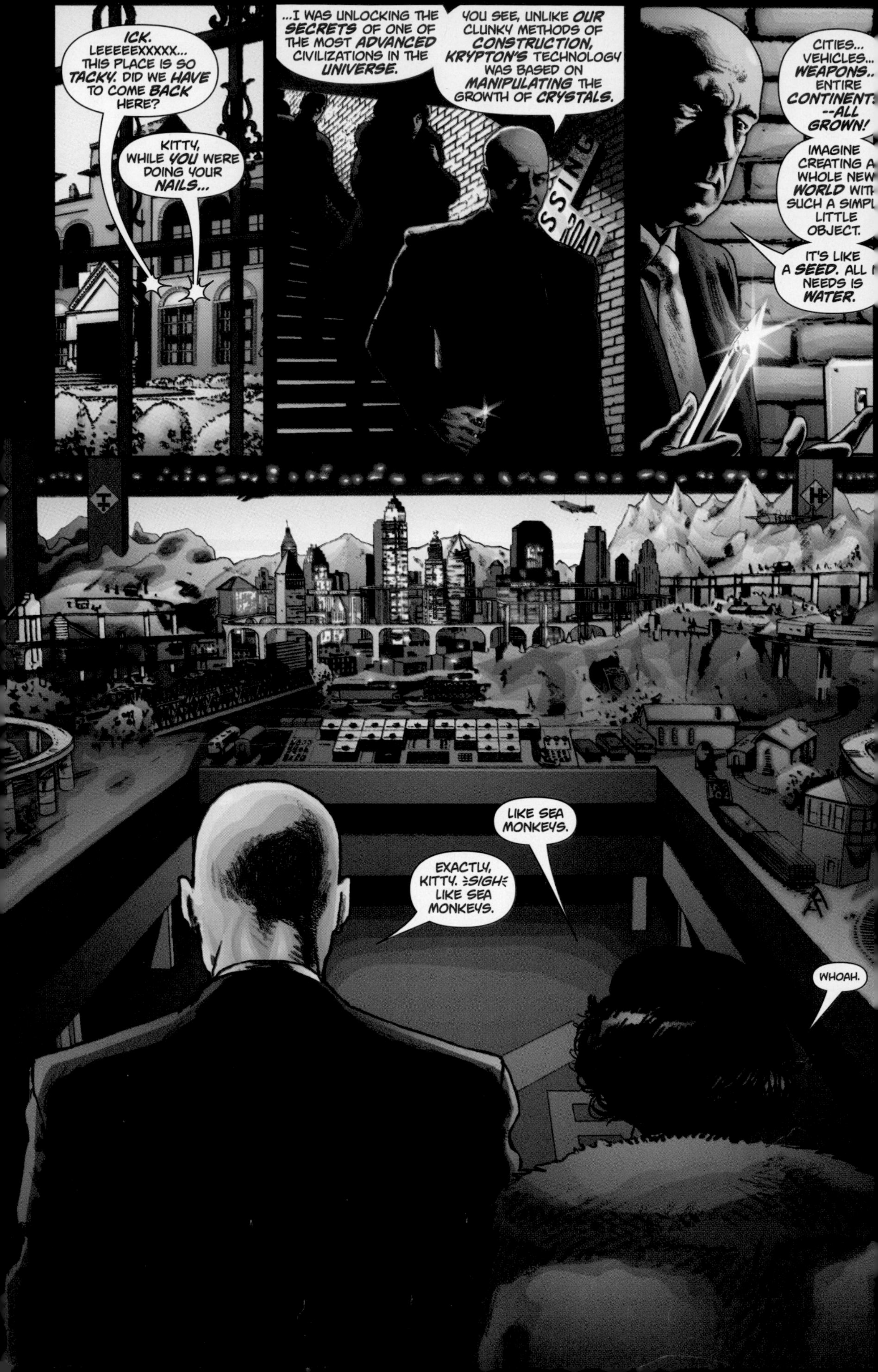
ICK. LEEEEEXXXXX... THIS PLACE IS SO TACKY. DID WE HAVE TO COME BACK HERE?
KITTY, WHILE YOU WERE DOING YOUR NAILS...
...I WAS UNLOCKING THE SECRETS OF ONE OF THE MOST ADVANCED CIVILIZATIONS IN THE UNIVERSE.
YOU SEE, UNLIKE OUR CLUNKY METHODS OF CONSTRUCTION, KRYPTON'S TECHNOLOGY WAS BASED ON MANIPULATING THE GROWTH OF CRYSTALS.
CITIES... VEHICLES... WEAPONS.. ENTIRE CONTINENT --ALL GROWN!
IMAGINE CREATING A WHOLE NEW WORLD WIT SUCH A SIMPL LITTLE OBJECT.
IT'S LIKE A SEED. ALL NEEDS IS WATER.
LIKE SEA MONKEYS.
EXACTLY, KITTY. *SIGH* LIKE SEA MONKEYS.
WHOAH.

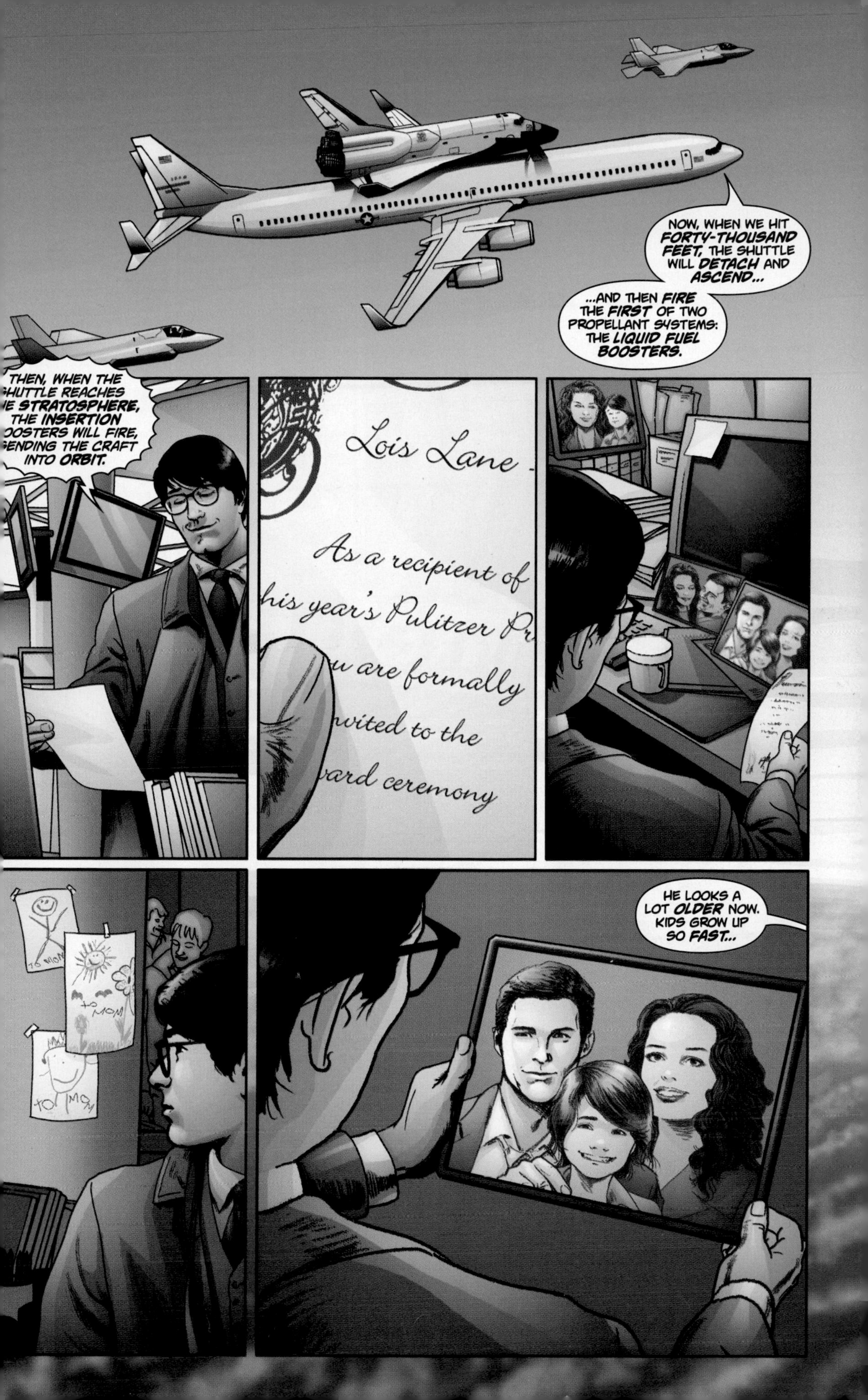
NOW, WHEN WE HIT FORTY-THOUSAND FEET, THE SHUTTLE WILL DETACH AND ASCEND...
...AND THEN FIRE THE FIRST OF TWO PROPELLANT SYSTEMS: THE LIQUID FUEL BOOSTERS.
THEN, WHEN THE HUTTLE REACHES E STRATOSPHERE, THE INSERTION OOSTERS WILL FIRE, ENDING THE CRAFT INTO ORBIT.
Lois Lane
As a recipient of
his year's Pulitzer Pr
u are formally
nvited to the
ard ceremony
TO MOM
TO MOM
TO MOM
HE LOOKS A LOT OLDER NOW. KIDS GROW UP SO FAST...

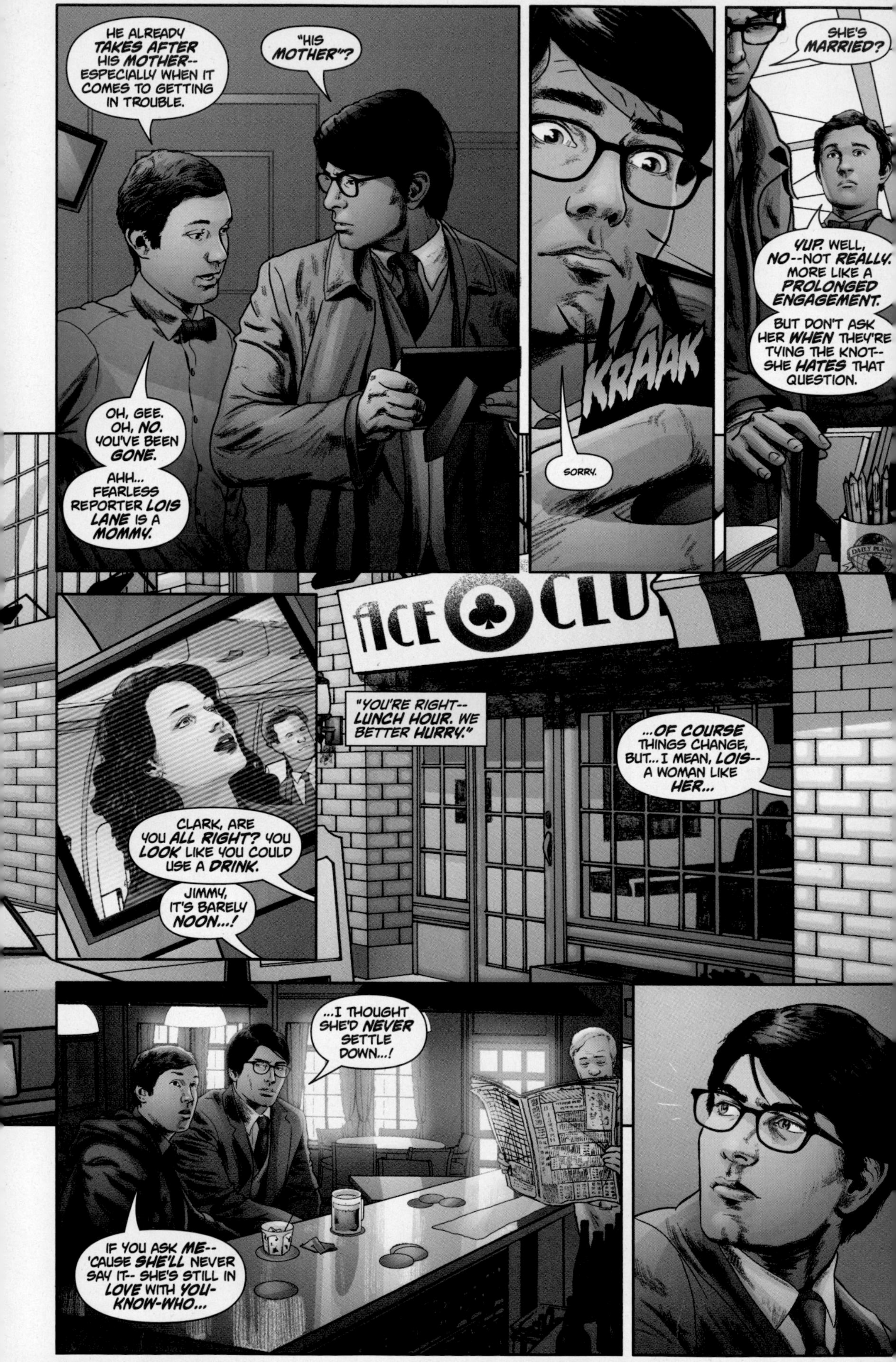

HE ALREADY TAKES AFTER HIS MOTHER-- ESPECIALLY WHEN IT COMES TO GETTING IN TROUBLE.
"HIS MOTHER"?
OH, GEE. OH, NO. YOU'VE BEEN GONE.
AHH... FEARLESS REPORTER LOIS LANE IS A MOMMY.
KRAAK
SORRY.
SHE'S MARRIED?
YUP. WELL, NO--NOT REALLY. MORE LIKE A PROLONGED ENGAGEMENT.
BUT DON'T ASK HER WHEN THEY'RE TYING THE KNOT-- SHE HATES THAT QUESTION.
ACE CLU
"YOU'RE RIGHT-- LUNCH HOUR. WE BETTER HURRY."
CLARK, ARE YOU ALL RIGHT? YOU LOOK LIKE YOU COULD USE A DRINK.
JIMMY, IT'S BARELY NOON...!
...OF COURSE THINGS CHANGE, BUT... I MEAN, LOIS-- A WOMAN LIKE HER...
...I THOUGHT SHE'D NEVER SETTLE DOWN...!
IF YOU ASK ME-- 'CAUSE SHE'LL NEVER SAY IT-- SHE'S STILL IN LOVE WITH YOU-KNOW-WHO...

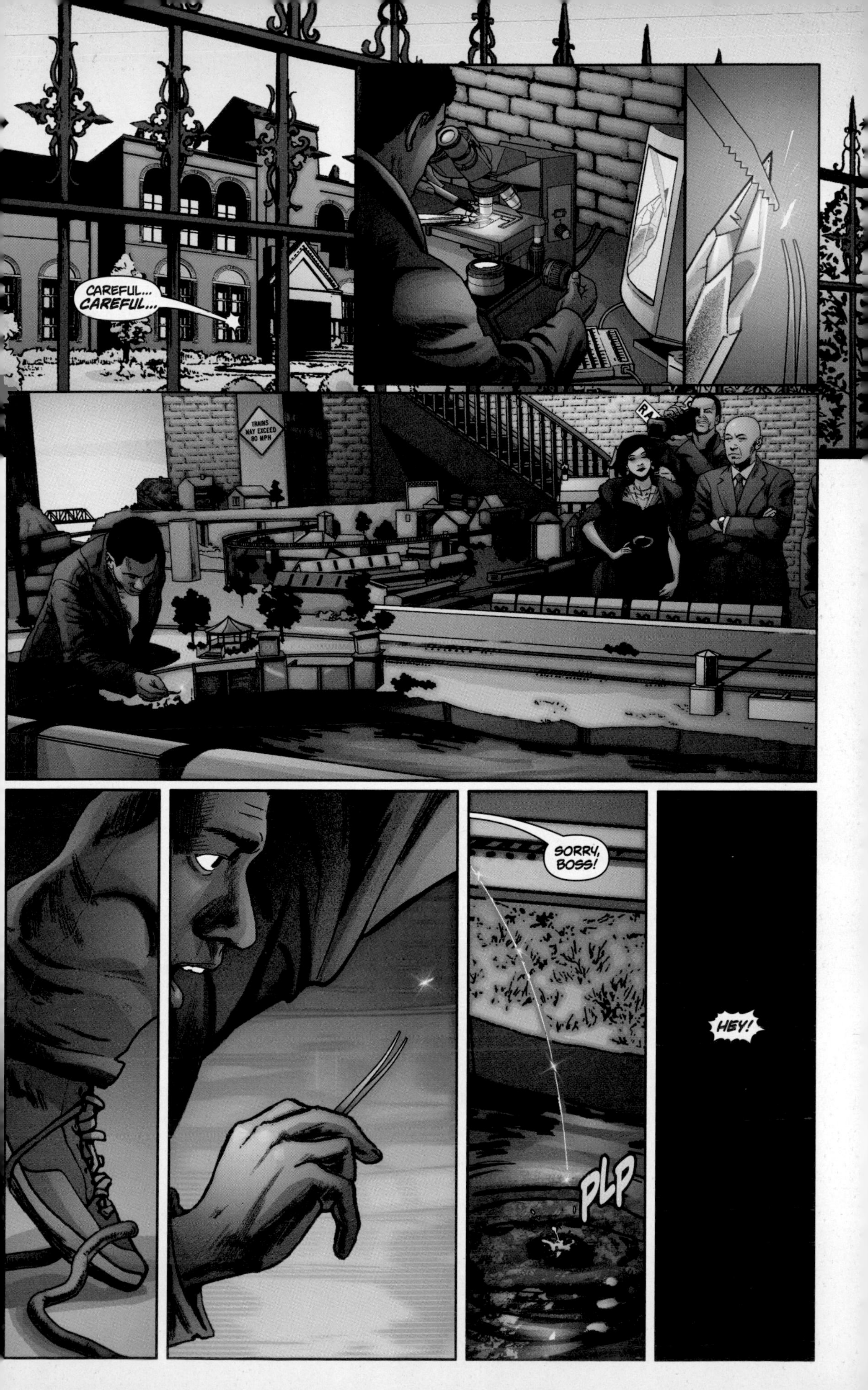
CAREFUL...
CAREFUL...
TRAINS
MAY EXCEED
80 MPH
SORRY,
BOSS!
PLP
HEY!

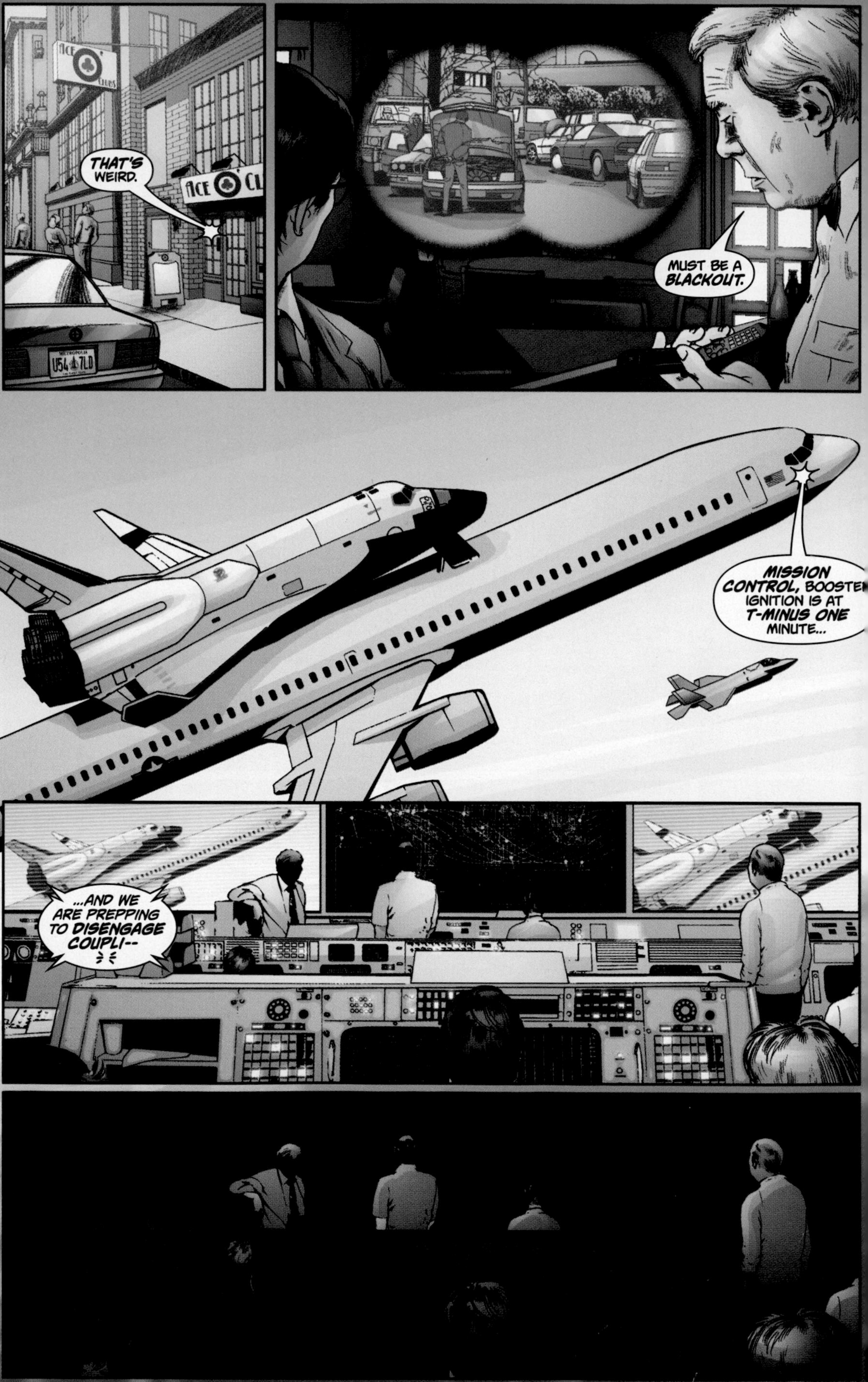
THAT'S WEIRD.
MUST BE A BLACKOUT.
MISSION CONTROL, BOOSTE IGNITION IS AT T-MINUS ONE MINUTE...
...AND WE ARE PREPPING TO DISENGAGE COUPLI--

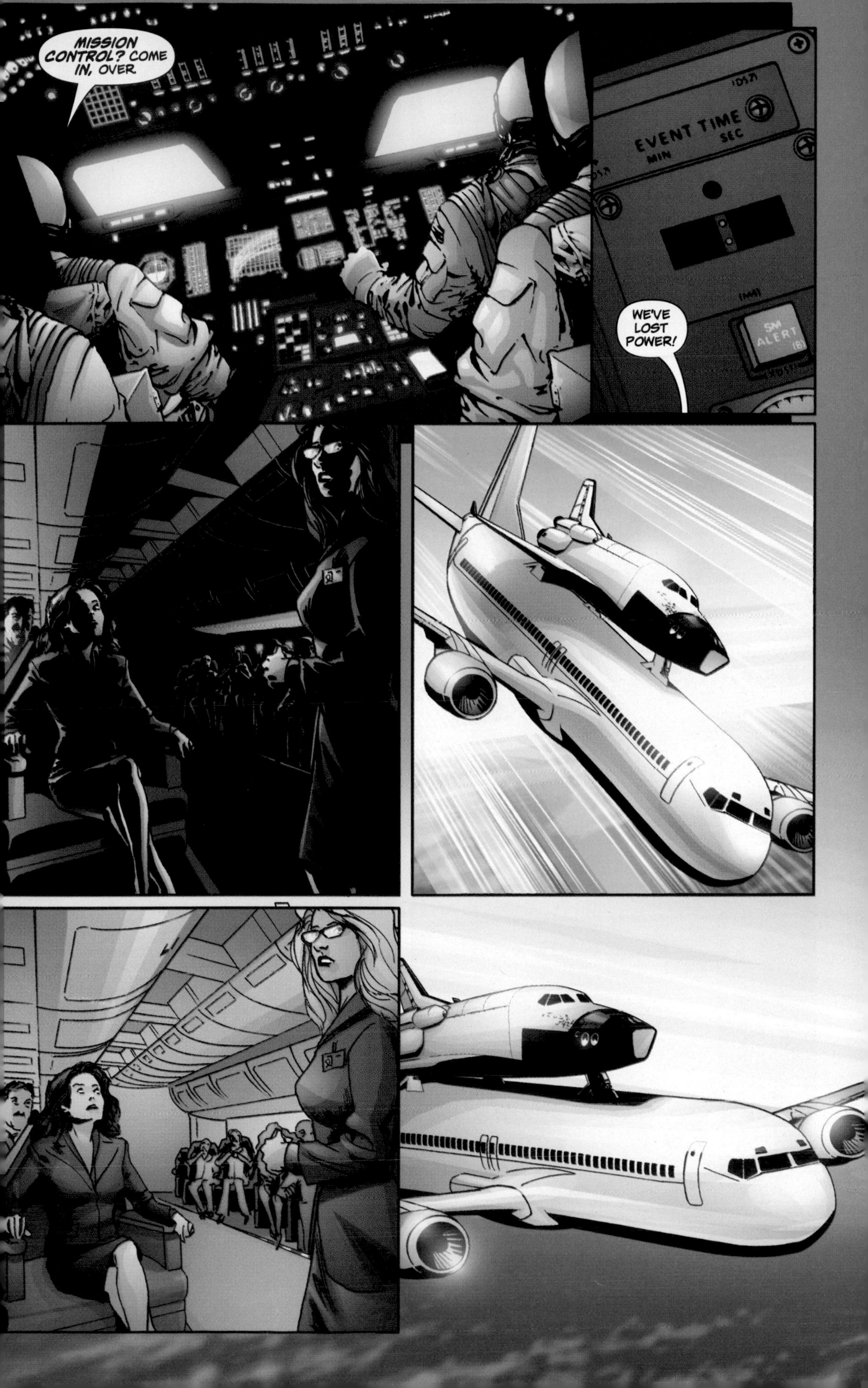
MISSION CONTROL? COME IN, OVER.
EVENT TIME
MIN
SEC
WE'VE LOST POWER!
SM ALERT

EXPLORER... NOT SURE WHAT JUST *HAPPENED*... BUT IT LOOKS LIKE WE'RE GOING TO HAVE TO *SCRUB* THE *LAUNCH*.

ROGER THAT. *ABORTING* BOOSTER IGNITION.

SIR, BOOSTERS ARE *NOT RESPONDING.* WE ARE *STILL* COUNTING DOWN FOR *IGNITION.*

CAN *WE* RELEASE THE COUPLINGS?

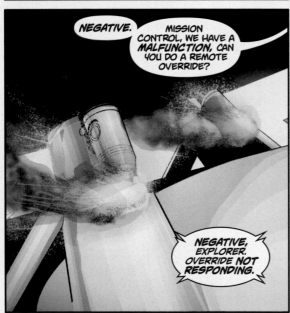

NEGATIVE.

MISSION CONTROL, WE HAVE A *MALFUNCTION,* CAN YOU DO A REMOTE OVERRIDE?

NEGATIVE, EXPLORER. OVERRIDE *NOT* RESPONDING.

MAYDAY! MAYDAY! BOOSTERS HAVE *FIRED* AND WE ARE *NOT DISENGAGED!* I REPEAT, WE ARE *NOT DISENGAGED!*

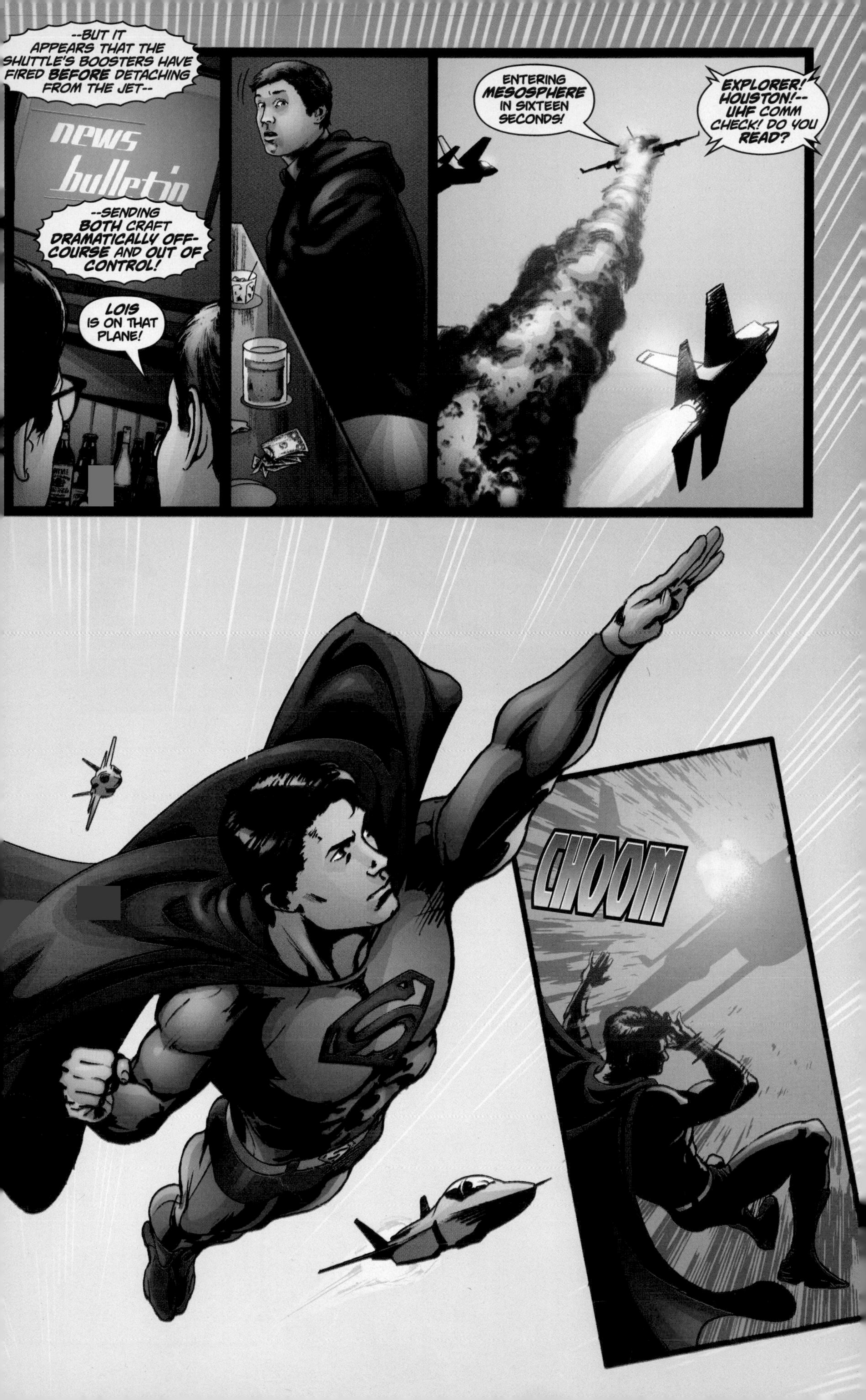
--BUT IT APPEARS THAT THE SHUTTLE'S BOOSTERS HAVE FIRED BEFORE DETACHING FROM THE JET--
news bulletin
--SENDING BOTH CRAFT DRAMATICALLY OFF-COURSE AND OUT OF CONTROL!
LOIS IS ON THAT PLANE!
ENTERING MESOSPHERE IN SIXTEEN SECONDS!
EXPLORER! HOUSTON!--UHF COMM CHECK! DO YOU READ?
CHOOM

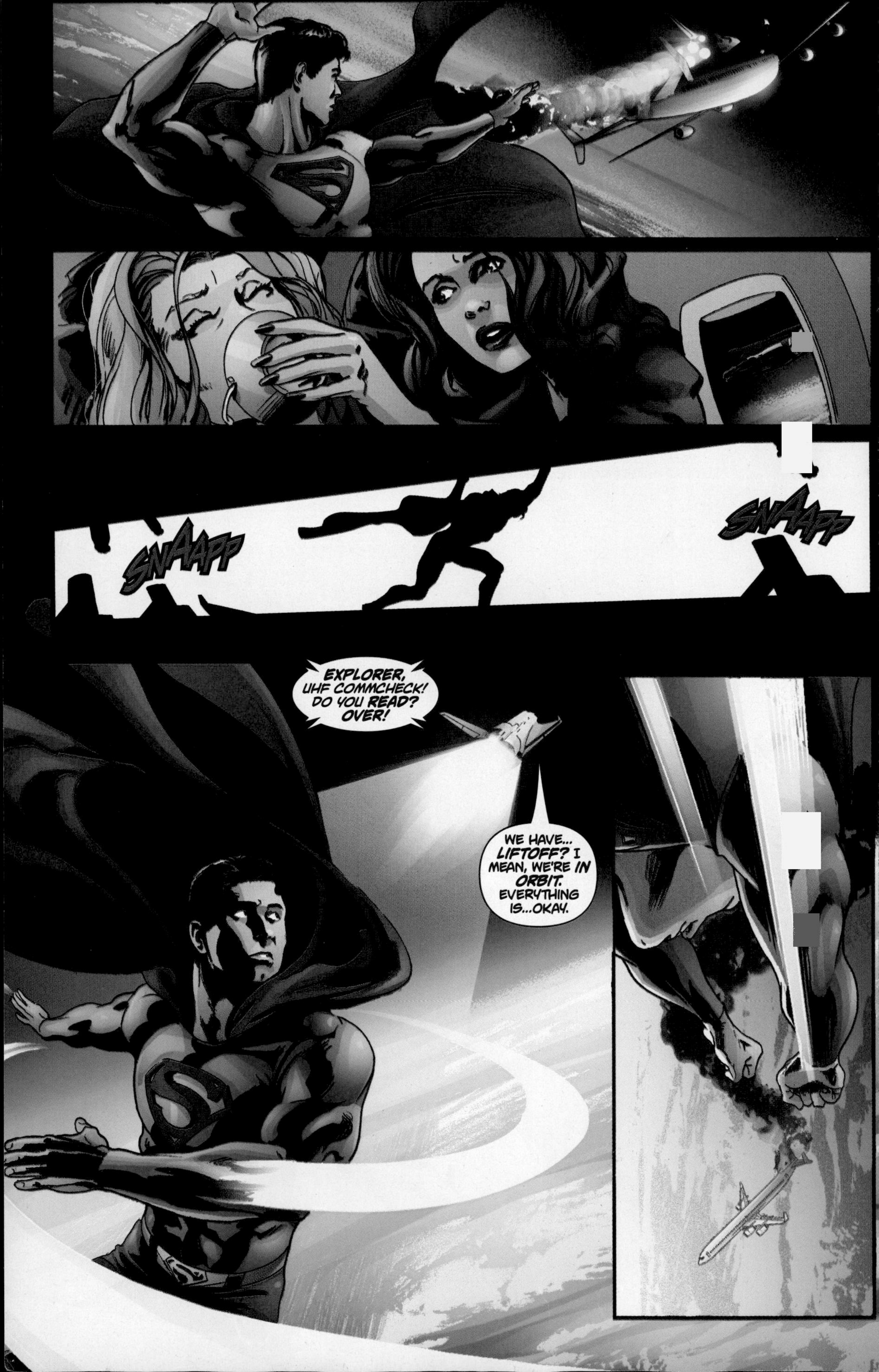
SNAAPP
SNAAPP
EXPLORER, UHF COMMCHECK! DO YOU READ? OVER!
WE HAVE... LIFTOFF? I MEAN, WE'RE IN ORBIT. EVERYTHING IS...OKAY.

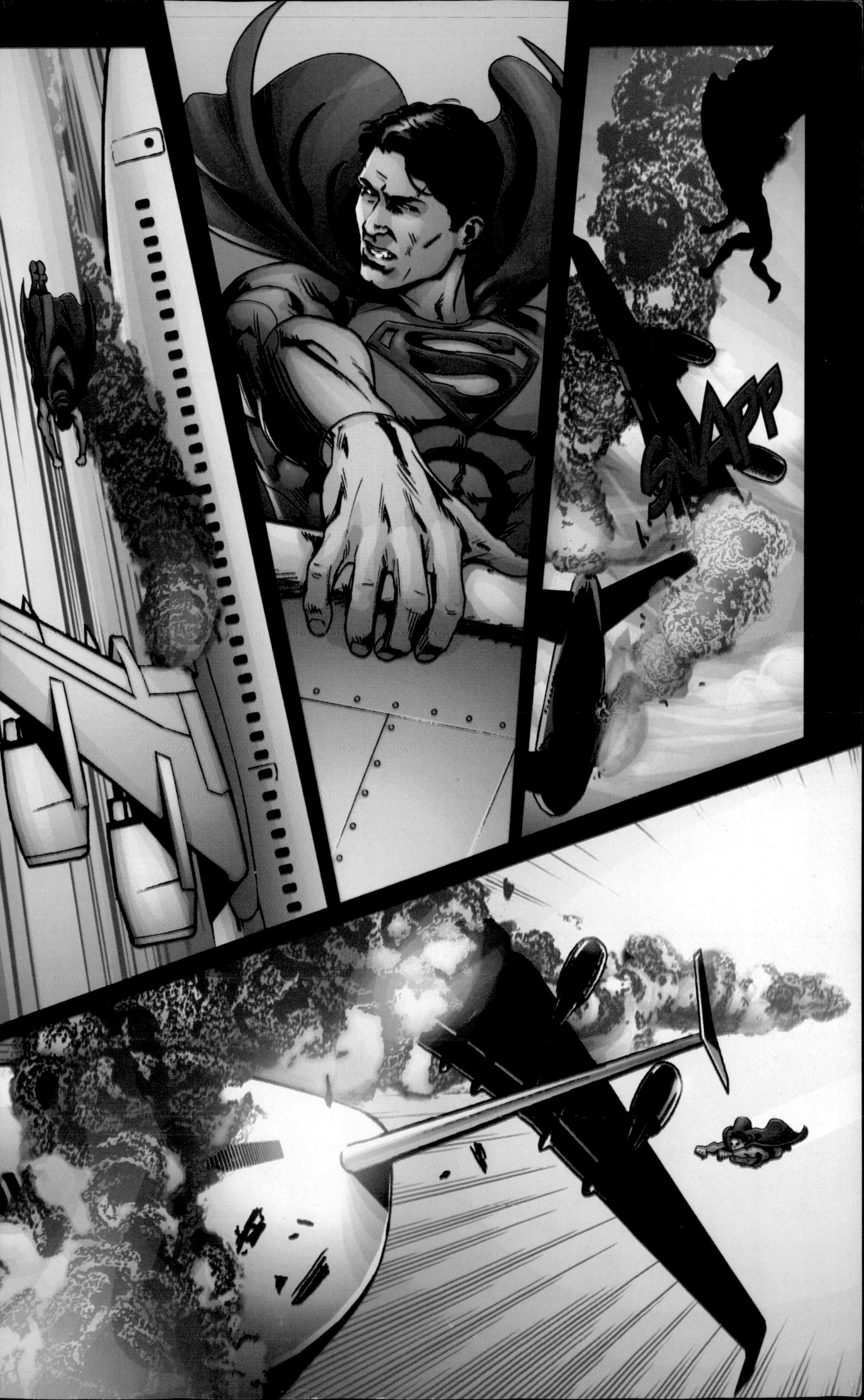
SNAPP

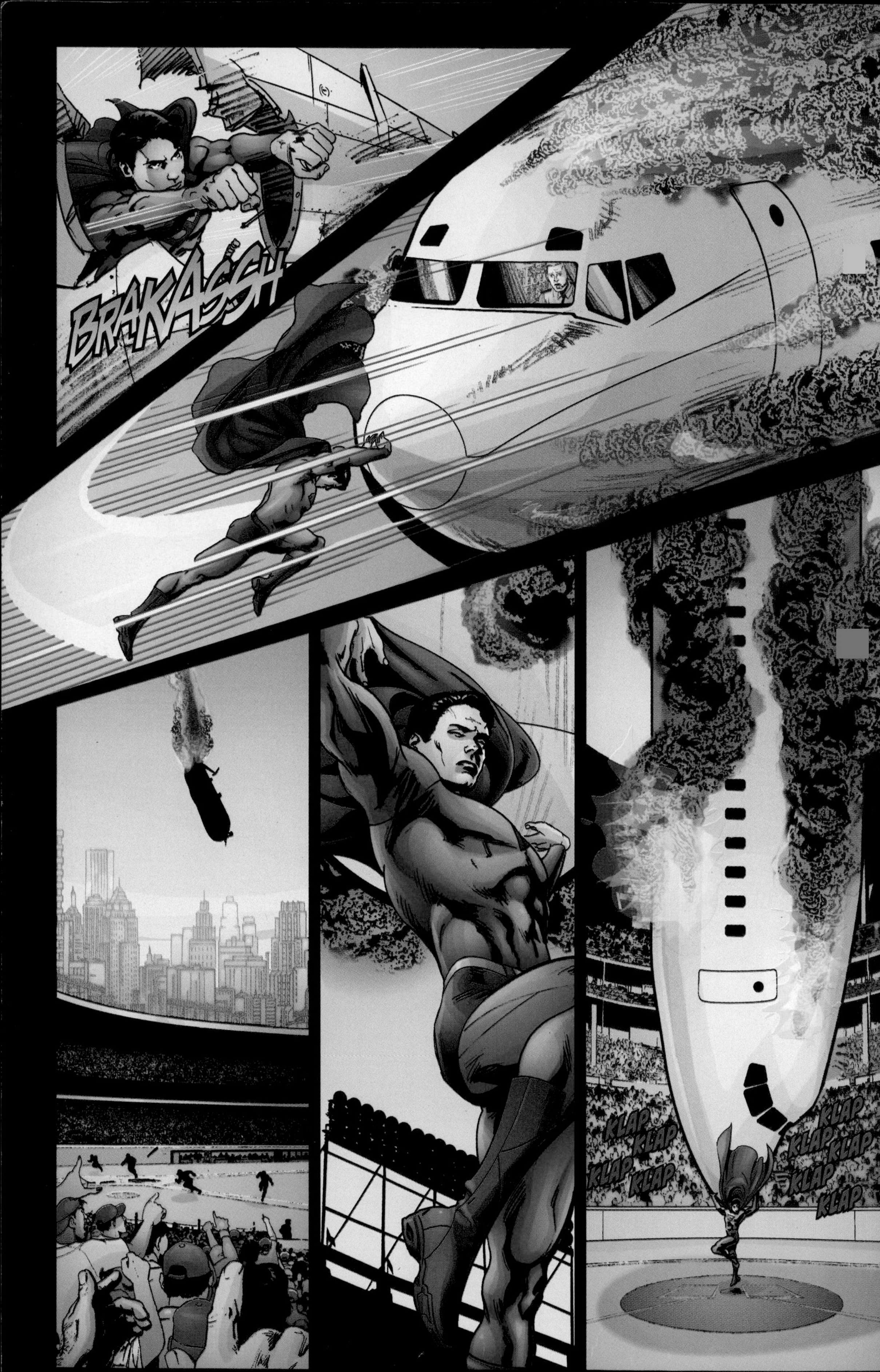
BRAKASSH
KLAP KLAP KLAP KLAP
KLAP KLAP KLAP KLAP KLAP KLAP

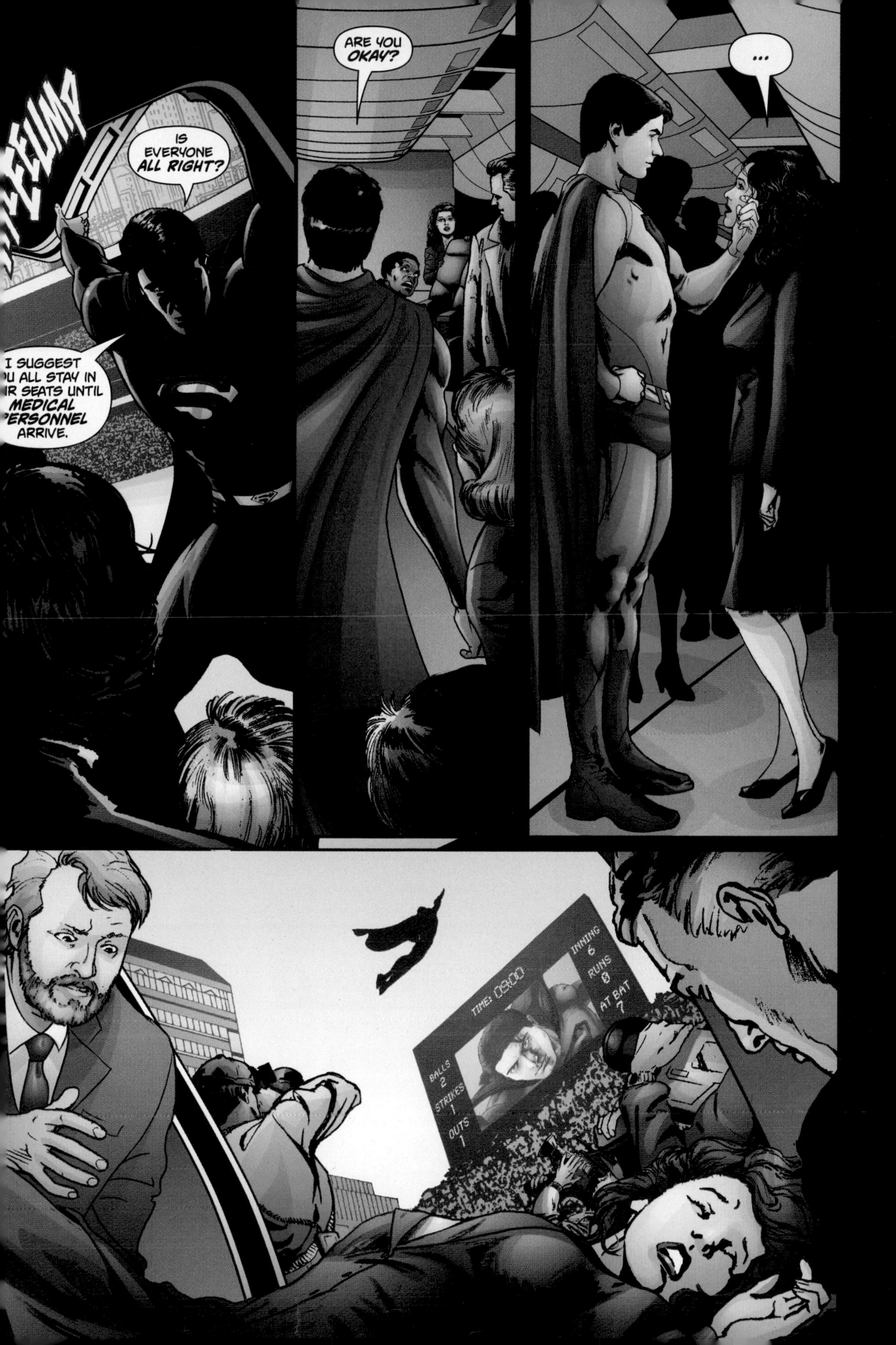

IS EVERYONE ALL RIGHT?
I SUGGEST
U ALL STAY IN
R SEATS UNTIL
MEDICAL
PERSONNEL
ARRIVE.
ARE YOU OKAY?
...
TIME: 09:00
INNING 6
RUNS 0
AT BAT 7
BALLS 2
STRIKES 1
OUTS 1

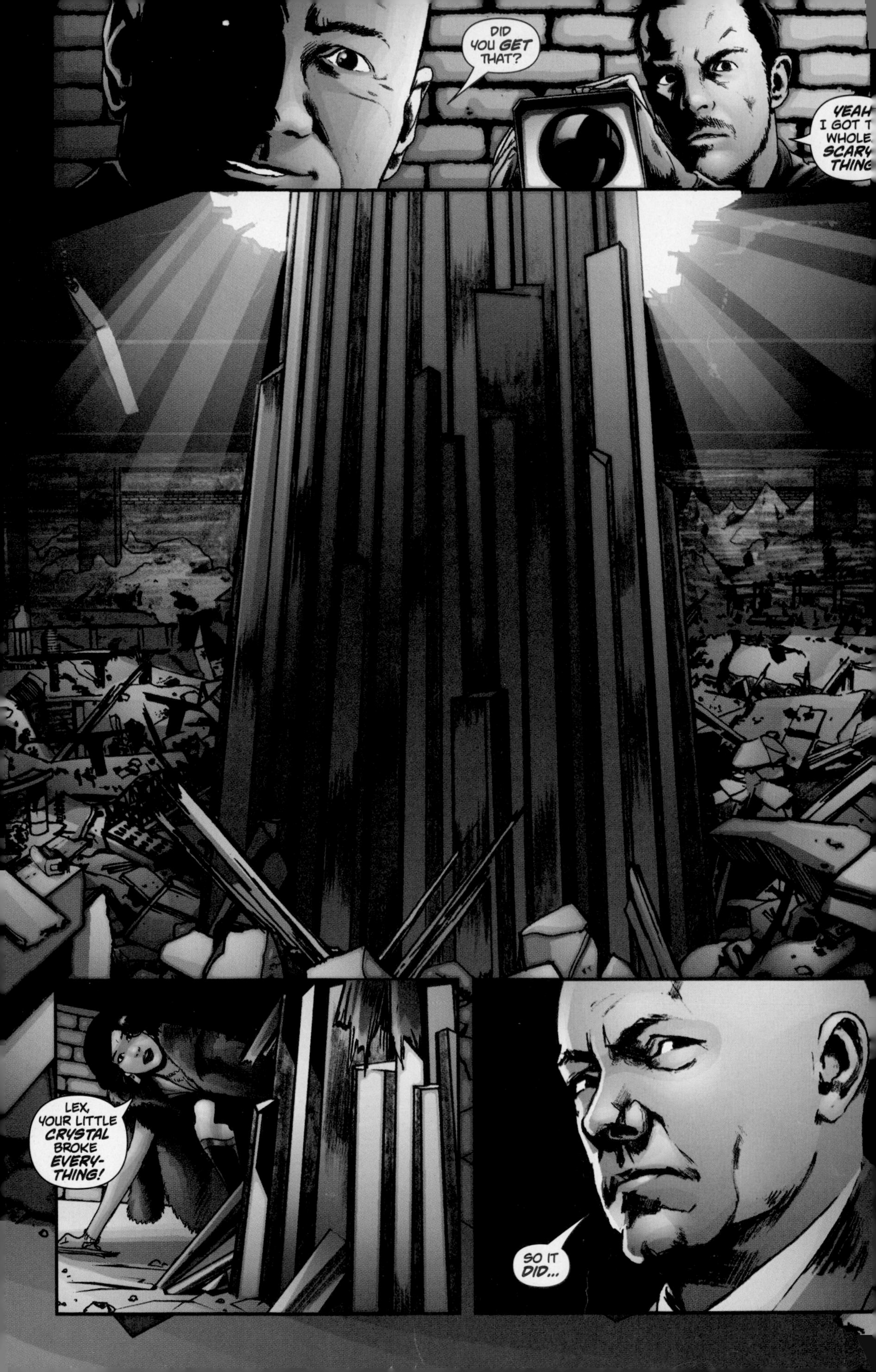
DID YOU GET THAT?
YEAH I GOT T WHOLE SCARY THING
LEX, YOUR LITTLE CRYSTAL BROKE EVERY-THING!
SO IT DID...

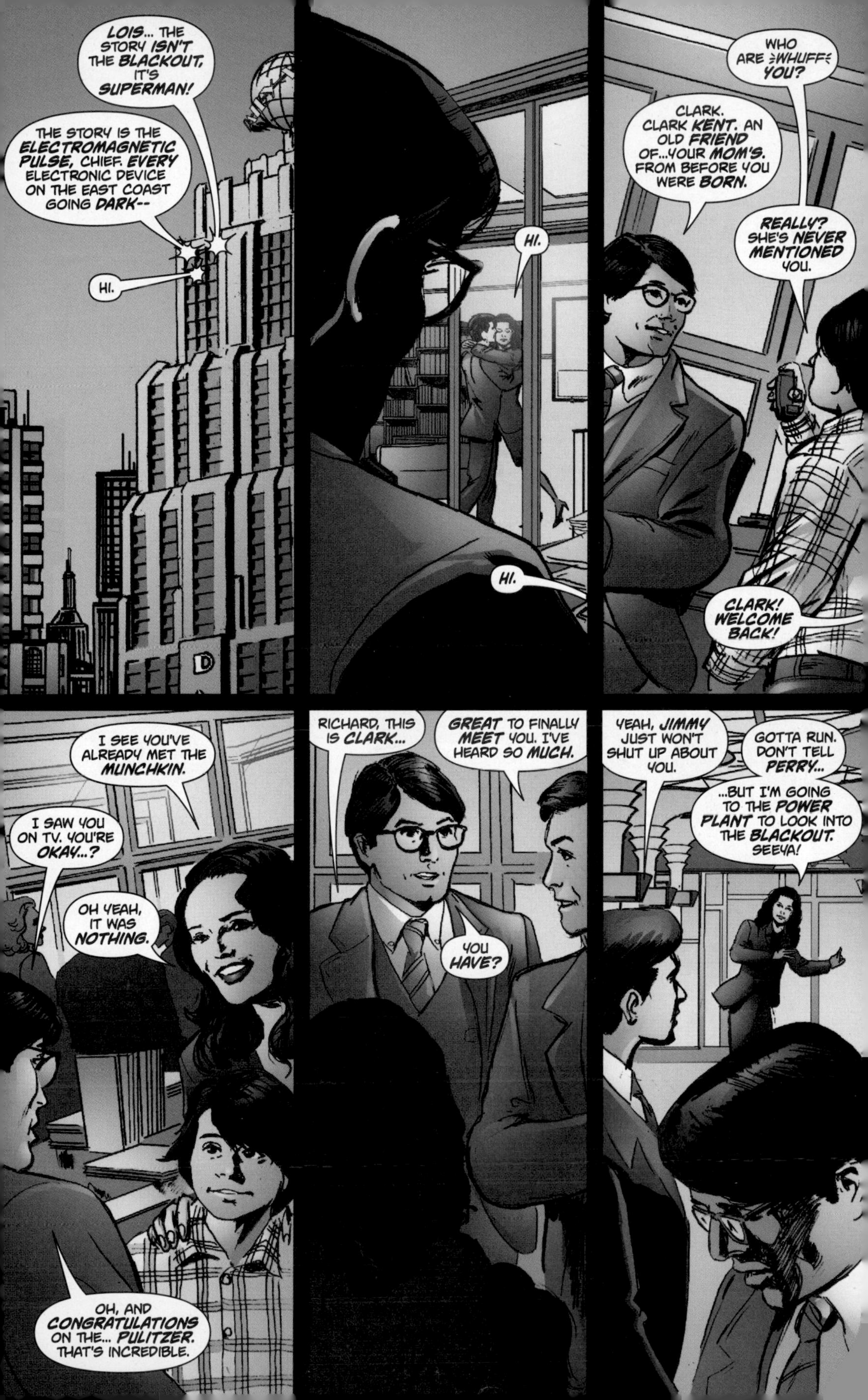
LOIS... THE STORY ISN'T THE BLACKOUT, IT'S SUPERMAN!
THE STORY IS THE ELECTROMAGNETIC PULSE, CHIEF. EVERY ELECTRONIC DEVICE ON THE EAST COAST GOING DARK--
HI.
HI.
HI.
WHO ARE WHUFF YOU?
CLARK. CLARK KENT. AN OLD FRIEND OF...YOUR MOM'S. FROM BEFORE YOU WERE BORN.
REALLY? SHE'S NEVER MENTIONED YOU.
CLARK! WELCOME BACK!
I SEE YOU'VE ALREADY MET THE MUNCHKIN.
I SAW YOU ON TV. YOU'RE OKAY...?
OH YEAH, IT WAS NOTHING.
OH, AND CONGRATULATIONS ON THE... PULITZER. THAT'S INCREDIBLE.
RICHARD, THIS IS CLARK...
GREAT TO FINALLY MEET YOU. I'VE HEARD SO MUCH.
YOU HAVE?
YEAH, JIMMY JUST WON'T SHUT UP ABOUT YOU.
GOTTA RUN. DON'T TELL PERRY...
...BUT I'M GOING TO THE POWER PLANT TO LOOK INTO THE BLACKOUT. SEEYA!

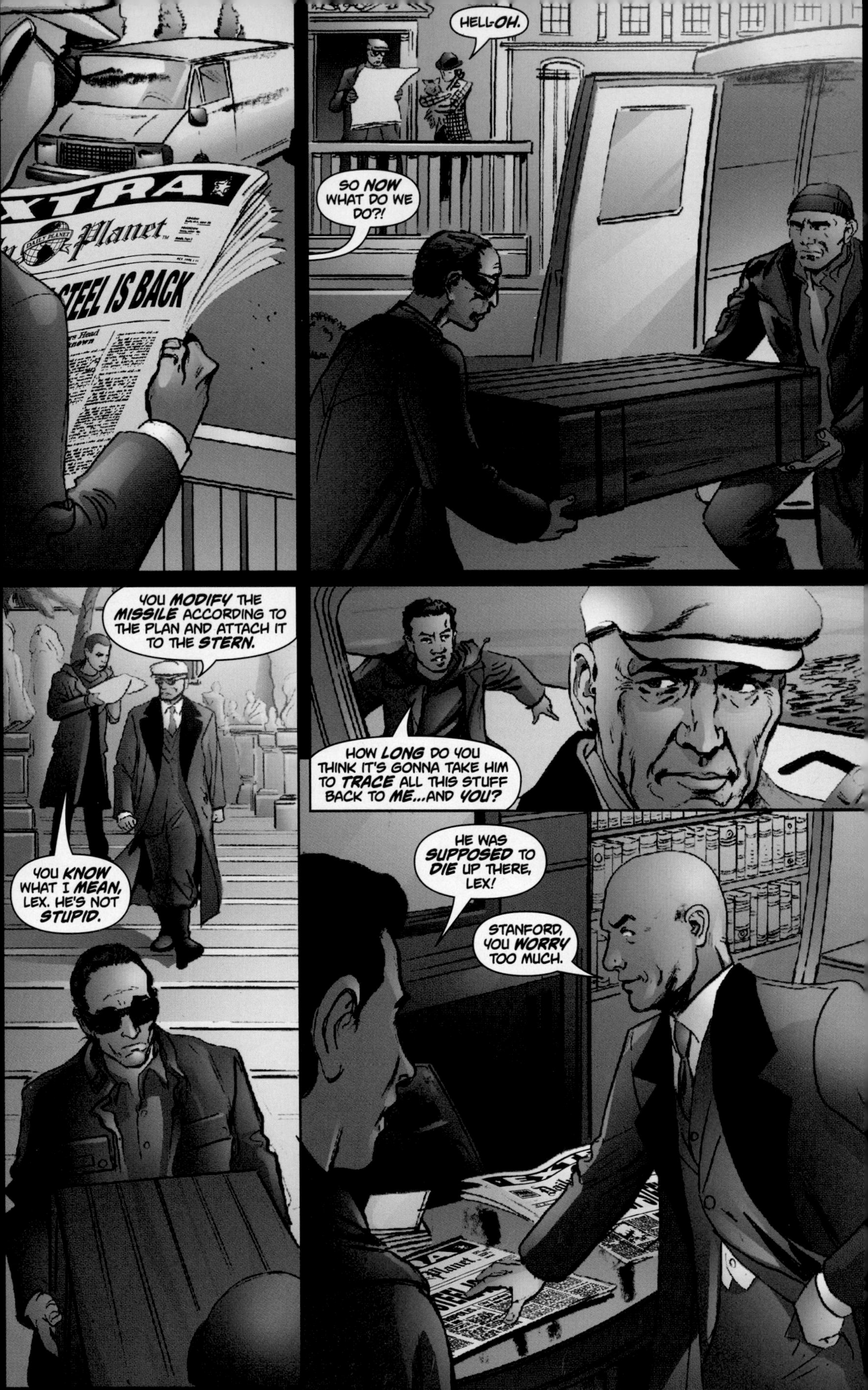
XTRA
Planet
STEEL IS BACK
HELL-OH.
SO NOW WHAT DO WE DO?!
YOU MODIFY THE MISSILE ACCORDING TO THE PLAN AND ATTACH IT TO THE STERN.
HOW LONG DO YOU THINK IT'S GONNA TAKE HIM TO TRACE ALL THIS STUFF BACK TO ME...AND YOU?
YOU KNOW WHAT I MEAN, LEX. HE'S NOT STUPID.
HE WAS SUPPOSED TO DIE UP THERE, LEX!
STANFORD, YOU WORRY TOO MUCH.

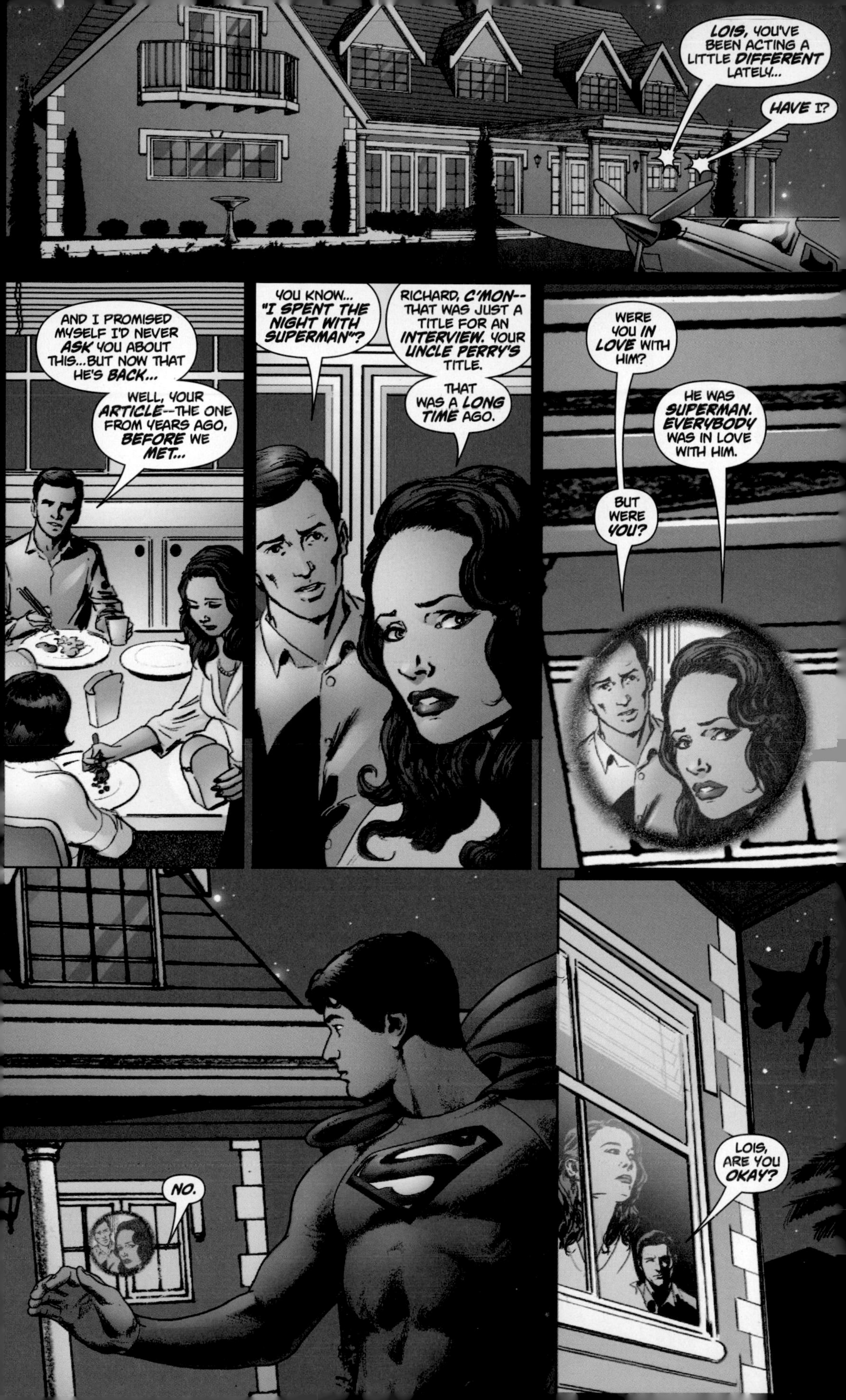

LOIS, YOU'VE BEEN ACTING A LITTLE DIFFERENT LATELY...
HAVE I?
AND I PROMISED MYSELF I'D NEVER ASK YOU ABOUT THIS...BUT NOW THAT HE'S BACK...
WELL, YOUR ARTICLE--THE ONE FROM YEARS AGO, BEFORE WE MET...
YOU KNOW... "I SPENT THE NIGHT WITH SUPERMAN"?
RICHARD, C'MON--THAT WAS JUST A TITLE FOR AN INTERVIEW. YOUR UNCLE PERRY'S TITLE.
THAT WAS A LONG TIME AGO.
WERE YOU IN LOVE WITH HIM?
HE WAS SUPERMAN. EVERYBODY WAS IN LOVE WITH HIM.
BUT WERE YOU?
NO.
LOIS, ARE YOU OKAY?

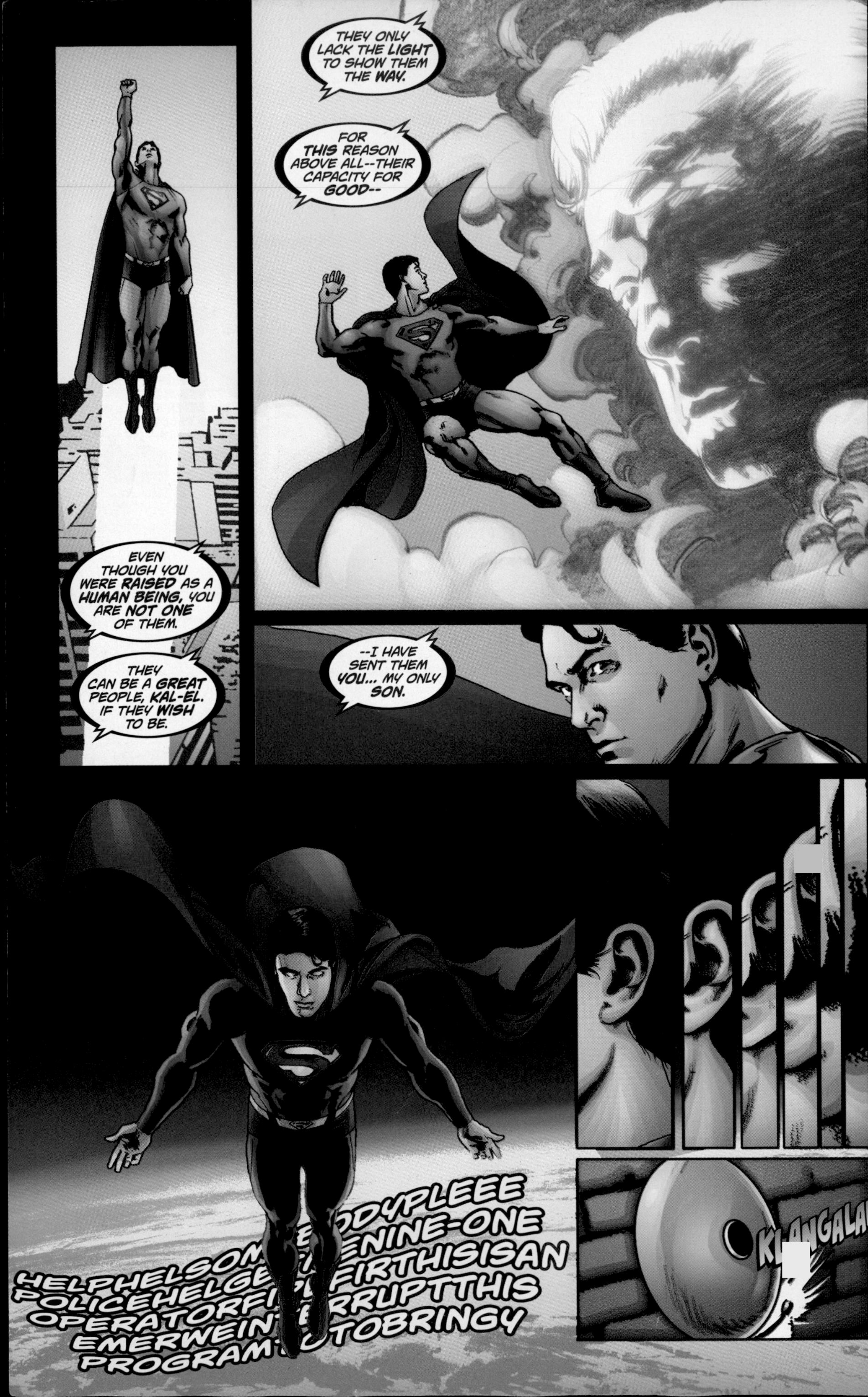
EVEN THOUGH YOU WERE RAISED AS A HUMAN BEING, YOU ARE NOT ONE OF THEM.
THEY CAN BE A GREAT PEOPLE, KAL-EL. IF THEY WISH TO BE.
THEY ONLY LACK THE LIGHT TO SHOW THEM THE WAY.
FOR THIS REASON ABOVE ALL--THEIR CAPACITY FOR GOOD--
--I HAVE SENT THEM YOU... MY ONLY SON.
HELPHELSOM BODYPLEEE
POLICEHELGE ENINE-ONE
OPERATORFI FIRTHISISAN
EMERWEINT RRUPTTHIS
PROGRAM TOBRINGY
KLANGALA

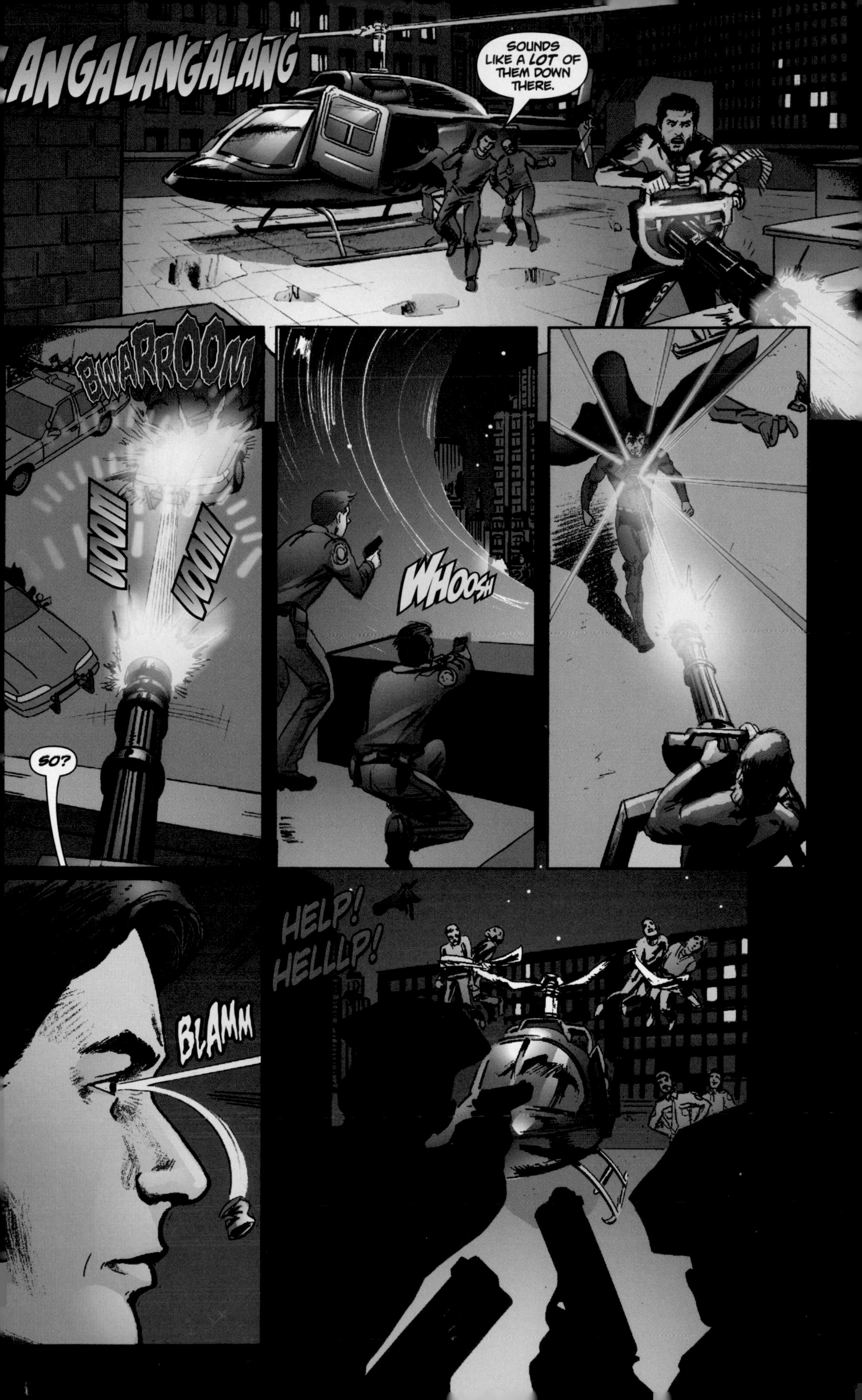
ANGALANGALANG
SOUNDS LIKE A LOT OF THEM DOWN THERE.
BWARROOM
VOOM
VOOM
SO?
WHOOSH
BLAMM
HELP! HELLLP!

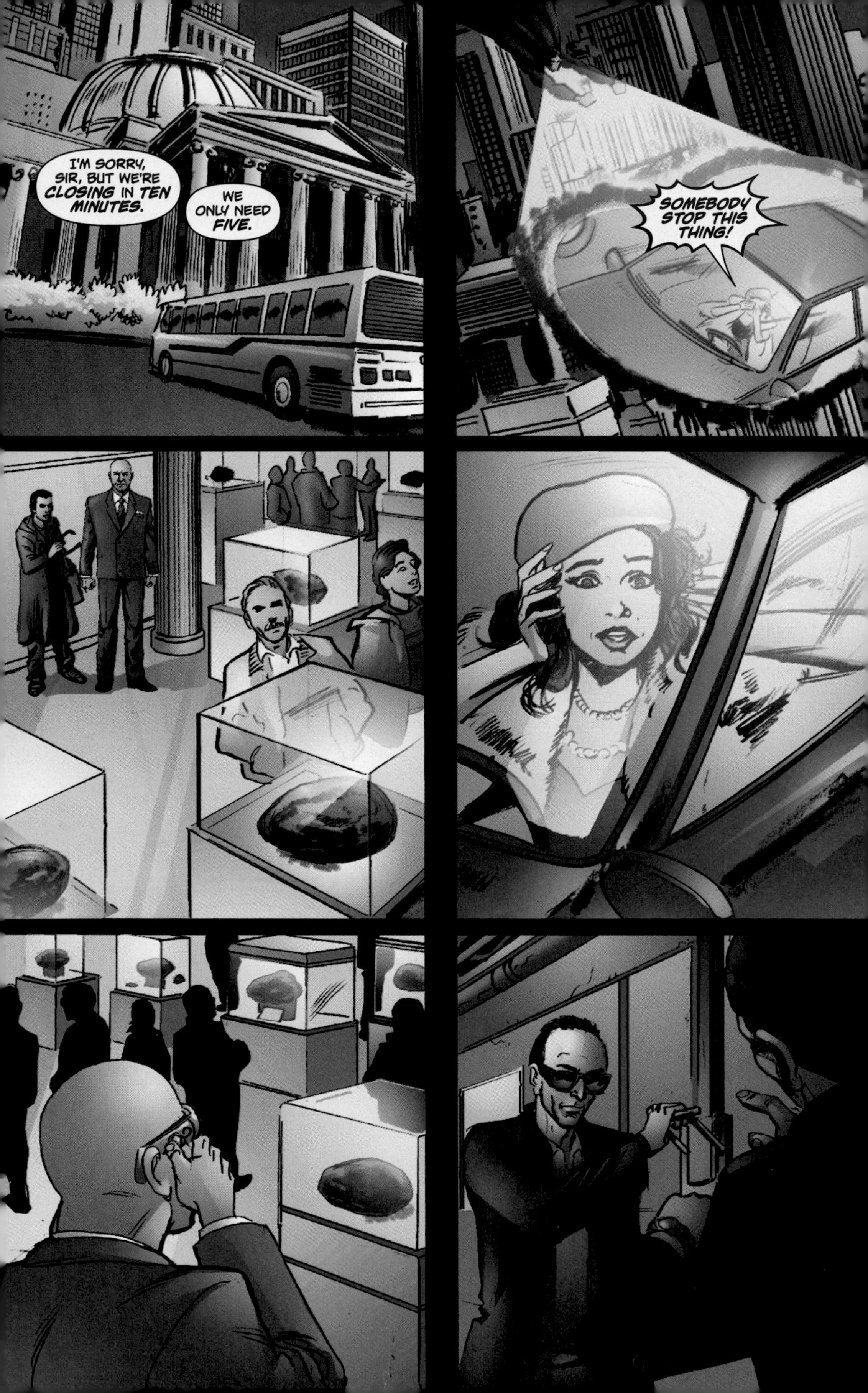
I'M SORRY, SIR, BUT WE'RE CLOSING IN TEN MINUTES.
WE ONLY NEED FIVE.
SOMEBODY STOP THIS THING!

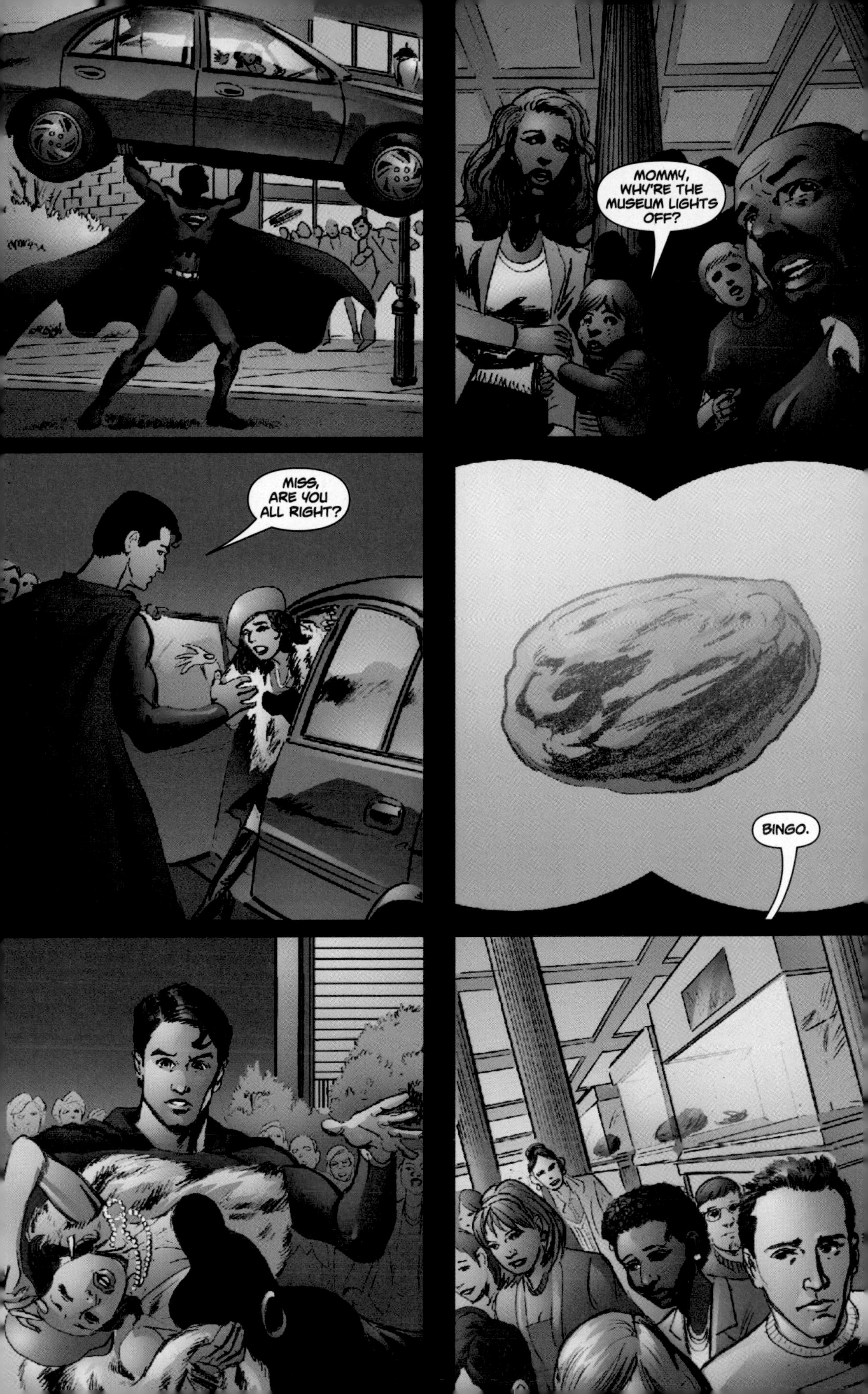
MOMMY, WHY'RE THE MUSEUM LIGHTS OFF?
MISS, ARE YOU ALL RIGHT?
BINGO.

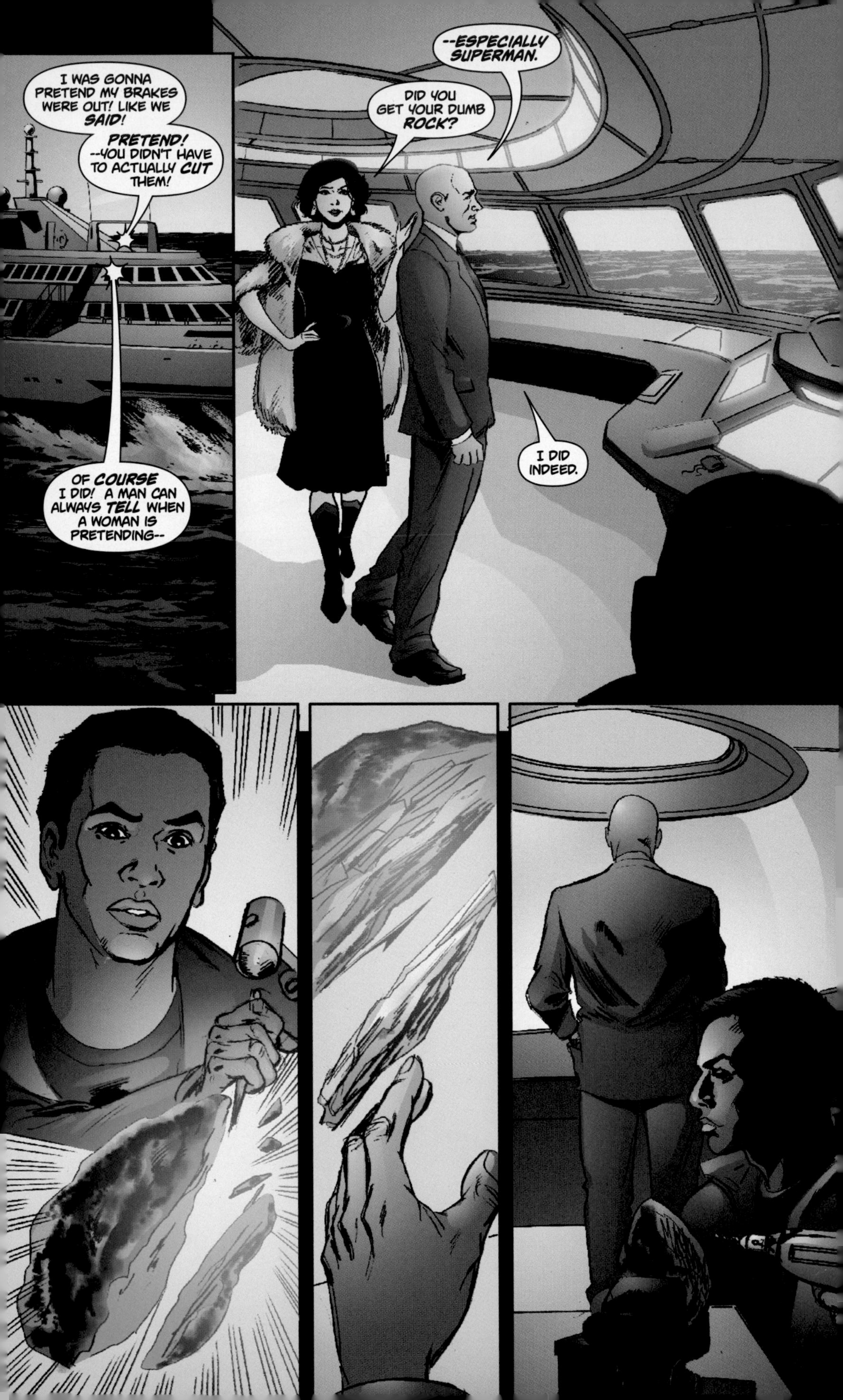
I WAS GONNA PRETEND MY BRAKES WERE OUT! LIKE WE SAID!
PRETEND! --YOU DIDN'T HAVE TO ACTUALLY CUT THEM!
OF COURSE I DID! A MAN CAN ALWAYS TELL WHEN A WOMAN IS PRETENDING--
--ESPECIALLY SUPERMAN.
DID YOU GET YOUR DUMB ROCK?
I DID INDEED.

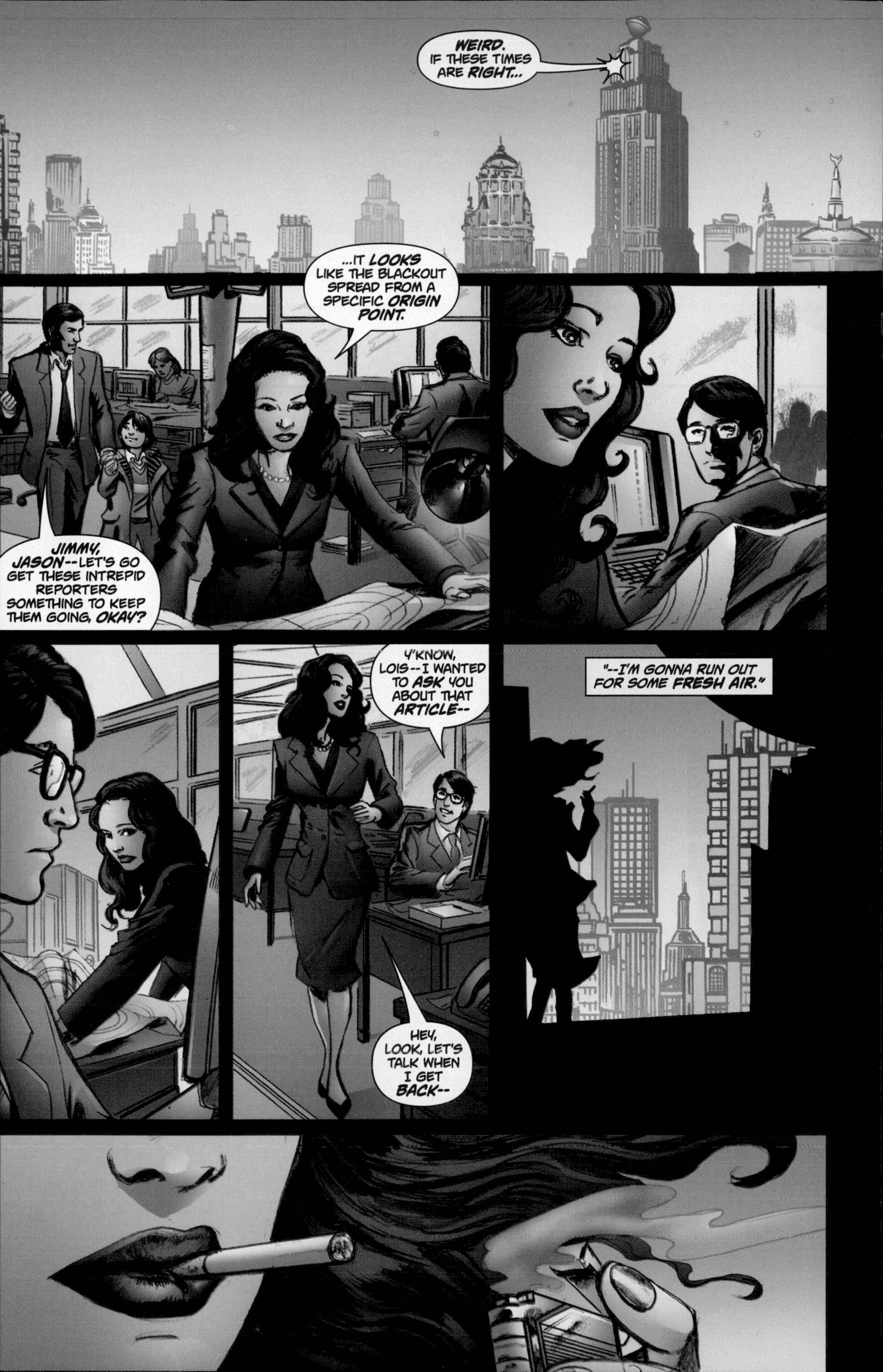
WEIRD. IF THESE TIMES ARE RIGHT...
...IT LOOKS LIKE THE BLACKOUT SPREAD FROM A SPECIFIC ORIGIN POINT.
JIMMY, JASON--LET'S GO GET THESE INTREPID REPORTERS SOMETHING TO KEEP THEM GOING, OKAY?
Y'KNOW, LOIS--I WANTED TO ASK YOU ABOUT THAT ARTICLE--
HEY, LOOK, LET'S TALK WHEN I GET BACK--
"--I'M GONNA RUN OUT FOR SOME FRESH AIR."

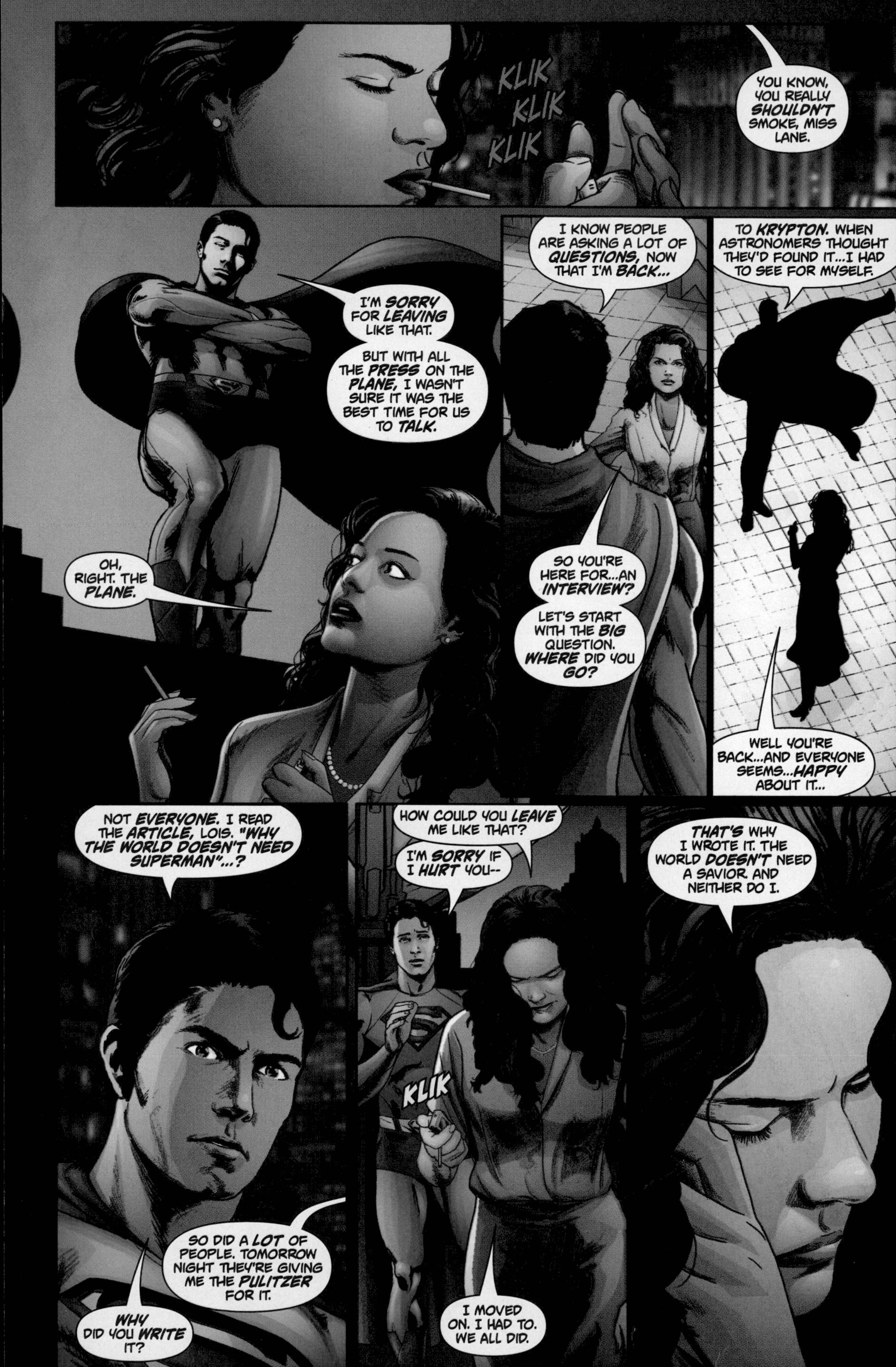
KLIK
KLIK
KLIK
YOU KNOW, YOU REALLY SHOULDN'T SMOKE, MISS LANE.
I'M SORRY FOR LEAVING LIKE THAT.
BUT WITH ALL THE PRESS ON THE PLANE, I WASN'T SURE IT WAS THE BEST TIME FOR US TO TALK.
OH, RIGHT. THE PLANE.
I KNOW PEOPLE ARE ASKING A LOT OF QUESTIONS, NOW THAT I'M BACK...
SO YOU'RE HERE FOR...AN INTERVIEW?
LET'S START WITH THE BIG QUESTION. WHERE DID YOU GO?
TO KRYPTON. WHEN ASTRONOMERS THOUGHT THEY'D FOUND IT...I HAD TO SEE FOR MYSELF.
WELL YOU'RE BACK...AND EVERYONE SEEMS...HAPPY ABOUT IT...
NOT EVERYONE. I READ THE ARTICLE, LOIS. "WHY THE WORLD DOESN'T NEED SUPERMAN"...?
SO DID A LOT OF PEOPLE. TOMORROW NIGHT THEY'RE GIVING ME THE PULITZER FOR IT.
WHY DID YOU WRITE IT?
HOW COULD YOU LEAVE ME LIKE THAT?
I'M SORRY IF I HURT YOU--
KLIK
I MOVED ON. I HAD TO. WE ALL DID.
THAT'S WHY I WROTE IT. THE WORLD DOESN'T NEED A SAVIOR. AND NEITHER DO I.

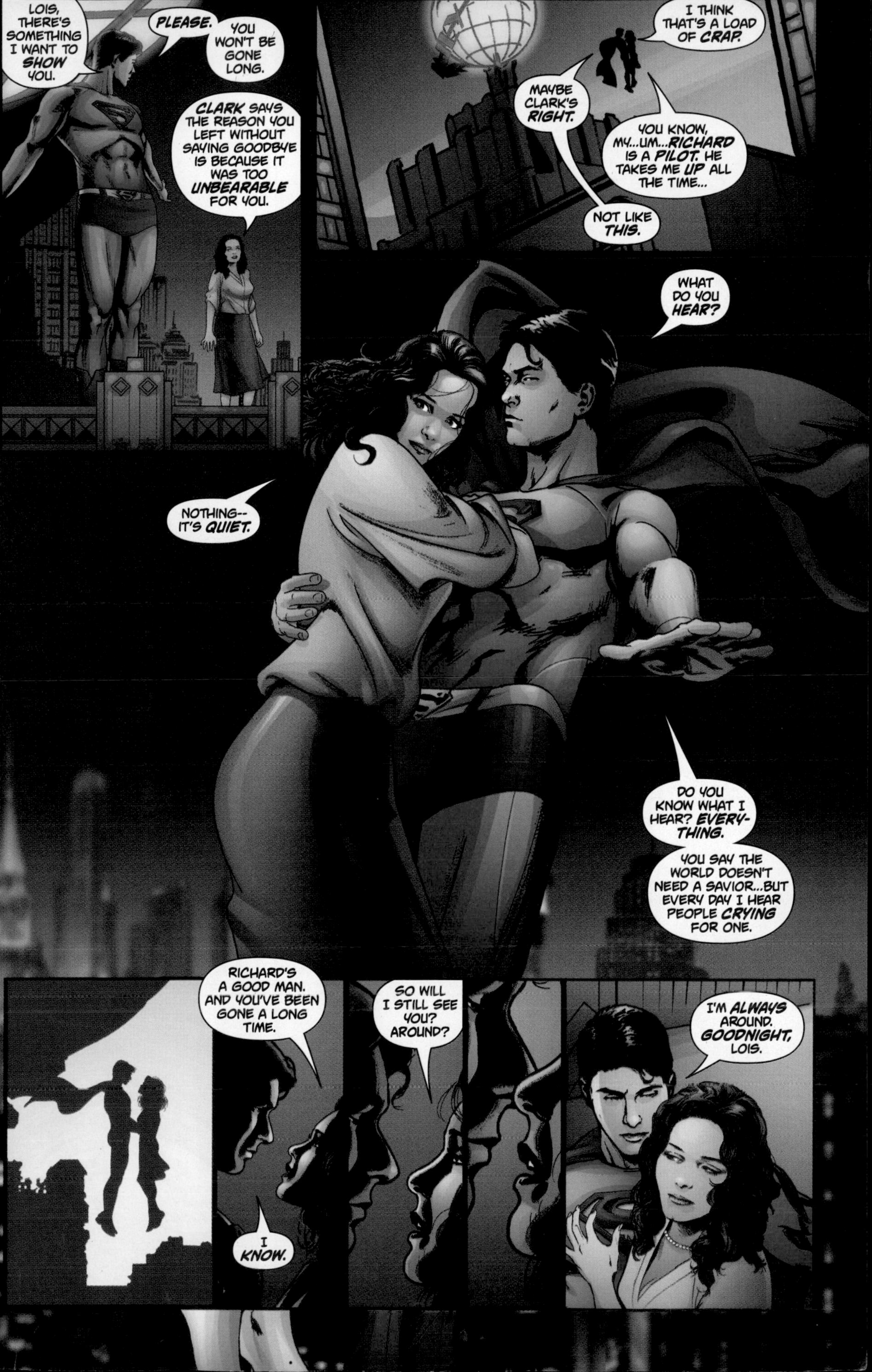
LOIS, THERE'S SOMETHING I WANT TO SHOW YOU.
PLEASE.
YOU WON'T BE GONE LONG.
CLARK SAYS THE REASON YOU LEFT WITHOUT SAYING GOODBYE IS BECAUSE IT WAS TOO UNBEARABLE FOR YOU.
I THINK THAT'S A LOAD OF CRAP.
MAYBE CLARK'S RIGHT.
YOU KNOW, MY...UM...RICHARD IS A PILOT. HE TAKES ME UP ALL THE TIME...
NOT LIKE THIS.
WHAT DO YOU HEAR?
NOTHING--IT'S QUIET.
DO YOU KNOW WHAT I HEAR? EVERY-THING.
YOU SAY THE WORLD DOESN'T NEED A SAVIOR...BUT EVERY DAY I HEAR PEOPLE CRYING FOR ONE.
RICHARD'S A GOOD MAN. AND YOU'VE BEEN GONE A LONG TIME.
I KNOW.
SO WILL I STILL SEE YOU? AROUND?
I'M ALWAYS AROUND. GOODNIGHT, LOIS.

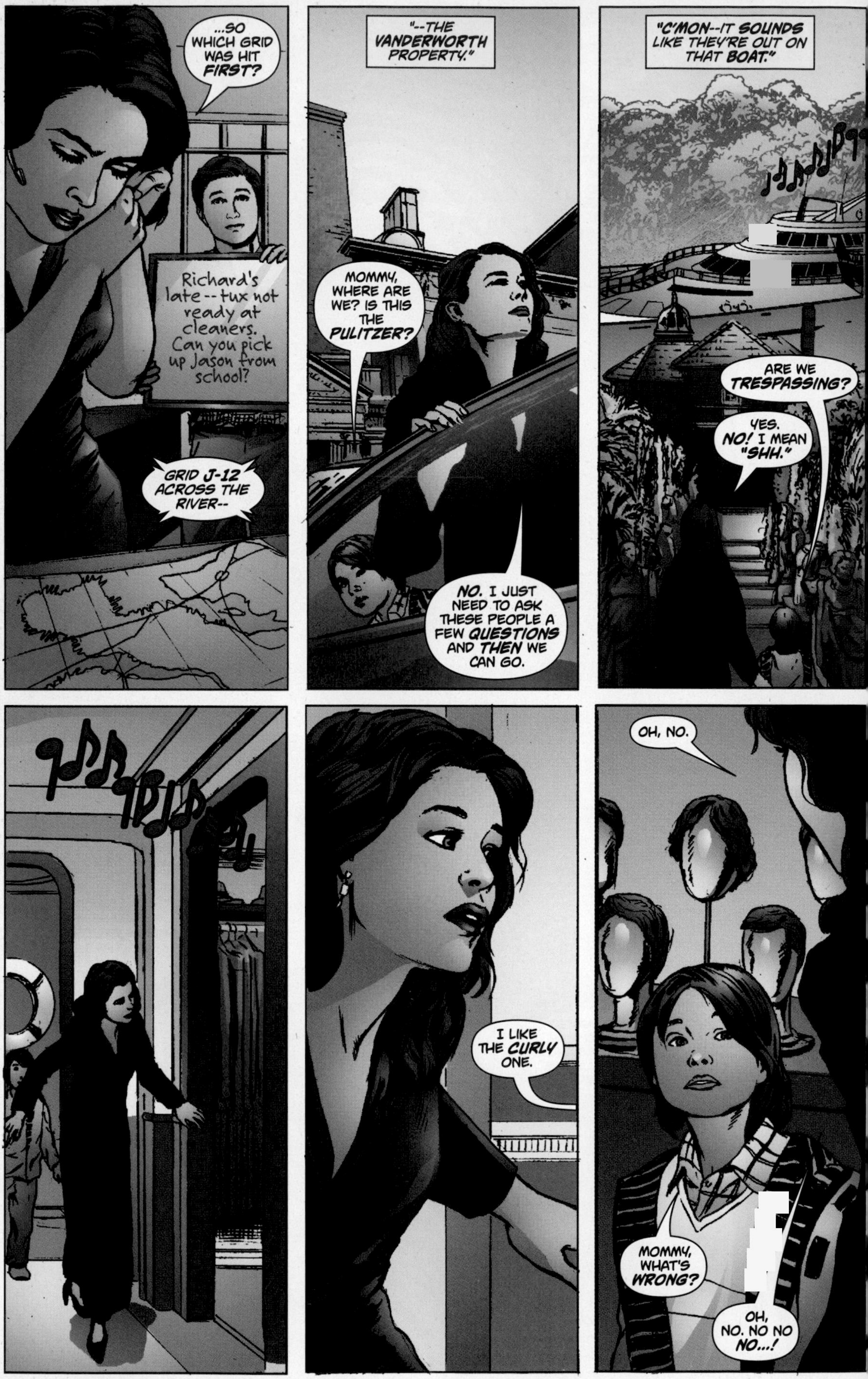
...SO WHICH GRID WAS HIT FIRST?
Richard's late -- tux not ready at cleaners. Can you pick up Jason from school?
GRID J-12 ACROSS THE RIVER--
"--THE VANDERWORTH PROPERTY."
MOMMY, WHERE ARE WE? IS THIS THE PULITZER?
NO. I JUST NEED TO ASK THESE PEOPLE A FEW QUESTIONS AND THEN WE CAN GO.
"C'MON--IT SOUNDS LIKE THEY'RE OUT ON THAT BOAT."
ARE WE TRESPASSING?
YES. NO! I MEAN "SHH."
I LIKE THE CURLY ONE.
OH, NO.
MOMMY, WHAT'S WRONG?
OH, NO. NO NO NO...!

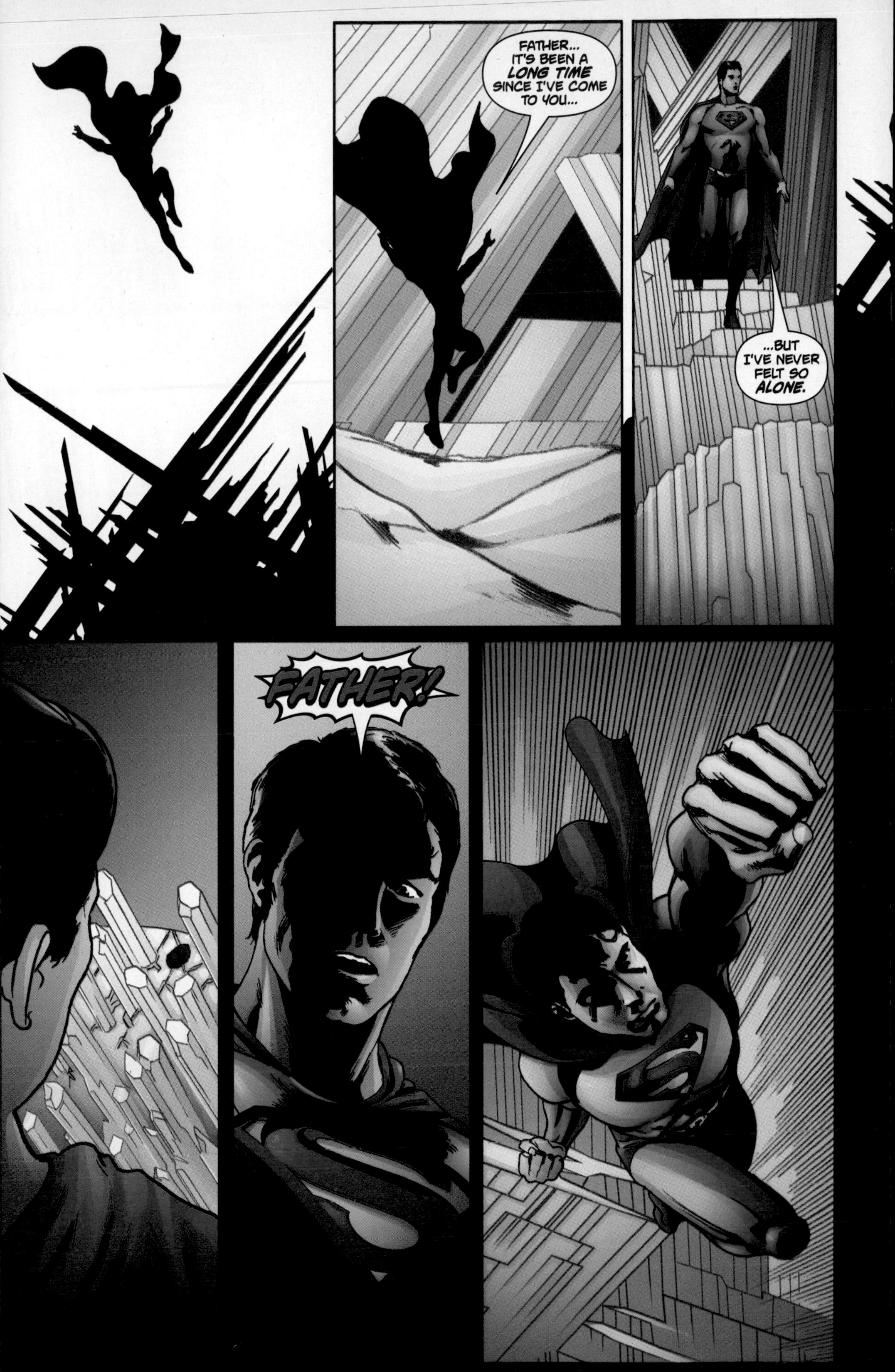
FATHER... IT'S BEEN A LONG TIME SINCE I'VE COME TO YOU...
...BUT I'VE NEVER FELT SO ALONE.
FATHER!

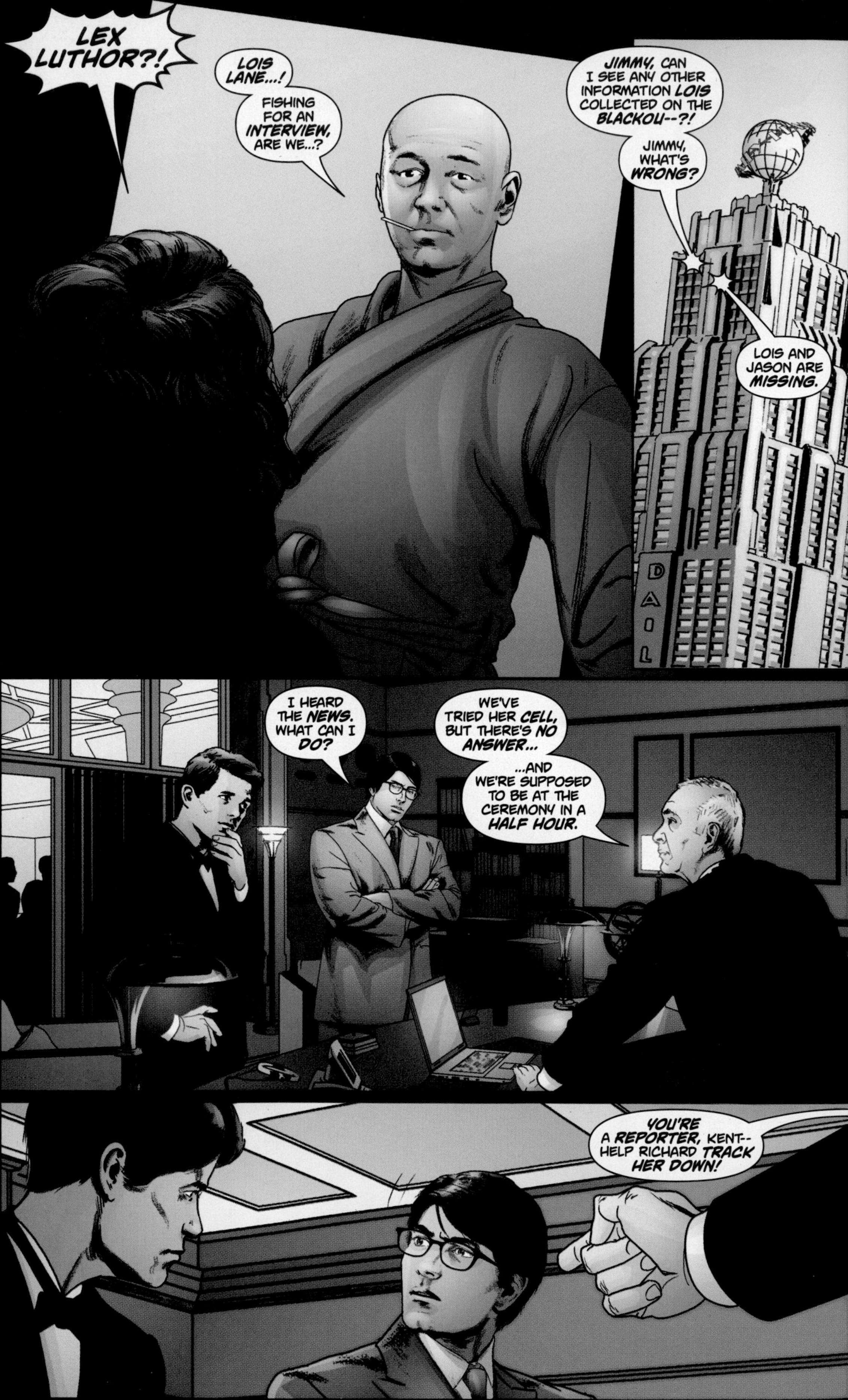
LEX LUTHOR?!
LOIS LANE...!
FISHING FOR AN INTERVIEW, ARE WE...?
JIMMY, CAN I SEE ANY OTHER INFORMATION LOIS COLLECTED ON THE BLACKOU--?!
JIMMY, WHAT'S WRONG?
LOIS AND JASON ARE MISSING.
DAIL
I HEARD THE NEWS. WHAT CAN I DO?
WE'VE TRIED HER CELL, BUT THERE'S NO ANSWER...
...AND WE'RE SUPPOSED TO BE AT THE CEREMONY IN A HALF HOUR.
YOU'RE A REPORTER, KENT-- HELP RICHARD TRACK HER DOWN!

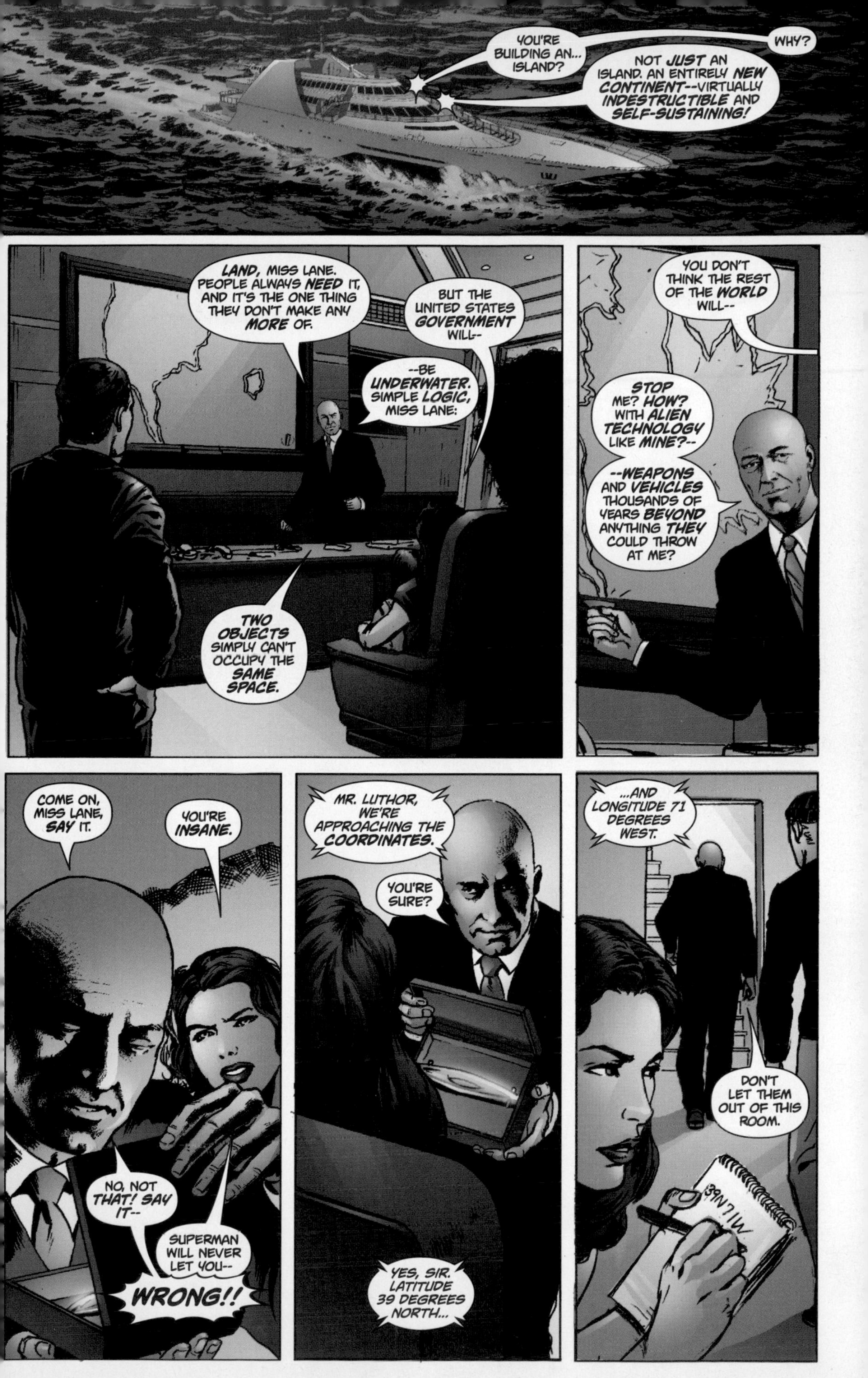
YOU'RE BUILDING AN... ISLAND?
WHY?
NOT JUST AN ISLAND. AN ENTIRELY NEW CONTINENT--VIRTUALLY INDESTRUCTIBLE AND SELF-SUSTAINING!
LAND, MISS LANE. PEOPLE ALWAYS NEED IT, AND IT'S THE ONE THING THEY DON'T MAKE ANY MORE OF.
BUT THE UNITED STATES GOVERNMENT WILL--
--BE UNDERWATER. SIMPLE LOGIC, MISS LANE:
TWO OBJECTS SIMPLY CAN'T OCCUPY THE SAME SPACE.
YOU DON'T THINK THE REST OF THE WORLD WILL--
STOP ME? HOW? WITH ALIEN TECHNOLOGY LIKE MINE?--
--WEAPONS AND VEHICLES THOUSANDS OF YEARS BEYOND ANYTHING THEY COULD THROW AT ME?
COME ON, MISS LANE, SAY IT.
YOU'RE INSANE.
NO, NOT THAT! SAY IT--
SUPERMAN WILL NEVER LET YOU--
WRONG!!
MR. LUTHOR, WE'RE APPROACHING THE COORDINATES.
YOU'RE SURE?
YES, SIR. LATITUDE 39 DEGREES NORTH...
...AND LONGITUDE 71 DEGREES WEST.
DON'T LET THEM OUT OF THIS ROOM.

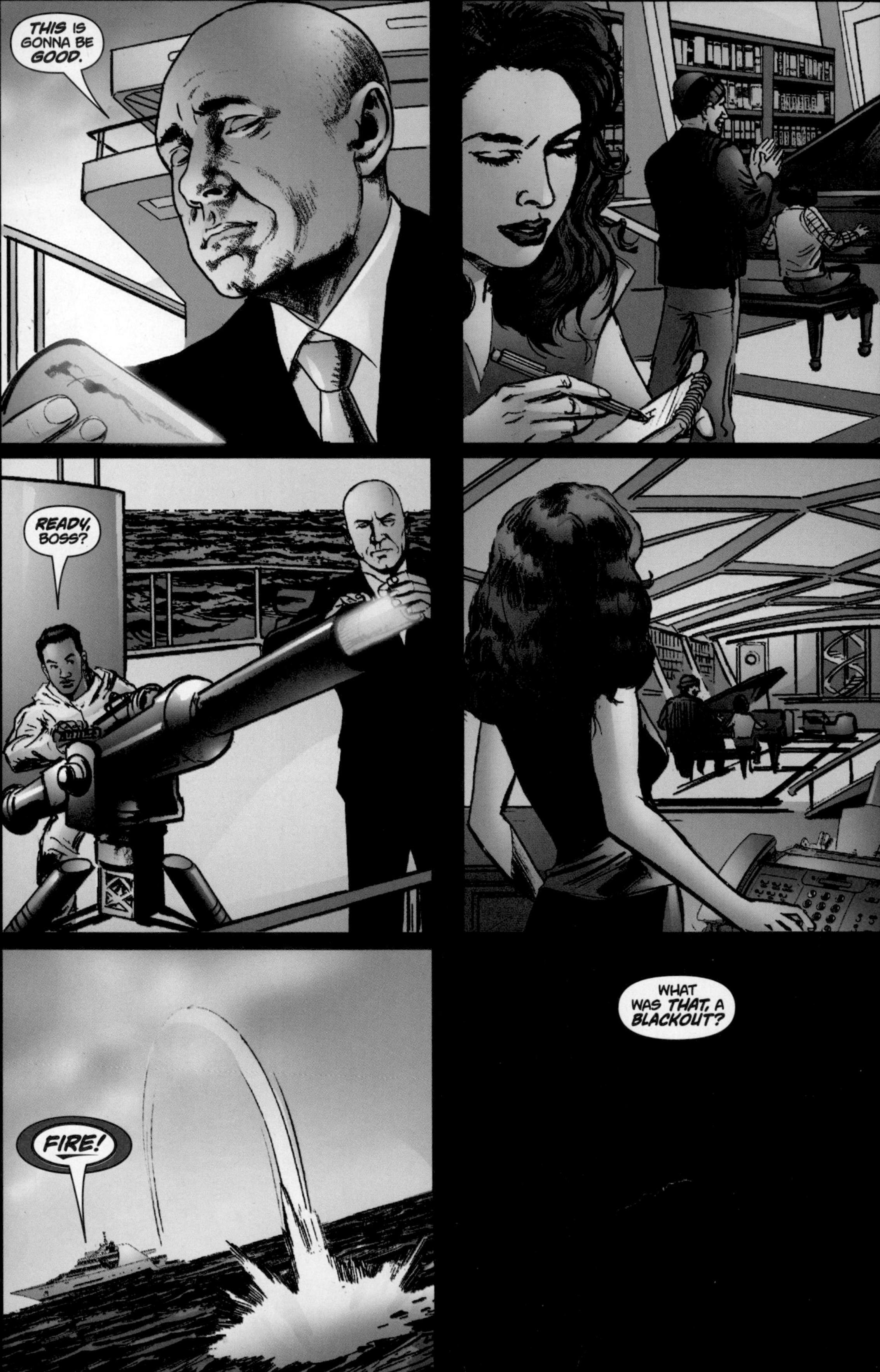
THIS IS GONNA BE GOOD.
READY, BOSS?
FIRE!
WHAT WAS THAT, A BLACKOUT?

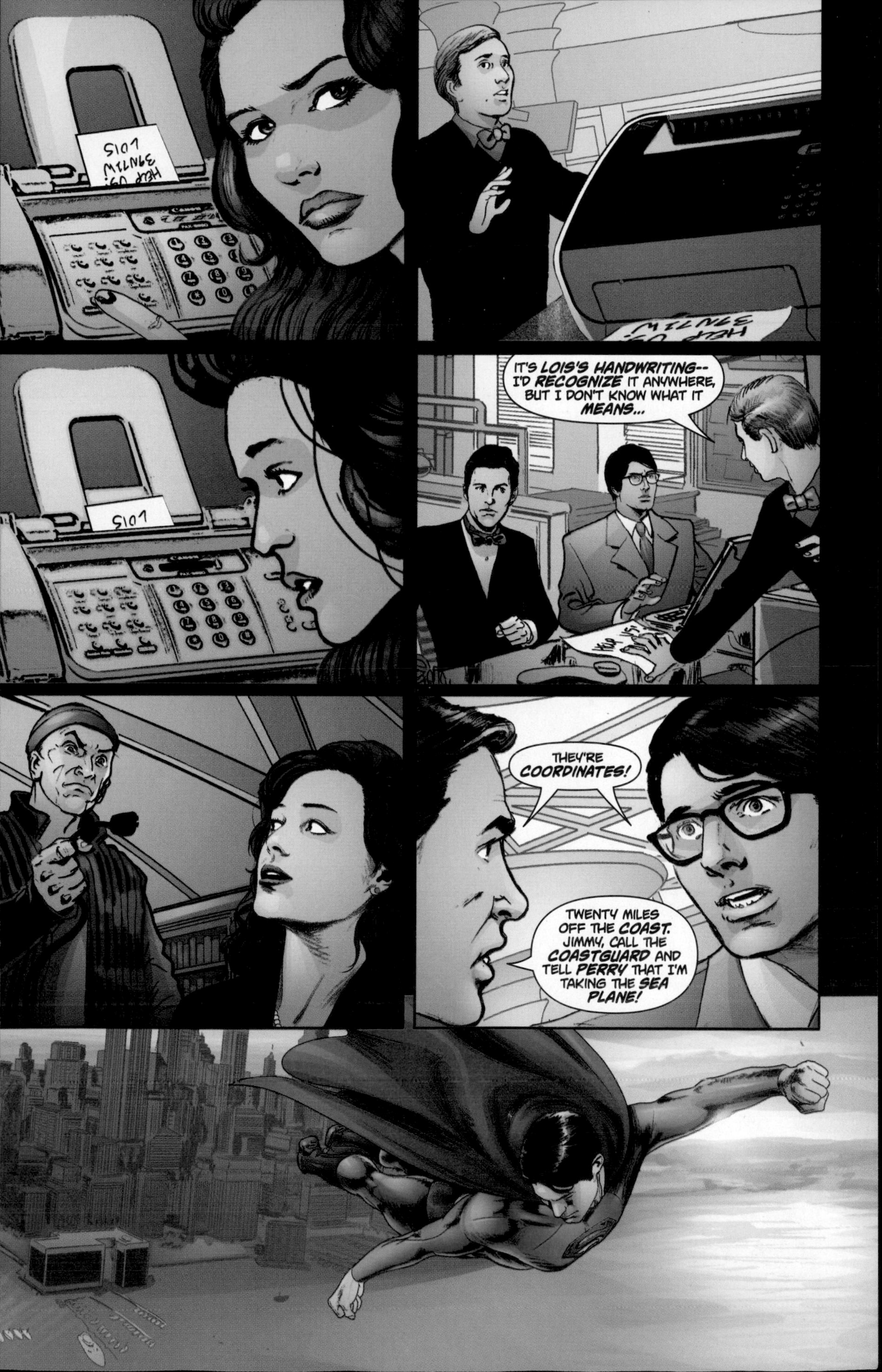
IT'S LOIS'S HANDWRITING-- I'D RECOGNIZE IT ANYWHERE, BUT I DON'T KNOW WHAT IT MEANS...
THEY'RE COORDINATES!
TWENTY MILES OFF THE COAST. JIMMY, CALL THE COASTGUARD AND TELL PERRY THAT I'M TAKING THE SEA PLANE!

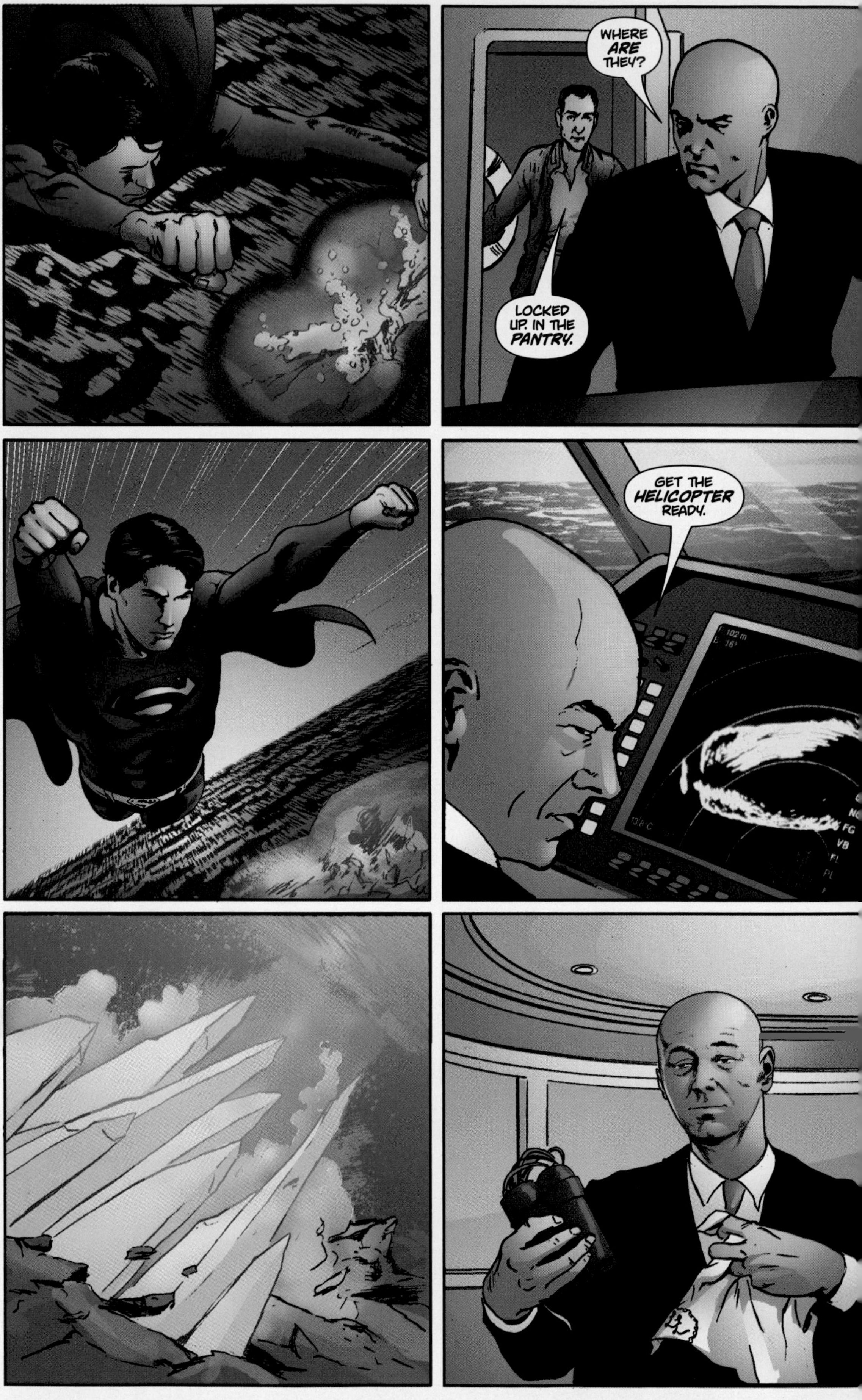
WHERE ARE THEY?
LOCKED UP. IN THE PANTRY.
GET THE HELICOPTER READY.

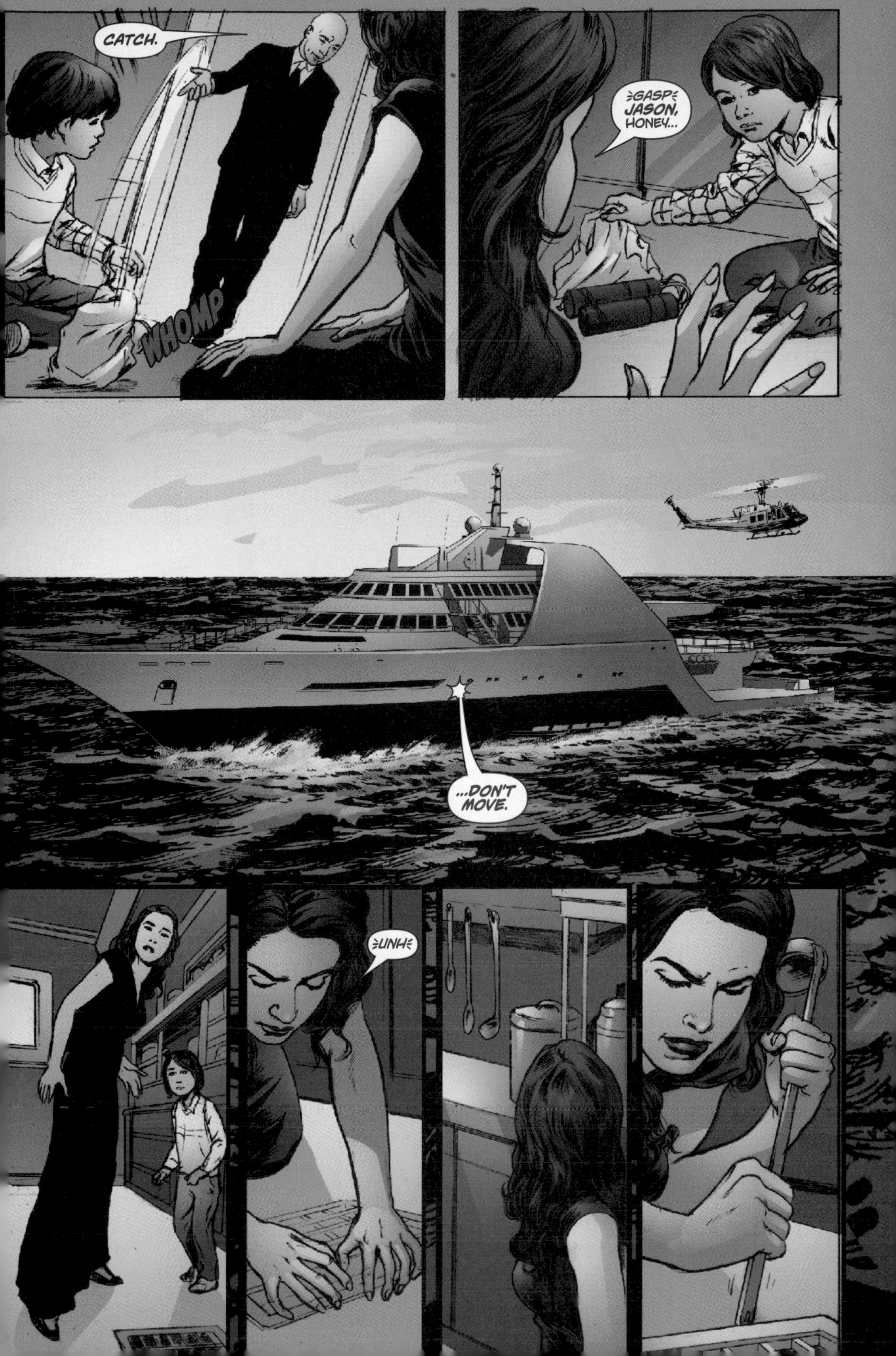
CATCH.
WHOMP
GASP JASON, HONEY...
...DON'T MOVE.
UNH

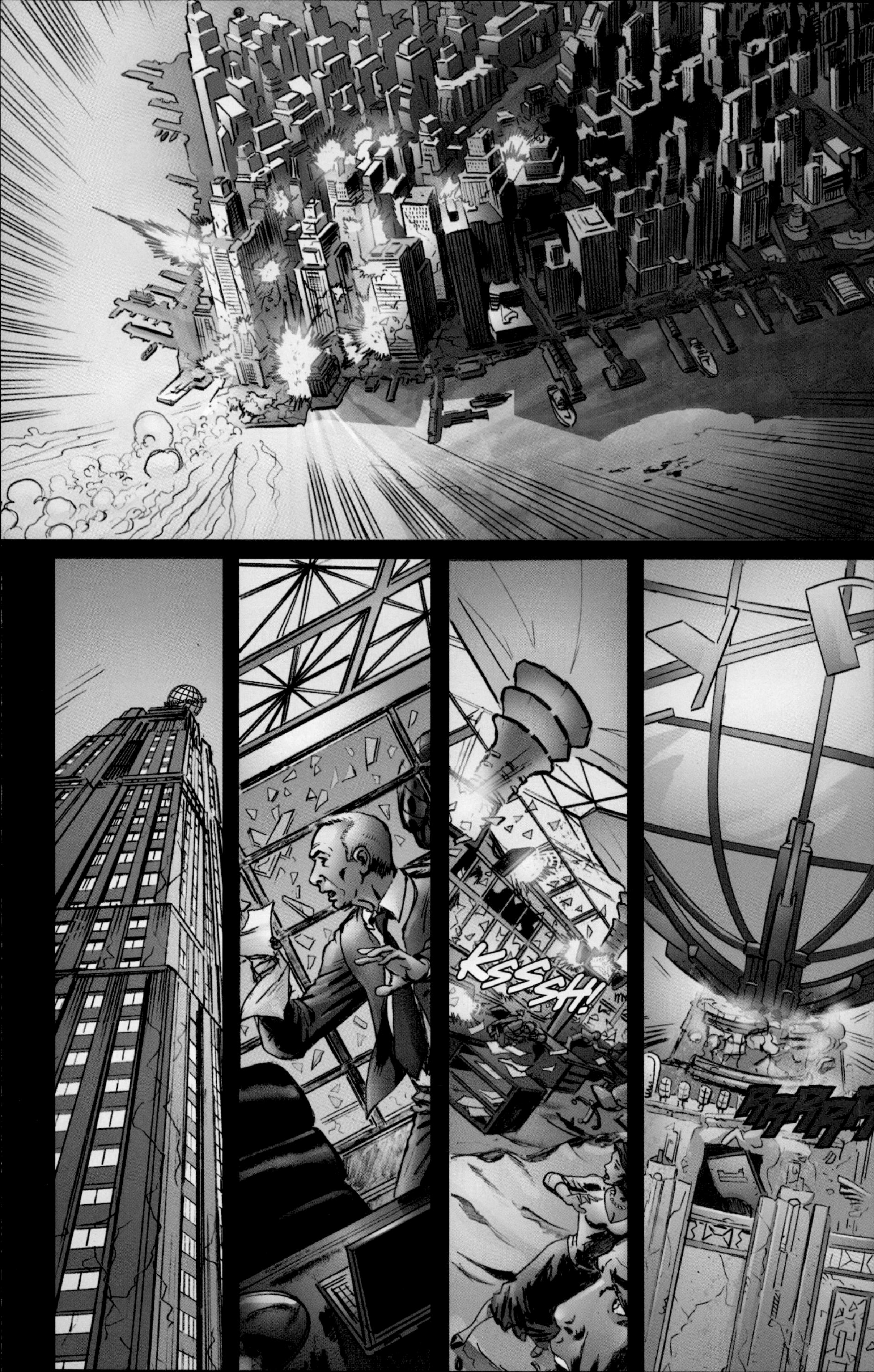
KSSSH!

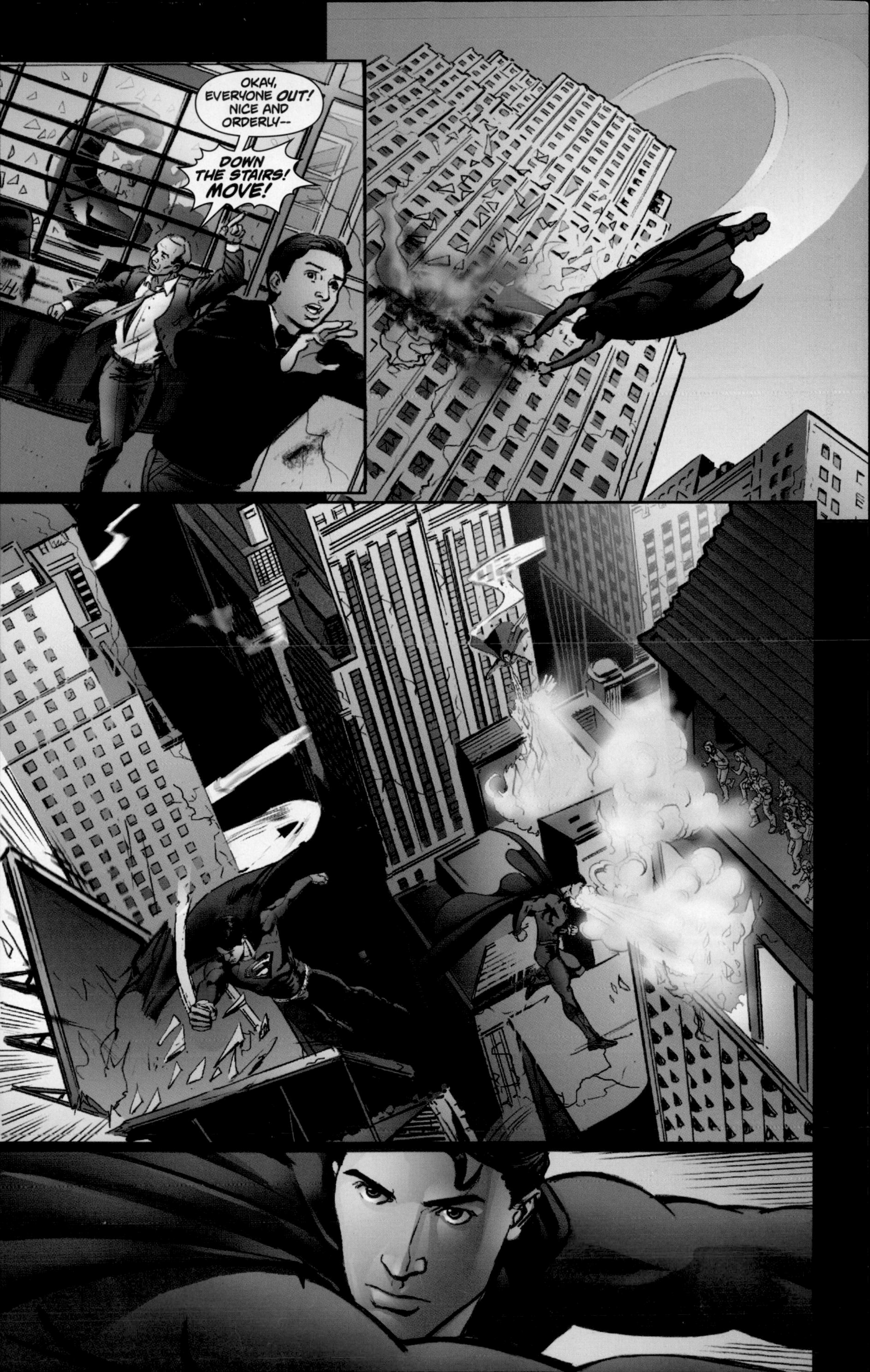
OKAY, EVERYONE OUT! NICE AND ORDERLY--
DOWN THE STAIRS! MOVE!

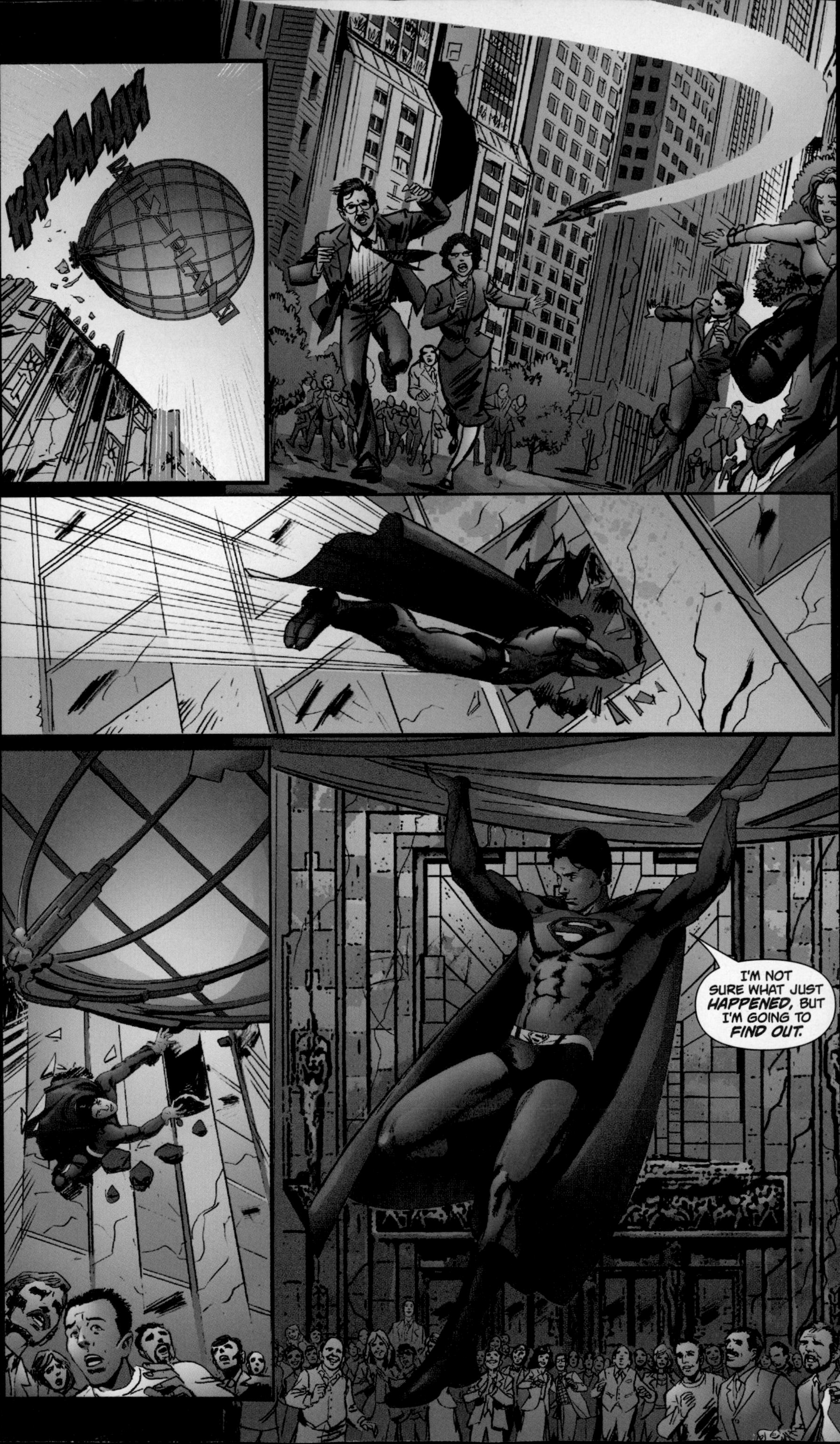
KARAAAK
I'M NOT SURE WHAT JUST HAPPENED, BUT I'M GOING TO FIND OUT.

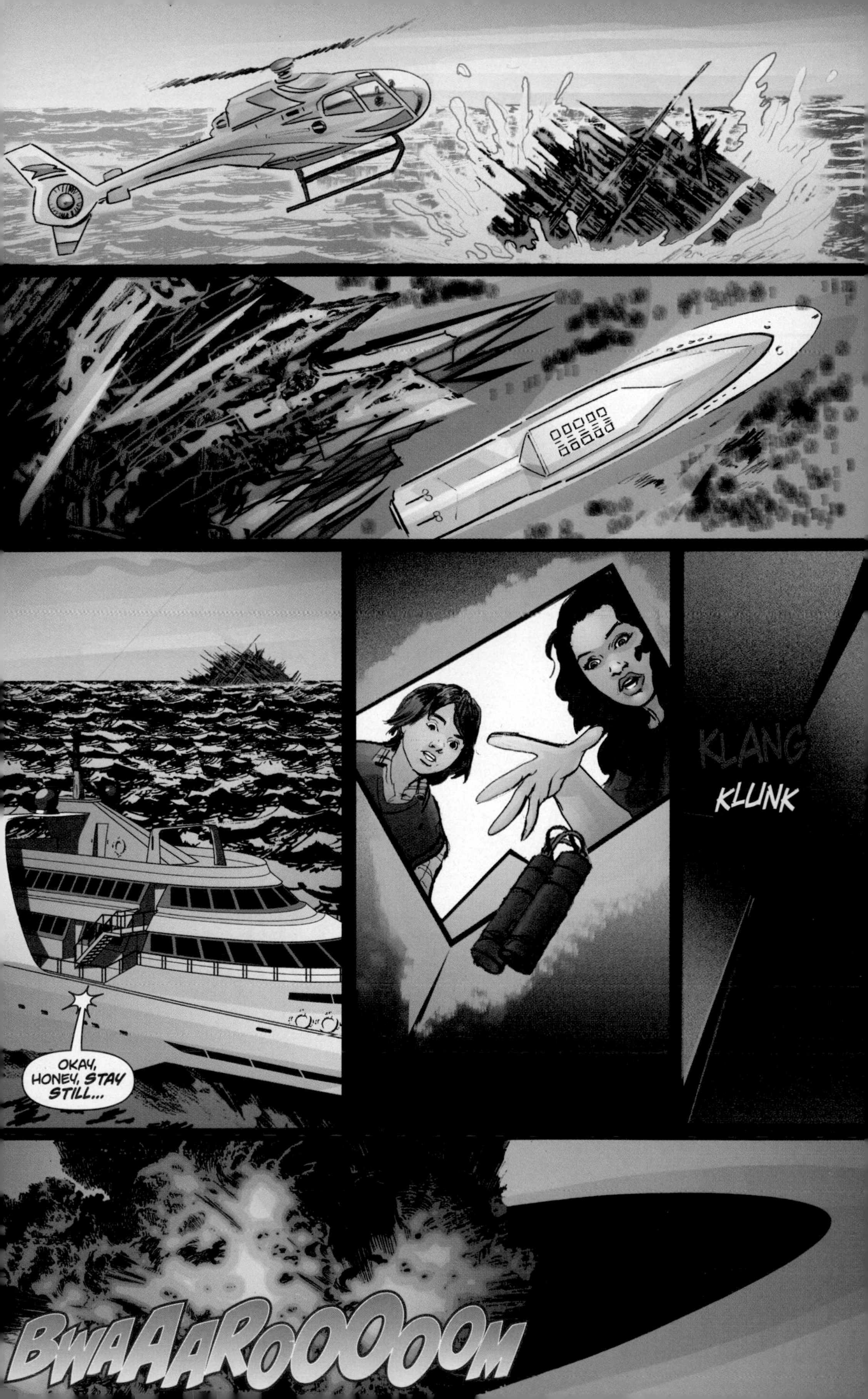
OKAY, HONEY, STAY STILL...
KLANG
KLUNK
BWAAAROOOOOOM

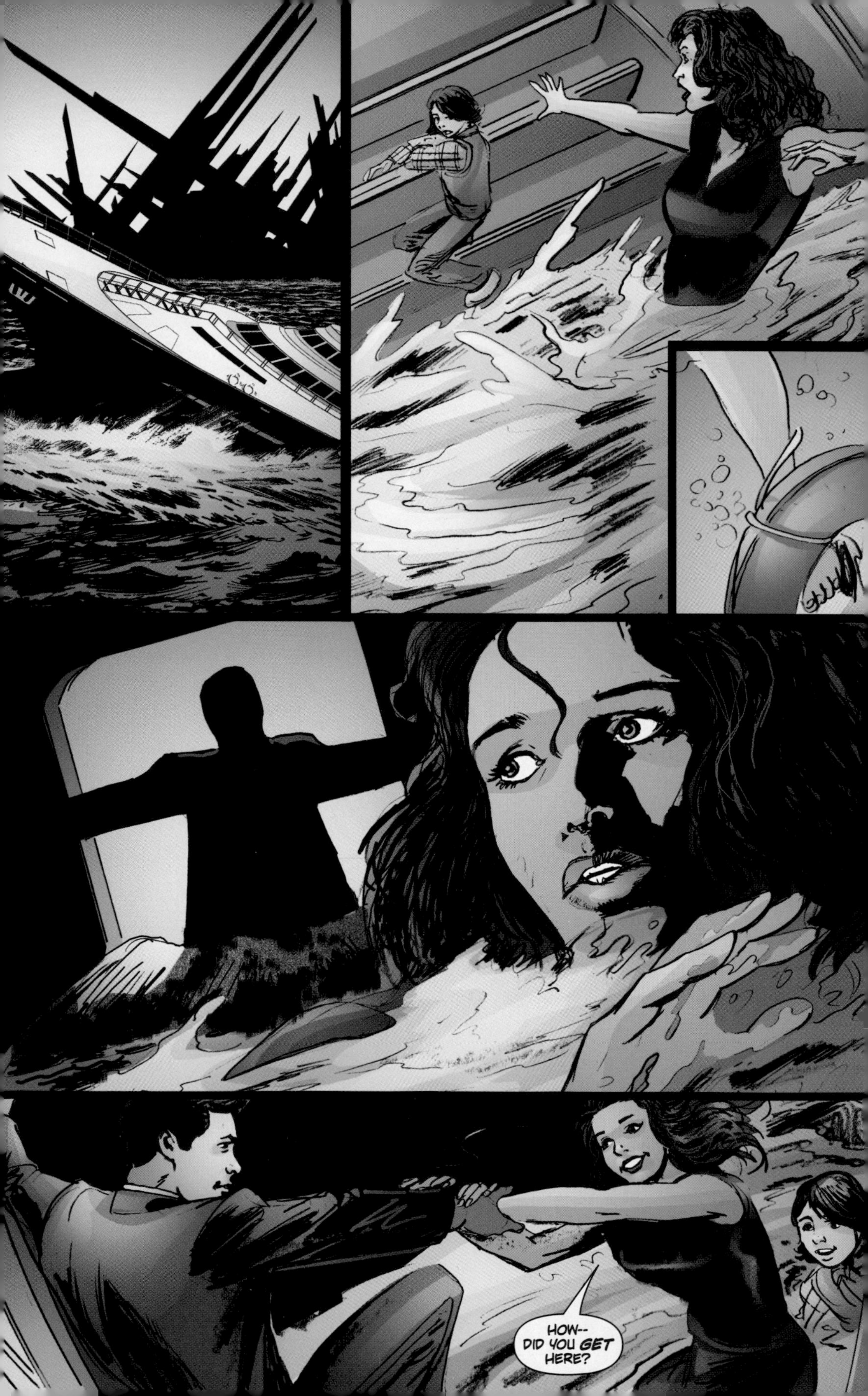
HOW--
DID YOU GET HERE?

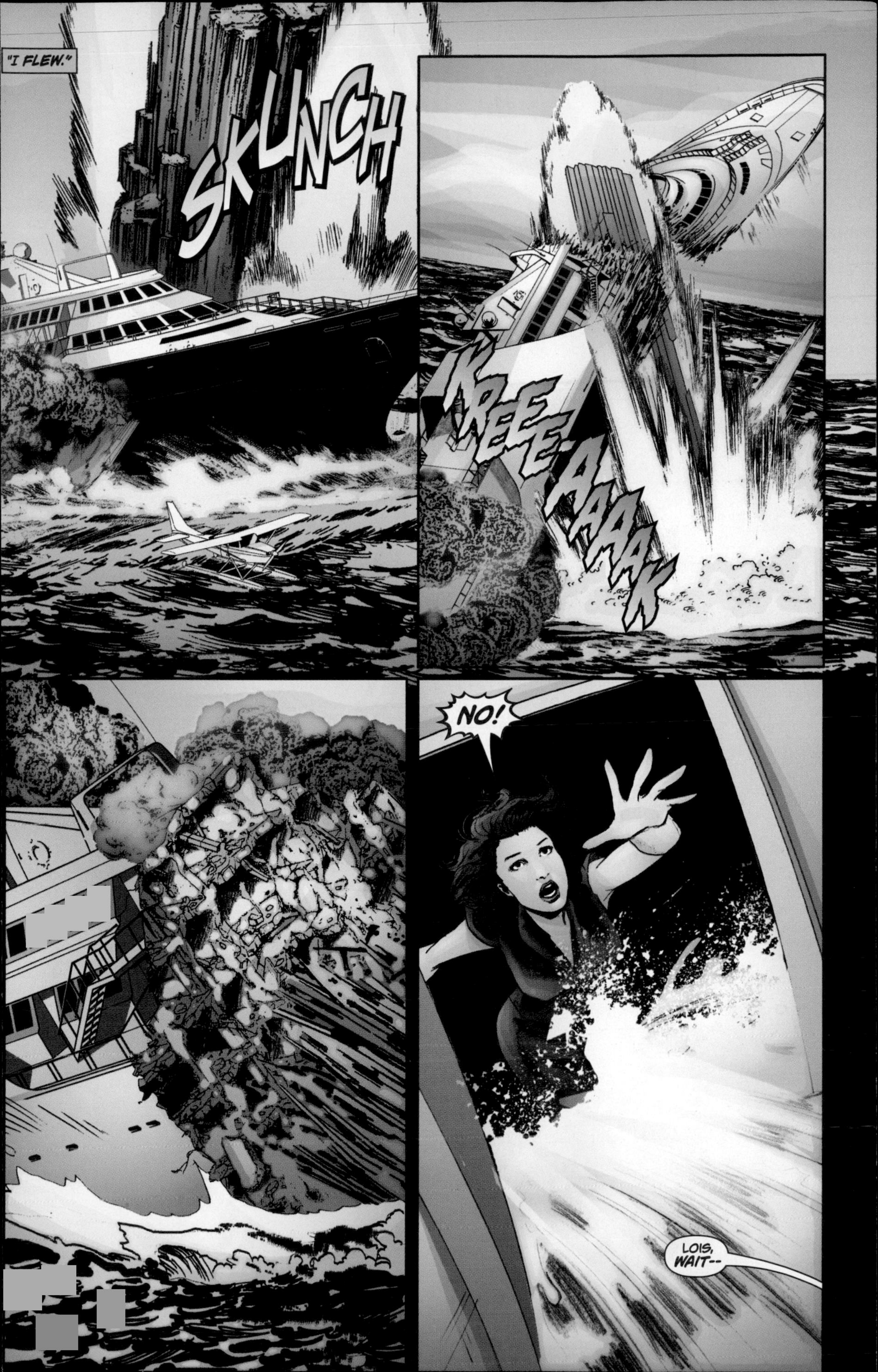
"I FLEW."
SKUNCH
KREEE-AAAAK
NO!
LOIS, WAIT--

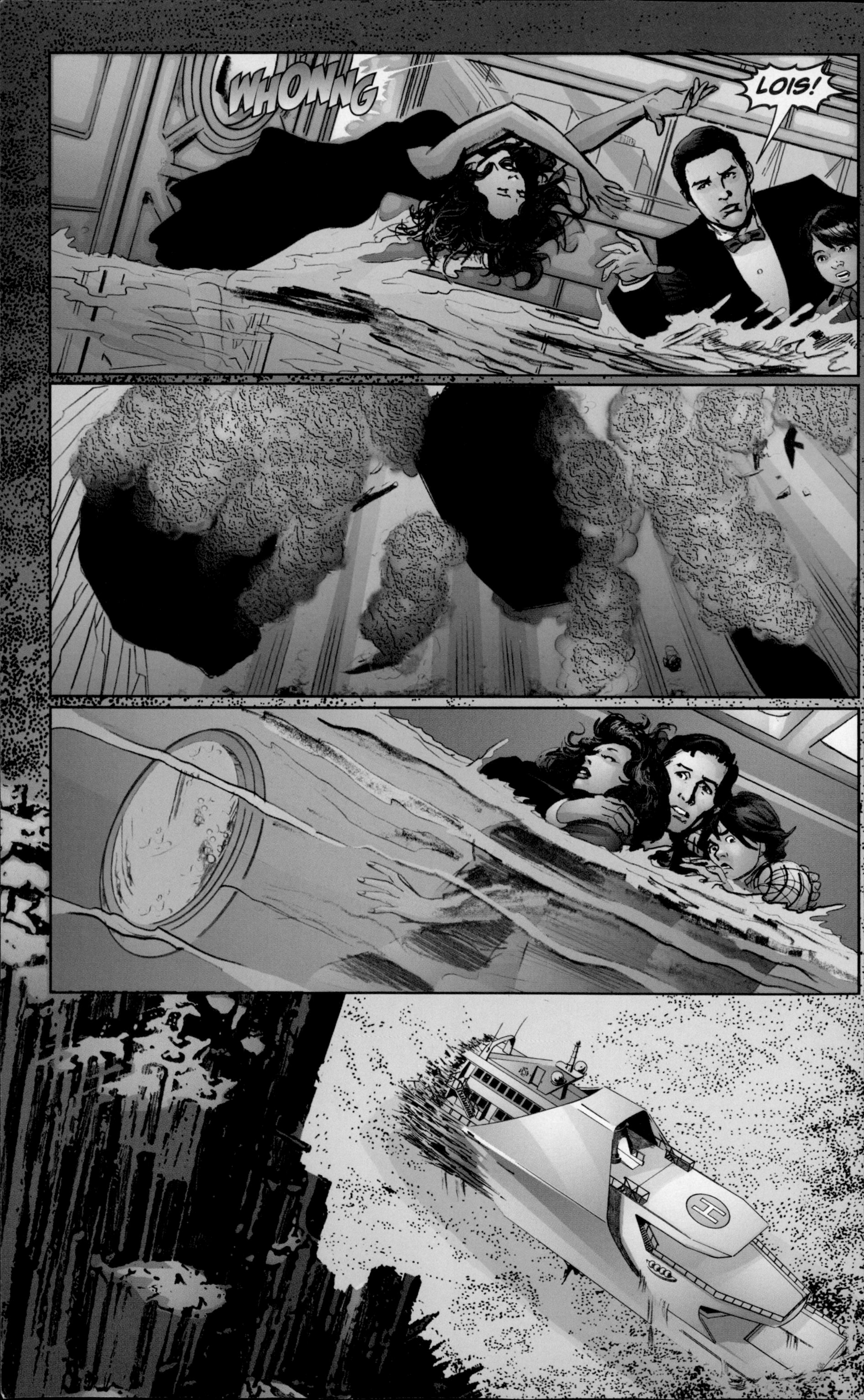
WHONNG
LOIS!

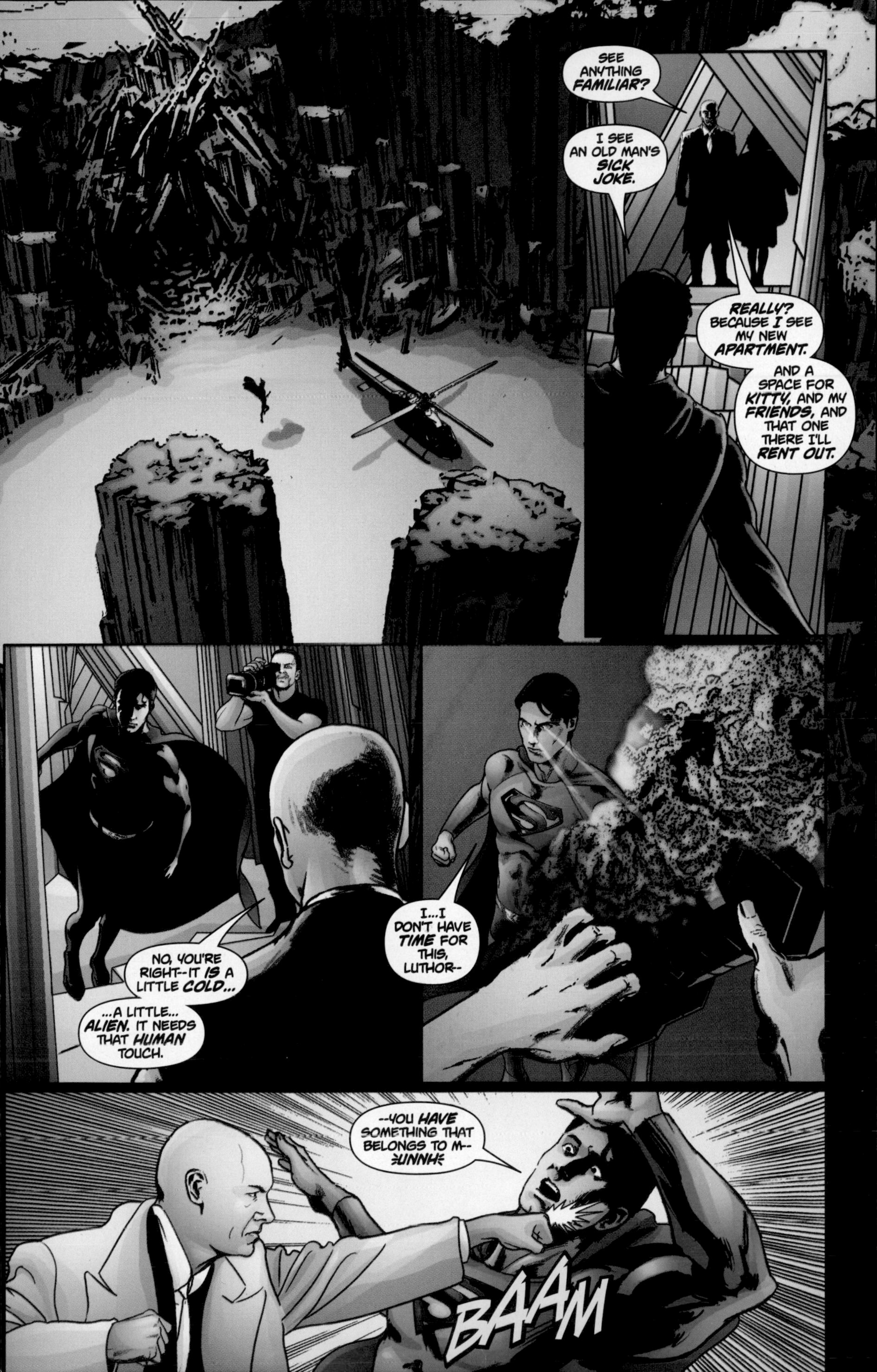
SEE ANYTHING FAMILIAR?
I SEE AN OLD MAN'S SICK JOKE.
REALLY? BECAUSE I SEE MY NEW APARTMENT.
AND A SPACE FOR KITTY, AND MY FRIENDS, AND THAT ONE THERE I'LL RENT OUT.
NO, YOU'RE RIGHT--IT IS A LITTLE COLD...
...A LITTLE... ALIEN. IT NEEDS THAT HUMAN TOUCH.
I...I DON'T HAVE TIME FOR THIS, LUTHOR--
--YOU HAVE SOMETHING THAT BELONGS TO M--UNNH!
BAAM

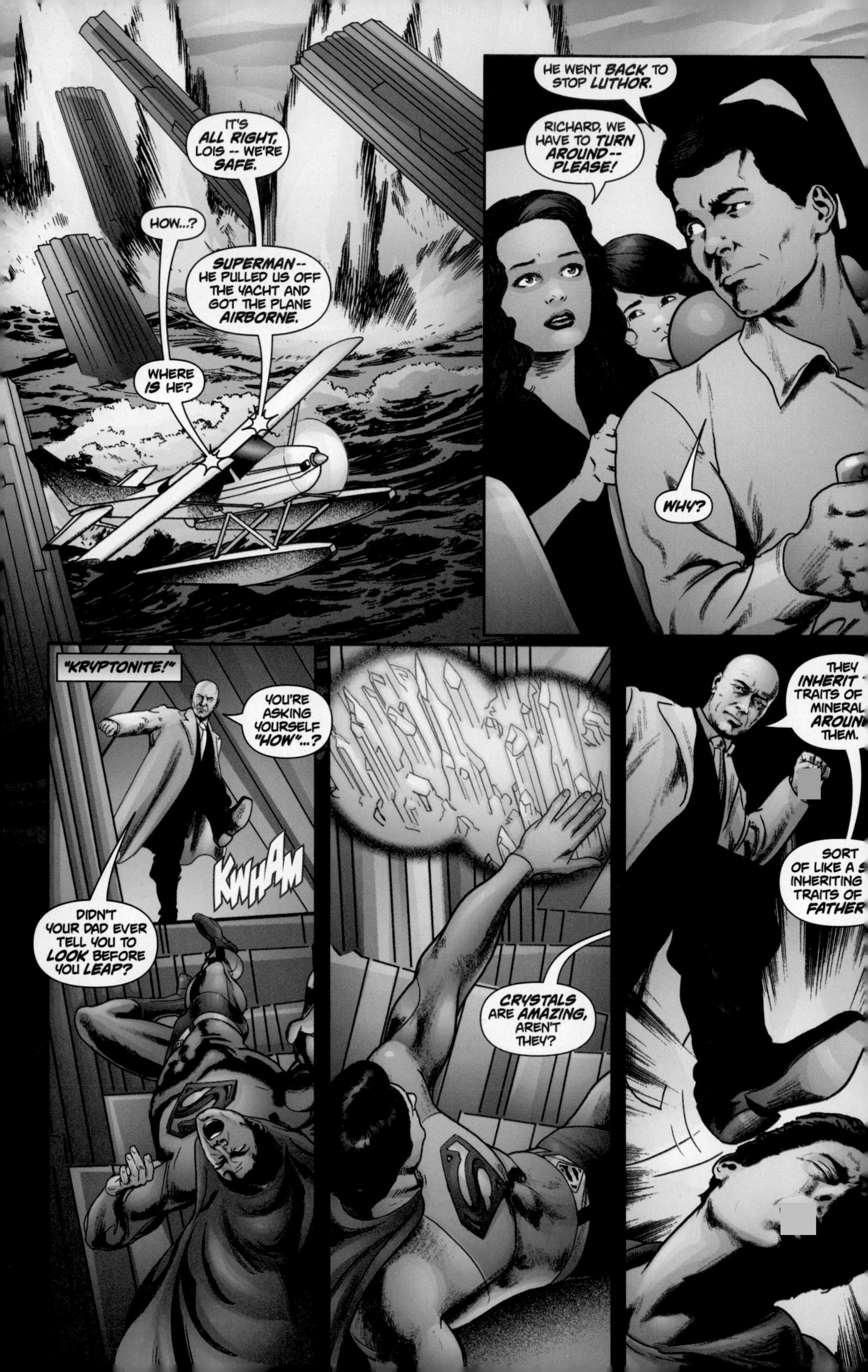

IT'S ALL RIGHT, LOIS -- WE'RE SAFE.
HOW...?
SUPERMAN-- HE PULLED US OFF THE YACHT AND GOT THE PLANE AIRBORNE.
WHERE IS HE?
HE WENT BACK TO STOP LUTHOR.
RICHARD, WE HAVE TO TURN AROUND-- PLEASE!
WHY?
"KRYPTONITE!"
YOU'RE ASKING YOURSELF "HOW"...?
DIDN'T YOUR DAD EVER TELL YOU TO LOOK BEFORE YOU LEAP?
KWHAM
CRYSTALS ARE AMAZING, AREN'T THEY?
THEY INHERIT TRAITS OF MINERAL AROUN THEM.
SORT OF LIKE A INHERITING TRAITS OF FATHER

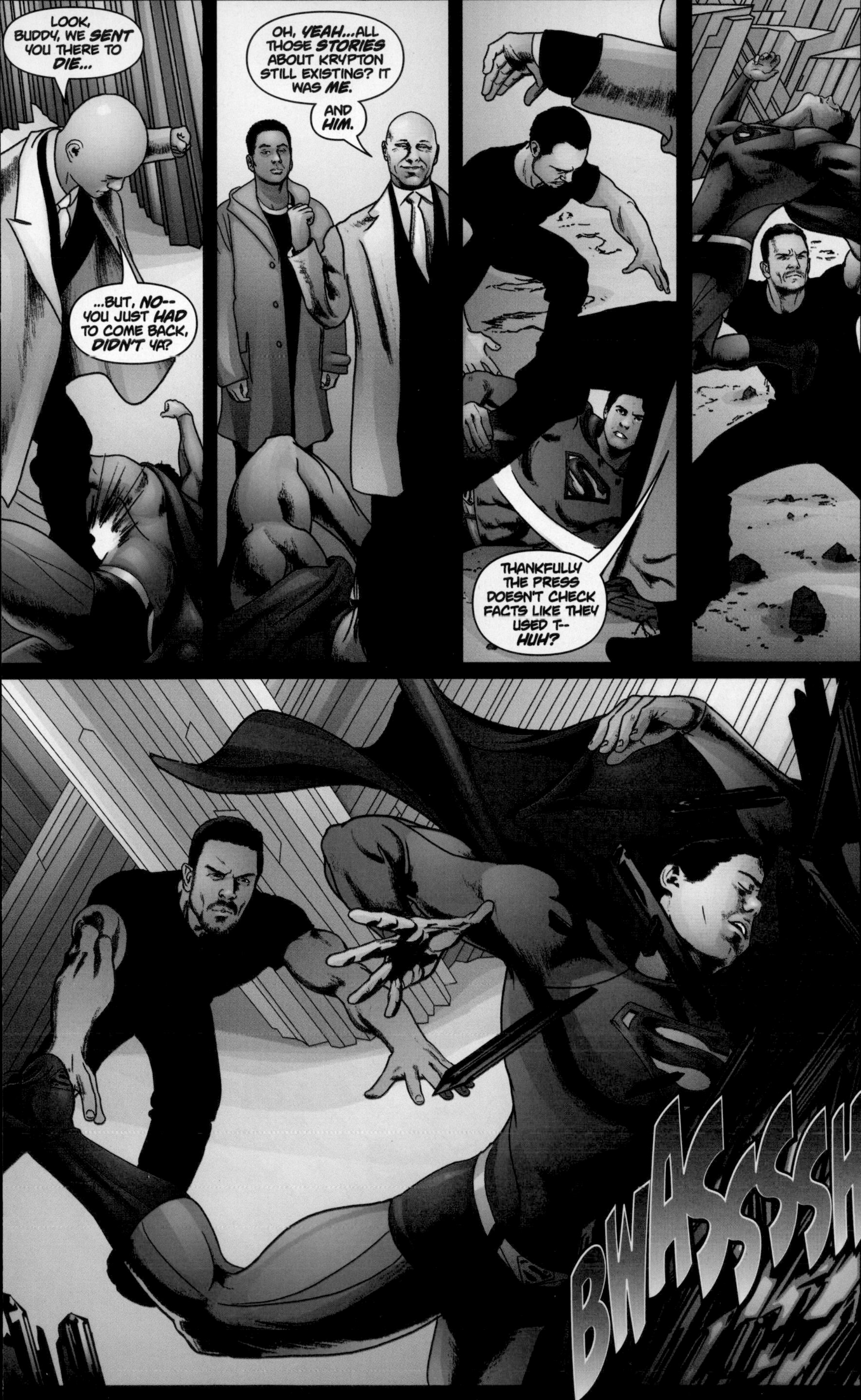
LOOK, BUDDY, WE SENT YOU THERE TO DIE...
...BUT, NO-- YOU JUST HAD TO COME BACK, DIDN'T YA?
OH, YEAH...ALL THOSE STORIES ABOUT KRYPTON STILL EXISTING? IT WAS ME.
AND HIM.
THANKFULLY THE PRESS DOESN'T CHECK FACTS LIKE THEY USED T-- HUH?
BWASSSH

HAGGHHH

KSHUKK

KRAK

NOW, FLY.

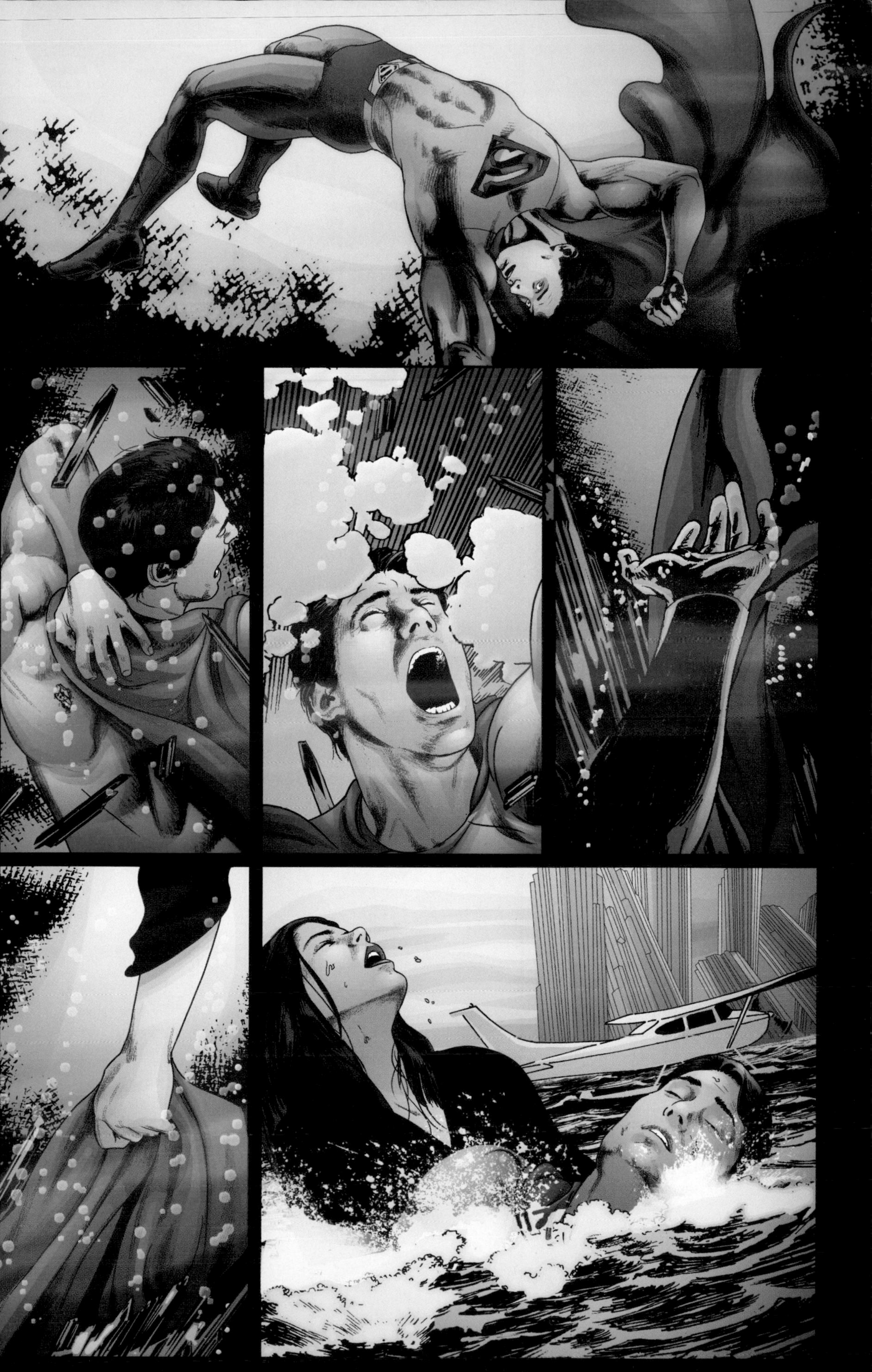

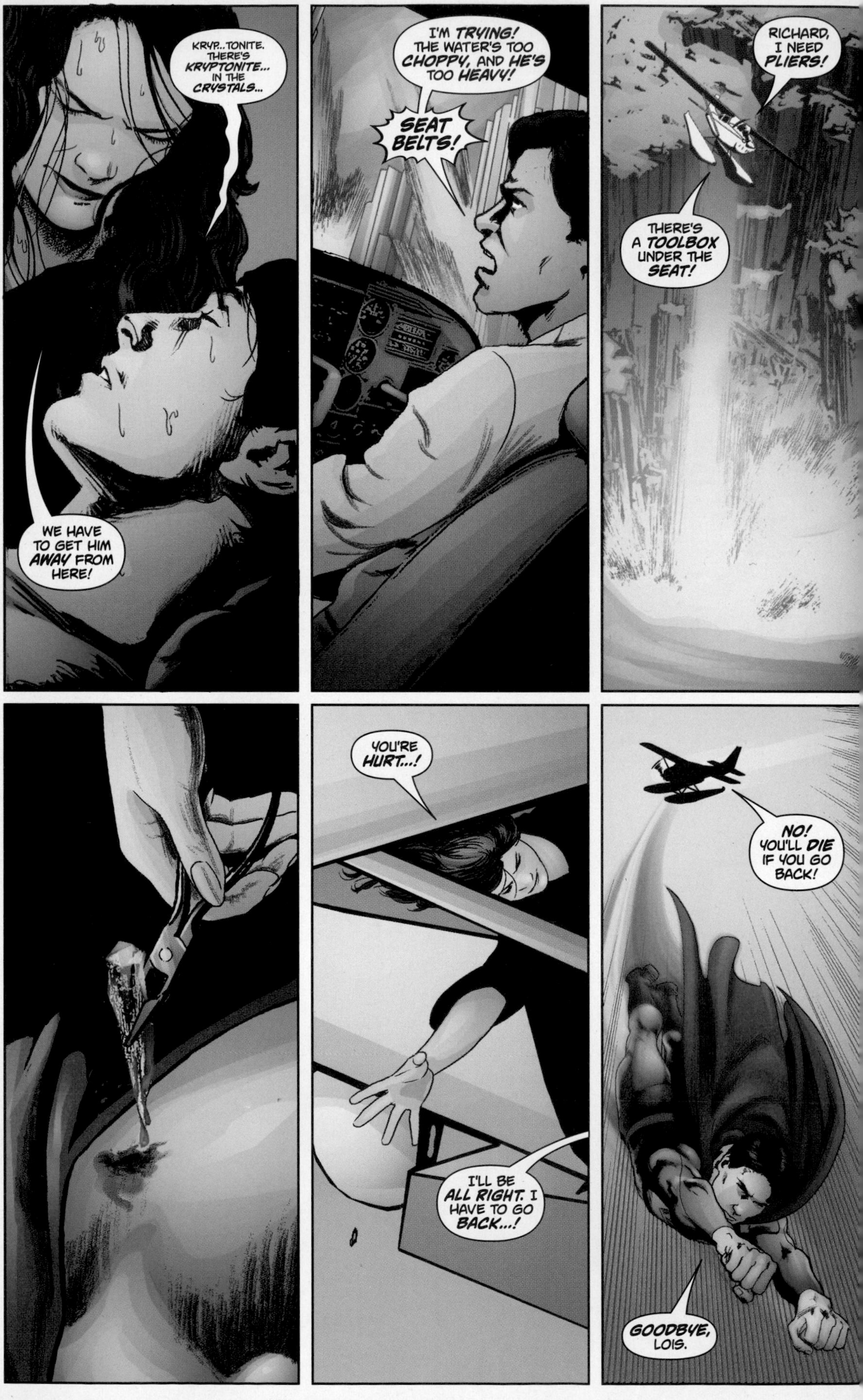
KRYP...TONITE. THERE'S KRYPTONITE... IN THE CRYSTALS...
WE HAVE TO GET HIM AWAY FROM HERE!
I'M TRYING! THE WATER'S TOO CHOPPY, AND HE'S TOO HEAVY!
SEAT BELTS!
RICHARD, I NEED PLIERS!
THERE'S A TOOLBOX UNDER THE SEAT!
YOU'RE HURT...!
I'LL BE ALL RIGHT. I HAVE TO GO BACK...!
NO! YOU'LL DIE IF YOU GO BACK!
GOODBYE, LOIS.

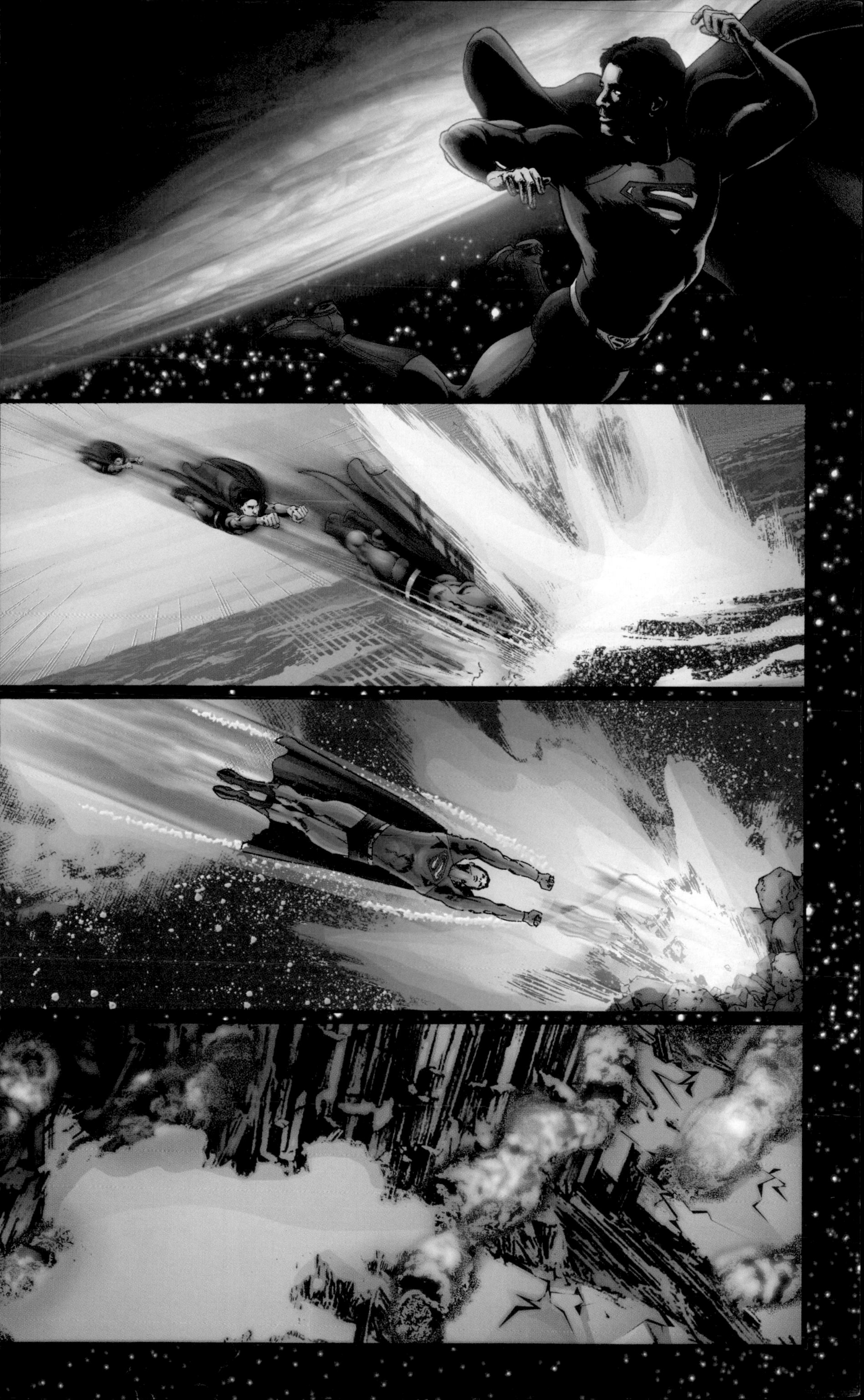

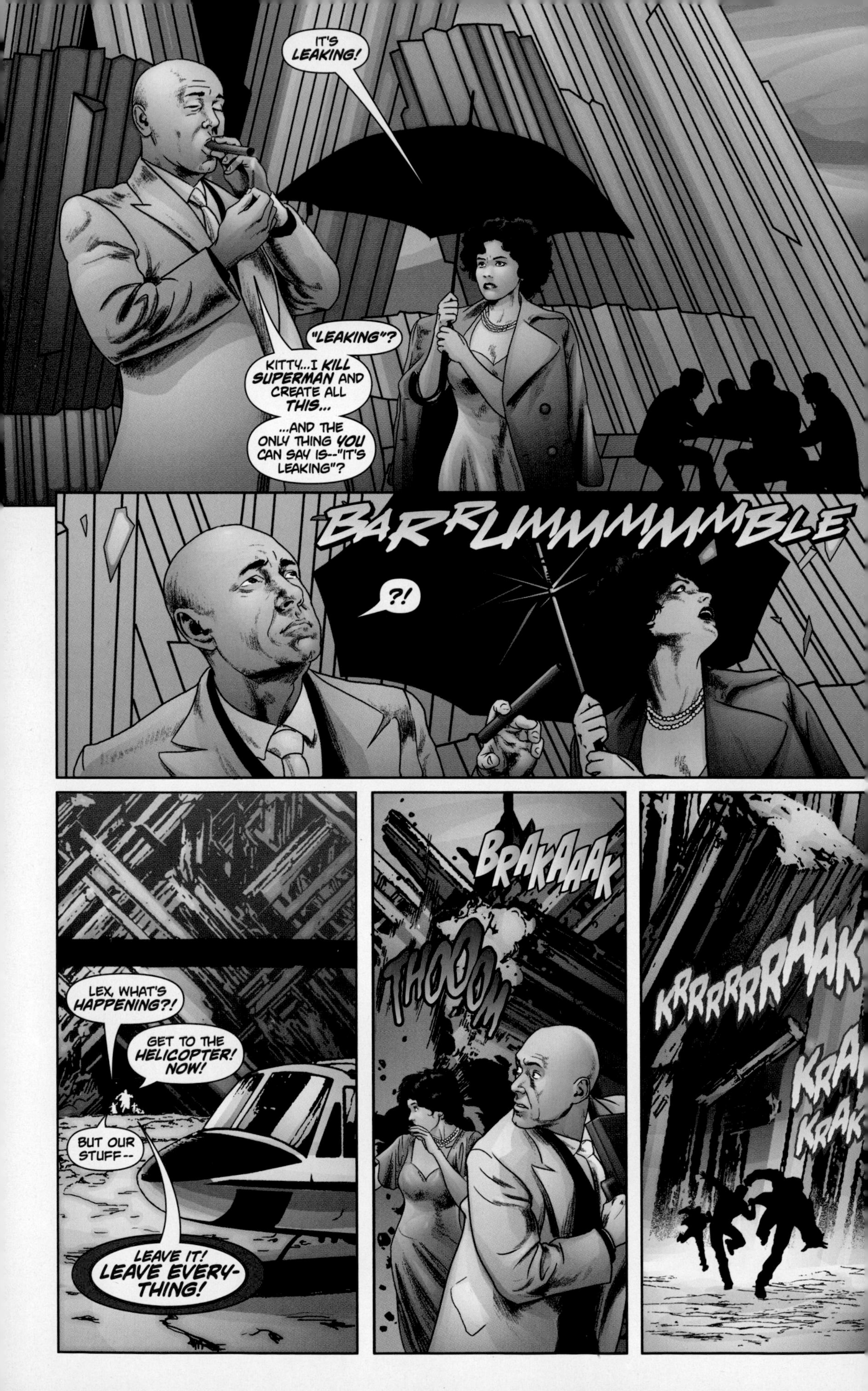
IT'S LEAKING!
"LEAKING"?
KITTY...I KILL SUPERMAN AND CREATE ALL THIS...
...AND THE ONLY THING YOU CAN SAY IS--"IT'S LEAKING"?
BARRUMMMMMBLE
?!
LEX, WHAT'S HAPPENING?!
GET TO THE HELICOPTER! NOW!
BUT OUR STUFF--
LEAVE IT! LEAVE EVERY-THING!
BRAKAAAK
THOOOM
KRRRRRRAAK
KRAK
KRAK

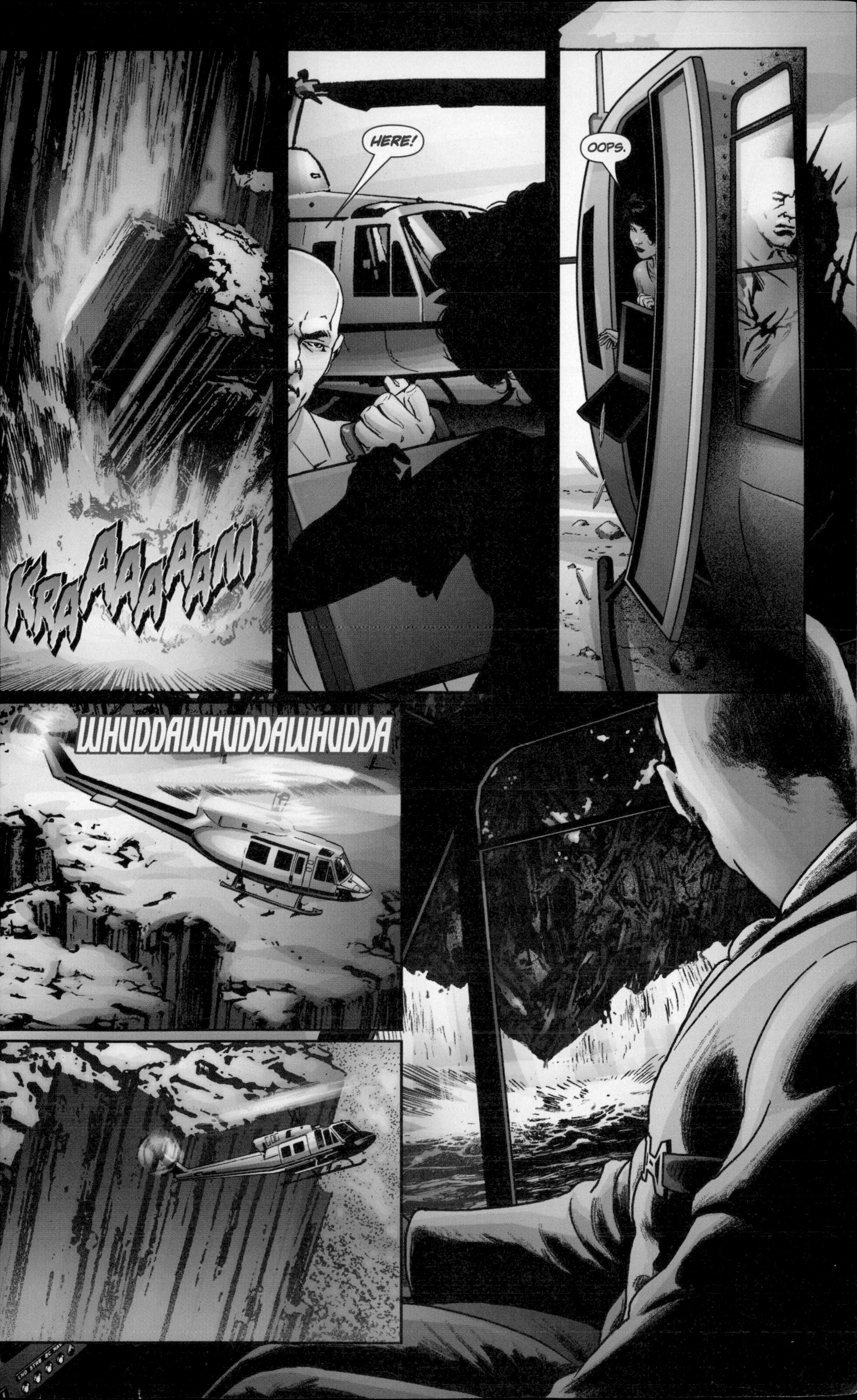
KRAAAAAAM
HERE!
OOPS.
WHUDDAWHUDDAWHUDDA

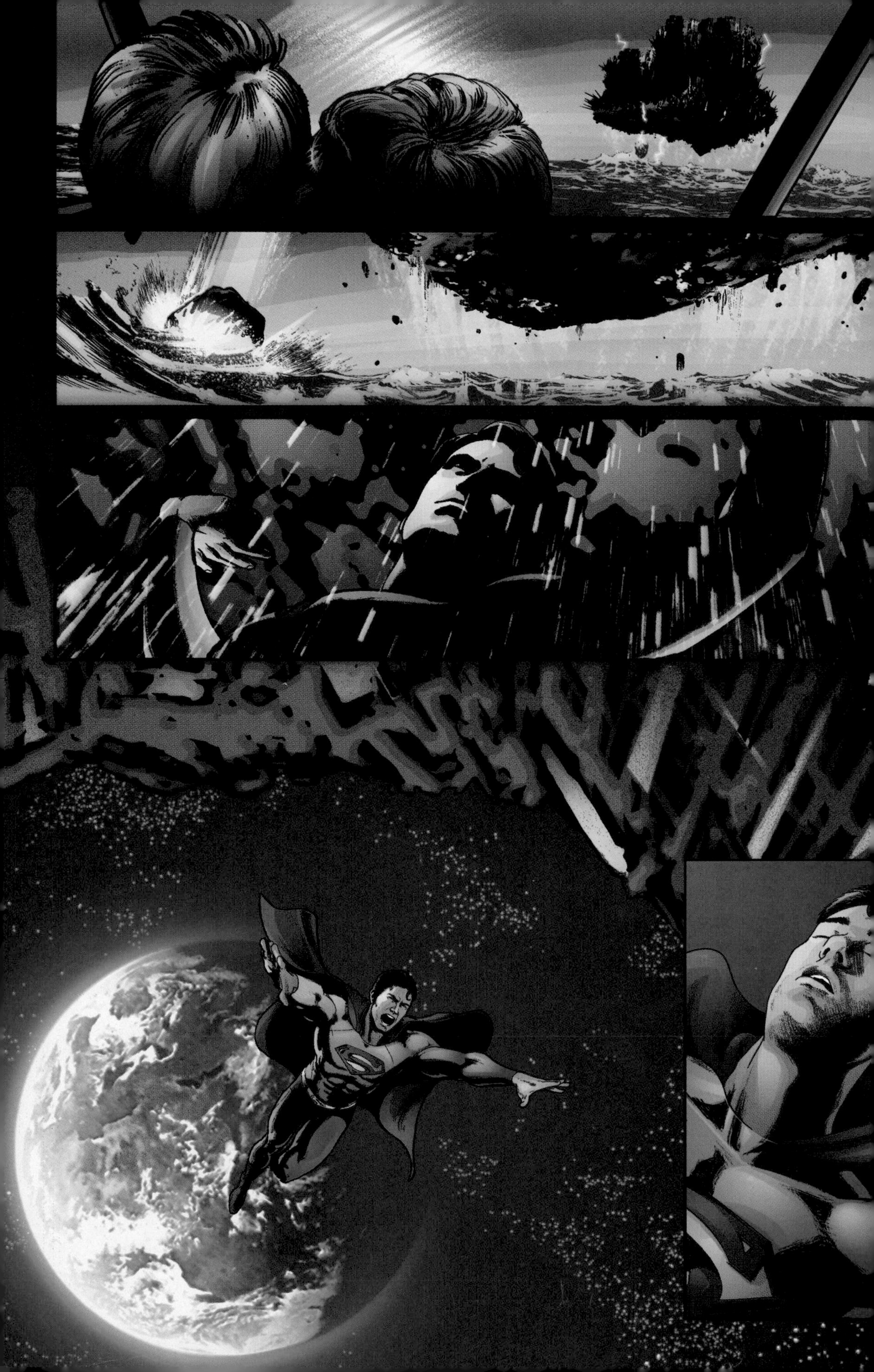

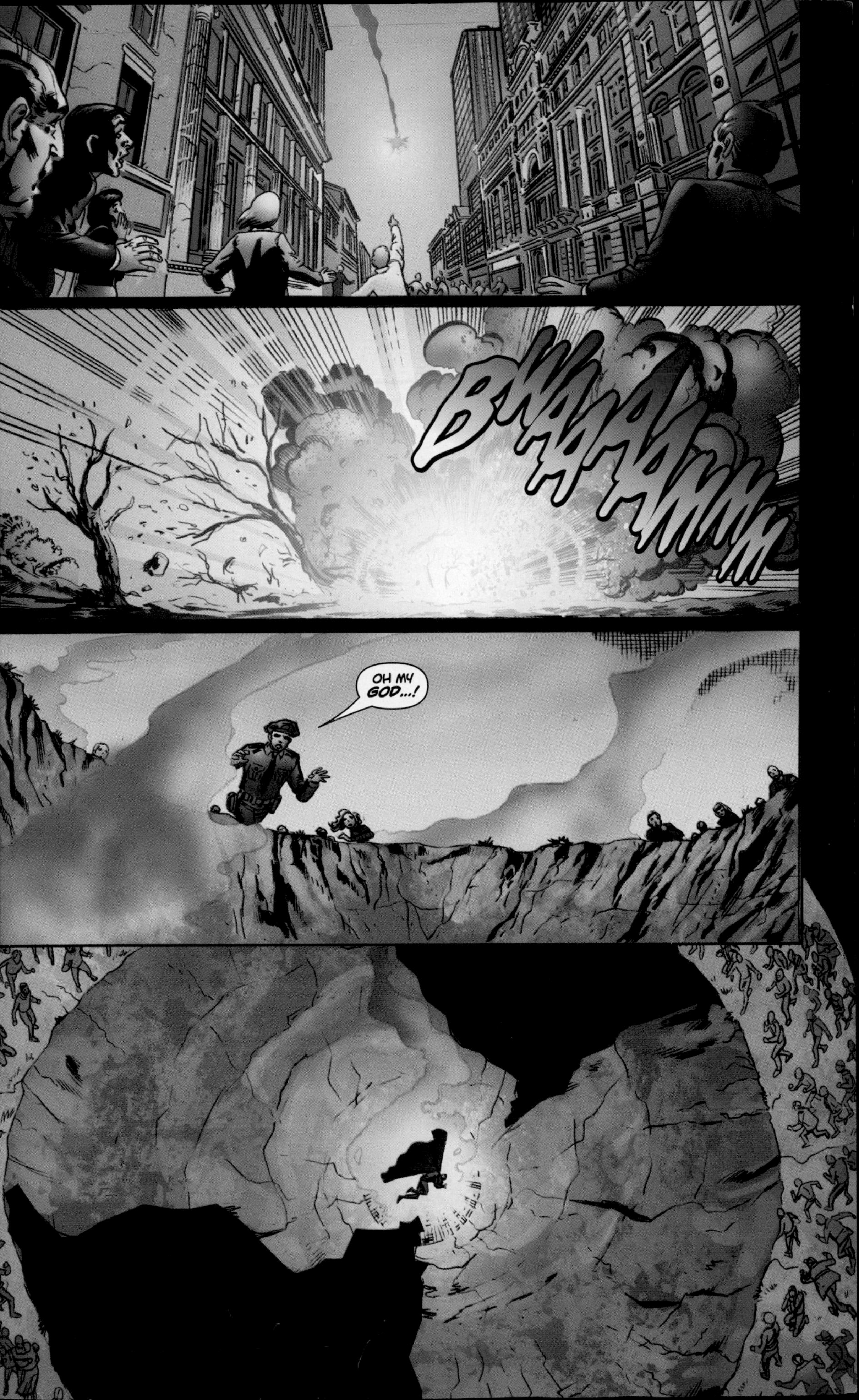
BWAAAAMMM
OH MY GOD...!

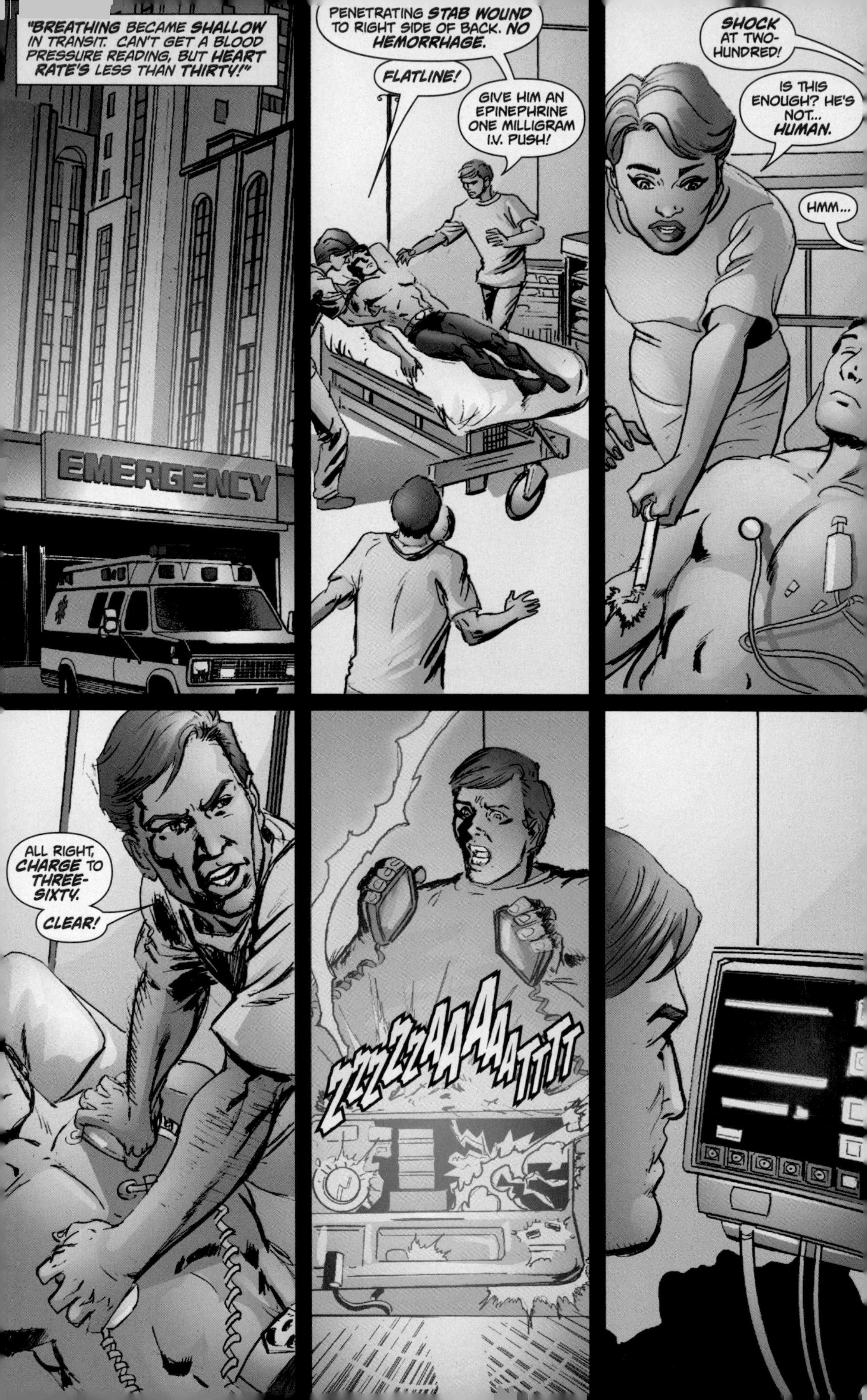
"BREATHING BECAME SHALLOW IN TRANSIT. CAN'T GET A BLOOD PRESSURE READING, BUT HEART RATE'S LESS THAN THIRTY!"
EMERGENCY
PENETRATING STAB WOUND TO RIGHT SIDE OF BACK. NO HEMORRHAGE.
FLATLINE!
GIVE HIM AN EPINEPHRINE ONE MILLIGRAM I.V. PUSH!
SHOCK AT TWO-HUNDRED!
IS THIS ENOUGH? HE'S NOT... HUMAN.
HMM...
ALL RIGHT, CHARGE TO THREE-SIXTY.
CLEAR!
ZZZZZAAAAAATTTT

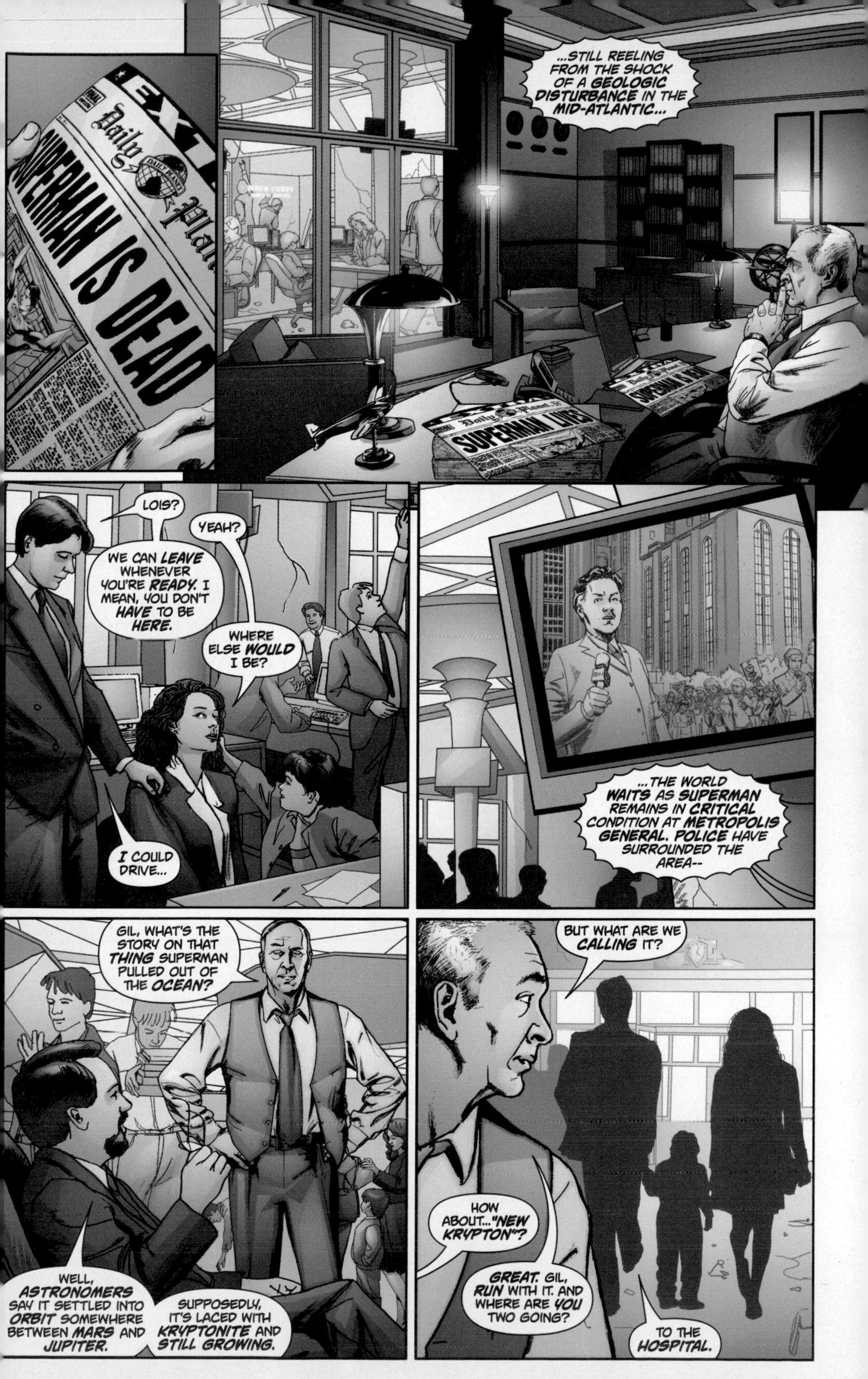
EXTRA
Daily Planet
SUPERMAN IS DEAD
...STILL REELING FROM THE SHOCK OF A GEOLOGIC DISTURBANCE IN THE MID-ATLANTIC...
Daily Planet
SUPERMAN LIVES
SUPERMAN IS DEAD
LOIS?
YEAH?
WE CAN LEAVE WHENEVER YOU'RE READY. I MEAN, YOU DON'T HAVE TO BE HERE.
WHERE ELSE WOULD I BE?
I COULD DRIVE...
...THE WORLD WAITS AS SUPERMAN REMAINS IN CRITICAL CONDITION AT METROPOLIS GENERAL. POLICE HAVE SURROUNDED THE AREA--
GIL, WHAT'S THE STORY ON THAT THING SUPERMAN PULLED OUT OF THE OCEAN?
WELL, ASTRONOMERS SAY IT SETTLED INTO ORBIT SOMEWHERE BETWEEN MARS AND JUPITER.
SUPPOSEDLY, IT'S LACED WITH KRYPTONITE AND STILL GROWING.
BUT WHAT ARE WE CALLING IT?
HOW ABOUT..."NEW KRYPTON"?
GREAT. GIL, RUN WITH IT. AND WHERE ARE YOU TWO GOING?
TO THE HOSPITAL.

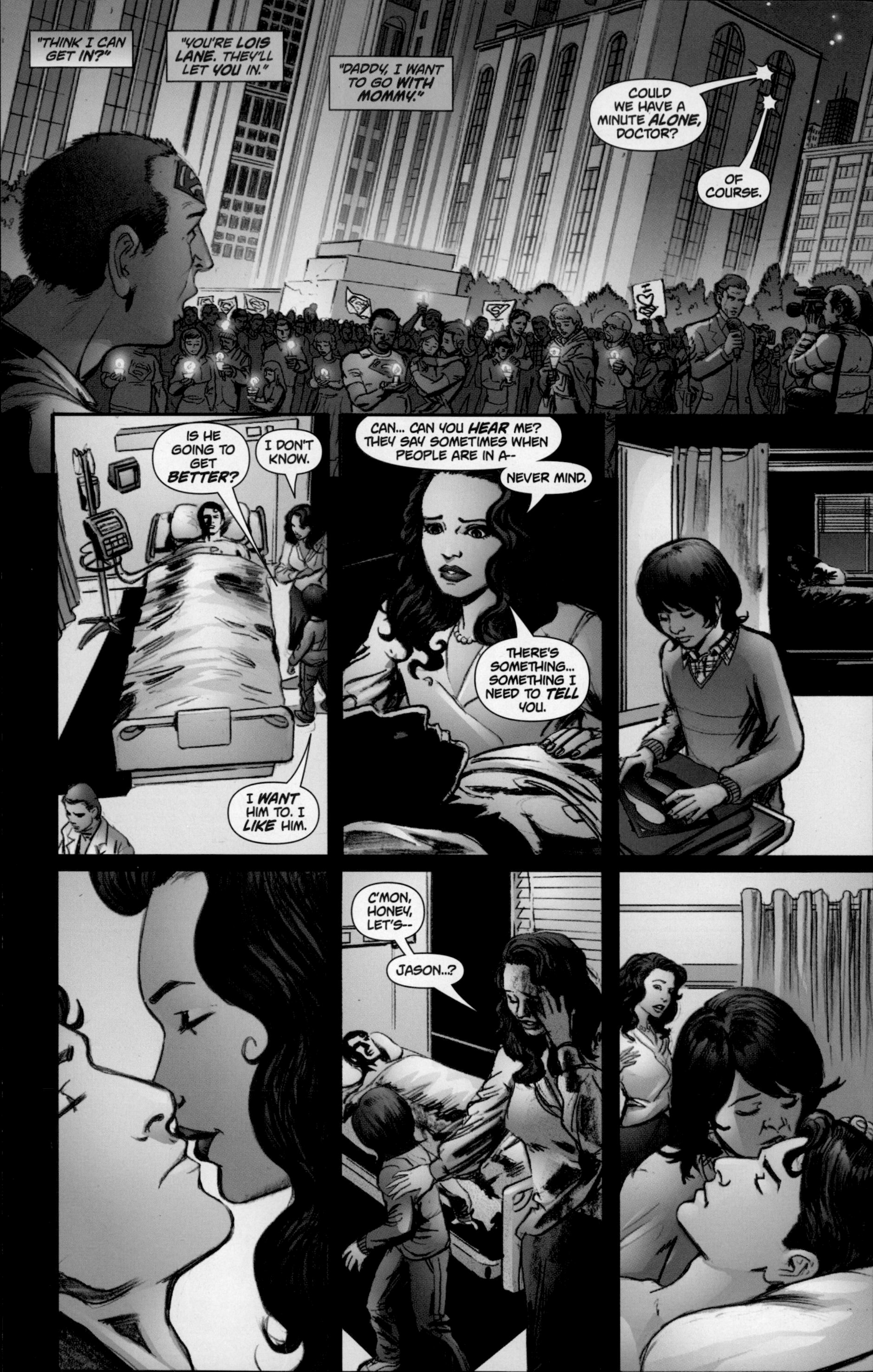
"THINK I CAN GET IN?"
"YOU'RE LOIS LANE. THEY'LL LET YOU IN."
"DADDY, I WANT TO GO WITH MOMMY."
COULD WE HAVE A MINUTE ALONE, DOCTOR?
OF COURSE.
IS HE GOING TO GET BETTER?
I DON'T KNOW.
I WANT HIM TO. I LIKE HIM.
CAN... CAN YOU HEAR ME? THEY SAY SOMETIMES WHEN PEOPLE ARE IN A--
NEVER MIND.
THERE'S SOMETHING... SOMETHING I NEED TO TELL YOU.
C'MON, HONEY, LET'S--
JASON..?

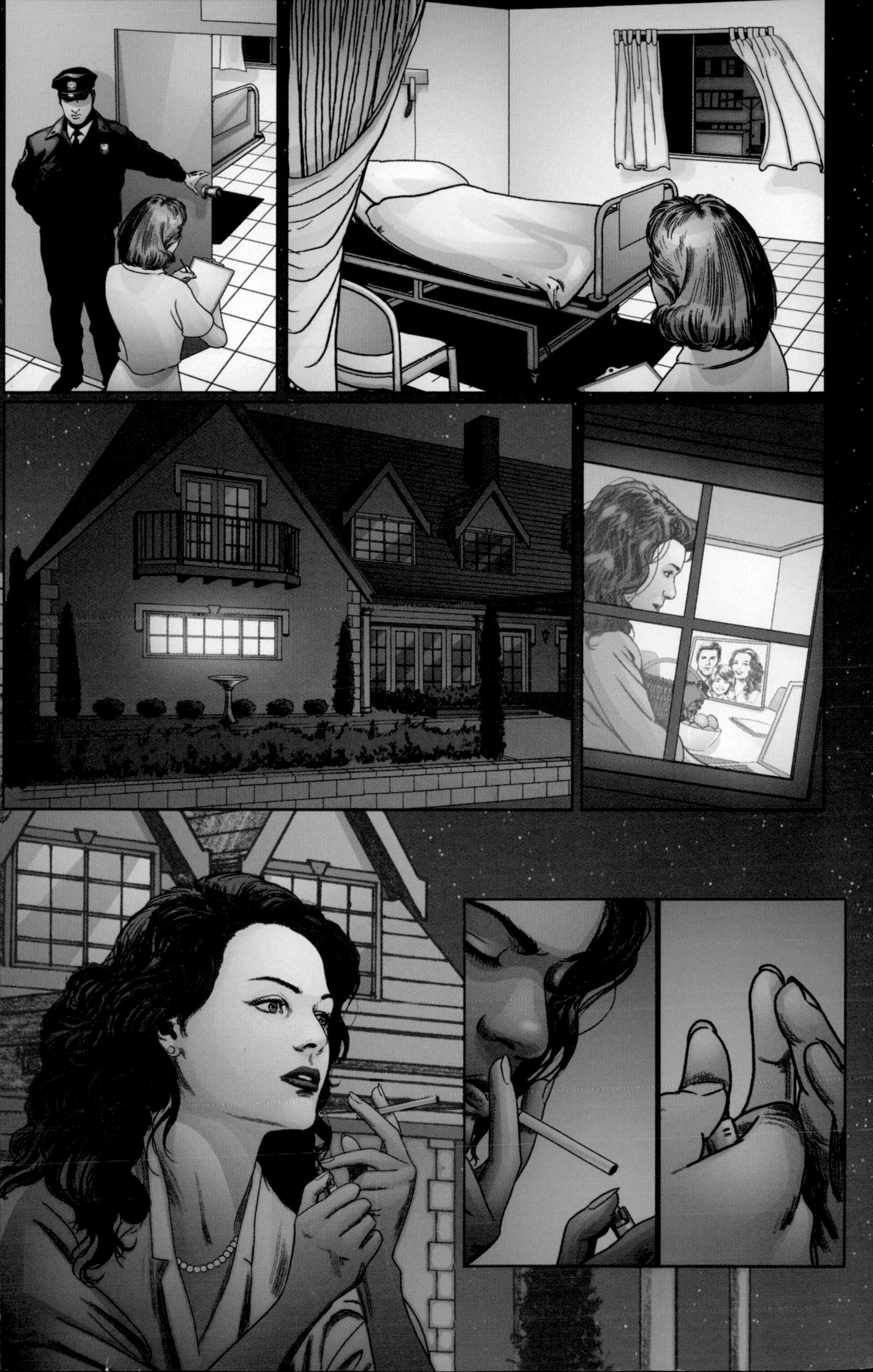

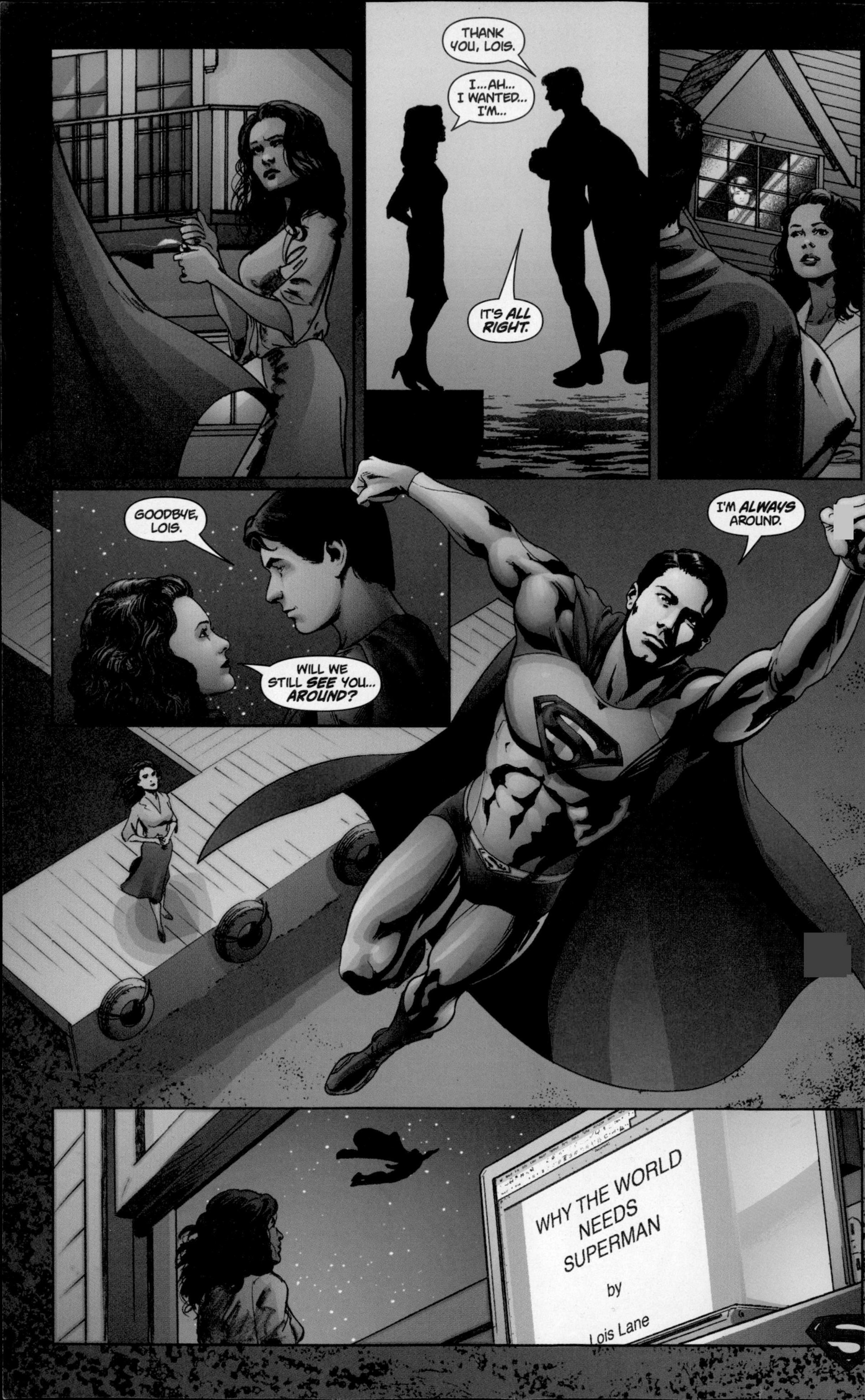
THANK YOU, LOIS.
I...AH... I WANTED... I'M...
IT'S ALL RIGHT.
GOODBYE, LOIS.
WILL WE STILL SEE YOU... AROUND?
I'M ALWAYS AROUND.
WHY THE WORLD NEEDS SUPERMAN
by
Lois Lane

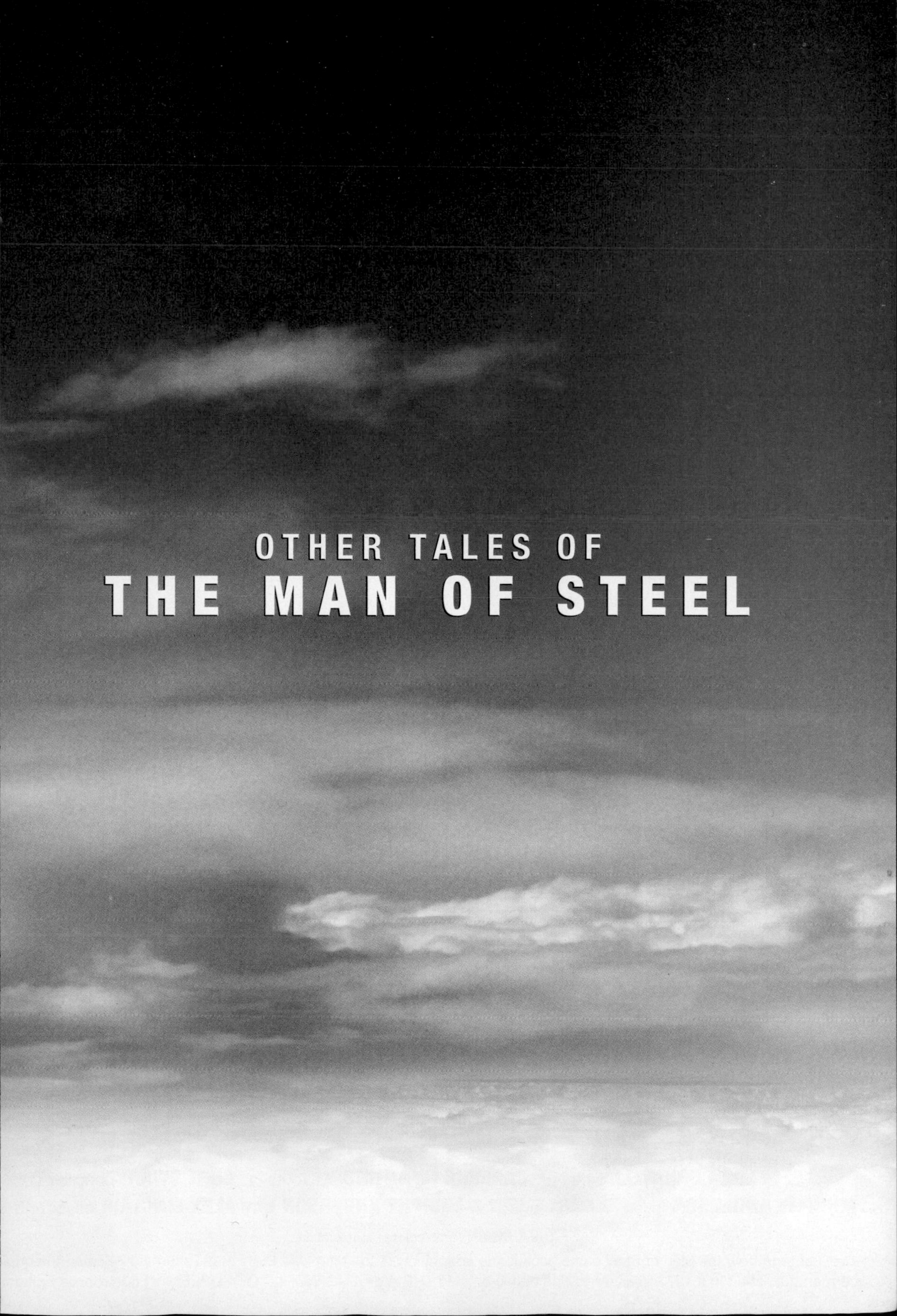

OTHER TALES OF

THE MAN OF STEEL

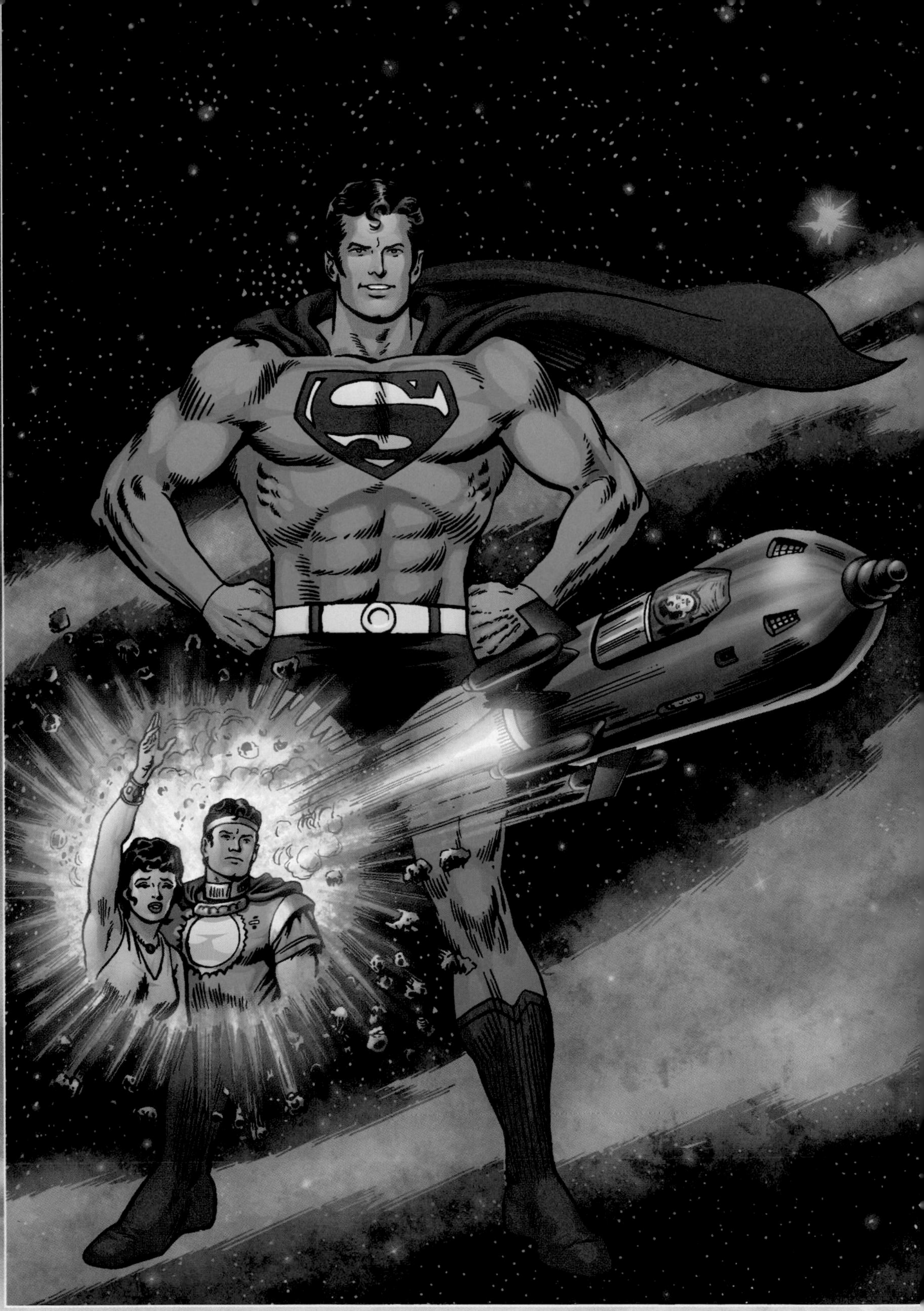

"The Origin of Superman"

E. NELSON BRIDWELL writer **CARMINE INFANTINO** Layouts **CURT SWAN** penciller
MURPHY ANDERSON inker **CURT SWAN & MURPHY ANDERSON WITH ALEX SINCLAIR** cover artist
DALE CRAIN art & color reconstruction

You've just read how the Man of Steel came back in the adaptation of the hit movie Superman Returns. Now read the origi
Superman published in a 1973 treasury-edition comic entitled THE AMAZING WORLD OF SUPERMAN (Metropolis Edition)

FASTER THAN A SPEEDING BULLET!

MORE POWERFUL THAN A LOCOMOTIVE!

ABLE TO LEAP TALL BUILDINGS AT A SINGLE BOUND!

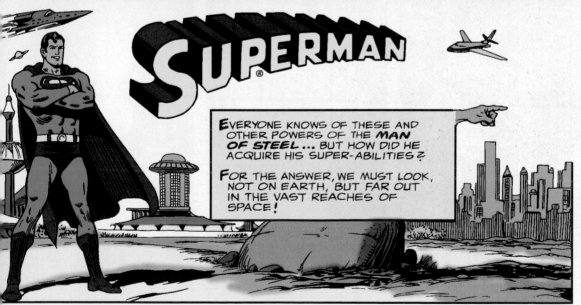

SUPERMAN

EVERYONE KNOWS OF THESE AND OTHER POWERS OF THE **MAN OF STEEL**... BUT HOW DID HE ACQUIRE HIS SUPER-ABILITIES?

FOR THE ANSWER, WE MUST LOOK, NOT ON EARTH, BUT FAR OUT IN THE VAST REACHES OF SPACE!

YEARS AGO, THE GIANT PLANET **KRYPTON** REVOLVED AROUND A GREAT **RED SUN**...

KRYPTON WAS INHABITED BY A HIGHLY INTELLIGENT CIVILIZATION. AMONG ITS FOREMOST CITIZENS WERE SCIENTIST **JOR-EL** AND HIS WIFE, **LARA**...

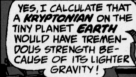

I'M WORRIED ABOUT OUR SON, **KAL-EL!**

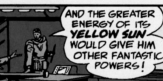

I KNOW...HE'S OVER A YEAR OLD AND HE HASN'T STARTED **READING** YET!

THE SCIENTISTS OF **KRYPTON** HAD STUDIED MANY DISTANT WORLDS, INCLUDING **EARTH**...

YES, I CALCULATE THAT A **KRYPTONIAN** ON THE TINY PLANET **EARTH** WOULD HAVE TREMENDOUS STRENGTH BECAUSE OF ITS LIGHTER GRAVITY!

AND THE GREATER ENERGY OF ITS **YELLOW SUN** WOULD GIVE HIM OTHER FANTASTIC POWERS!

BUT THE TIME CAME WHEN **KRYPTON** WAS SHAKEN BY MYSTERIOUS RUMBLINGS...

ANOTHER **GROUND-QUAKE!**

THERE HAVE BEEN SIMILAR ONES ALL OVER THE PLANET!

IN THE **HALL OF WISDOM**, THE RULING **SCIENCE COUNCIL** AWAITED AN ANNOUNCEMENT FROM ONE OF ITS MEMBERS...

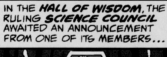

WHAT DO YOU SUPPOSE HE HAS ON HIS MIND?

WE'LL SOON KNOW...HERE HE COMES!

FELLOW SCIENTISTS, **KRYPTON IS DOOMED!**

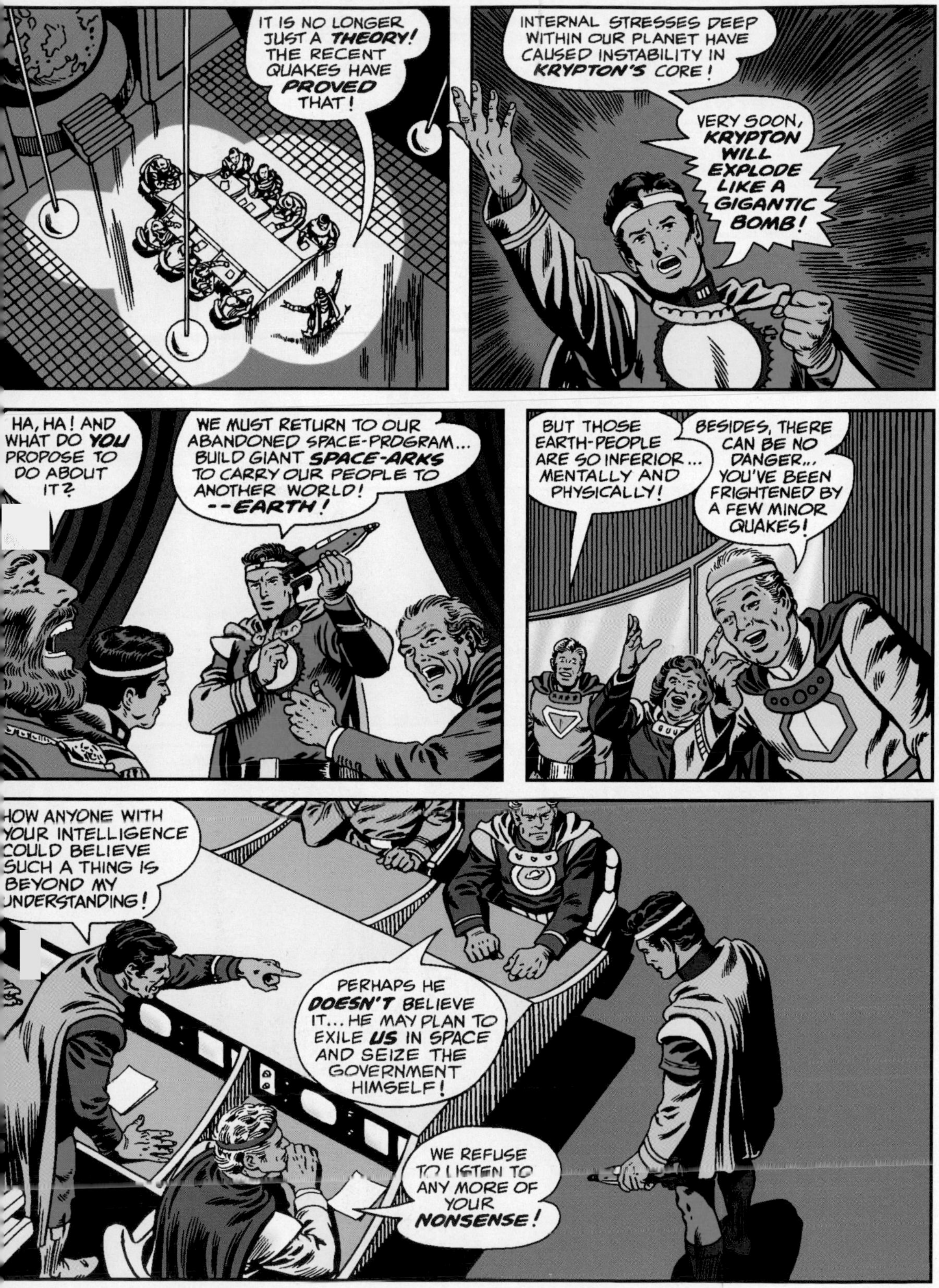
IT IS NO LONGER JUST A THEORY! THE RECENT QUAKES HAVE PROVED THAT!
INTERNAL STRESSES DEEP WITHIN OUR PLANET HAVE CAUSED INSTABILITY IN KRYPTON'S CORE!
VERY SOON, KRYPTON WILL EXPLODE LIKE A GIGANTIC BOMB!
HA, HA! AND WHAT DO YOU PROPOSE TO DO ABOUT IT?
WE MUST RETURN TO OUR ABANDONED SPACE-PROGRAM... BUILD GIANT SPACE-ARKS TO CARRY OUR PEOPLE TO ANOTHER WORLD! --EARTH!
BUT THOSE EARTH-PEOPLE ARE SO INFERIOR... MENTALLY AND PHYSICALLY!
BESIDES, THERE CAN BE NO DANGER... YOU'VE BEEN FRIGHTENED BY A FEW MINOR QUAKES!
HOW ANYONE WITH YOUR INTELLIGENCE COULD BELIEVE SUCH A THING IS BEYOND MY UNDERSTANDING!
PERHAPS HE DOESN'T BELIEVE IT... HE MAY PLAN TO EXILE US IN SPACE AND SEIZE THE GOVERNMENT HIMSELF!
WE REFUSE TO LISTEN TO ANY MORE OF YOUR NONSENSE!

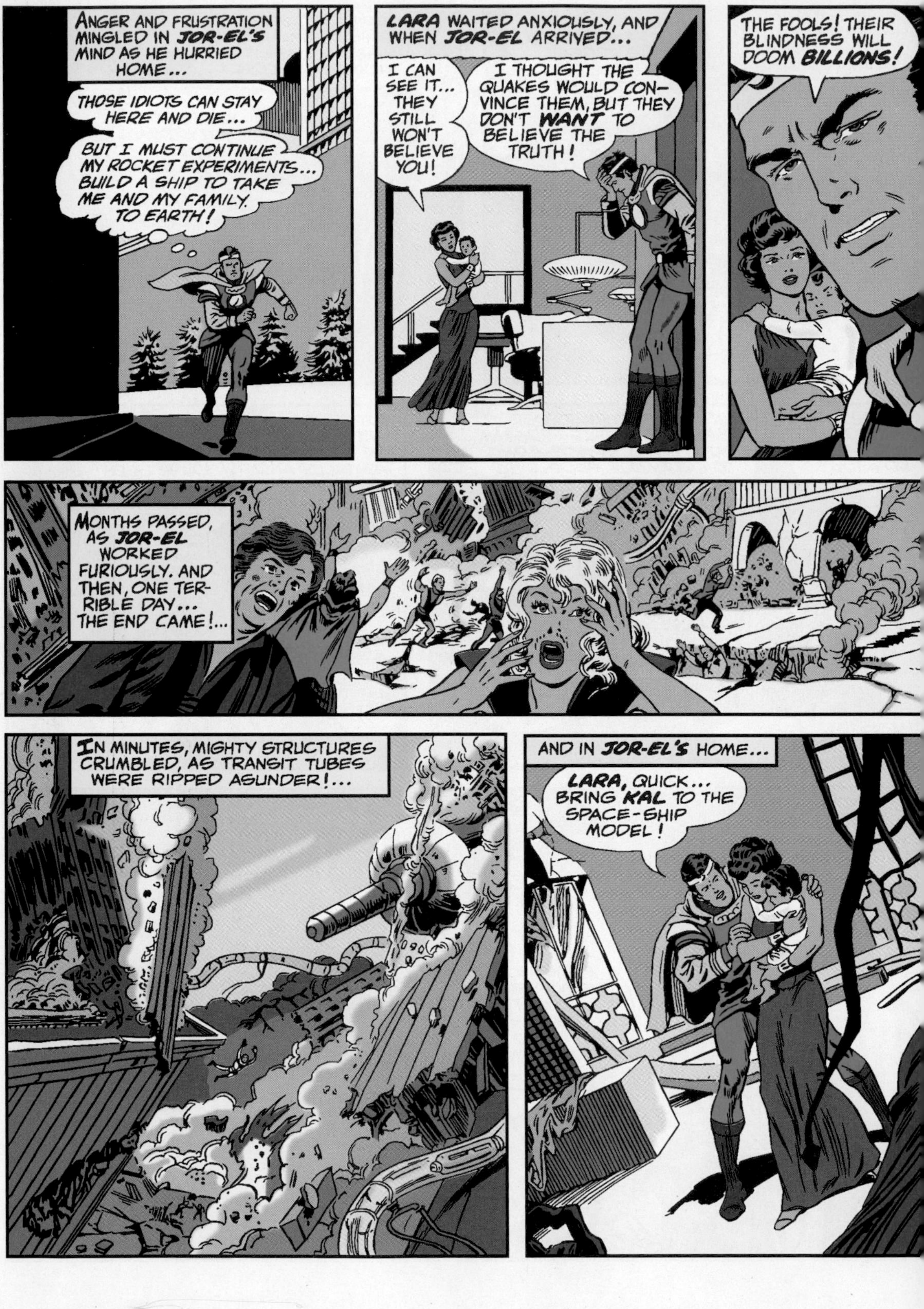

ANGER AND FRUSTRATION MINGLED IN JOR-EL'S MIND AS HE HURRIED HOME...
THOSE IDIOTS CAN STAY HERE AND DIE...
BUT I MUST CONTINUE MY ROCKET EXPERIMENTS... BUILD A SHIP TO TAKE ME AND MY FAMILY TO EARTH!
LARA WAITED ANXIOUSLY, AND WHEN JOR-EL ARRIVED...
I CAN SEE IT... THEY STILL WON'T BELIEVE YOU!
I THOUGHT THE QUAKES WOULD CONVINCE THEM, BUT THEY DON'T WANT TO BELIEVE THE TRUTH!
THE FOOLS! THEIR BLINDNESS WILL DOOM BILLIONS!
MONTHS PASSED, AS JOR-EL WORKED FURIOUSLY. AND THEN, ONE TERRIBLE DAY... THE END CAME!...
IN MINUTES, MIGHTY STRUCTURES CRUMBLED, AS TRANSIT TUBES WERE RIPPED ASUNDER!...
AND IN JOR-EL'S HOME...
LARA, QUICK... BRING KAL TO THE SPACE-SHIP MODEL!

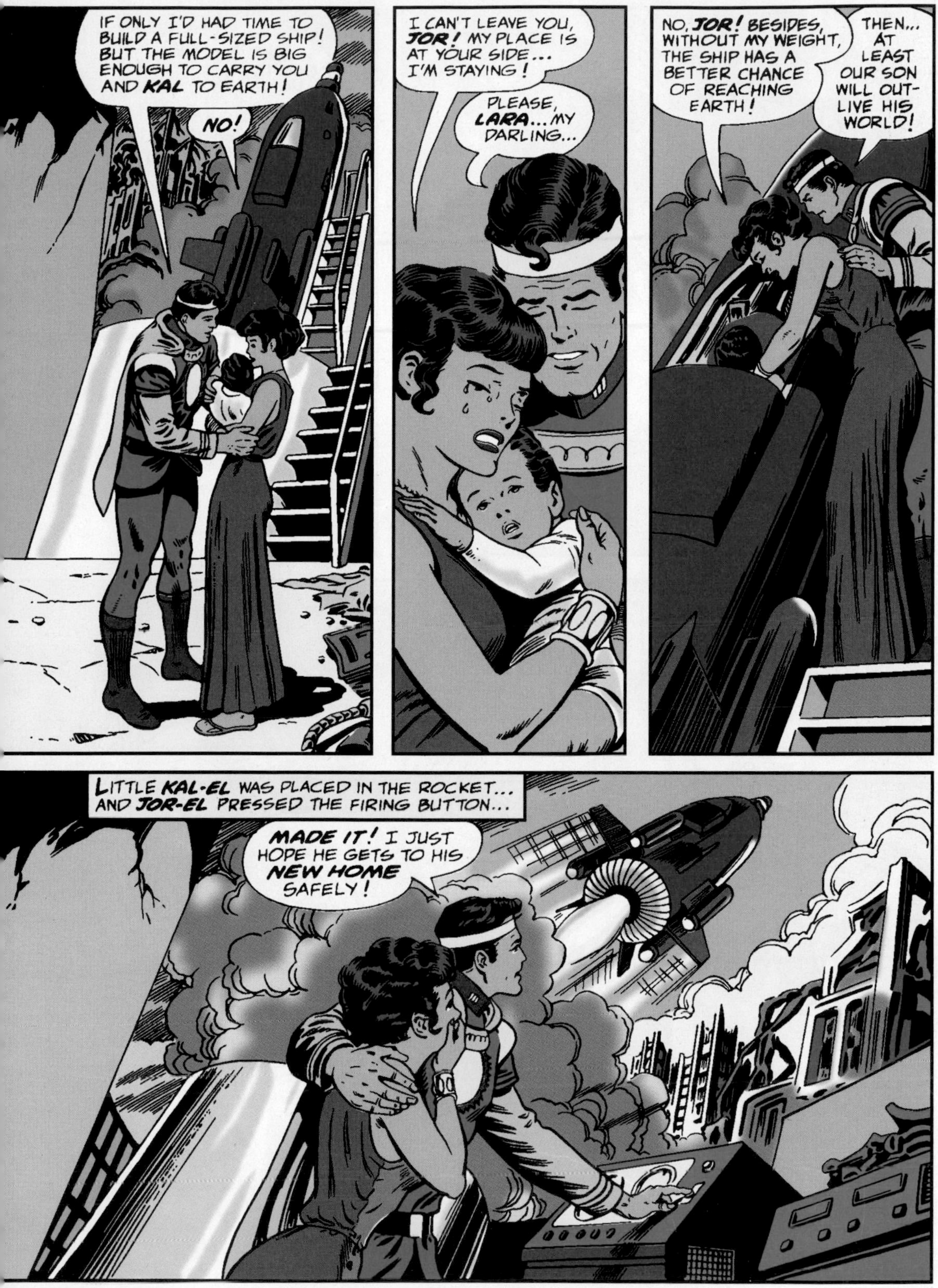
IF ONLY I'D HAD TIME TO BUILD A FULL-SIZED SHIP! BUT THE MODEL IS BIG ENOUGH TO CARRY YOU AND KAL TO EARTH!
NO!
I CAN'T LEAVE YOU, JOR! MY PLACE IS AT YOUR SIDE... I'M STAYING!
PLEASE, LARA... MY DARLING...
NO, JOR! BESIDES, WITHOUT MY WEIGHT, THE SHIP HAS A BETTER CHANCE OF REACHING EARTH!
THEN... AT LEAST OUR SON WILL OUT-LIVE HIS WORLD!
LITTLE KAL-EL WAS PLACED IN THE ROCKET... AND JOR-EL PRESSED THE FIRING BUTTON...
MADE IT! I JUST HOPE HE GETS TO HIS NEW HOME SAFELY!

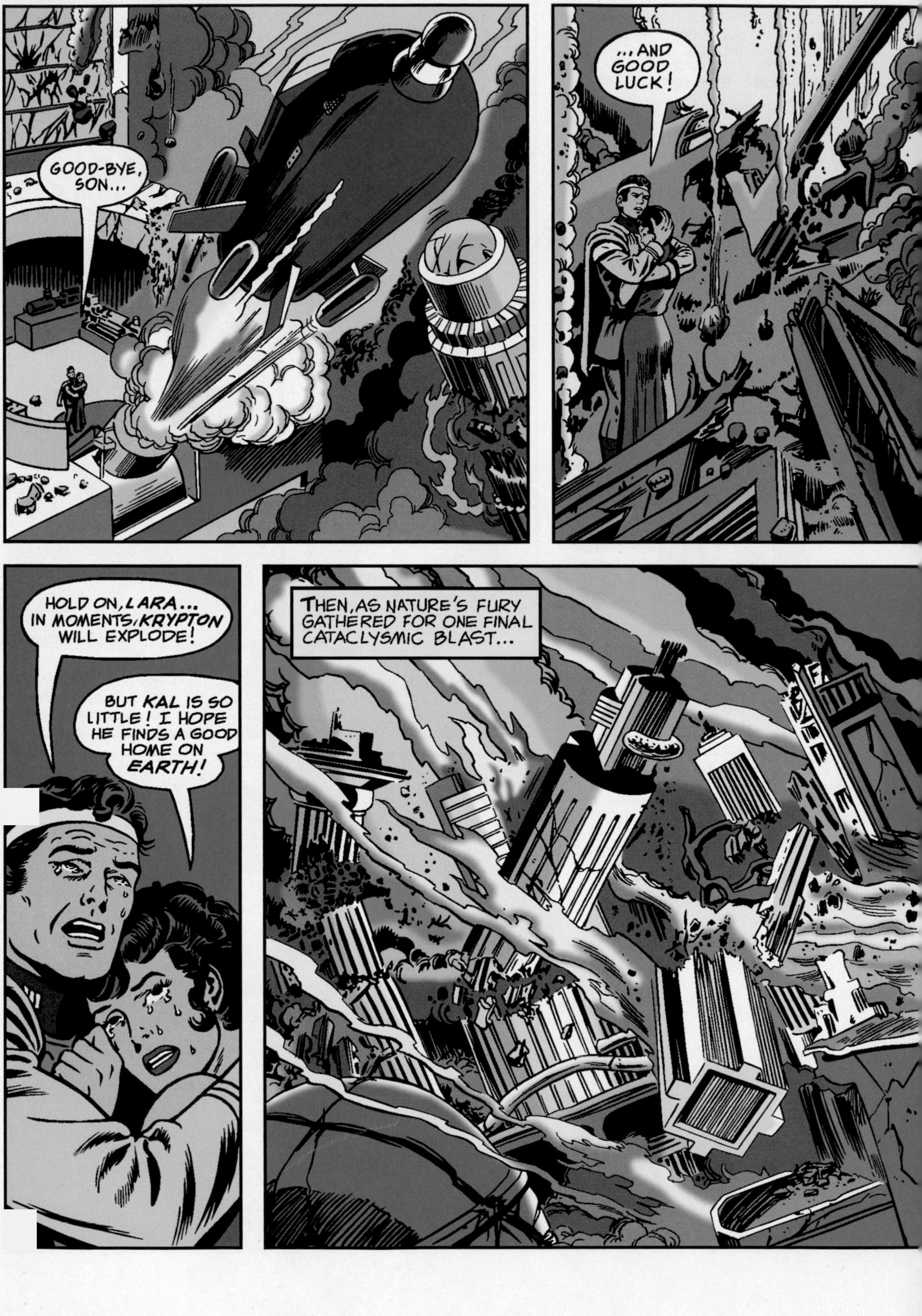
GOOD-BYE, SON...
...AND GOOD LUCK!
HOLD ON, LARA... IN MOMENTS, KRYPTON WILL EXPLODE!
BUT KAL IS SO LITTLE! I HOPE HE FINDS A GOOD HOME ON EARTH!
THEN, AS NATURE'S FURY GATHERED FOR ONE FINAL CATACLYSMIC BLAST...

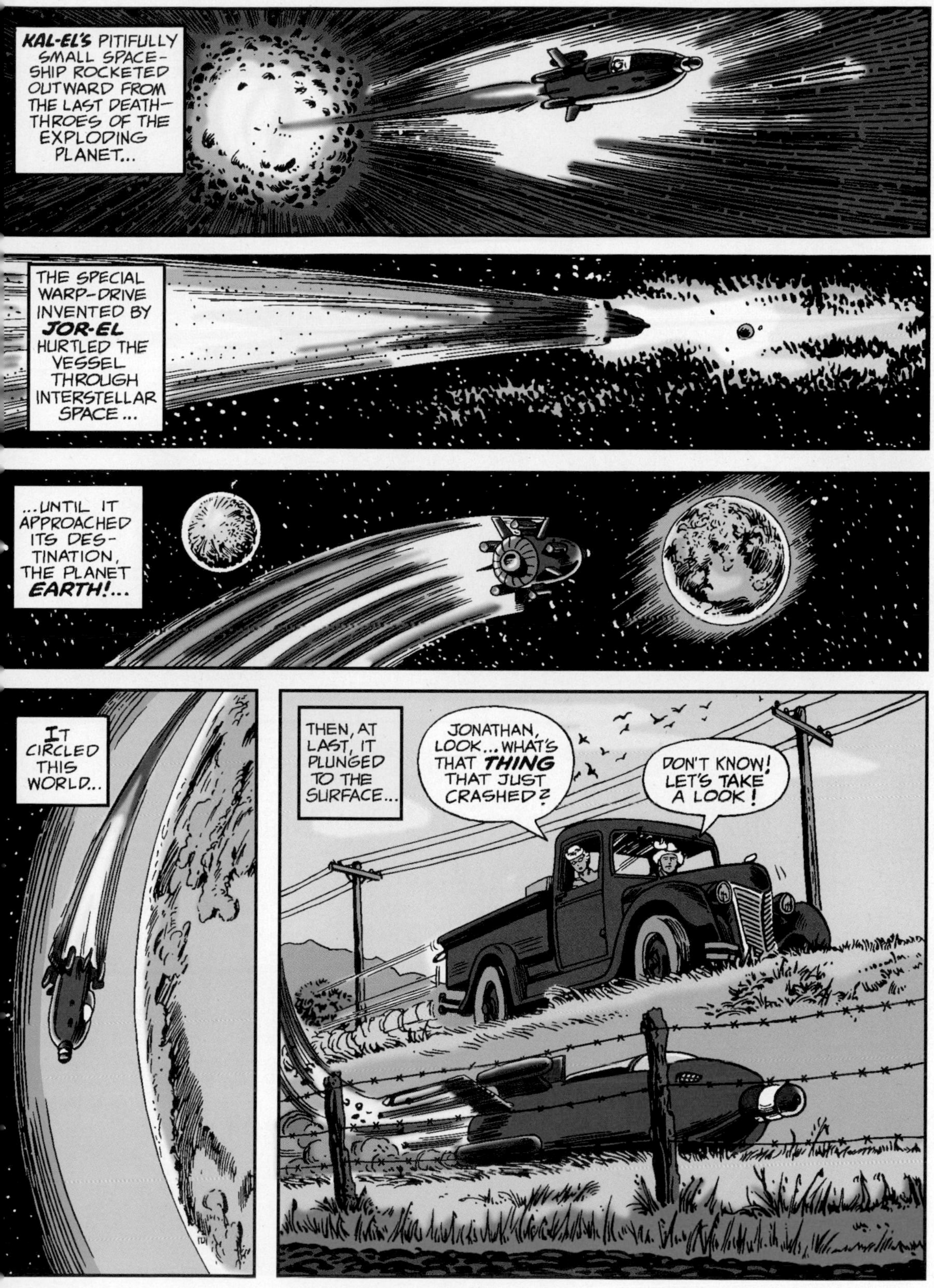
KAL-EL'S PITIFULLY SMALL SPACE-SHIP ROCKETED OUTWARD FROM THE LAST DEATH-THROES OF THE EXPLODING PLANET...
THE SPECIAL WARP-DRIVE INVENTED BY JOR-EL HURTLED THE VESSEL THROUGH INTERSTELLAR SPACE...
...UNTIL IT APPROACHED ITS DESTINATION, THE PLANET EARTH!...
IT CIRCLED THIS WORLD...
THEN, AT LAST, IT PLUNGED TO THE SURFACE...
JONATHAN, LOOK... WHAT'S THAT THING THAT JUST CRASHED?
DON'T KNOW! LET'S TAKE A LOOK!

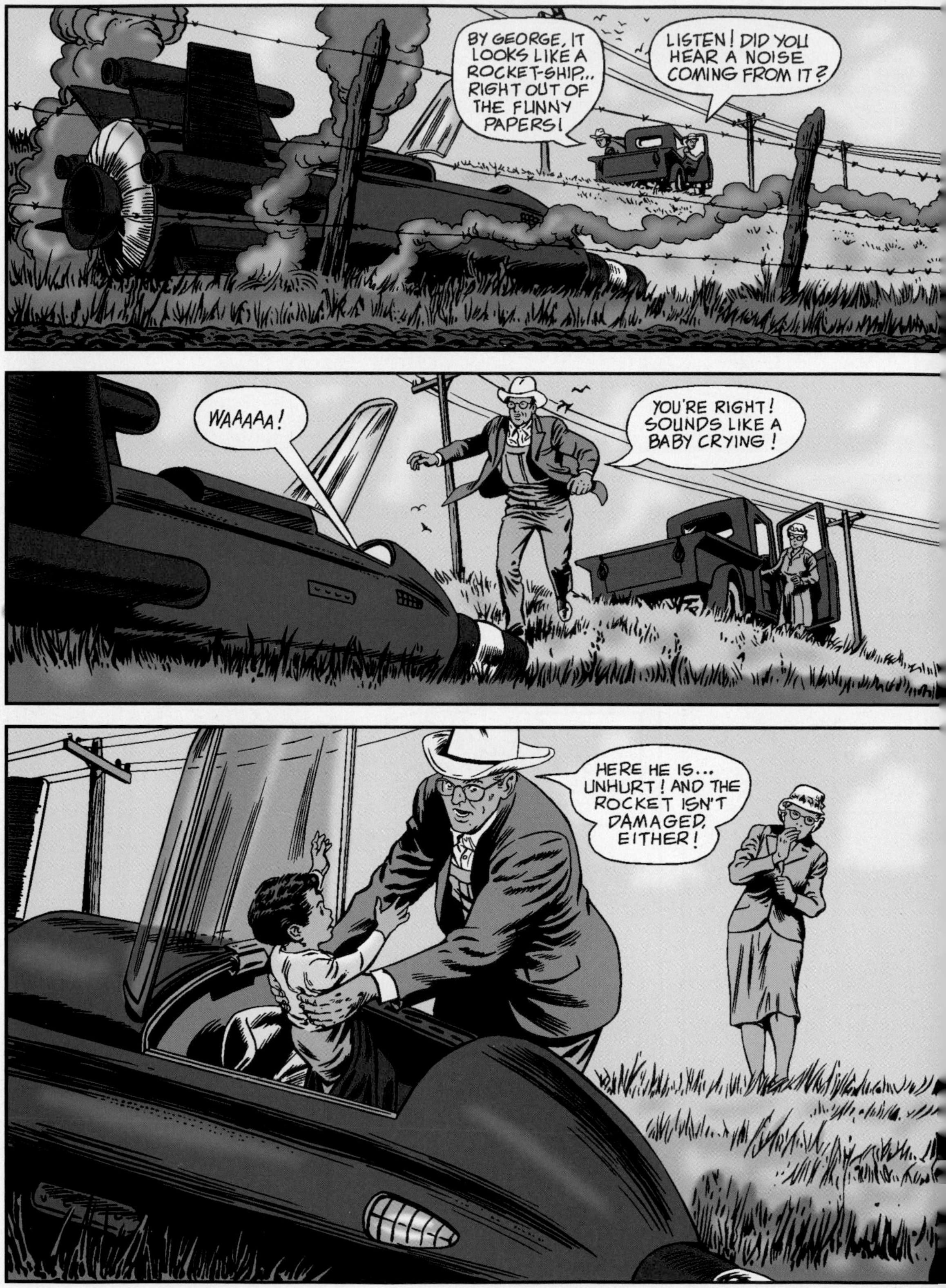
BY GEORGE, IT LOOKS LIKE A ROCKET-SHIP... RIGHT OUT OF THE FUNNY PAPERS!
LISTEN! DID YOU HEAR A NOISE COMING FROM IT?
WAAAAA!
YOU'RE RIGHT! SOUNDS LIKE A BABY CRYING!
HERE HE IS... UNHURT! AND THE ROCKET ISN'T DAMAGED, EITHER!

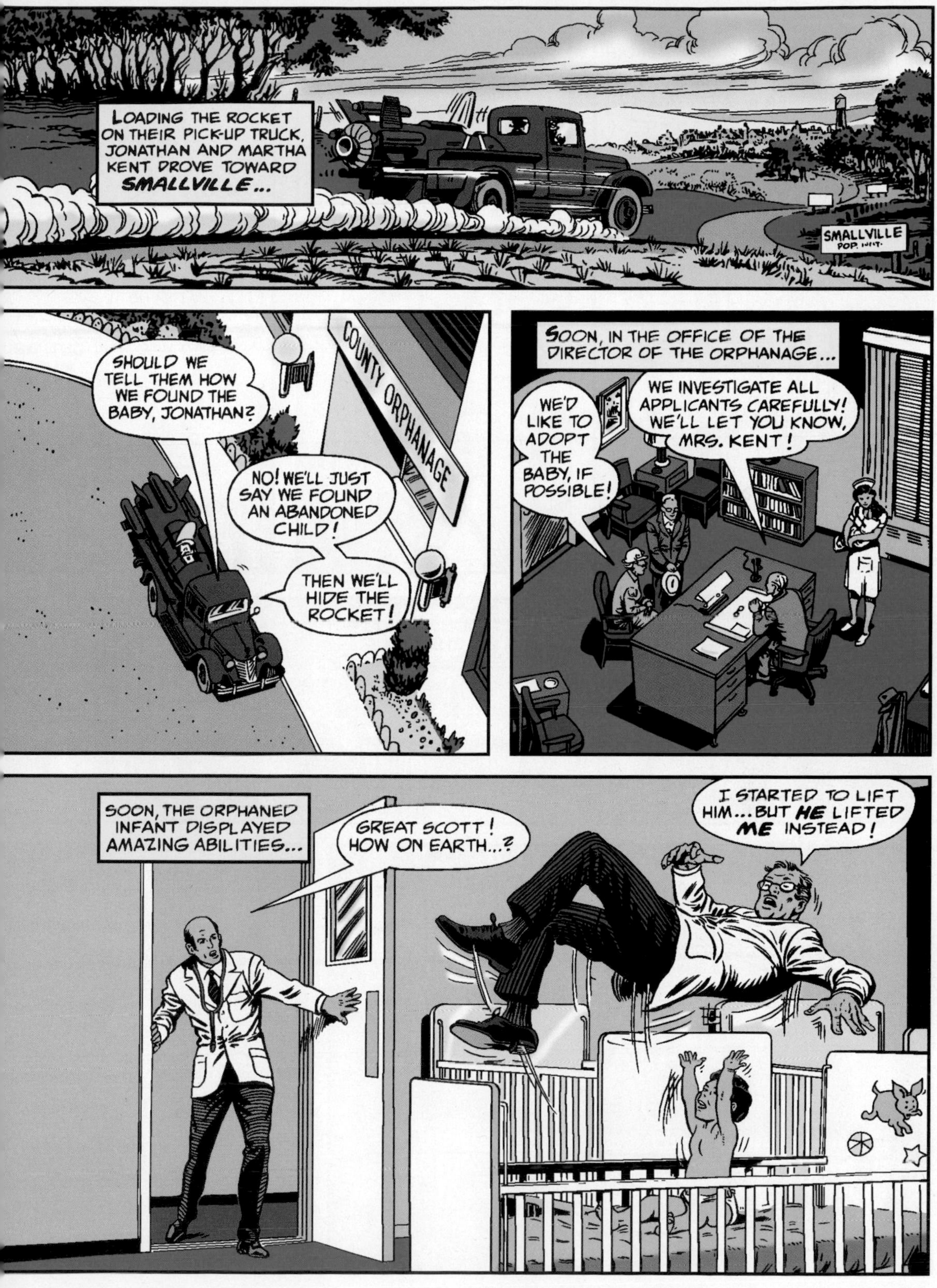
LOADING THE ROCKET ON THEIR PICK-UP TRUCK, JONATHAN AND MARTHA KENT DROVE TOWARD SMALLVILLE...
SMALLVILLE
SHOULD WE TELL THEM HOW WE FOUND THE BABY, JONATHAN?
NO! WE'LL JUST SAY WE FOUND AN ABANDONED CHILD!
THEN WE'LL HIDE THE ROCKET!
COUNTY ORPHANAGE
SOON, IN THE OFFICE OF THE DIRECTOR OF THE ORPHANAGE...
WE'D LIKE TO ADOPT THE BABY, IF POSSIBLE!
WE INVESTIGATE ALL APPLICANTS CAREFULLY! WE'LL LET YOU KNOW, MRS. KENT!
SOON, THE ORPHANED INFANT DISPLAYED AMAZING ABILITIES...
GREAT SCOTT! HOW ON EARTH...?
I STARTED TO LIFT HIM... BUT HE LIFTED ME INSTEAD!

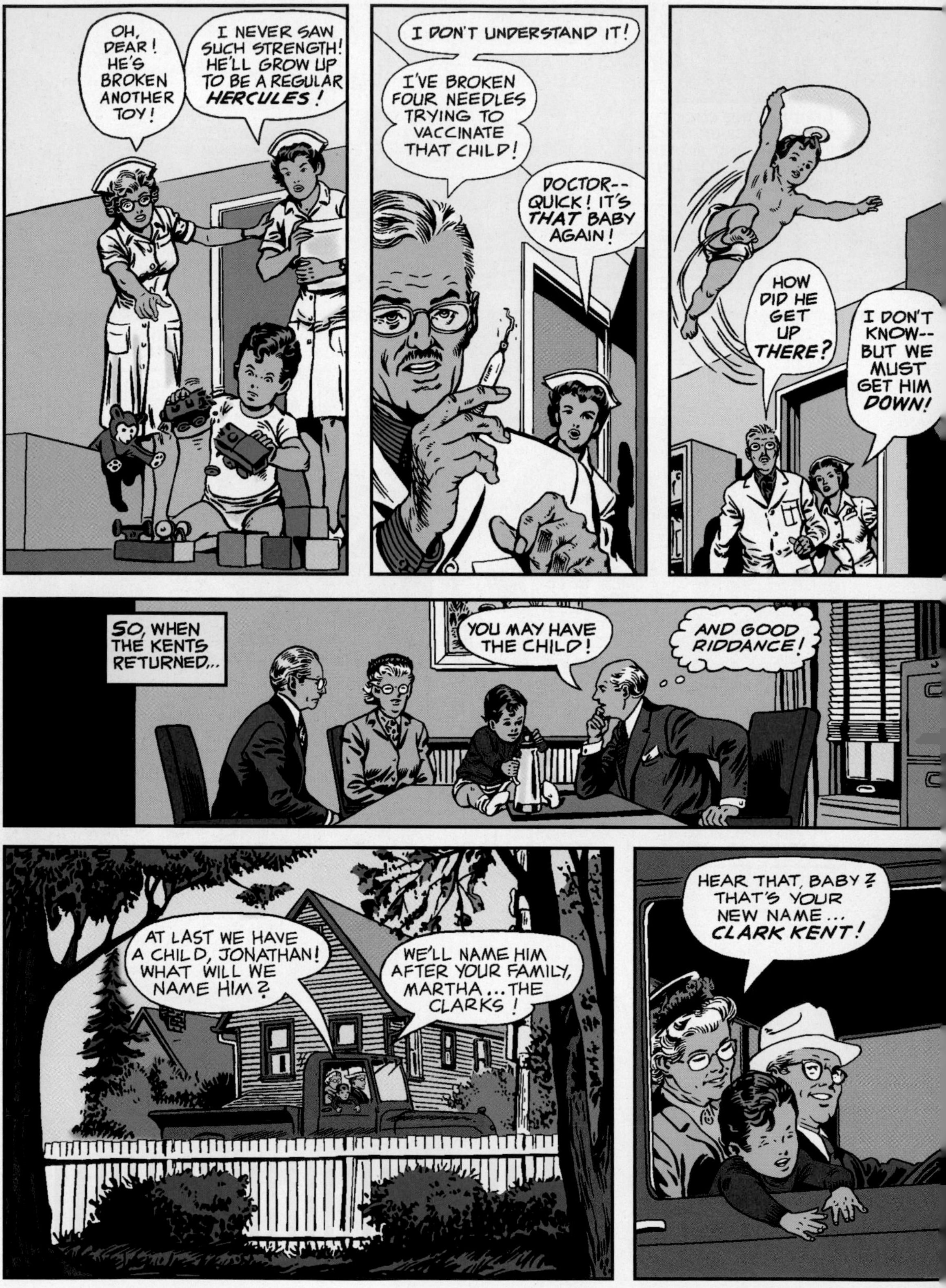

OH, DEAR! HE'S BROKEN ANOTHER TOY!
I NEVER SAW SUCH STRENGTH! HE'LL GROW UP TO BE A REGULAR HERCULES!
I DON'T UNDERSTAND IT!
I'VE BROKEN FOUR NEEDLES TRYING TO VACCINATE THAT CHILD!
DOCTOR-- QUICK! IT'S THAT BABY AGAIN!
HOW DID HE GET UP THERE?
I DON'T KNOW-- BUT WE MUST GET HIM DOWN!
SO, WHEN THE KENTS RETURNED...
YOU MAY HAVE THE CHILD!
AND GOOD RIDDANCE!
AT LAST WE HAVE A CHILD, JONATHAN! WHAT WILL WE NAME HIM?
WE'LL NAME HIM AFTER YOUR FAMILY, MARTHA... THE CLARKS!
HEAR THAT, BABY? THAT'S YOUR NEW NAME... CLARK KENT!

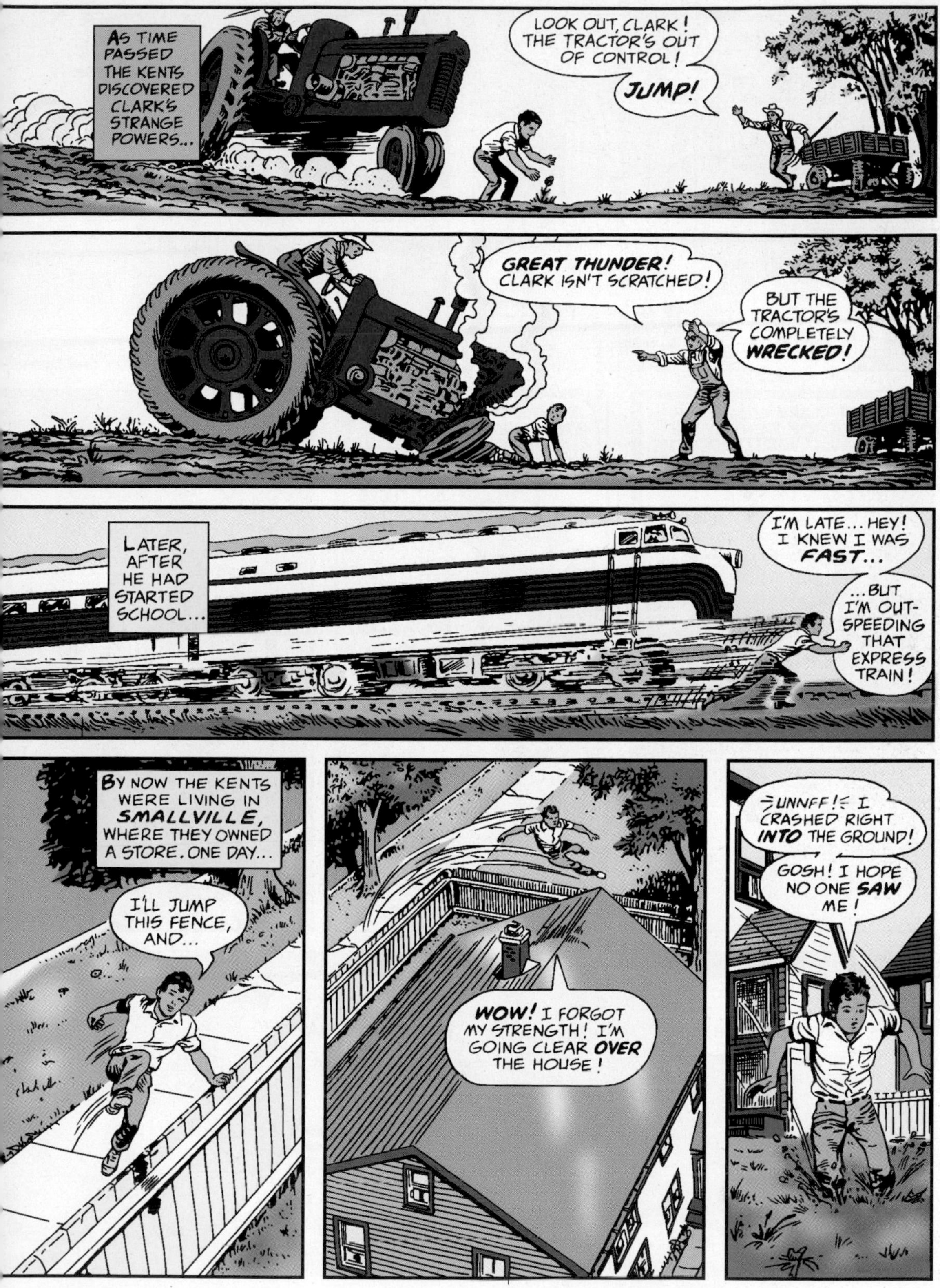
AS TIME PASSED THE KENTS DISCOVERED CLARK'S STRANGE POWERS...
LOOK OUT, CLARK! THE TRACTOR'S OUT OF CONTROL!
JUMP!
GREAT THUNDER! CLARK ISN'T SCRATCHED!
BUT THE TRACTOR'S COMPLETELY WRECKED!
LATER, AFTER HE HAD STARTED SCHOOL...
I'M LATE... HEY! I KNEW I WAS FAST...
...BUT I'M OUT-SPEEDING THAT EXPRESS TRAIN!
BY NOW THE KENTS WERE LIVING IN SMALLVILLE, WHERE THEY OWNED A STORE. ONE DAY...
I'LL JUMP THIS FENCE, AND...
WOW! I FORGOT MY STRENGTH! I'M GOING CLEAR OVER THE HOUSE!
UNNFF! I CRASHED RIGHT INTO THE GROUND!
GOSH! I HOPE NO ONE SAW ME!

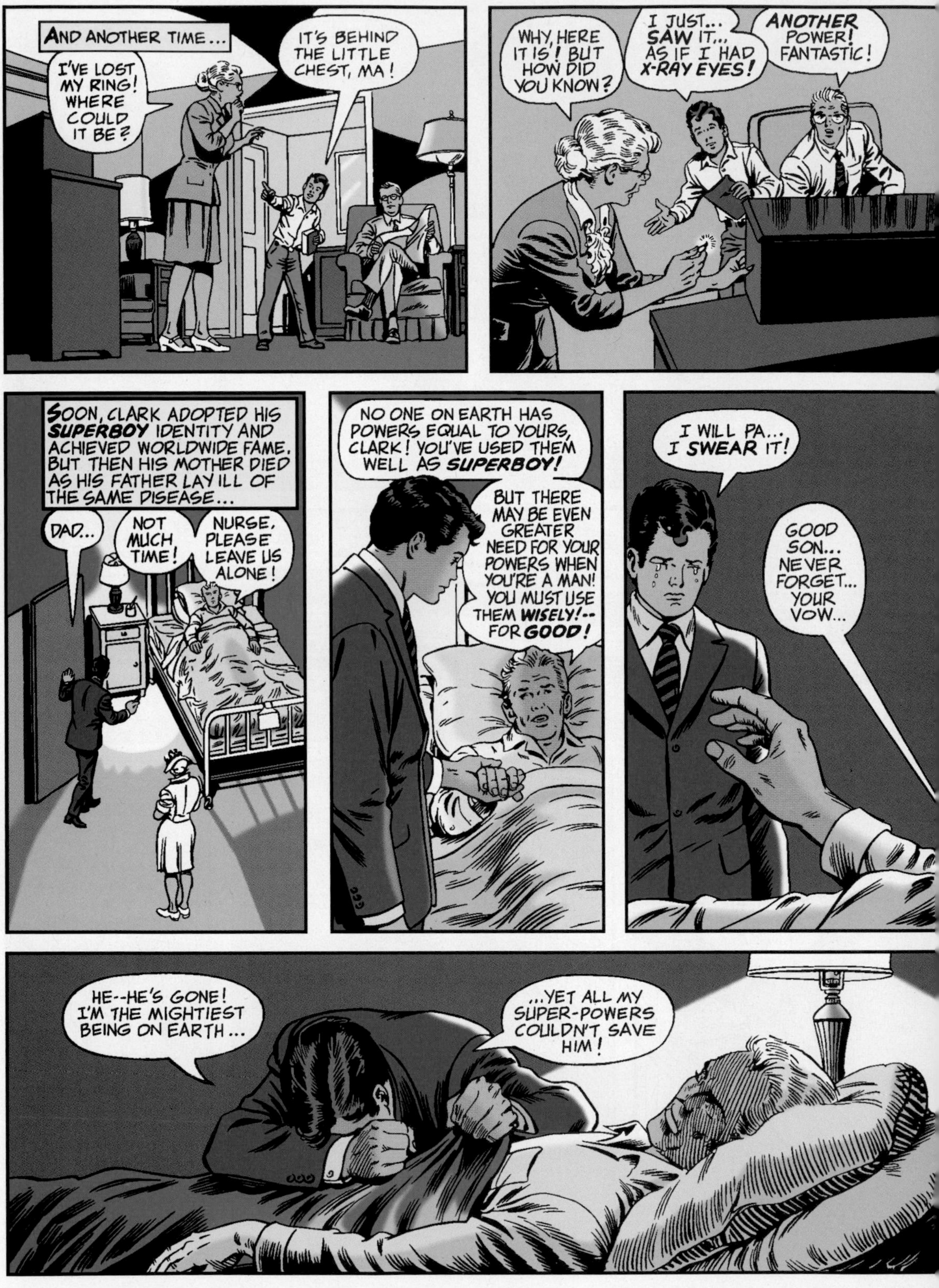
AND ANOTHER TIME...
I'VE LOST MY RING! WHERE COULD IT BE?
IT'S BEHIND THE LITTLE CHEST, MA!
WHY, HERE IT IS! BUT HOW DID YOU KNOW?
I JUST... SAW IT... AS IF I HAD X-RAY EYES!
ANOTHER POWER! FANTASTIC!
SOON, CLARK ADOPTED HIS SUPERBOY IDENTITY AND ACHIEVED WORLDWIDE FAME. BUT THEN HIS MOTHER DIED AS HIS FATHER LAY ILL OF THE SAME DISEASE...
DAD...
NOT MUCH TIME!
NURSE, PLEASE LEAVE US ALONE!
NO ONE ON EARTH HAS POWERS EQUAL TO YOURS, CLARK! YOU'VE USED THEM WELL AS SUPERBOY!
BUT THERE MAY BE EVEN GREATER NEED FOR YOUR POWERS WHEN YOU'RE A MAN! YOU MUST USE THEM WISELY!--FOR GOOD!
I WILL PA... I SWEAR IT!
GOOD SON... NEVER FORGET... YOUR VOW...
HE--HE'S GONE! I'M THE MIGHTIEST BEING ON EARTH...
...YET ALL MY SUPER-POWERS COULDN'T SAVE HIM!

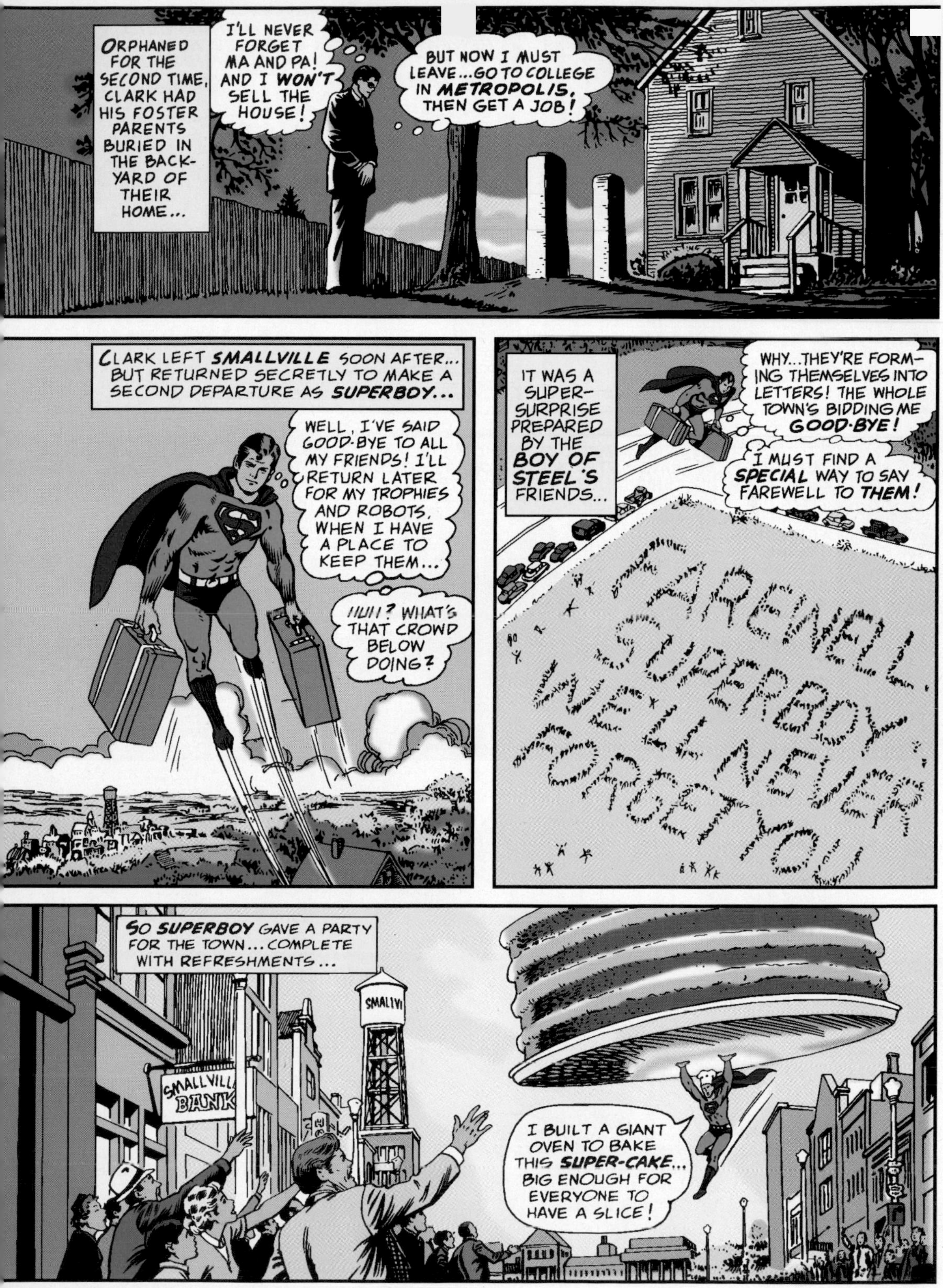
ORPHANED FOR THE SECOND TIME, CLARK HAD HIS FOSTER PARENTS BURIED IN THE BACK-YARD OF THEIR HOME...
I'LL NEVER FORGET MA AND PA! AND I WON'T SELL THE HOUSE!
BUT NOW I MUST LEAVE...GO TO COLLEGE IN METROPOLIS, THEN GET A JOB!
CLARK LEFT SMALLVILLE SOON AFTER... BUT RETURNED SECRETLY TO MAKE A SECOND DEPARTURE AS SUPERBOY...
WELL, I'VE SAID GOOD-BYE TO ALL MY FRIENDS! I'LL RETURN LATER FOR MY TROPHIES AND ROBOTS, WHEN I HAVE A PLACE TO KEEP THEM...
HUH? WHAT'S THAT CROWD BELOW DOING?
IT WAS A SUPER-SURPRISE PREPARED BY THE BOY OF STEEL'S FRIENDS...
WHY...THEY'RE FORMING THEMSELVES INTO LETTERS! THE WHOLE TOWN'S BIDDING ME GOOD-BYE!
I MUST FIND A SPECIAL WAY TO SAY FAREWELL TO THEM!
FAREWELL SUPERBOY WE'LL NEVER FORGET YOU!
SO SUPERBOY GAVE A PARTY FOR THE TOWN... COMPLETE WITH REFRESHMENTS...
SMALLVILLE BANK
I BUILT A GIANT OVEN TO BAKE THIS SUPER-CAKE... BIG ENOUGH FOR EVERYONE TO HAVE A SLICE!

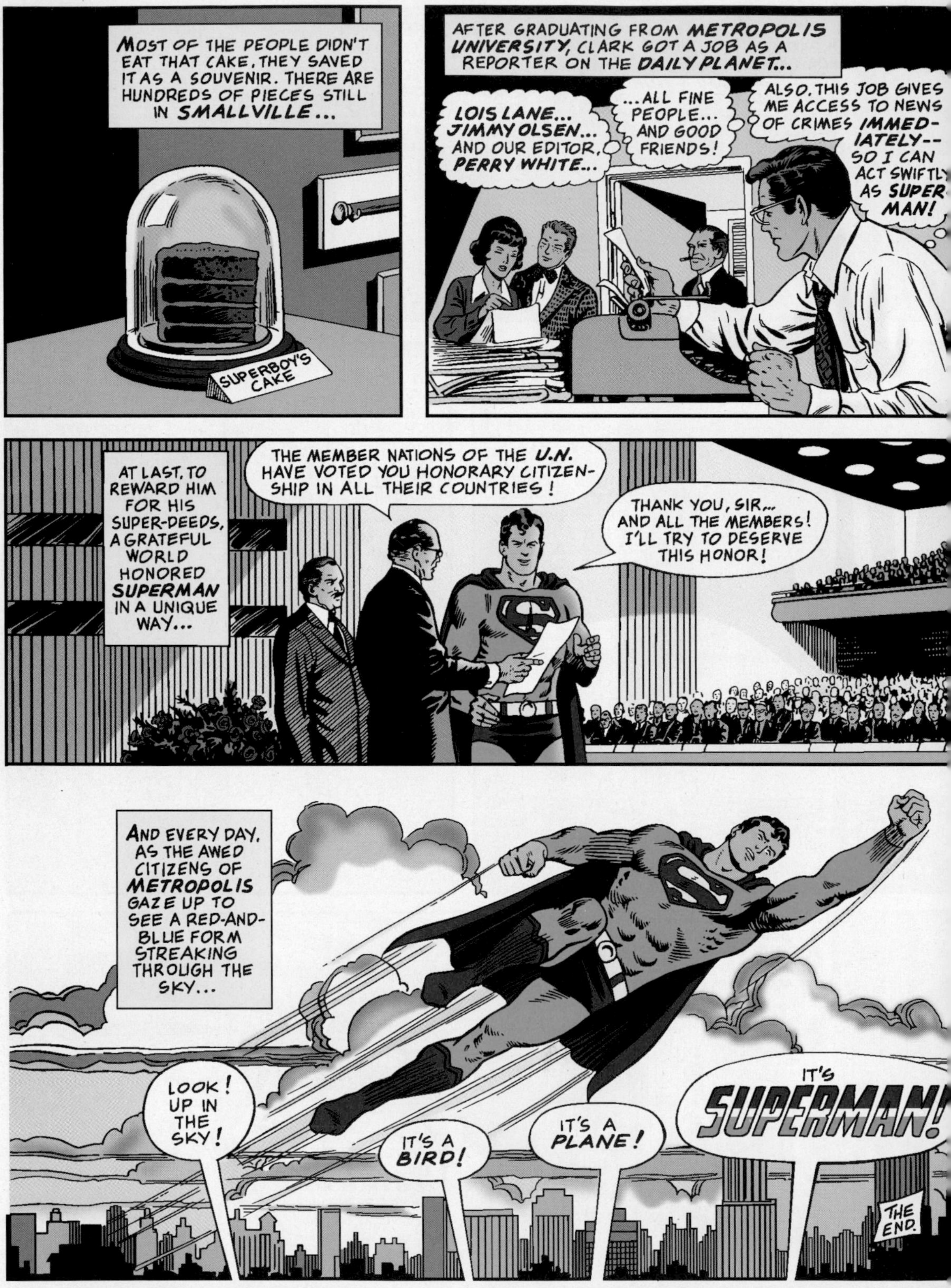
MOST OF THE PEOPLE DIDN'T EAT THAT CAKE. THEY SAVED IT AS A SOUVENIR. THERE ARE HUNDREDS OF PIECES STILL IN SMALLVILLE...
SUPERBOY'S CAKE
AFTER GRADUATING FROM METROPOLIS UNIVERSITY, CLARK GOT A JOB AS A REPORTER ON THE DAILY PLANET...
LOIS LANE... JIMMY OLSEN... AND OUR EDITOR, PERRY WHITE...
...ALL FINE PEOPLE... AND GOOD FRIENDS!
ALSO, THIS JOB GIVES ME ACCESS TO NEWS OF CRIMES IMMED-IATELY-- SO I CAN ACT SWIFTLY AS SUPERMAN!
AT LAST, TO REWARD HIM FOR HIS SUPER-DEEDS, A GRATEFUL WORLD HONORED SUPERMAN IN A UNIQUE WAY...
THE MEMBER NATIONS OF THE U.N. HAVE VOTED YOU HONORARY CITIZEN-SHIP IN ALL THEIR COUNTRIES!
THANK YOU, SIR... AND ALL THE MEMBERS! I'LL TRY TO DESERVE THIS HONOR!
AND EVERY DAY, AS THE AWED CITIZENS OF METROPOLIS GAZE UP TO SEE A RED-AND-BLUE FORM STREAKING THROUGH THE SKY...
LOOK! UP IN THE SKY!
IT'S A BIRD!
IT'S A PLANE!
IT'S SUPERMAN!
THE END.

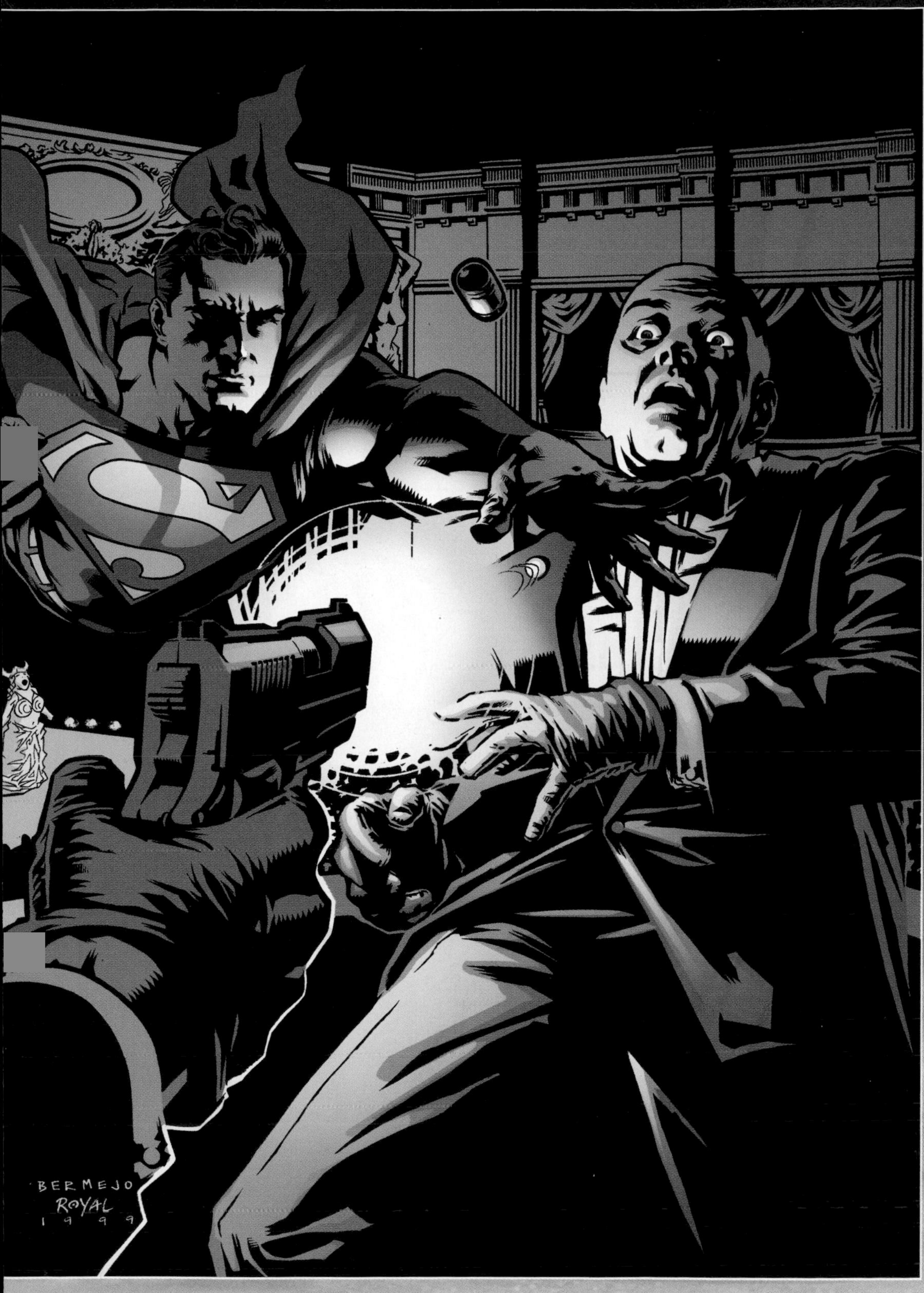
BERMEJO
ROYAL
1999

"A Night at the Opera"

STUART IMMONEN plotter **MARK MILLAR** scripter **YANICK PAQUETTE** penciller
XTER VINES, RICH FABER & JIM ROYAL inkers **GLENN WHITMORE** colorist **BILL OAKLEY** letterer
LEE BERMEJO & JIM ROYAL WITH LIQUID cover artists

uperman's archnemesis, Lex Luthor, is once again up to no good in this story from THE ADVENTURES OF SUPERMAN.

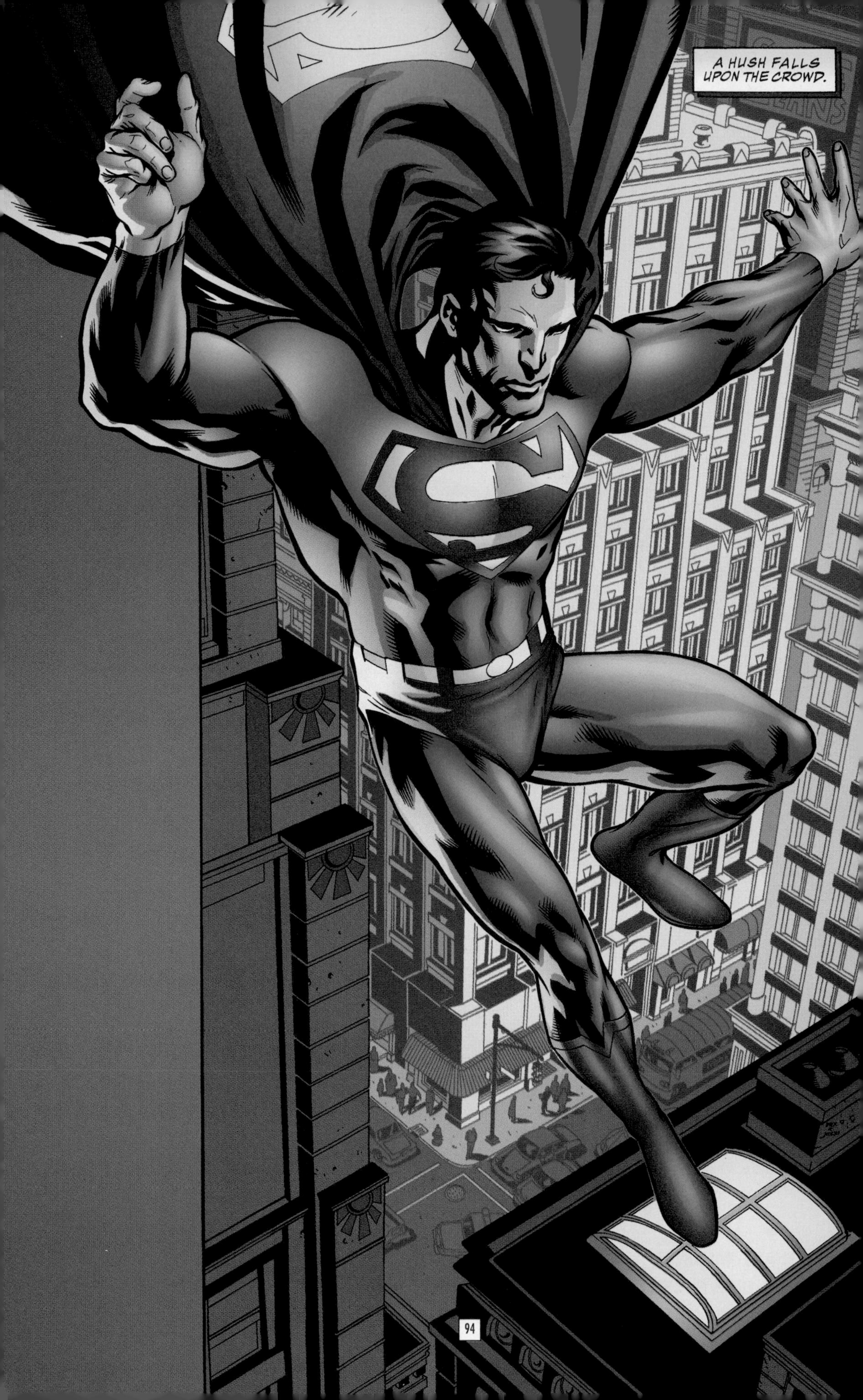
A HUSH FALLS
UPON THE CROWD.

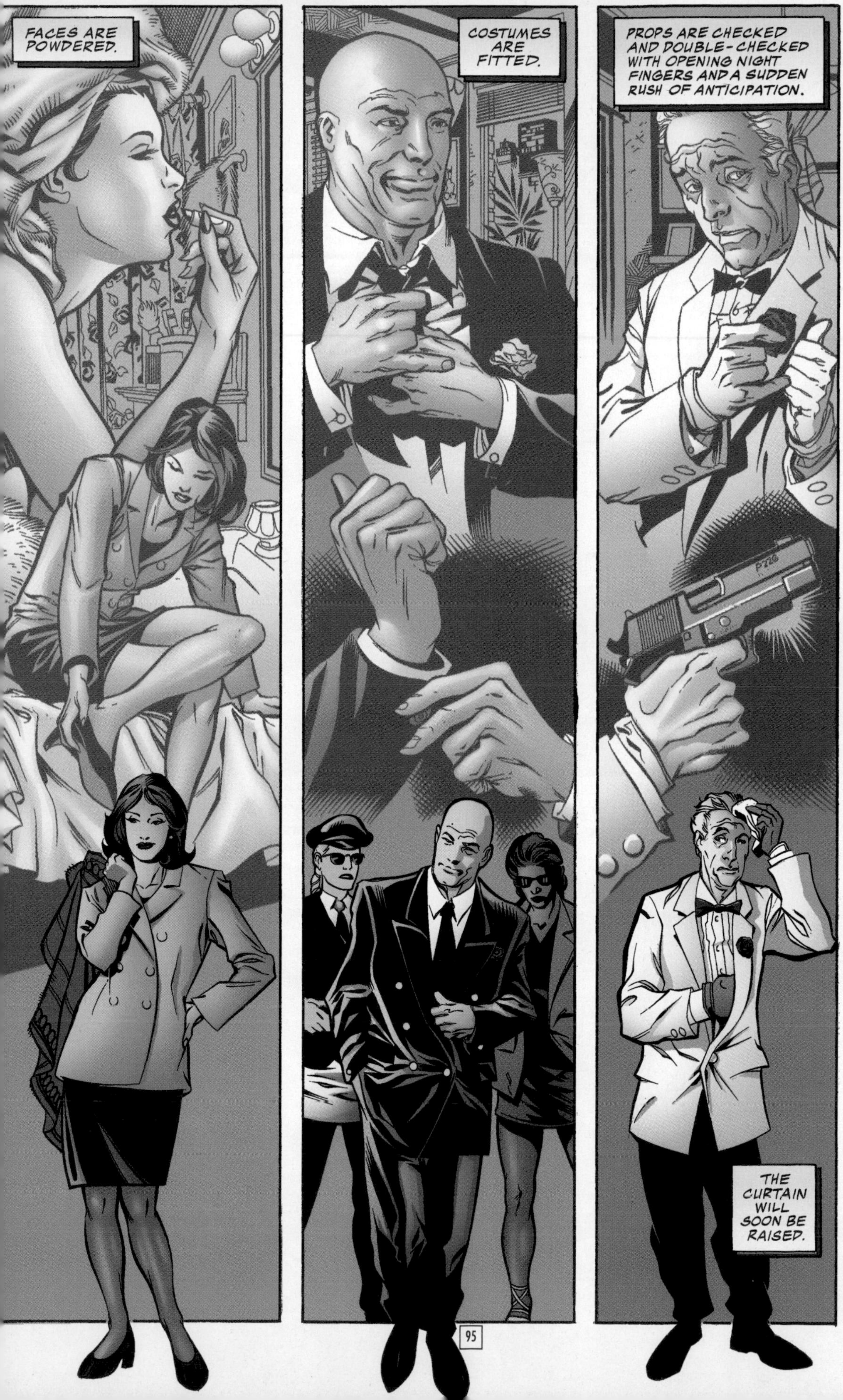
FACES ARE POWDERED.
COSTUMES ARE FITTED.
PROPS ARE CHECKED AND DOUBLE-CHECKED WITH OPENING NIGHT FINGERS AND A SUDDEN RUSH OF ANTICIPATION.
THE CURTAIN WILL SOON BE RAISED.

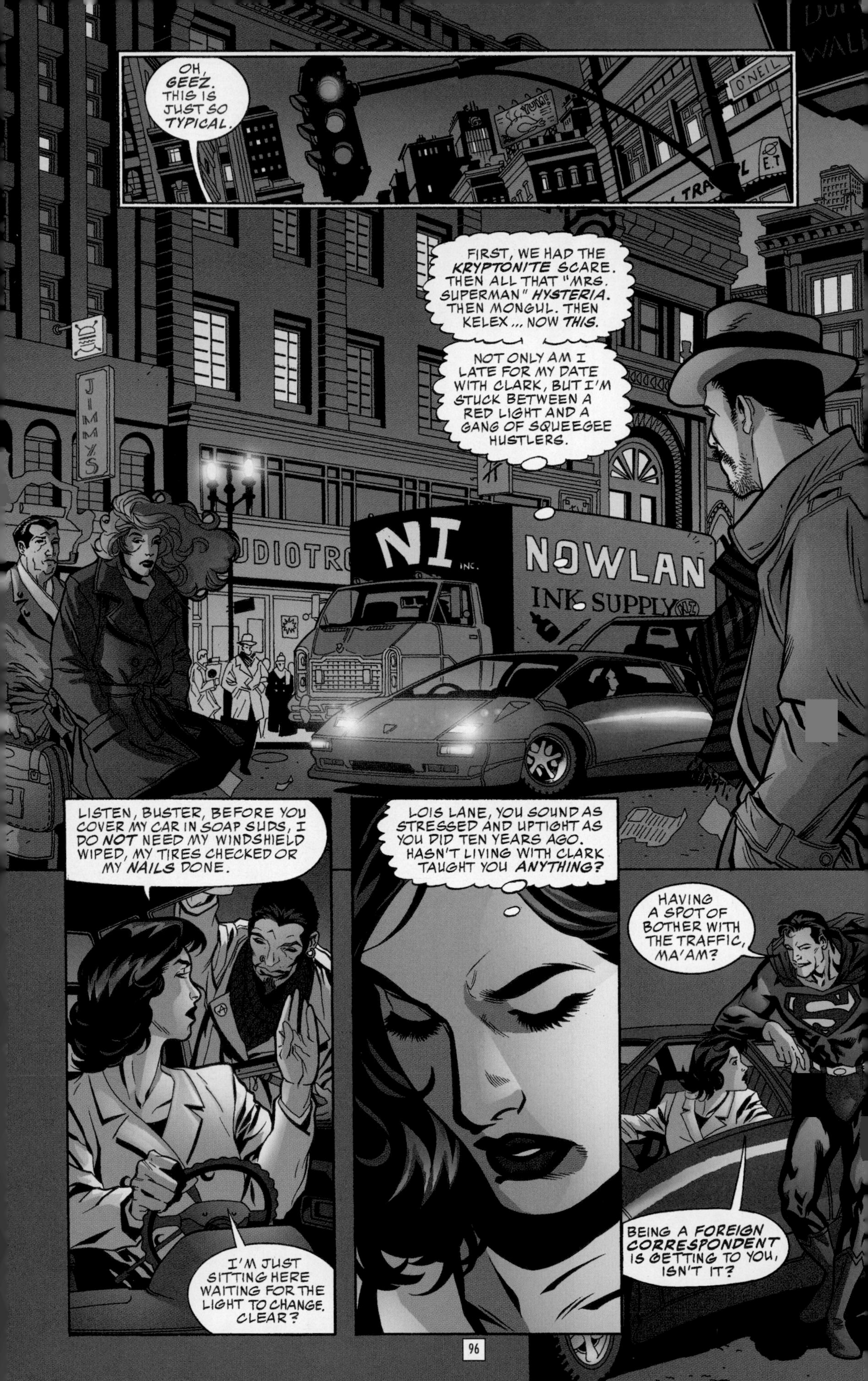
OH, GEEZ. THIS IS JUST SO TYPICAL.
O'NEIL
FIRST, WE HAD THE KRYPTONITE SCARE. THEN ALL THAT "MRS. SUPERMAN" HYSTERIA. THEN MONGUL. THEN KELEX ... NOW THIS.
NOT ONLY AM I LATE FOR MY DATE WITH CLARK, BUT I'M STUCK BETWEEN A RED LIGHT AND A GANG OF SQUEEGEE HUSTLERS.
JIMMY'S
NI INC.
NOWLAN
INK SUPPLY
LISTEN, BUSTER, BEFORE YOU COVER MY CAR IN SOAP SUDS, I DO NOT NEED MY WINDSHIELD WIPED, MY TIRES CHECKED OR MY NAILS DONE.
I'M JUST SITTING HERE WAITING FOR THE LIGHT TO CHANGE. CLEAR?
LOIS LANE, YOU SOUND AS STRESSED AND UPTIGHT AS YOU DID TEN YEARS AGO. HASN'T LIVING WITH CLARK TAUGHT YOU ANYTHING?
HAVING A SPOT OF BOTHER WITH THE TRAFFIC, MA'AM?
BEING A FOREIGN CORRESPONDENT IS GETTING TO YOU, ISN'T IT?

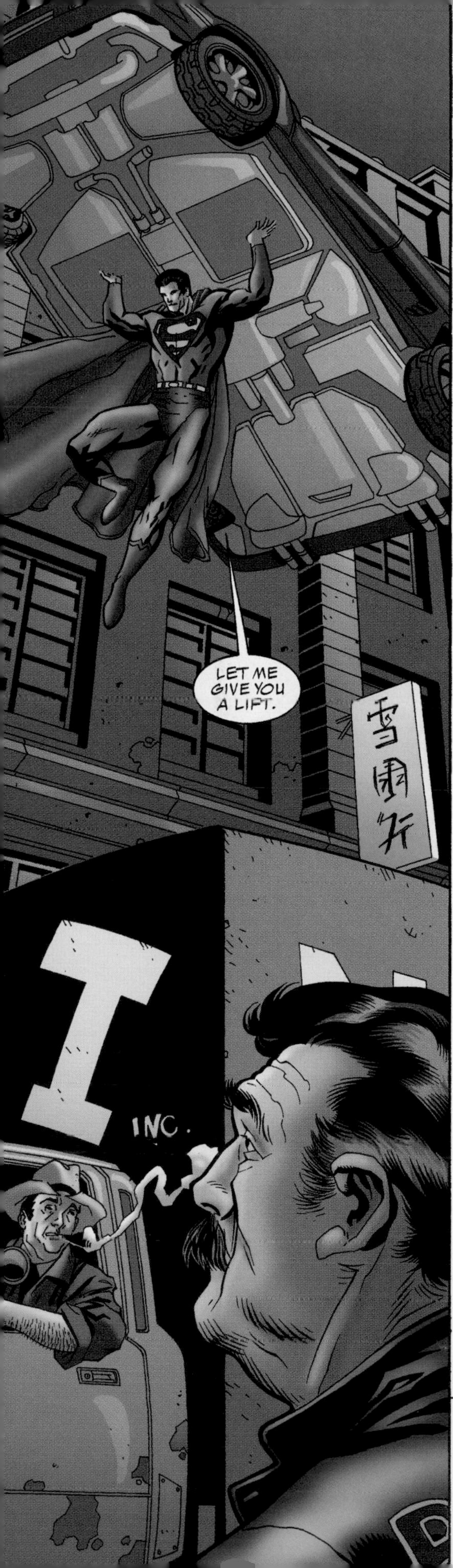
LET ME GIVE YOU A LIFT.
INC.

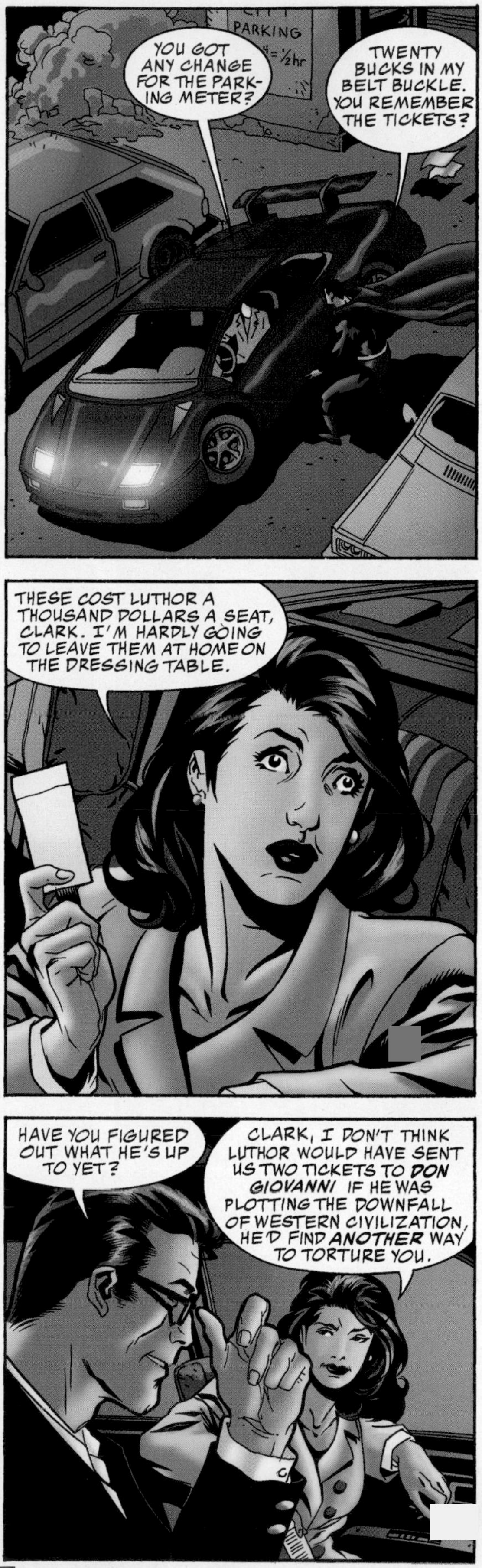
PARKING
YOU GOT ANY CHANGE FOR THE PARK-ING METER?
TWENTY BUCKS IN MY BELT BUCKLE. YOU REMEMBER THE TICKETS?
THESE COST LUTHOR A THOUSAND DOLLARS A SEAT, CLARK. I'M HARDLY GOING TO LEAVE THEM AT HOME ON THE DRESSING TABLE.
HAVE YOU FIGURED OUT WHAT HE'S UP TO YET?
CLARK, I DON'T THINK LUTHOR WOULD HAVE SENT US TWO TICKETS TO DON GIOVANNI IF HE WAS PLOTTING THE DOWNFALL OF WESTERN CIVILIZATION. HE'D FIND ANOTHER WAY TO TORTURE YOU.

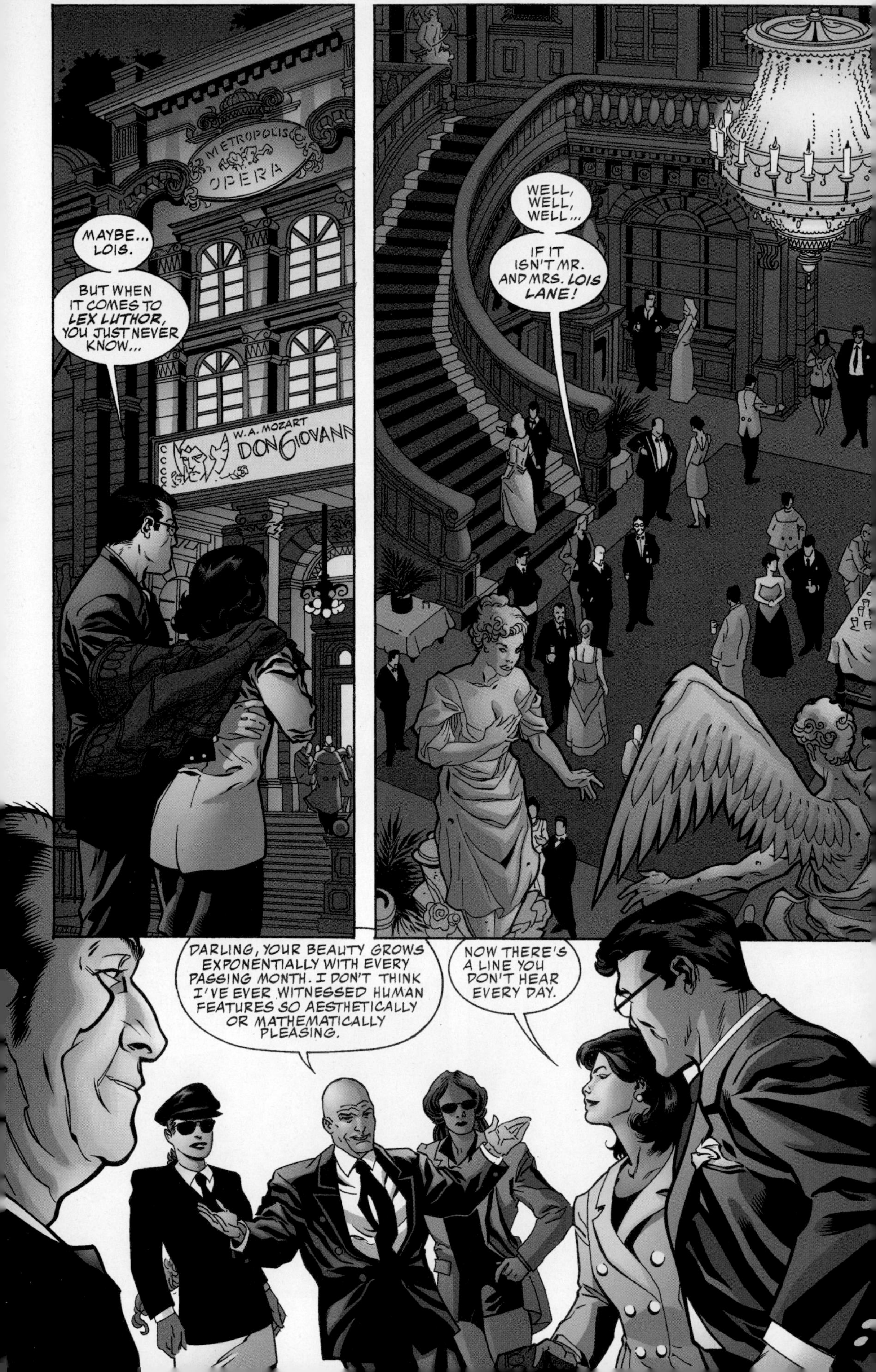
METROPOLIS OPERA
MAYBE... LOIS.
BUT WHEN IT COMES TO LEX LUTHOR, YOU JUST NEVER KNOW...
W. A. MOZART DON GIOVANNI
WELL, WELL, WELL...
IF IT ISN'T MR. AND MRS. LOIS LANE!
DARLING, YOUR BEAUTY GROWS EXPONENTIALLY WITH EVERY PASSING MONTH. I DON'T THINK I'VE EVER WITNESSED HUMAN FEATURES SO AESTHETICALLY OR MATHEMATICALLY PLEASING.
NOW THERE'S A LINE YOU DON'T HEAR EVERY DAY.

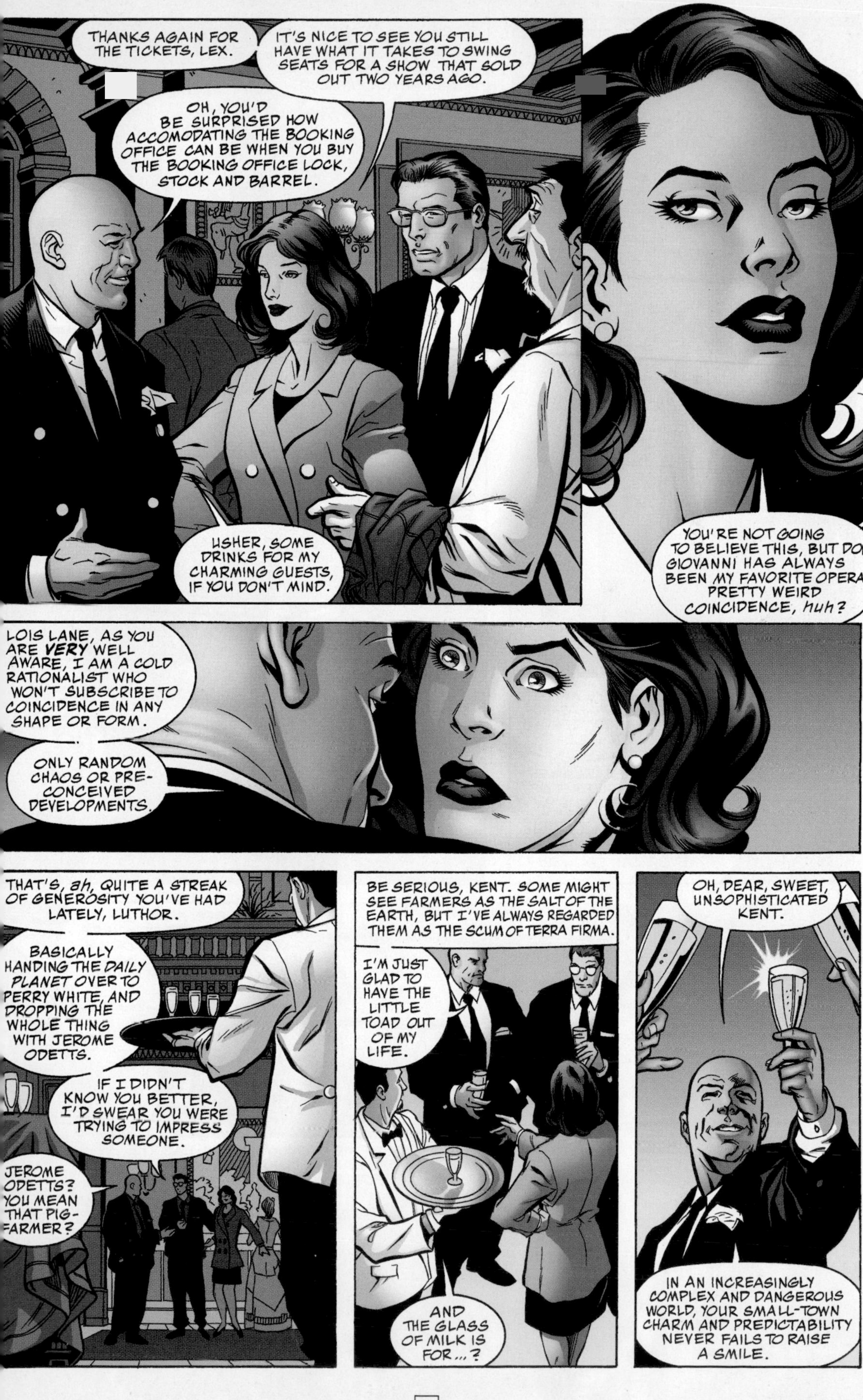
THANKS AGAIN FOR THE TICKETS, LEX.
IT'S NICE TO SEE YOU STILL HAVE WHAT IT TAKES TO SWING SEATS FOR A SHOW THAT SOLD OUT TWO YEARS AGO.
OH, YOU'D BE SURPRISED HOW ACCOMODATING THE BOOKING OFFICE CAN BE WHEN YOU BUY THE BOOKING OFFICE LOCK, STOCK AND BARREL.
USHER, SOME DRINKS FOR MY CHARMING GUESTS, IF YOU DON'T MIND.
YOU'RE NOT GOING TO BELIEVE THIS, BUT DON GIOVANNI HAS ALWAYS BEEN MY FAVORITE OPERA. PRETTY WEIRD COINCIDENCE, *huh*?
LOIS LANE, AS YOU ARE **VERY** WELL AWARE, I AM A COLD RATIONALIST WHO WON'T SUBSCRIBE TO COINCIDENCE IN ANY SHAPE OR FORM.
ONLY RANDOM CHAOS OR PRE-CONCEIVED DEVELOPMENTS.
THAT'S, *ah*, QUITE A STREAK OF GENEROSITY YOU'VE HAD LATELY, LUTHOR.
BASICALLY HANDING THE *DAILY PLANET* OVER TO PERRY WHITE, AND DROPPING THE WHOLE THING WITH JEROME ODETTS.
IF I DIDN'T KNOW YOU BETTER, I'D SWEAR YOU WERE TRYING TO IMPRESS SOMEONE.
JEROME ODETTS? YOU MEAN THAT PIG-FARMER?
BE SERIOUS, KENT. SOME MIGHT SEE FARMERS AS THE SALT OF THE EARTH, BUT I'VE ALWAYS REGARDED THEM AS THE SCUM OF TERRA FIRMA.
I'M JUST GLAD TO HAVE THE LITTLE TOAD OUT OF MY LIFE.
AND THE GLASS OF MILK IS FOR...?
OH, DEAR, SWEET, UNSOPHISTICATED KENT.
IN AN INCREASINGLY COMPLEX AND DANGEROUS WORLD, YOUR SMALL-TOWN CHARM AND PREDICTABILITY NEVER FAILS TO RAISE A SMILE.

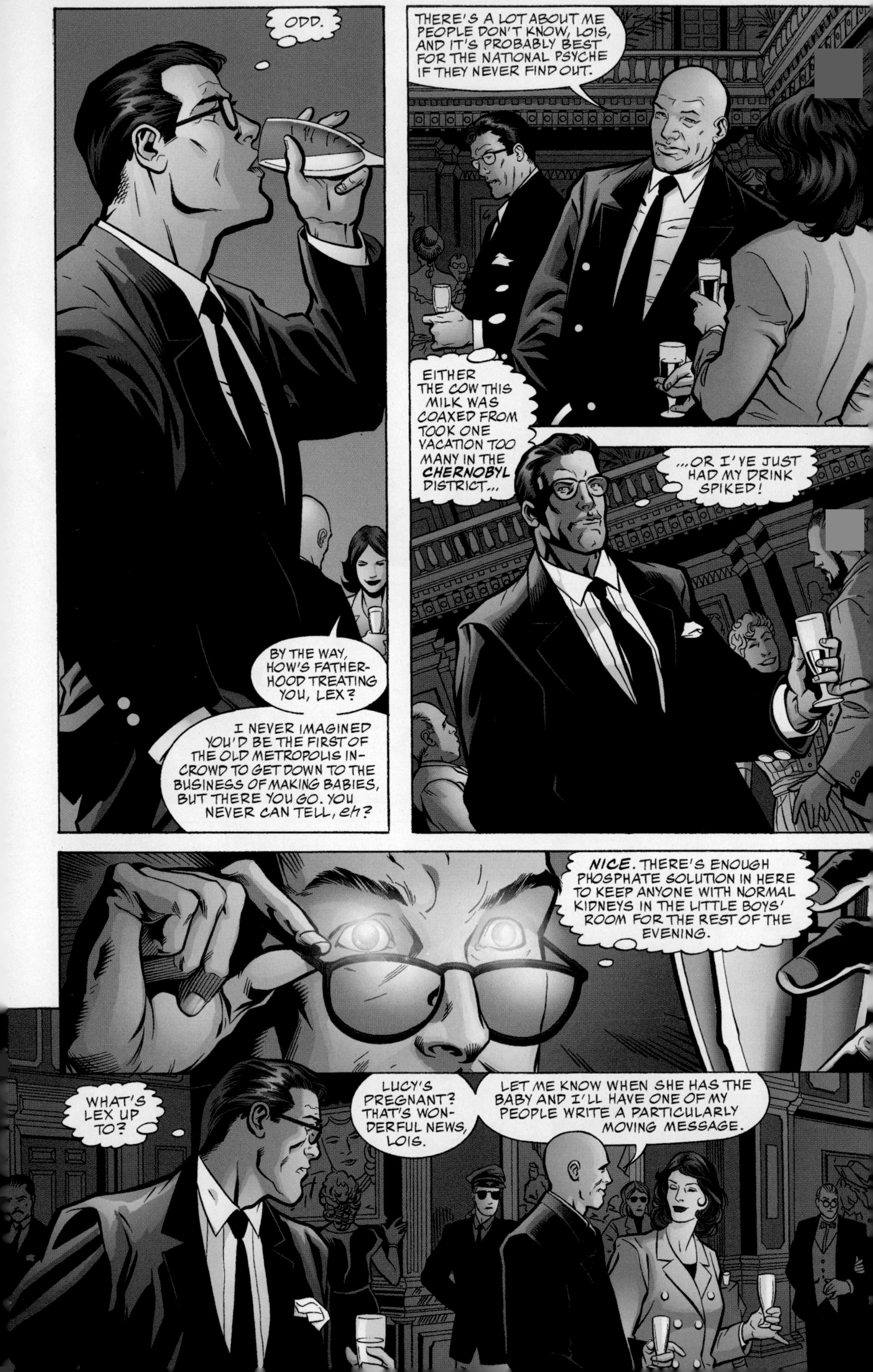
ODD.
THERE'S A LOT ABOUT ME PEOPLE DON'T KNOW, LOIS, AND IT'S PROBABLY BEST FOR THE NATIONAL PSYCHE IF THEY NEVER FIND OUT.
EITHER THE COW THIS MILK WAS COAXED FROM TOOK ONE VACATION TOO MANY IN THE CHERNOBYL DISTRICT...
...OR I'VE JUST HAD MY DRINK SPIKED!
BY THE WAY, HOW'S FATHER-HOOD TREATING YOU, LEX?
I NEVER IMAGINED YOU'D BE THE FIRST OF THE OLD METROPOLIS IN-CROWD TO GET DOWN TO THE BUSINESS OF MAKING BABIES, BUT THERE YOU GO. YOU NEVER CAN TELL, eh?
NICE. THERE'S ENOUGH PHOSPHATE SOLUTION IN HERE TO KEEP ANYONE WITH NORMAL KIDNEYS IN THE LITTLE BOYS' ROOM FOR THE REST OF THE EVENING.
WHAT'S LEX UP TO?
LUCY'S PREGNANT? THAT'S WON-DERFUL NEWS, LOIS.
LET ME KNOW WHEN SHE HAS THE BABY AND I'LL HAVE ONE OF MY PEOPLE WRITE A PARTICULARLY MOVING MESSAGE.

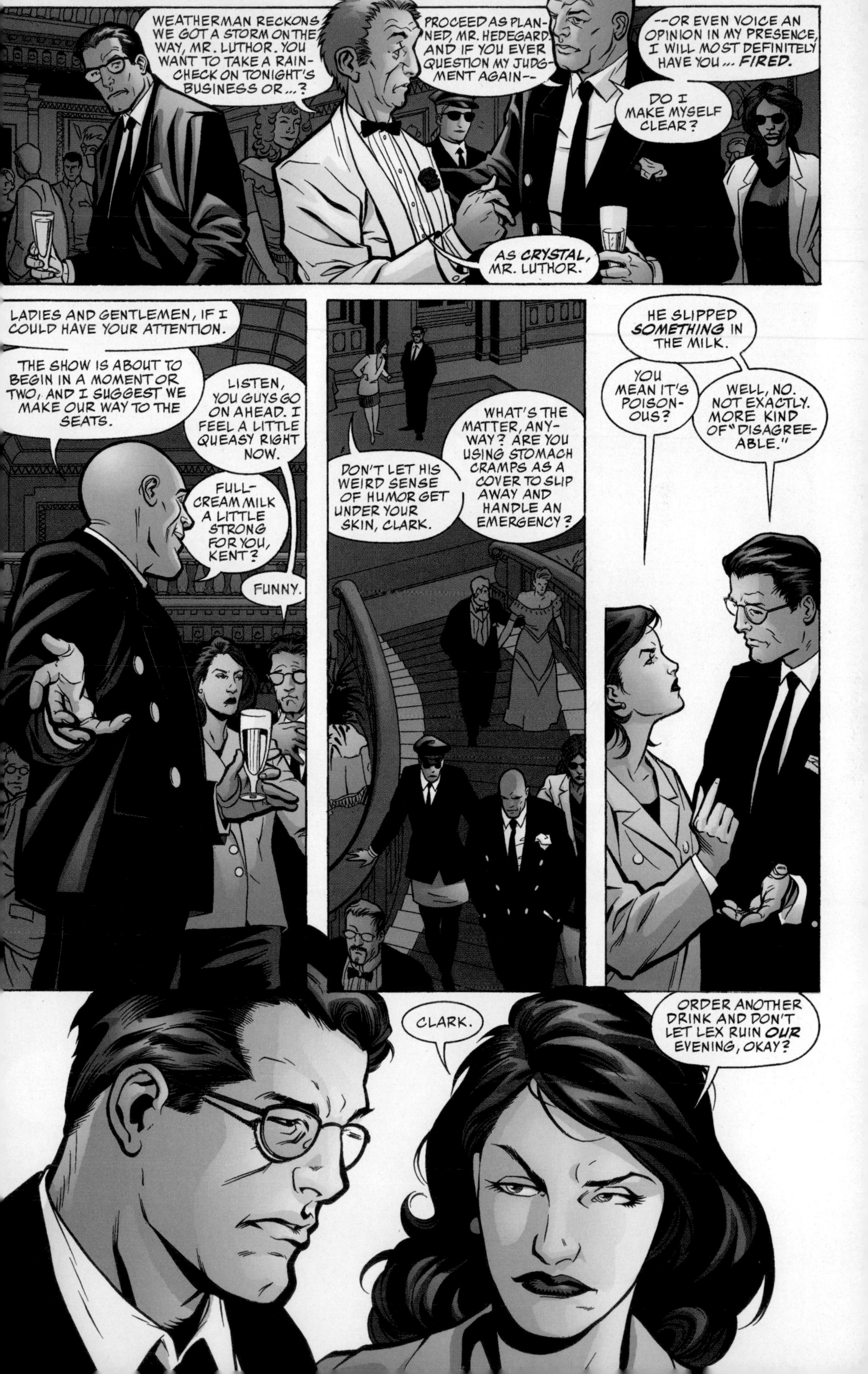
WEATHERMAN RECKONS WE GOT A STORM ON THE WAY, MR. LUTHOR. YOU WANT TO TAKE A RAIN-CHECK ON TONIGHT'S BUSINESS OR ...?
PROCEED AS PLANNED, MR. HEDEGARD. AND IF YOU EVER QUESTION MY JUDGMENT AGAIN--
--OR EVEN VOICE AN OPINION IN MY PRESENCE, I WILL MOST DEFINITELY HAVE YOU ... FIRED.
DO I MAKE MYSELF CLEAR?
AS CRYSTAL, MR. LUTHOR.
LADIES AND GENTLEMEN, IF I COULD HAVE YOUR ATTENTION.
THE SHOW IS ABOUT TO BEGIN IN A MOMENT OR TWO, AND I SUGGEST WE MAKE OUR WAY TO THE SEATS.
LISTEN, YOU GUYS GO ON AHEAD. I FEEL A LITTLE QUEASY RIGHT NOW.
FULL-CREAM MILK A LITTLE STRONG FOR YOU, KENT?
FUNNY.
DON'T LET HIS WEIRD SENSE OF HUMOR GET UNDER YOUR SKIN, CLARK.
WHAT'S THE MATTER, ANYWAY? ARE YOU USING STOMACH CRAMPS AS A COVER TO SLIP AWAY AND HANDLE AN EMERGENCY?
HE SLIPPED SOMETHING IN THE MILK.
YOU MEAN IT'S POISONOUS?
WELL, NO. NOT EXACTLY. MORE KIND OF "DISAGREEABLE."
CLARK.
ORDER ANOTHER DRINK AND DON'T LET LEX RUIN OUR EVENING, OKAY?

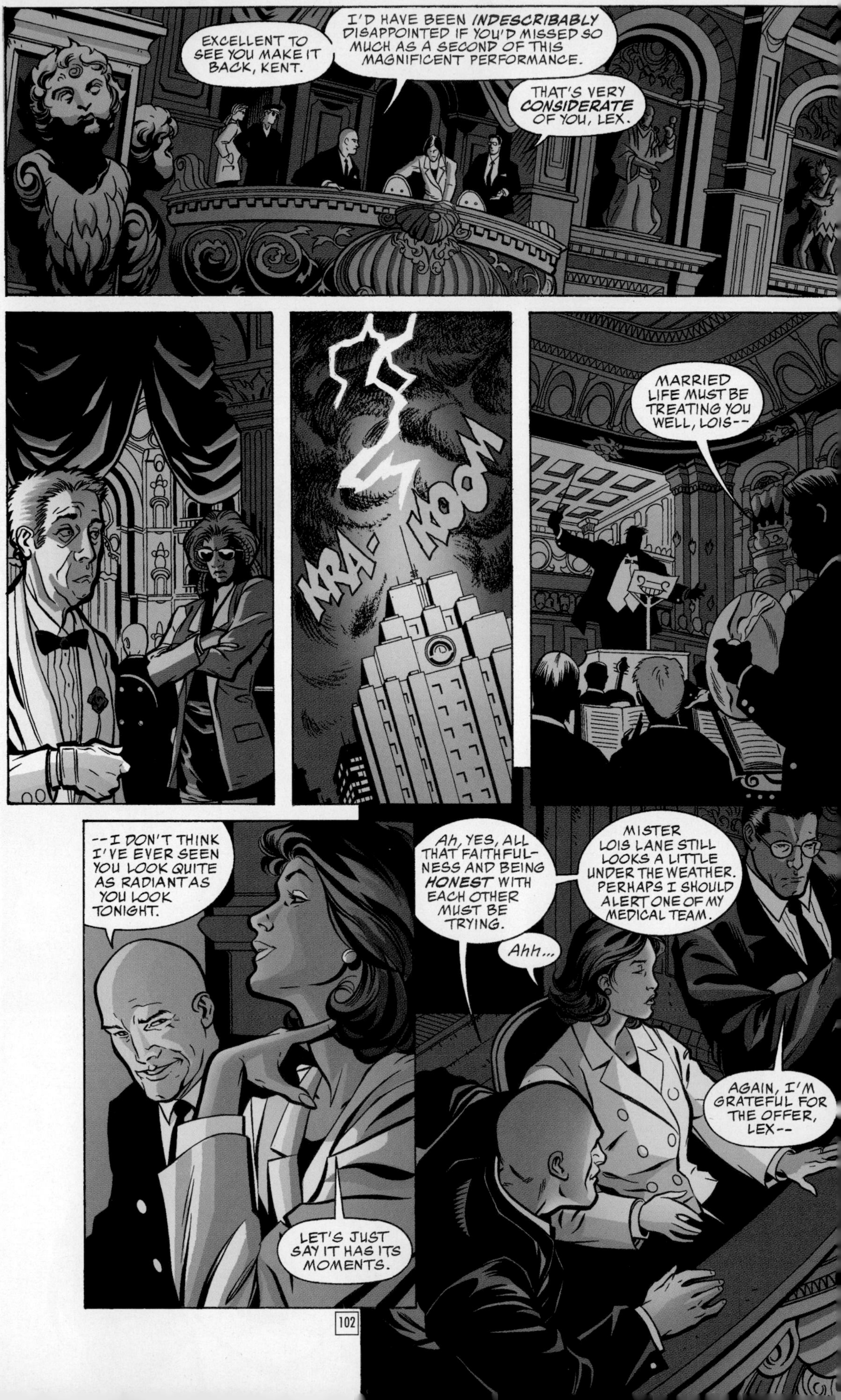
EXCELLENT TO SEE YOU MAKE IT BACK, KENT.
I'D HAVE BEEN *INDESCRIBABLY* DISAPPOINTED IF YOU'D MISSED SO MUCH AS A SECOND OF THIS MAGNIFICENT PERFORMANCE.
THAT'S VERY *CONSIDERATE* OF YOU, LEX.
KRA-KOOM
MARRIED LIFE MUST BE TREATING YOU WELL, LOIS--
--I DON'T THINK I'VE EVER SEEN YOU LOOK QUITE AS RADIANT AS YOU LOOK TONIGHT.
LET'S JUST SAY IT HAS ITS MOMENTS.
Ah, YES, ALL THAT FAITHFULNESS AND BEING ***HONEST*** *WITH EACH OTHER MUST BE TRYING.*
Ahh...
MISTER LOIS LANE STILL LOOKS A LITTLE UNDER THE WEATHER. PERHAPS I SHOULD ALERT ONE OF MY MEDICAL TEAM.
AGAIN, I'M GRATEFUL FOR THE OFFER, LEX--

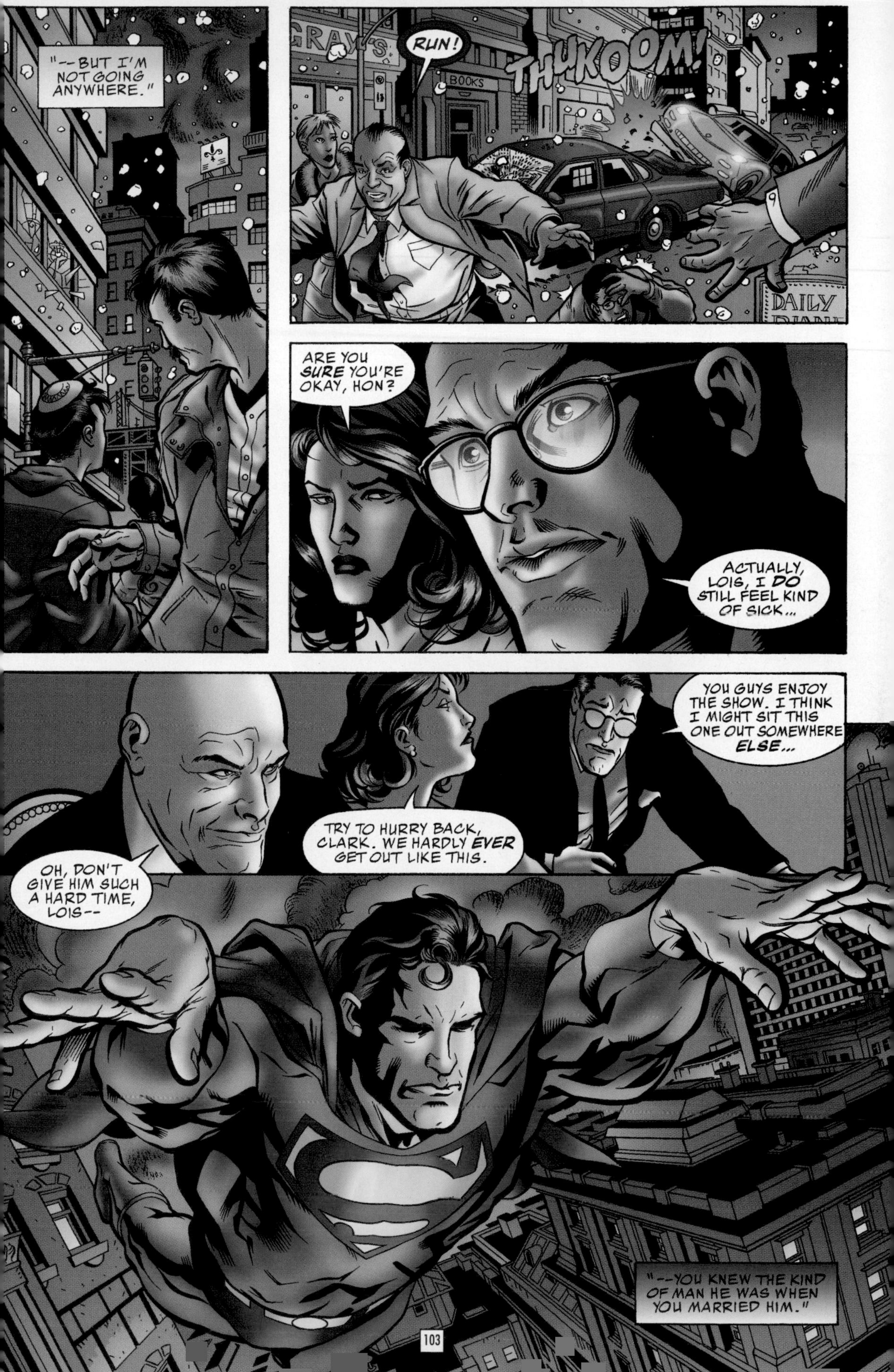
"--BUT I'M NOT GOING ANYWHERE."
GRAY'S
BOOKS
RUN!
THUKOOM!
DAILY
ARE YOU SURE YOU'RE OKAY, HON?
ACTUALLY, LOIS, I DO STILL FEEL KIND OF SICK...
YOU GUYS ENJOY THE SHOW. I THINK I MIGHT SIT THIS ONE OUT SOMEWHERE ELSE...
TRY TO HURRY BACK, CLARK. WE HARDLY EVER GET OUT LIKE THIS.
OH, DON'T GIVE HIM SUCH A HARD TIME, LOIS--
"--YOU KNEW THE KIND OF MAN HE WAS WHEN YOU MARRIED HIM."

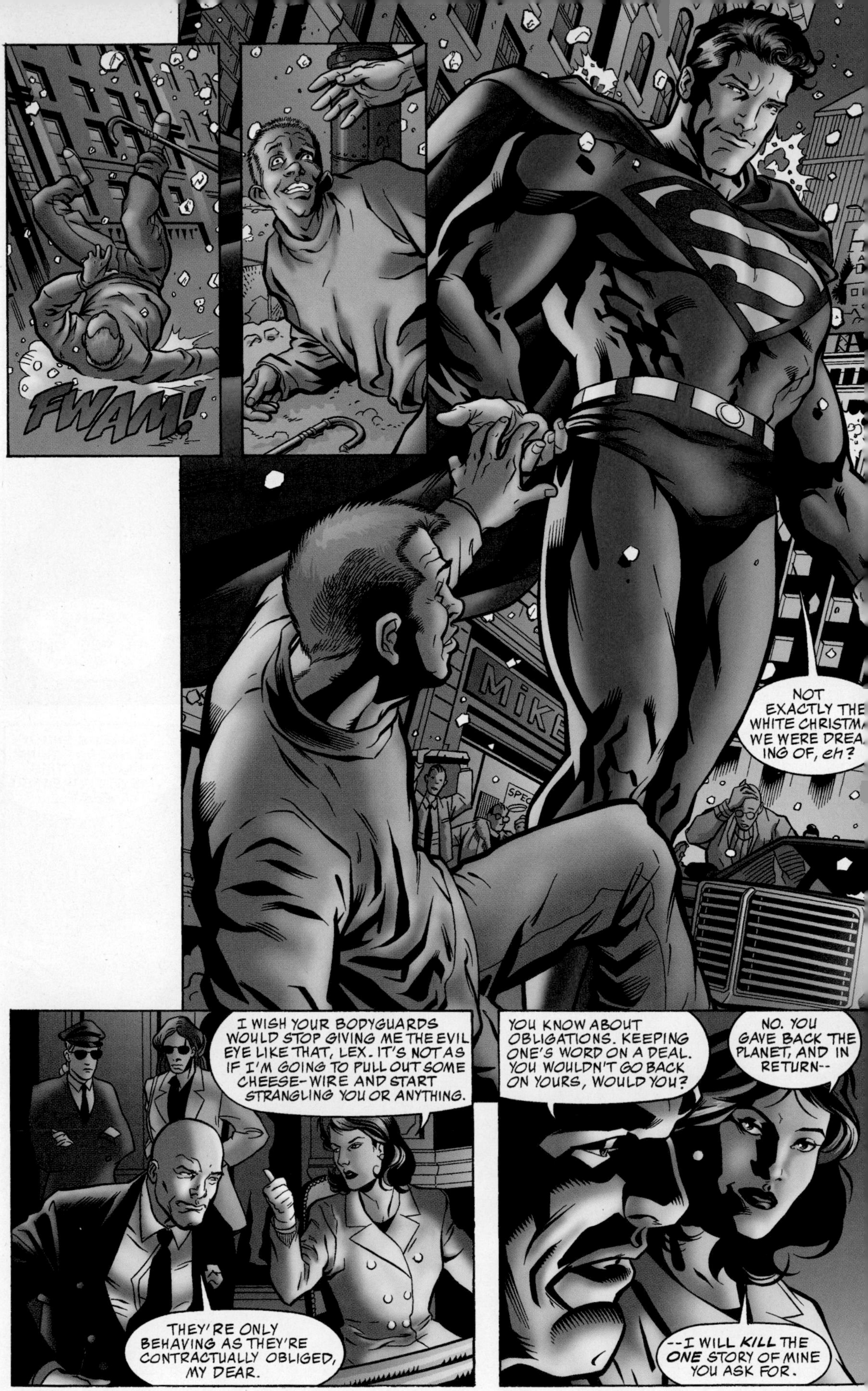
FWAM!
NOT EXACTLY THE WHITE CHRISTM WE WERE DREA ING OF, eh?
MIKE
I WISH YOUR BODYGUARDS WOULD STOP GIVING ME THE EVIL EYE LIKE THAT, LEX. IT'S NOT AS IF I'M GOING TO PULL OUT SOME CHEESE-WIRE AND START STRANGLING YOU OR ANYTHING.
THEY'RE ONLY BEHAVING AS THEY'RE CONTRACTUALLY OBLIGED, MY DEAR.
YOU KNOW ABOUT OBLIGATIONS. KEEPING ONE'S WORD ON A DEAL. YOU WOULDN'T GO BACK ON YOURS, WOULD YOU?
NO. YOU GAVE BACK THE PLANET, AND IN RETURN--
--I WILL KILL THE ONE STORY OF MINE YOU ASK FOR.

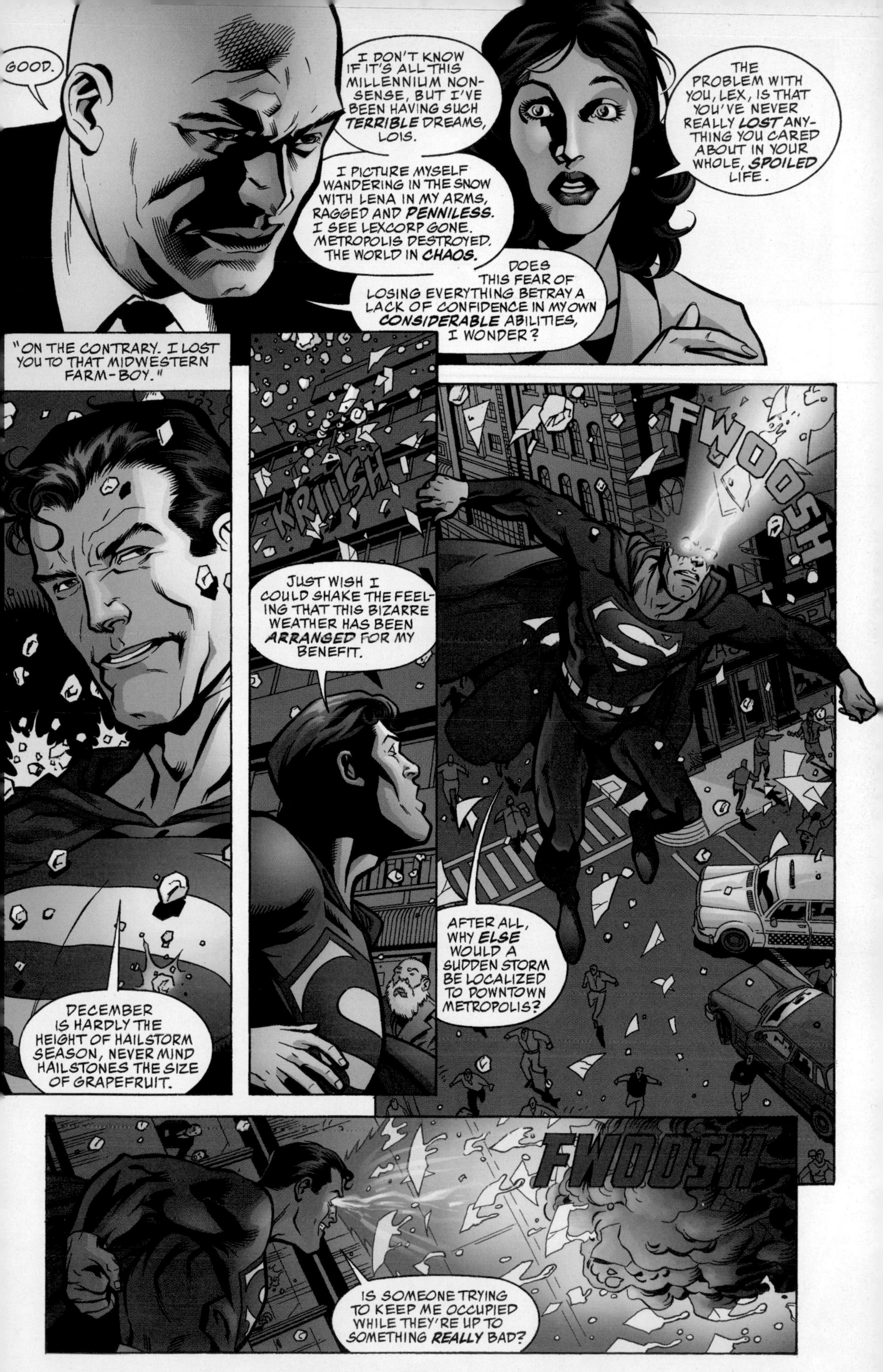
GOOD.
I DON'T KNOW IF IT'S ALL THIS MILLENNIUM NON-SENSE, BUT I'VE BEEN HAVING SUCH TERRIBLE DREAMS, LOIS.
I PICTURE MYSELF WANDERING IN THE SNOW WITH LENA IN MY ARMS, RAGGED AND PENNILESS. I SEE LEXCORP GONE. METROPOLIS DESTROYED. THE WORLD IN CHAOS.
DOES THIS FEAR OF LOSING EVERYTHING BETRAY A LACK OF CONFIDENCE IN MY OWN CONSIDERABLE ABILITIES, I WONDER?
THE PROBLEM WITH YOU, LEX, IS THAT YOU'VE NEVER REALLY LOST ANY-THING YOU CARED ABOUT IN YOUR WHOLE, SPOILED LIFE.
"ON THE CONTRARY. I LOST YOU TO THAT MIDWESTERN FARM-BOY."
DECEMBER IS HARDLY THE HEIGHT OF HAILSTORM SEASON, NEVER MIND HAILSTONES THE SIZE OF GRAPEFRUIT.
KRIIISH
JUST WISH I COULD SHAKE THE FEEL-ING THAT THIS BIZARRE WEATHER HAS BEEN ARRANGED FOR MY BENEFIT.
FWOOSH
AFTER ALL, WHY ELSE WOULD A SUDDEN STORM BE LOCALIZED TO DOWNTOWN METROPOLIS?
FWOOSH
IS SOMEONE TRYING TO KEEP ME OCCUPIED WHILE THEY'RE UP TO SOMETHING REALLY BAD?

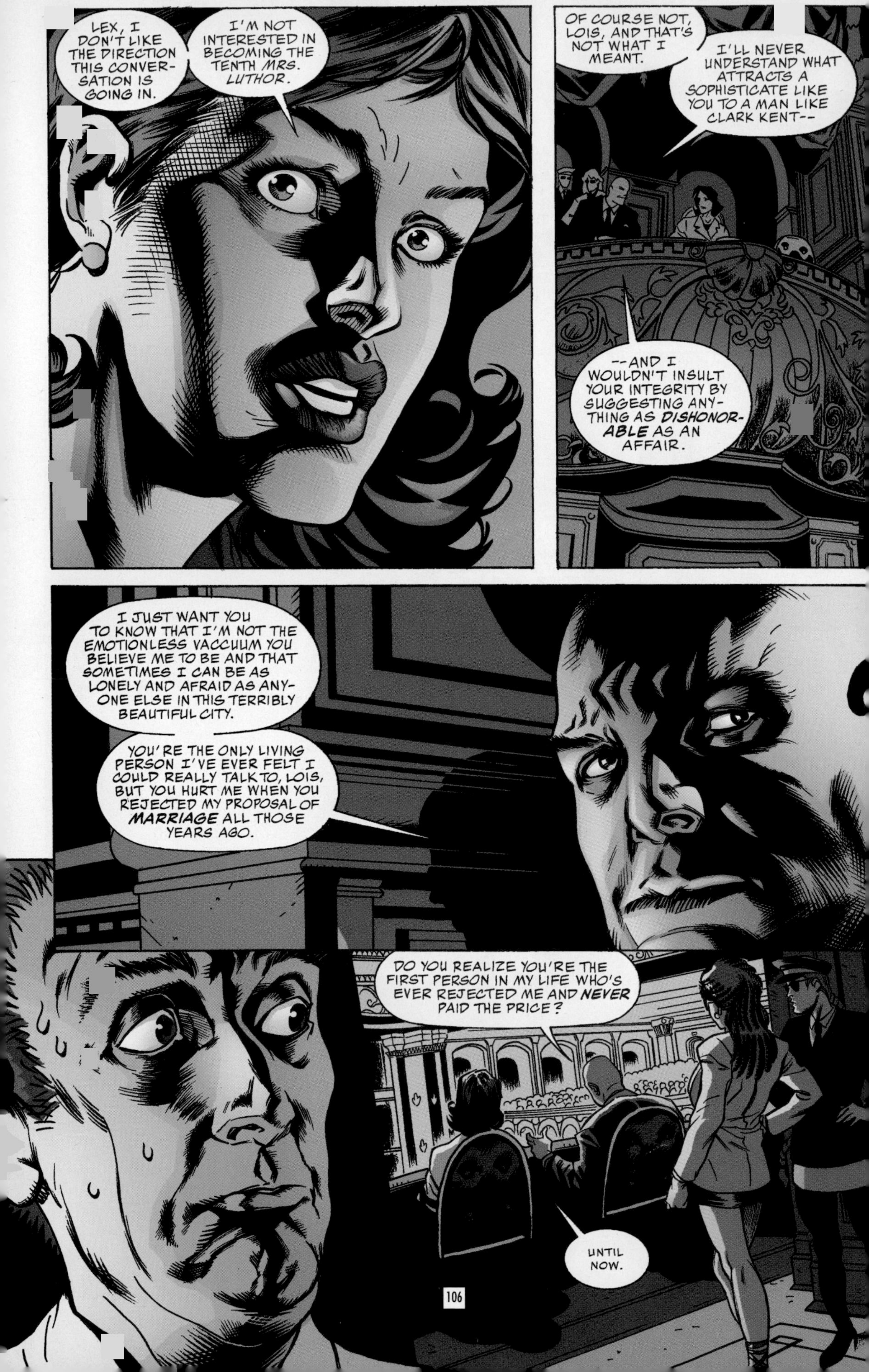
LEX, I DON'T LIKE THE DIRECTION THIS CONVER-SATION IS GOING IN.
I'M NOT INTERESTED IN BECOMING THE TENTH MRS. LUTHOR.
OF COURSE NOT, LOIS, AND THAT'S NOT WHAT I MEANT.
I'LL NEVER UNDERSTAND WHAT ATTRACTS A SOPHISTICATE LIKE YOU TO A MAN LIKE CLARK KENT--
--AND I WOULDN'T INSULT YOUR INTEGRITY BY SUGGESTING ANY-THING AS DISHONOR-ABLE AS AN AFFAIR.
I JUST WANT YOU TO KNOW THAT I'M NOT THE EMOTIONLESS VACCUUM YOU BELIEVE ME TO BE AND THAT SOMETIMES I CAN BE AS LONELY AND AFRAID AS ANY-ONE ELSE IN THIS TERRIBLY BEAUTIFUL CITY.
YOU'RE THE ONLY LIVING PERSON I'VE EVER FELT I COULD REALLY TALK TO, LOIS, BUT YOU HURT ME WHEN YOU REJECTED MY PROPOSAL OF MARRIAGE ALL THOSE YEARS AGO.
DO YOU REALIZE YOU'RE THE FIRST PERSON IN MY LIFE WHO'S EVER REJECTED ME AND NEVER PAID THE PRICE?
UNTIL NOW.

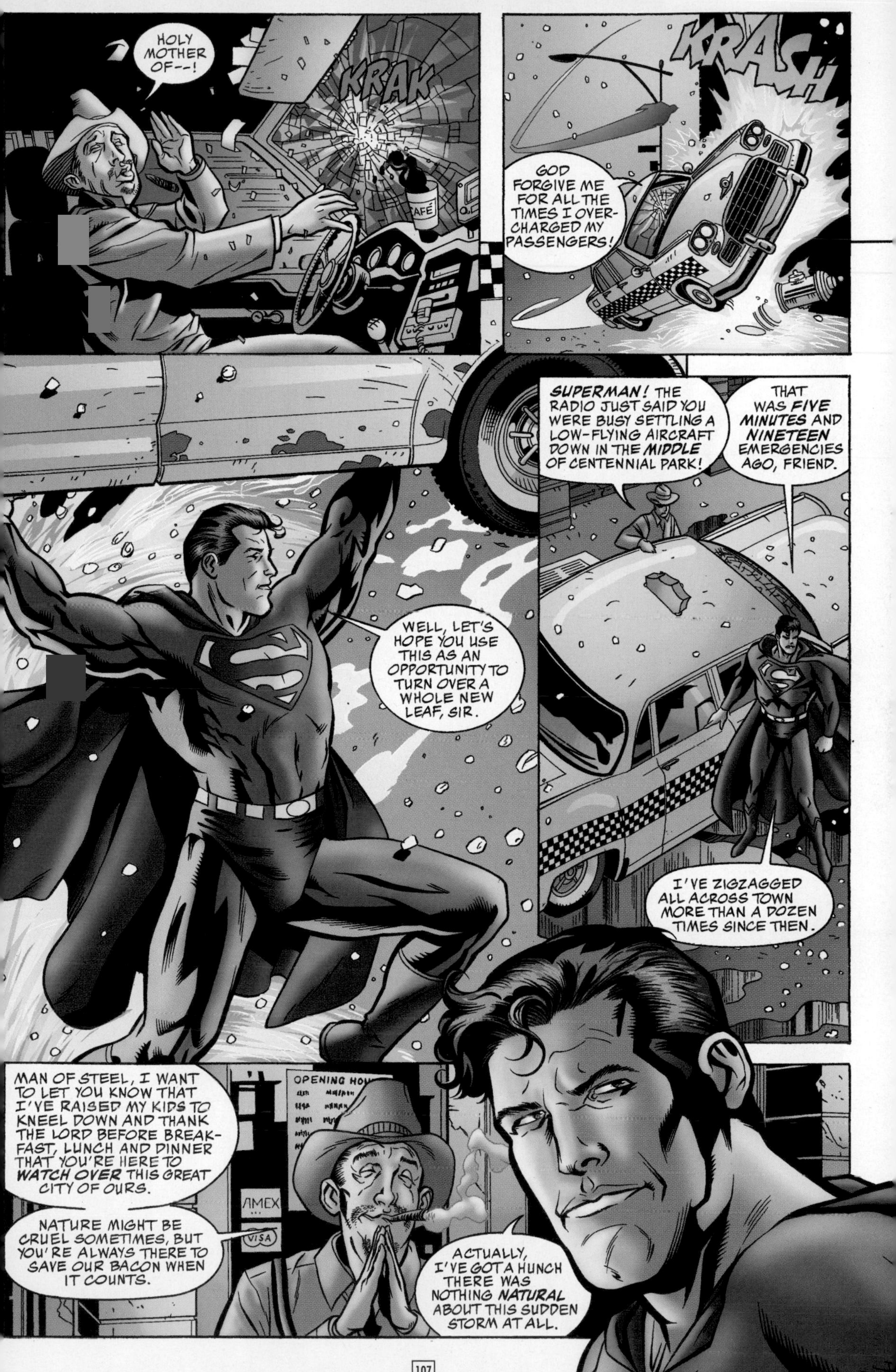
HOLY MOTHER OF--!
KRAK
KRASH
GOD FORGIVE ME FOR ALL THE TIMES I OVER-CHARGED MY PASSENGERS!
WELL, LET'S HOPE YOU USE THIS AS AN OPPORTUNITY TO TURN OVER A WHOLE NEW LEAF, SIR.
SUPERMAN! THE RADIO JUST SAID YOU WERE BUSY SETTLING A LOW-FLYING AIRCRAFT DOWN IN THE MIDDLE OF CENTENNIAL PARK!
THAT WAS FIVE MINUTES AND NINETEEN EMERGENCIES AGO, FRIEND.
I'VE ZIGZAGGED ALL ACROSS TOWN MORE THAN A DOZEN TIMES SINCE THEN.
MAN OF STEEL, I WANT TO LET YOU KNOW THAT I'VE RAISED MY KIDS TO KNEEL DOWN AND THANK THE LORD BEFORE BREAK-FAST, LUNCH AND DINNER THAT YOU'RE HERE TO WATCH OVER THIS GREAT CITY OF OURS.
NATURE MIGHT BE CRUEL SOMETIMES, BUT YOU'RE ALWAYS THERE TO SAVE OUR BACON WHEN IT COUNTS.
ACTUALLY, I'VE GOT A HUNCH THERE WAS NOTHING NATURAL ABOUT THIS SUDDEN STORM AT ALL.

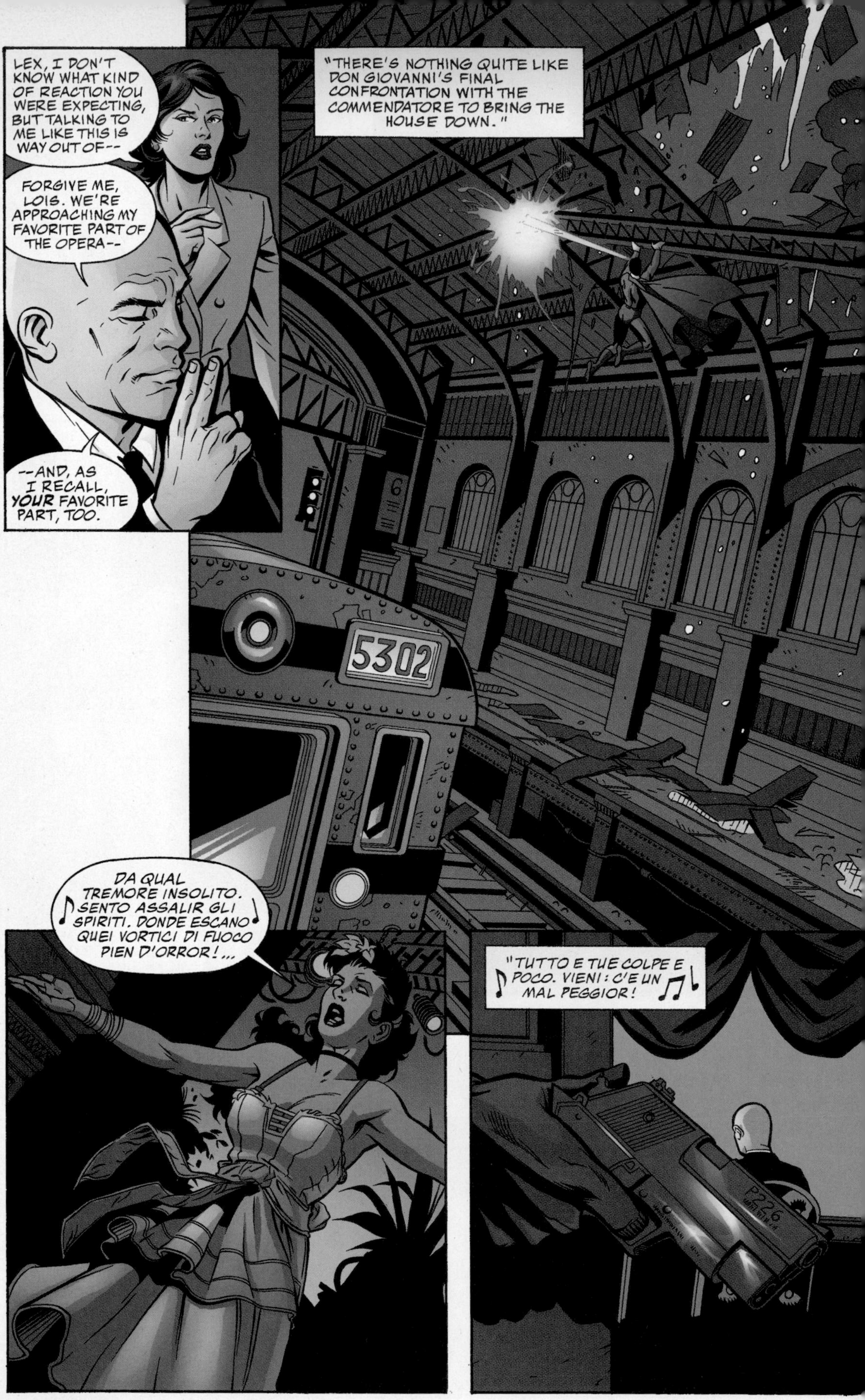

LEX, I DON'T KNOW WHAT KIND OF REACTION YOU WERE EXPECTING, BUT TALKING TO ME LIKE THIS IS WAY OUT OF--
FORGIVE ME, LOIS. WE'RE APPROACHING MY FAVORITE PART OF THE OPERA--
--AND, AS I RECALL, YOUR FAVORITE PART, TOO.
"THERE'S NOTHING QUITE LIKE DON GIOVANNI'S FINAL CONFRONTATION WITH THE COMMENDATORE TO BRING THE HOUSE DOWN."
6
5302
DA QUAL TREMORE INSOLITO. SENTO ASSALIR GLI SPIRITI. DONDE ESCANO QUEI VORTICI DI FUOCO PIEN D'ORROR!...
"TUTTO E TUE COLPE E POCO. VIENI: C'E UN MAL PEGGIOR!
P226

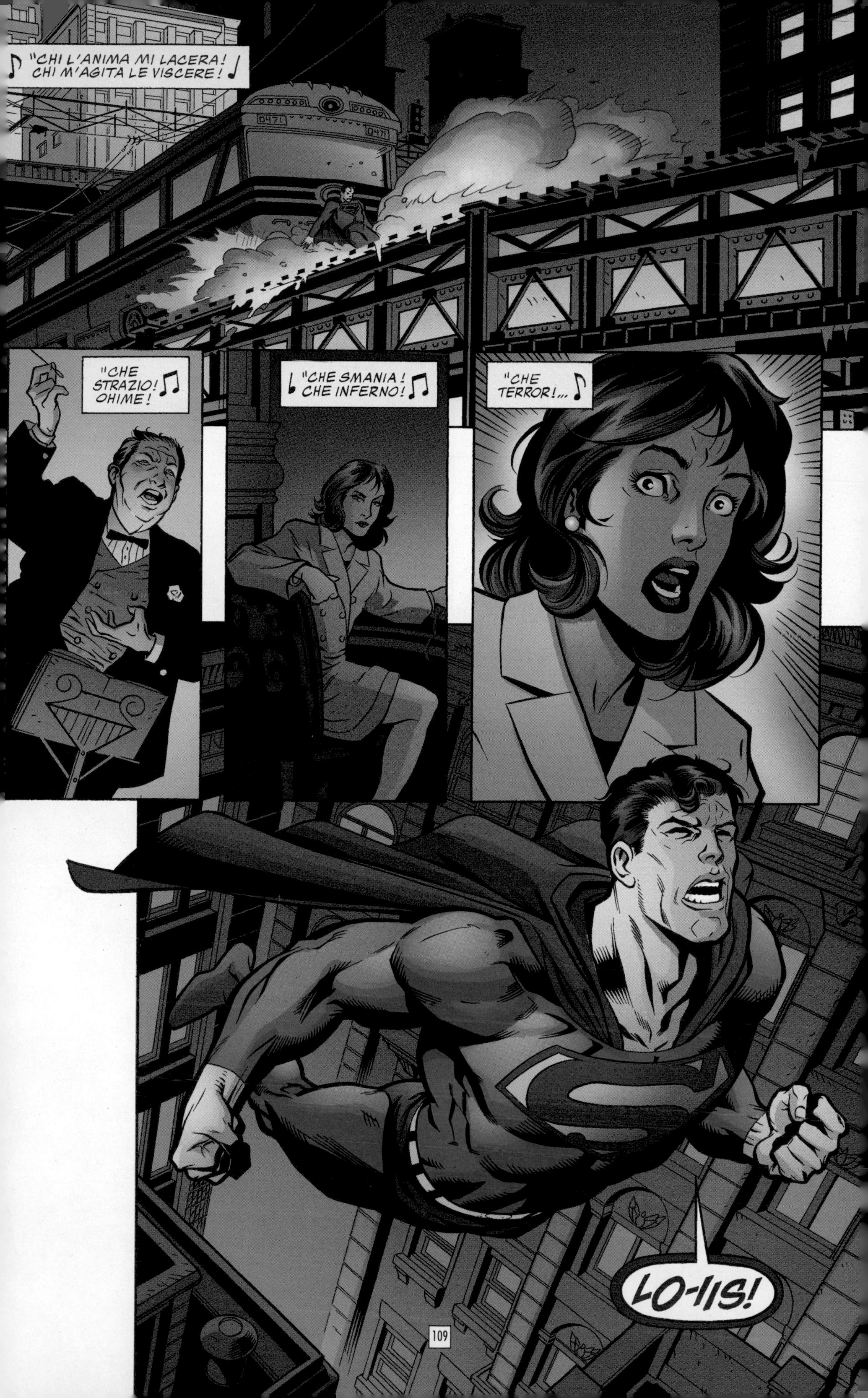
"CHI L'ANIMA MI LACERA! CHI M'AGITA LE VISCERE!
"CHE STRAZIO! OHIME!
"CHE SMANIA! CHE INFERNO!
"CHE TERROR!...
LO-IIS!

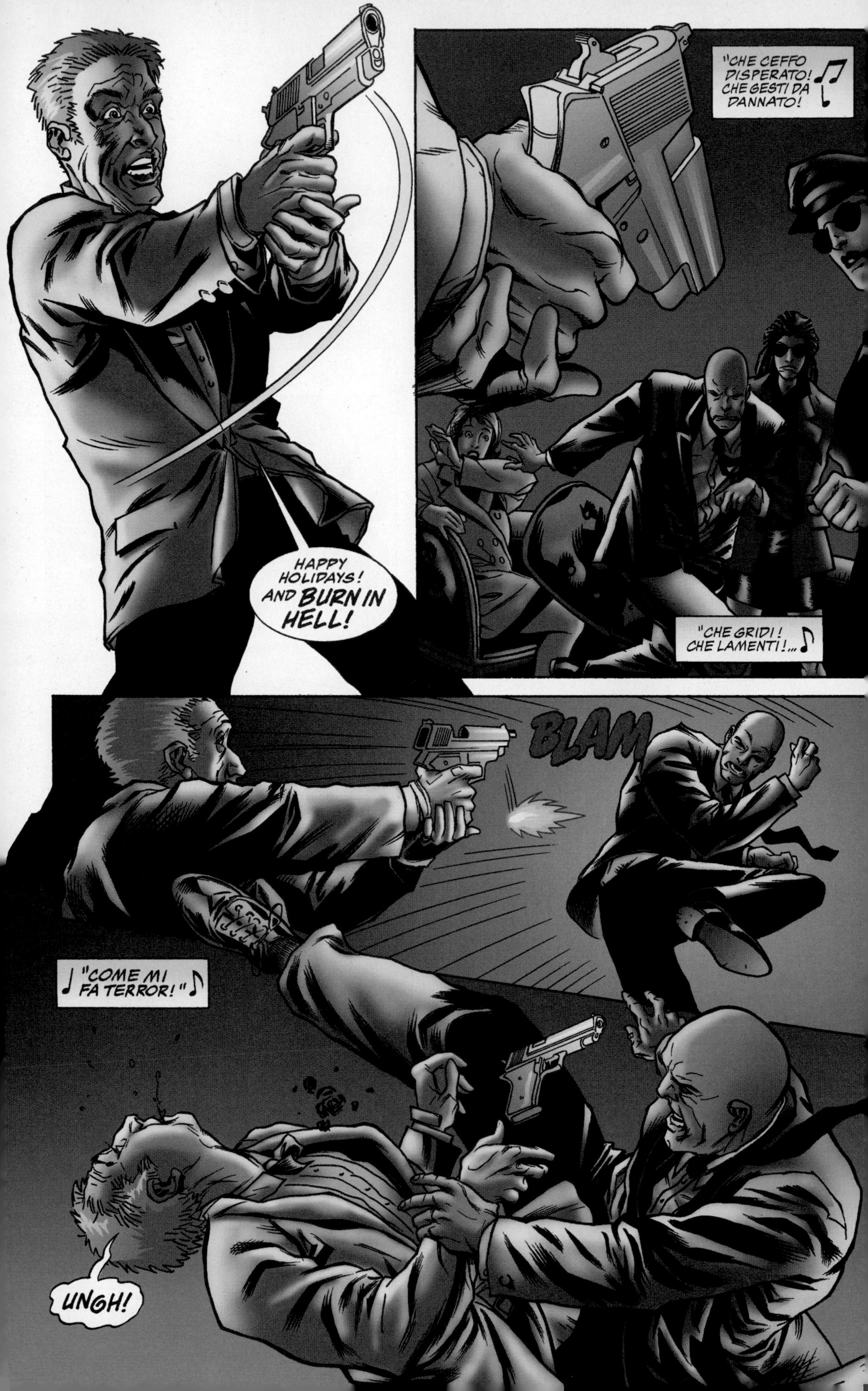
HAPPY HOLIDAYS! AND BURN IN HELL!
"CHE CEFFO DISPERATO! CHE GESTI DA DANNATO!
"CHE GRIDI! CHE LAMENTI!...
BLAM
"COME MI FA TERROR!"
UNGH!

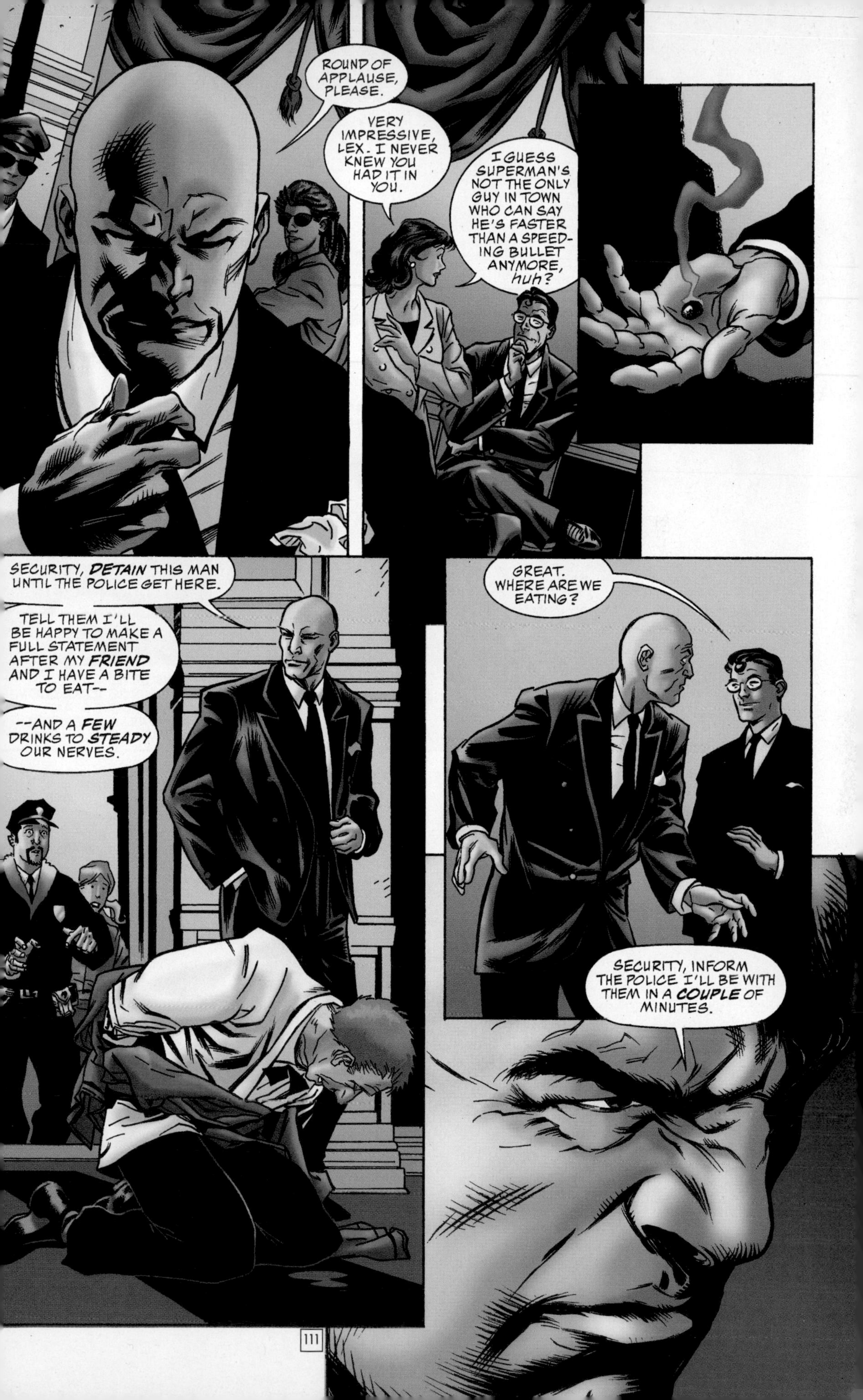
ROUND OF APPLAUSE, PLEASE.
VERY IMPRESSIVE, LEX. I NEVER KNEW YOU HAD IT IN YOU.
I GUESS SUPERMAN'S NOT THE ONLY GUY IN TOWN WHO CAN SAY HE'S FASTER THAN A SPEEDING BULLET ANYMORE, huh?
SECURITY, DETAIN THIS MAN UNTIL THE POLICE GET HERE.
TELL THEM I'LL BE HAPPY TO MAKE A FULL STATEMENT AFTER MY FRIEND AND I HAVE A BITE TO EAT--
--AND A FEW DRINKS TO STEADY OUR NERVES.
GREAT. WHERE ARE WE EATING?
SECURITY, INFORM THE POLICE I'LL BE WITH THEM IN A COUPLE OF MINUTES.

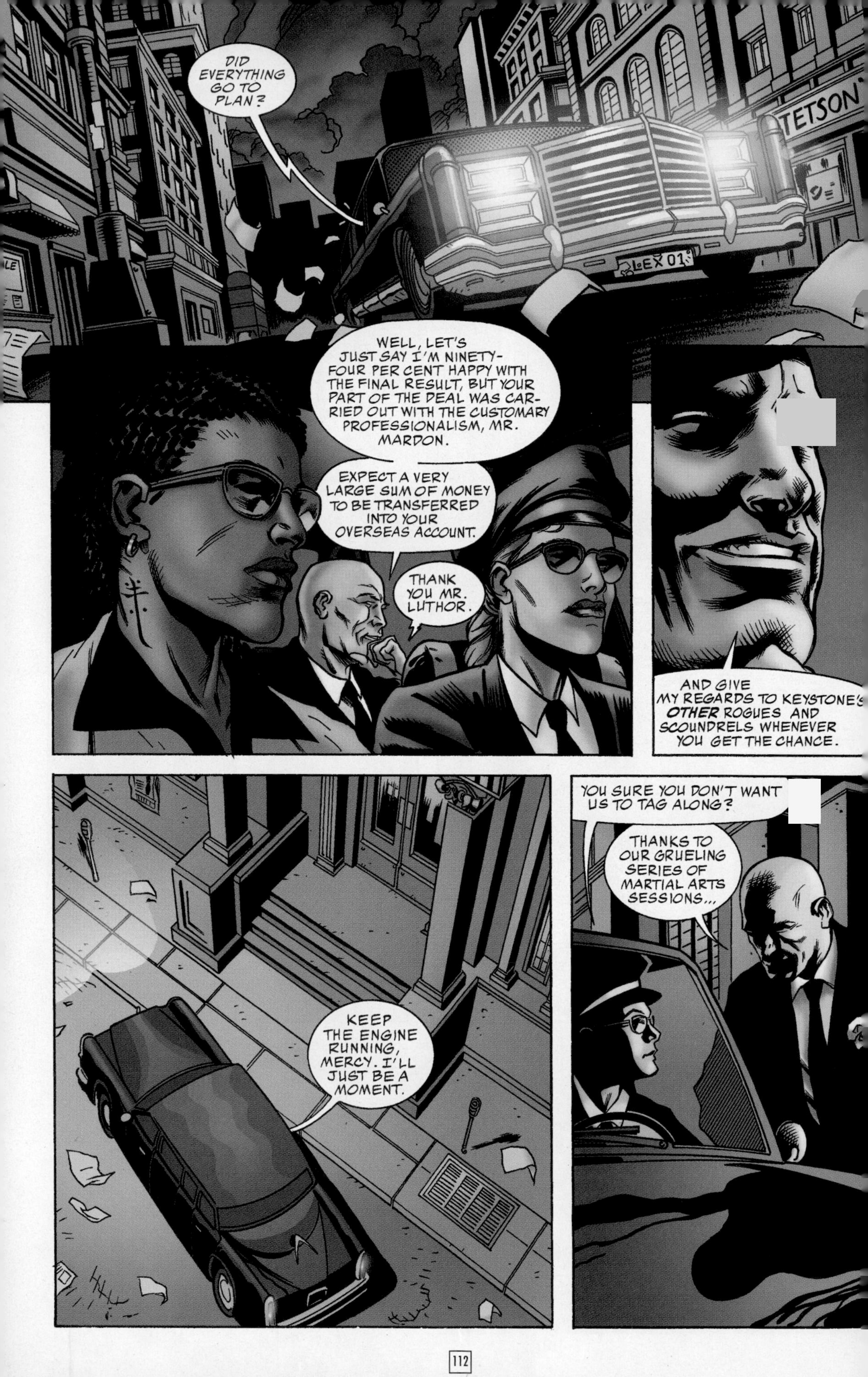
DID EVERYTHING GO TO PLAN?
TETSON
LEX 01
WELL, LET'S JUST SAY I'M NINETY-FOUR PER CENT HAPPY WITH THE FINAL RESULT, BUT YOUR PART OF THE DEAL WAS CARRIED OUT WITH THE CUSTOMARY PROFESSIONALISM, MR. MARDON.
EXPECT A VERY LARGE SUM OF MONEY TO BE TRANSFERRED INTO YOUR OVERSEAS ACCOUNT.
THANK YOU MR. LUTHOR.
AND GIVE MY REGARDS TO KEYSTONE'S *OTHER* ROGUES AND SCOUNDRELS WHENEVER YOU GET THE CHANCE.
KEEP THE ENGINE RUNNING, MERCY. I'LL JUST BE A MOMENT.
YOU SURE YOU DON'T WANT US TO TAG ALONG?
THANKS TO OUR GRUELING SERIES OF MARTIAL ARTS SESSIONS...

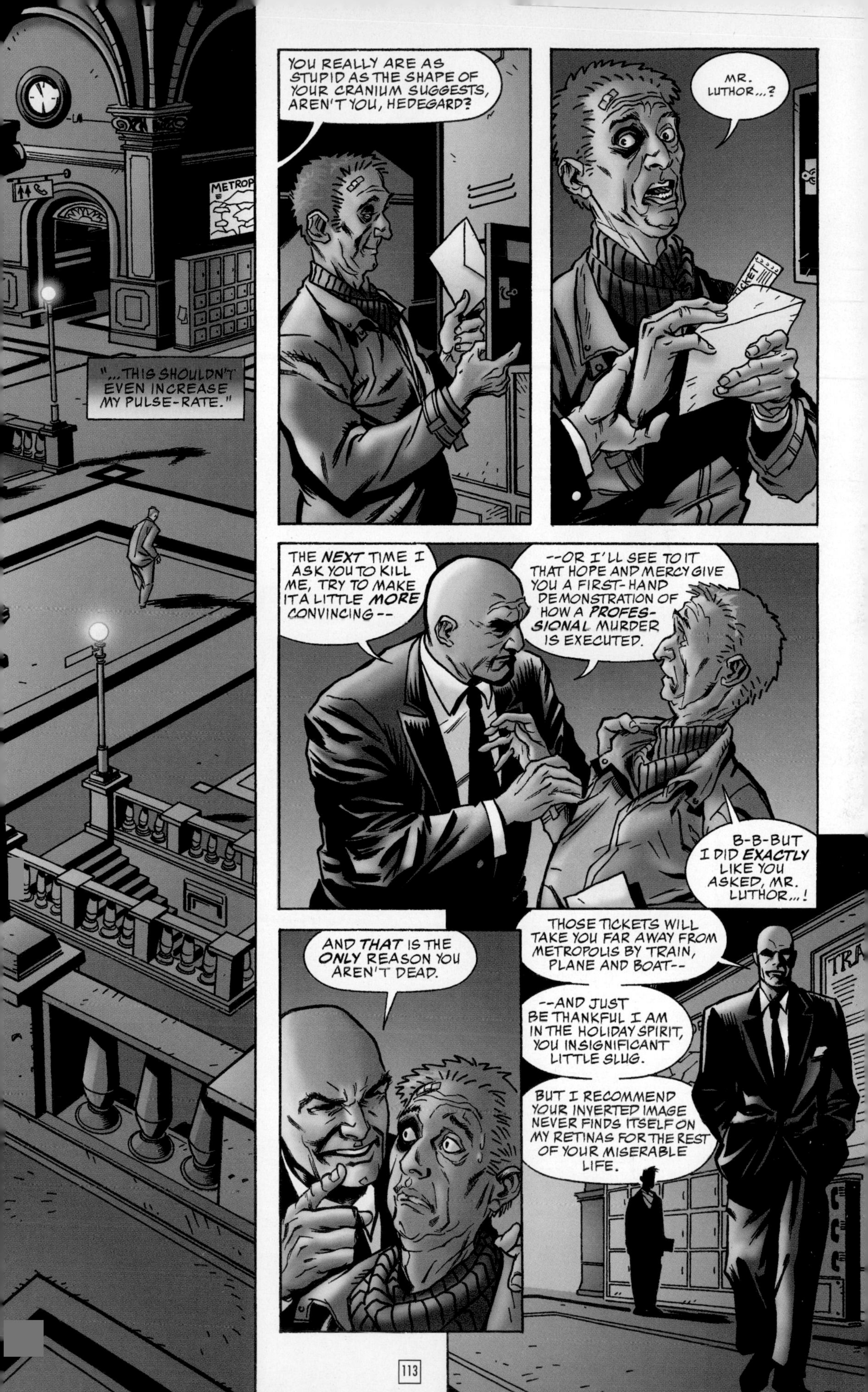

METROP
"...THIS SHOULDN'T EVEN INCREASE MY PULSE-RATE."
YOU REALLY ARE AS STUPID AS THE SHAPE OF YOUR CRANIUM SUGGESTS, AREN'T YOU, HEDEGARD?
MR. LUTHOR...?
THE NEXT TIME I ASK YOU TO KILL ME, TRY TO MAKE IT A LITTLE MORE CONVINCING--
--OR I'LL SEE TO IT THAT HOPE AND MERCY GIVE YOU A FIRST-HAND DEMONSTRATION OF HOW A PROFESSIONAL MURDER IS EXECUTED.
B-B-BUT I DID EXACTLY LIKE YOU ASKED, MR. LUTHOR...!
AND THAT IS THE ONLY REASON YOU AREN'T DEAD.
THOSE TICKETS WILL TAKE YOU FAR AWAY FROM METROPOLIS BY TRAIN, PLANE AND BOAT--
--AND JUST BE THANKFUL I AM IN THE HOLIDAY SPIRIT, YOU INSIGNIFICANT LITTLE SLUG.
BUT I RECOMMEND YOUR INVERTED IMAGE NEVER FINDS ITSELF ON MY RETINAS FOR THE REST OF YOUR MISERABLE LIFE.

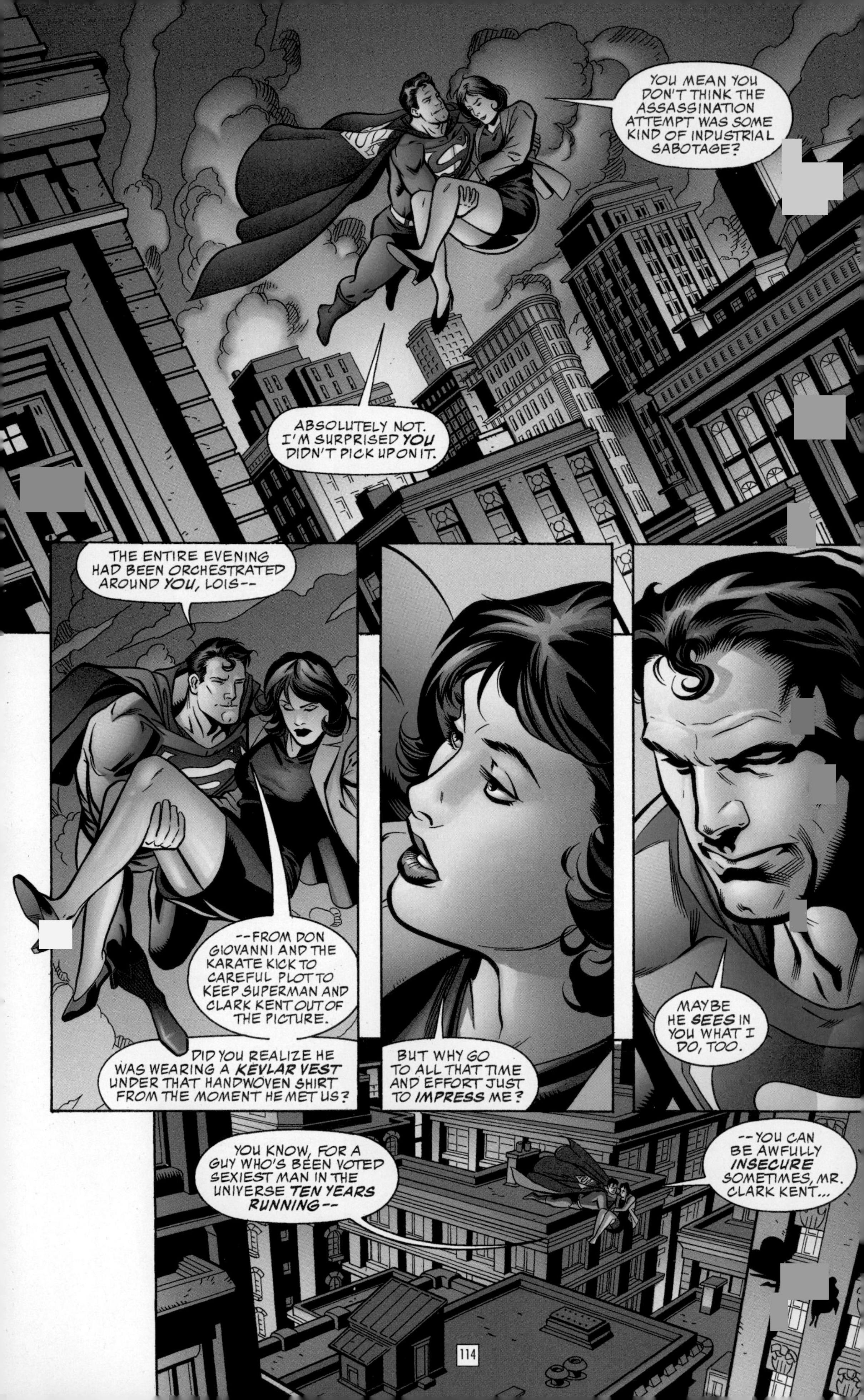
YOU MEAN YOU DON'T THINK THE ASSASSINATION ATTEMPT WAS SOME KIND OF INDUSTRIAL SABOTAGE?
ABSOLUTELY NOT. I'M SURPRISED YOU DIDN'T PICK UP ON IT.
THE ENTIRE EVENING HAD BEEN ORCHESTRATED AROUND YOU, LOIS--
--FROM DON GIOVANNI AND THE KARATE KICK TO CAREFUL PLOT TO KEEP SUPERMAN AND CLARK KENT OUT OF THE PICTURE.
DID YOU REALIZE HE WAS WEARING A KEVLAR VEST UNDER THAT HANDWOVEN SHIRT FROM THE MOMENT HE MET US?
BUT WHY GO TO ALL THAT TIME AND EFFORT JUST TO IMPRESS ME?
MAYBE HE SEES IN YOU WHAT I DO, TOO.
YOU KNOW, FOR A GUY WHO'S BEEN VOTED SEXIEST MAN IN THE UNIVERSE TEN YEARS RUNNING--
--YOU CAN BE AWFULLY INSECURE SOMETIMES, MR. CLARK KENT...

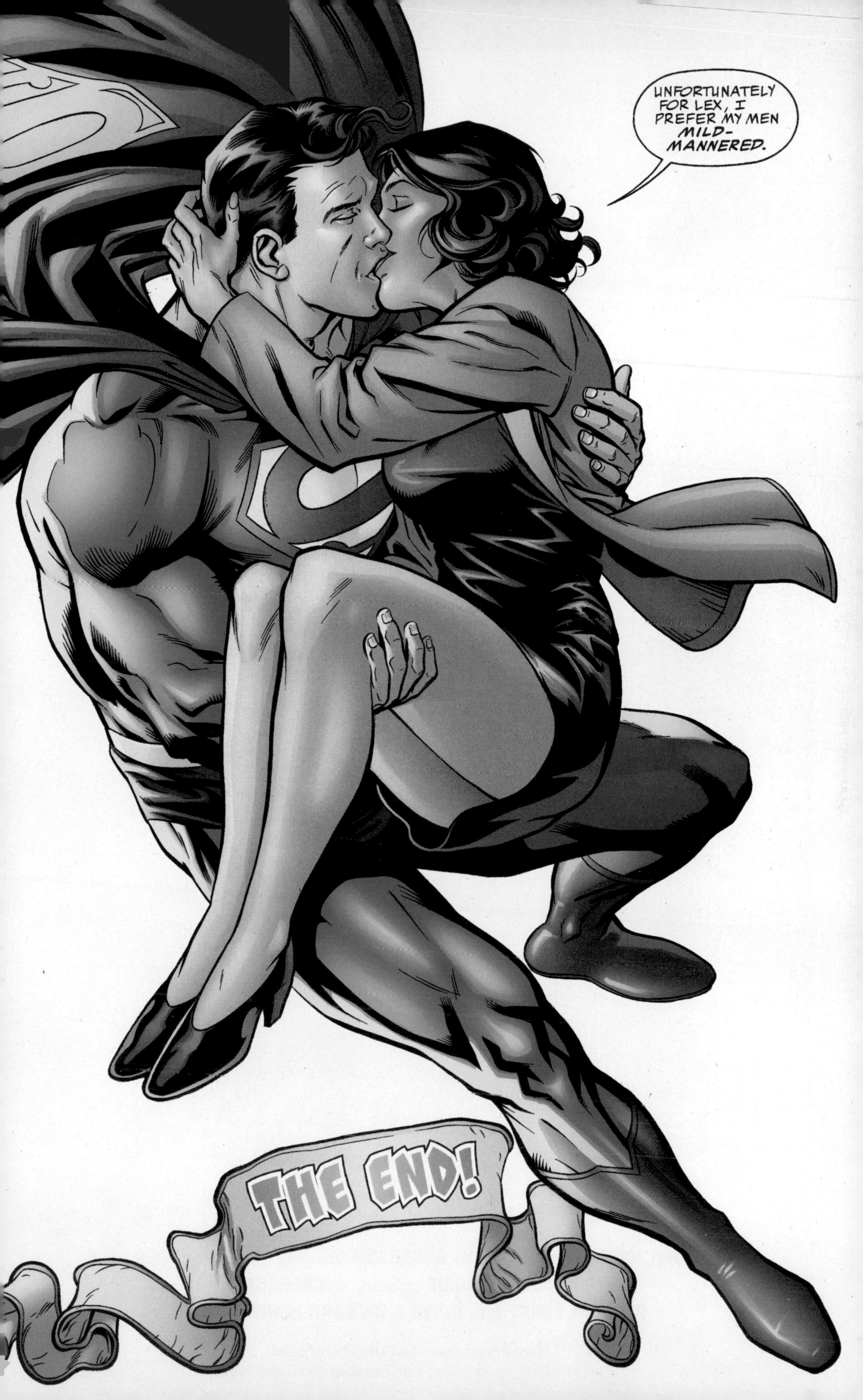
UNFORTUNATELY FOR LEX, I PREFER MY MEN MILD-MANNERED.
THE END!

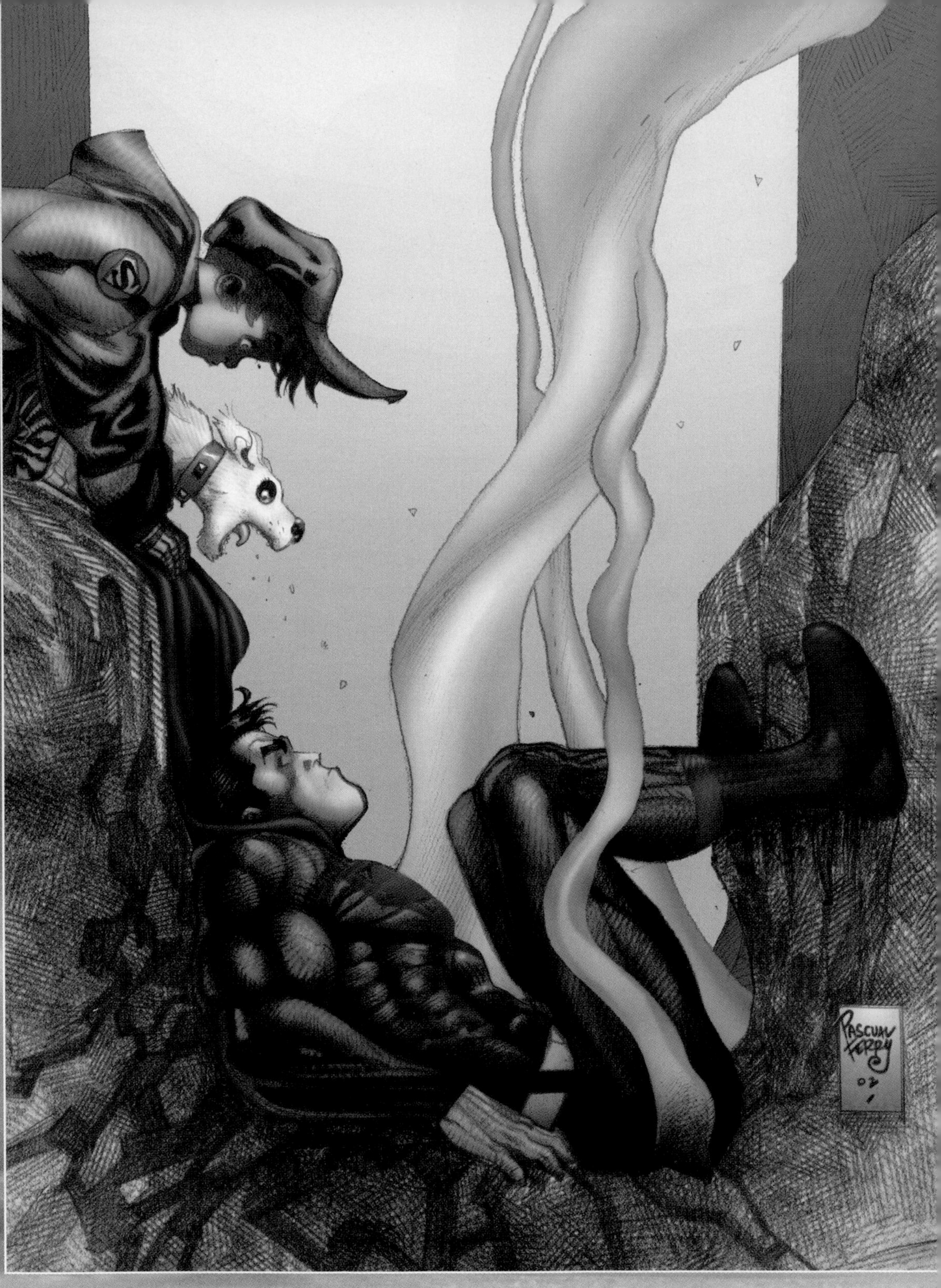
PASCUAL FERRY

"The Second Landing"

GEOFF JOHNS writer **BRENT ANDERSON** penciller **RAY SNYDER** inker
TANYA & RICHARD HORIE colorists **COMICRAFT** letterer
PASCUAL FERRY WITH TANYA & RICHARD HORIE cover artists

From the pages of the SUPERMAN comic...
What's more American than baseball and Superman?

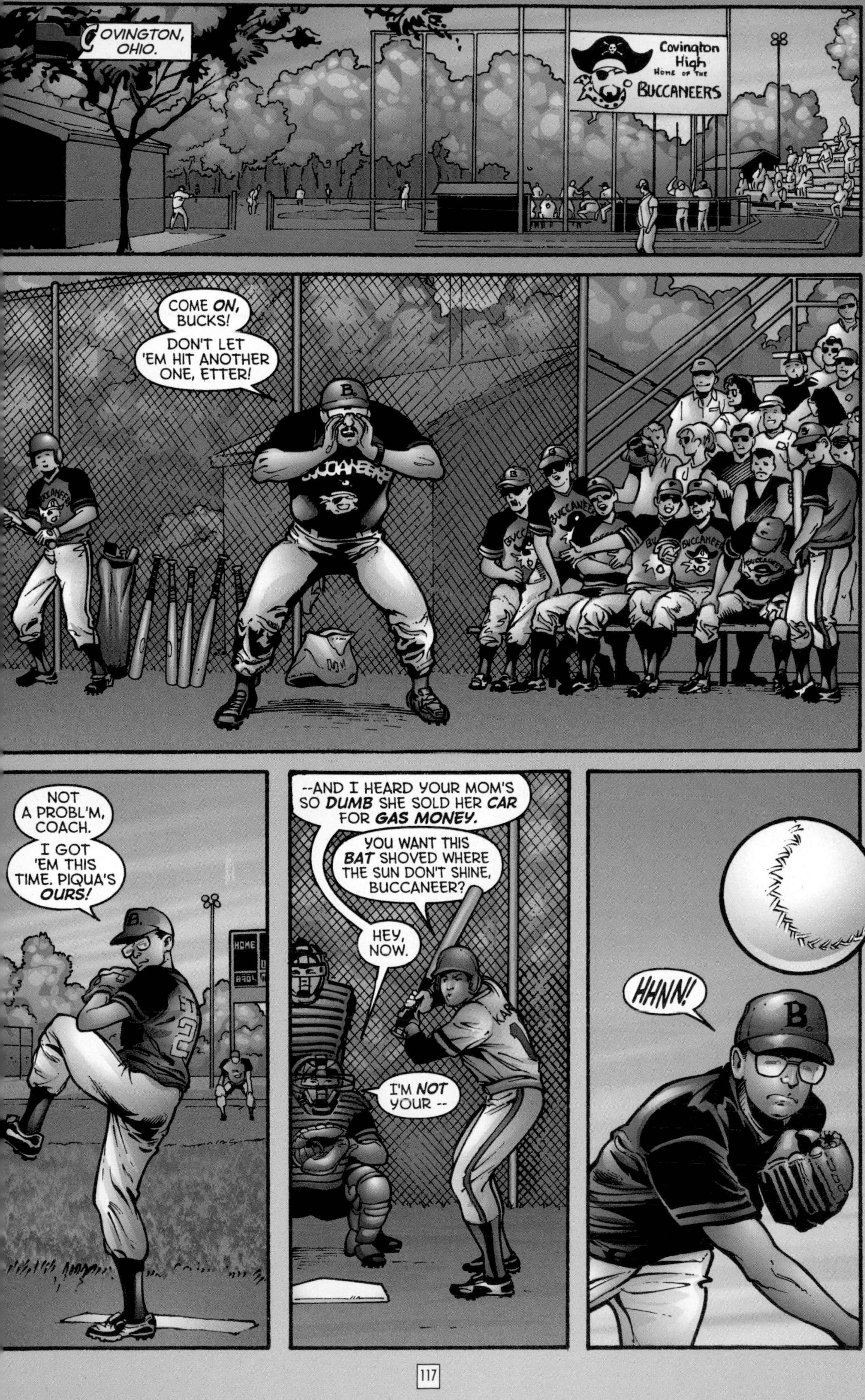
COVINGTON, OHIO.
Covington High Home of the BUCCANEERS
COME ON, BUCKS!
DON'T LET 'EM HIT ANOTHER ONE, ETTER!
NOT A PROBL'M, COACH.
I GOT 'EM THIS TIME. PIQUA'S OURS!
--AND I HEARD YOUR MOM'S SO DUMB SHE SOLD HER CAR FOR GAS MONEY.
YOU WANT THIS BAT SHOVED WHERE THE SUN DON'T SHINE, BUCCANEER?
HEY, NOW.
I'M NOT YOUR --
HHNN!

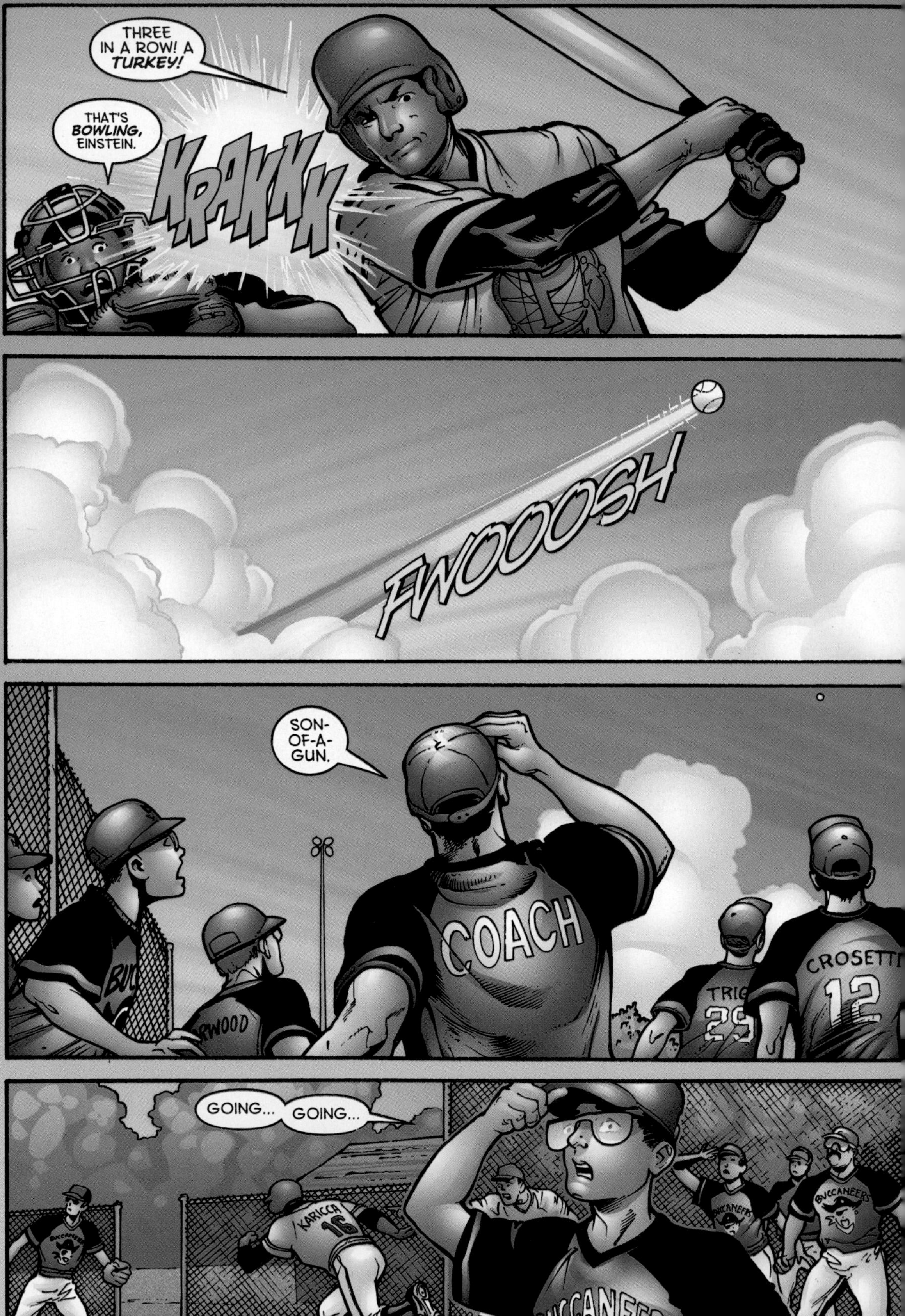
THREE IN A ROW! A TURKEY!
THAT'S BOWLING, EINSTEIN.
KRAKKK
FWOOOOSH
SON-OF-A-GUN.
COACH
CROSETTI 12
GOING... GOING...
BUCCANEERS

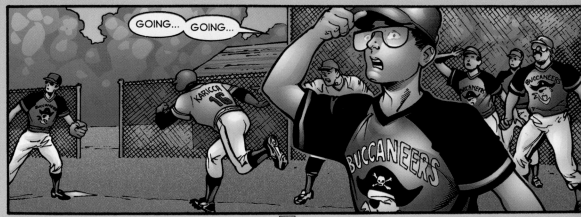

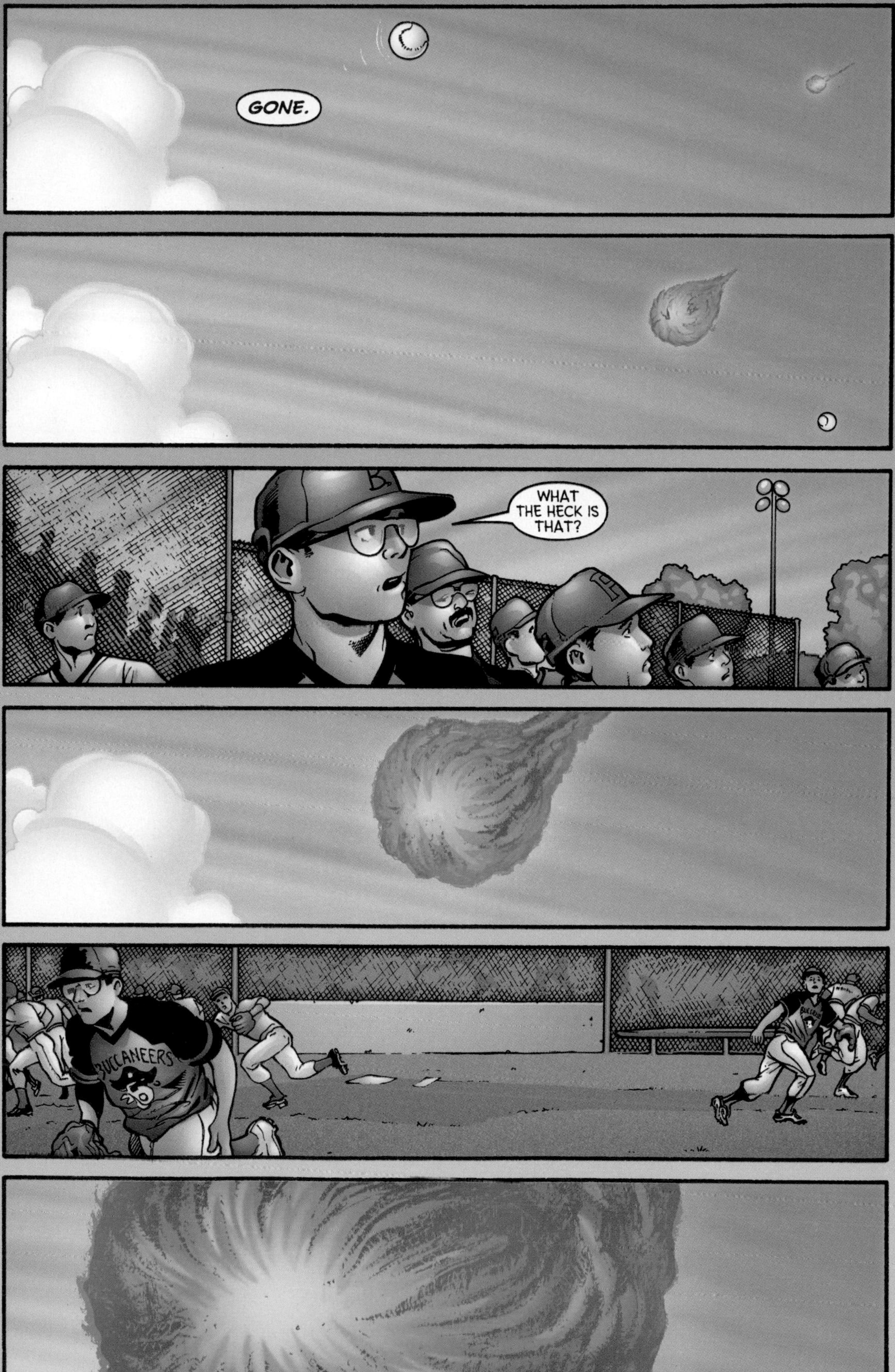
GONE.
WHAT THE HECK IS THAT?
BUCCANEERS

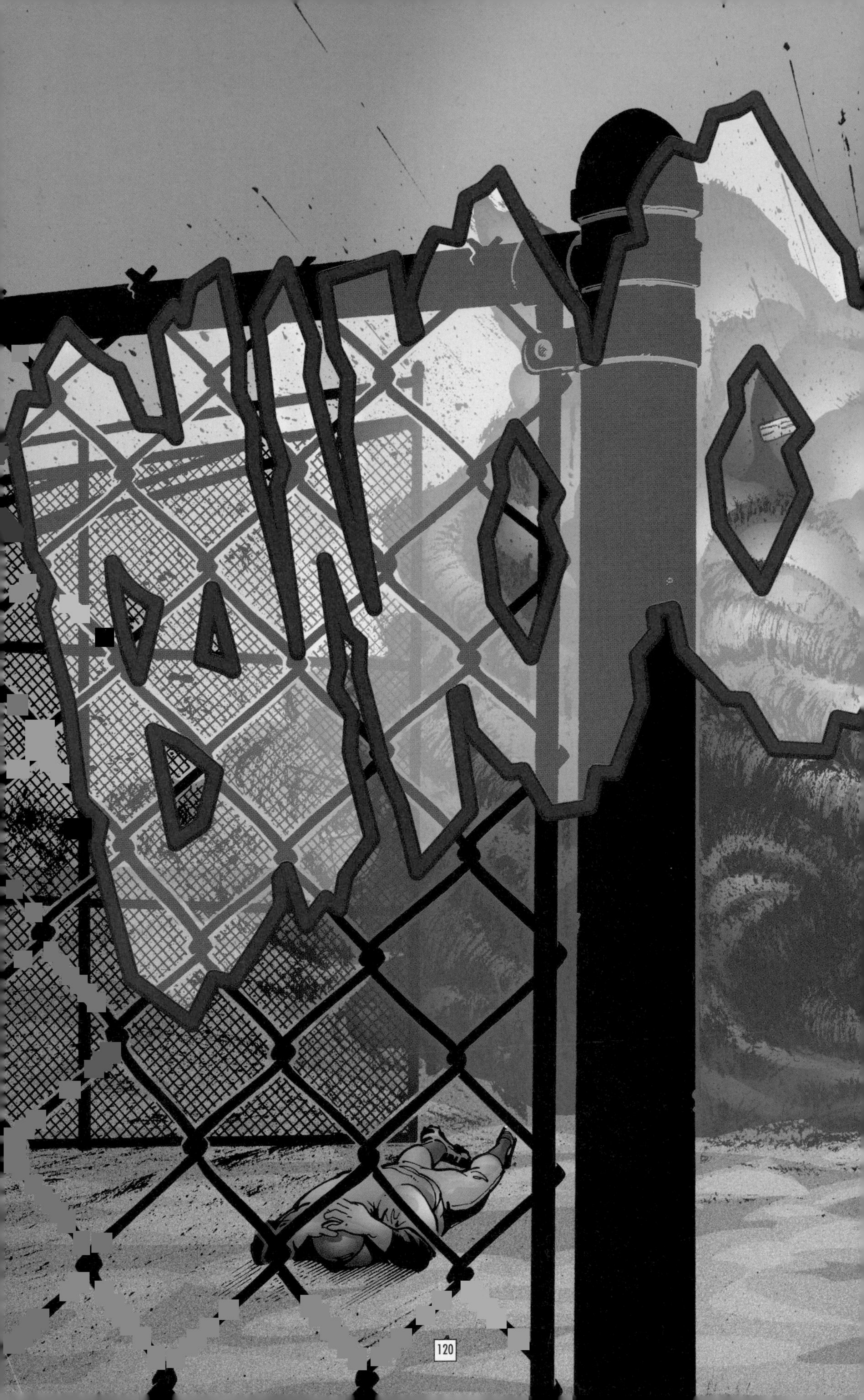

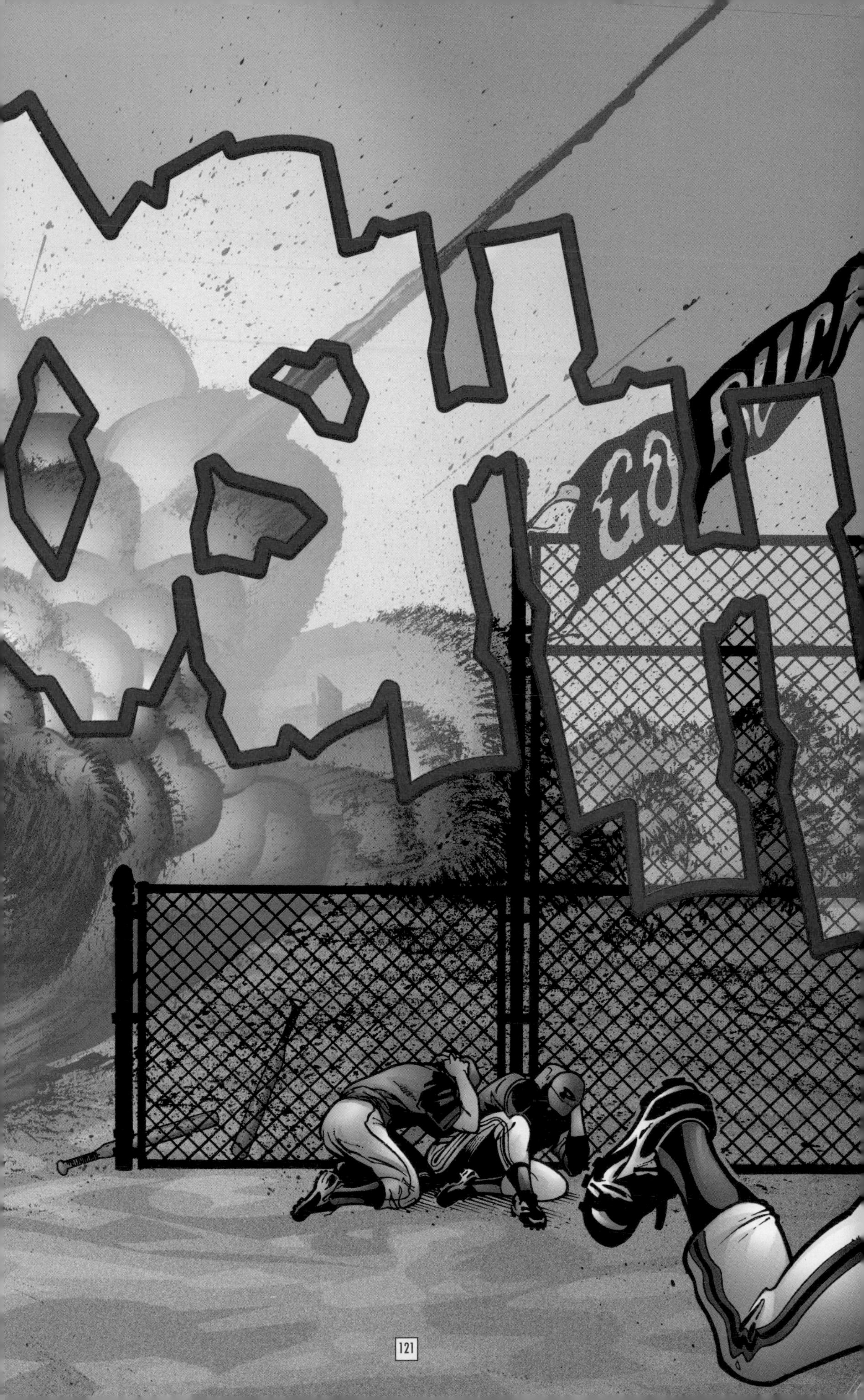
GO

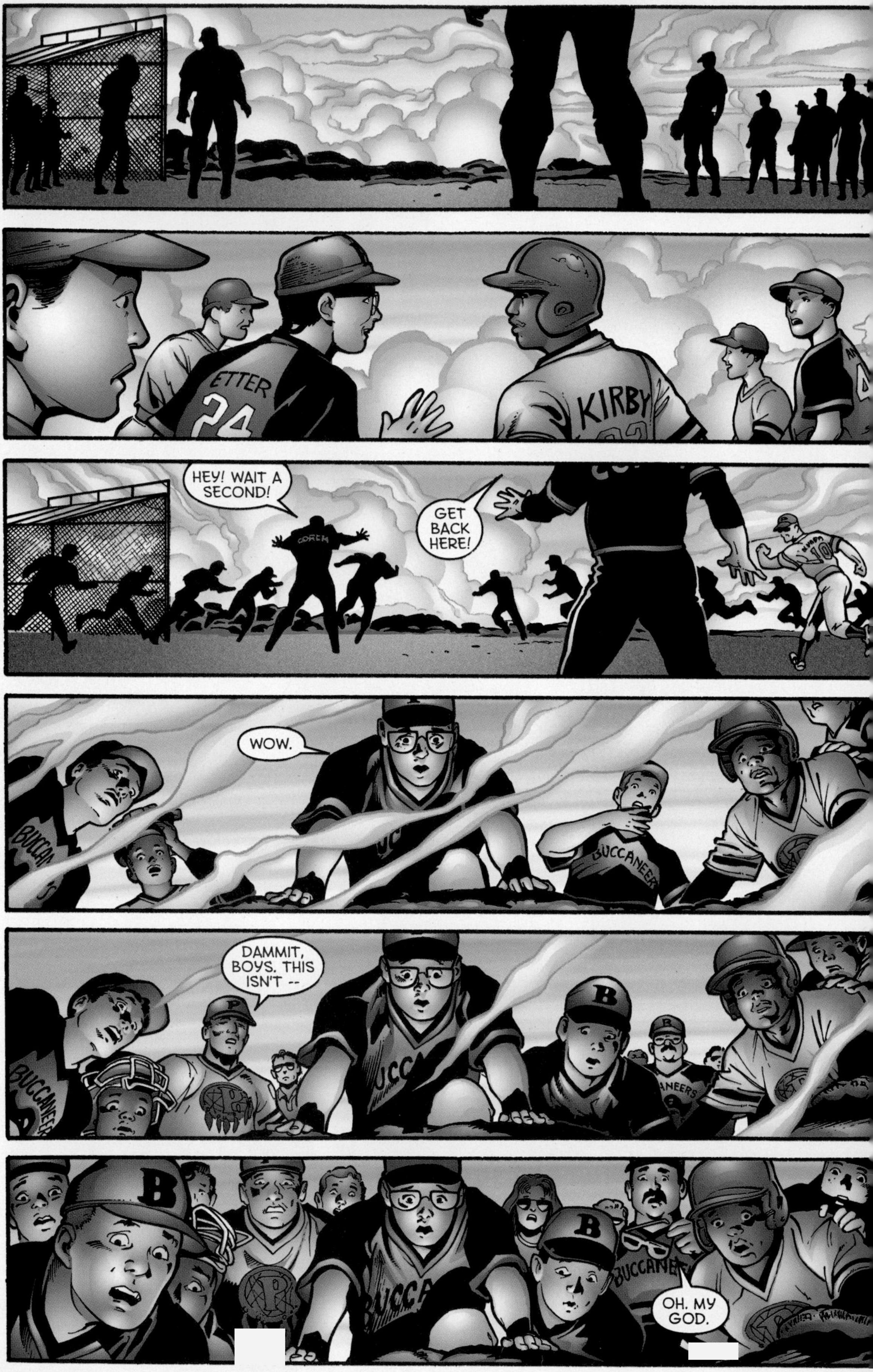
HEY! WAIT A SECOND!
GET BACK HERE!
WOW.
DAMMIT, BOYS. THIS ISN'T --
OH. MY GOD.

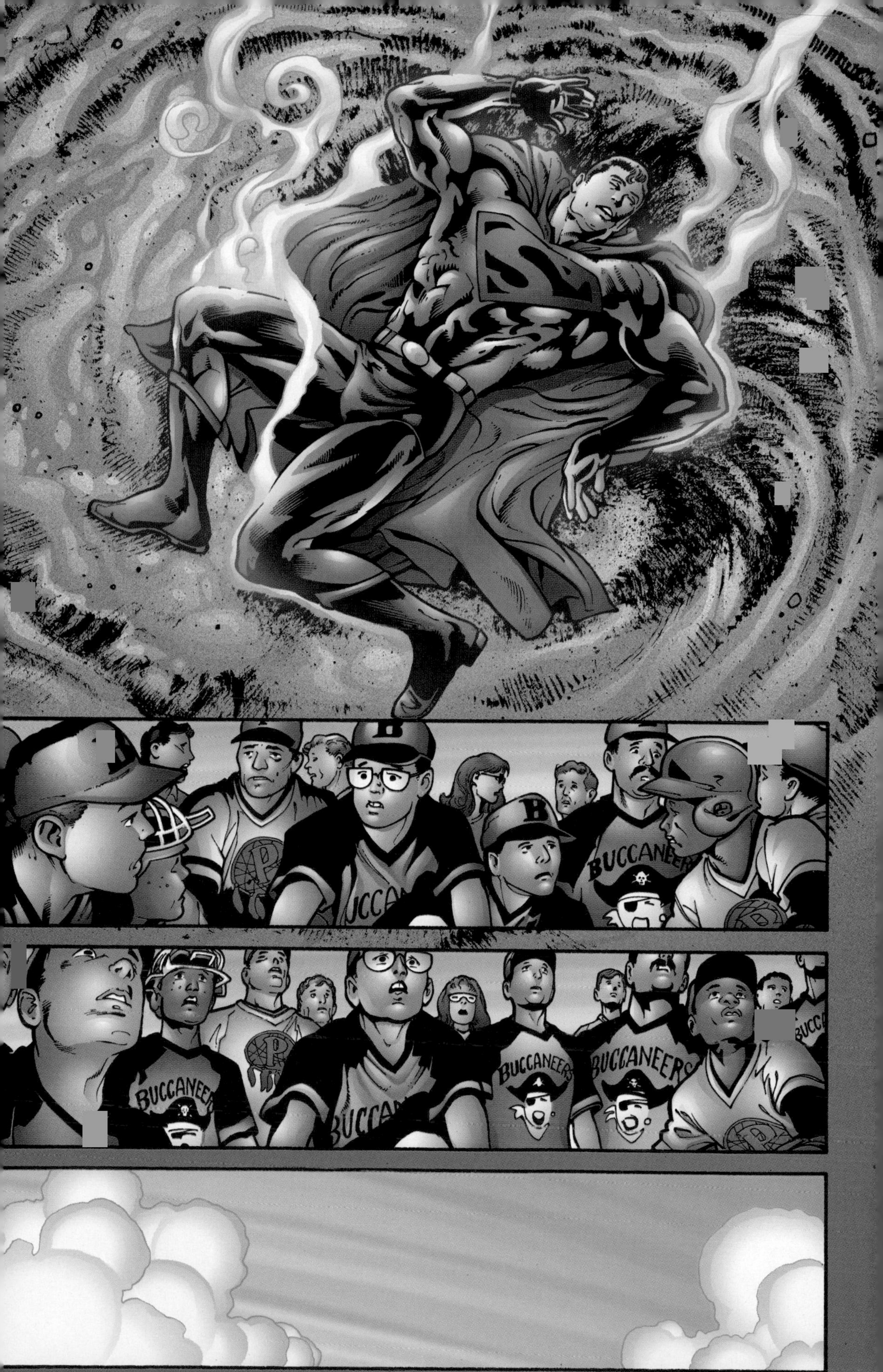
BUCCANEERS
BUCCANEERS

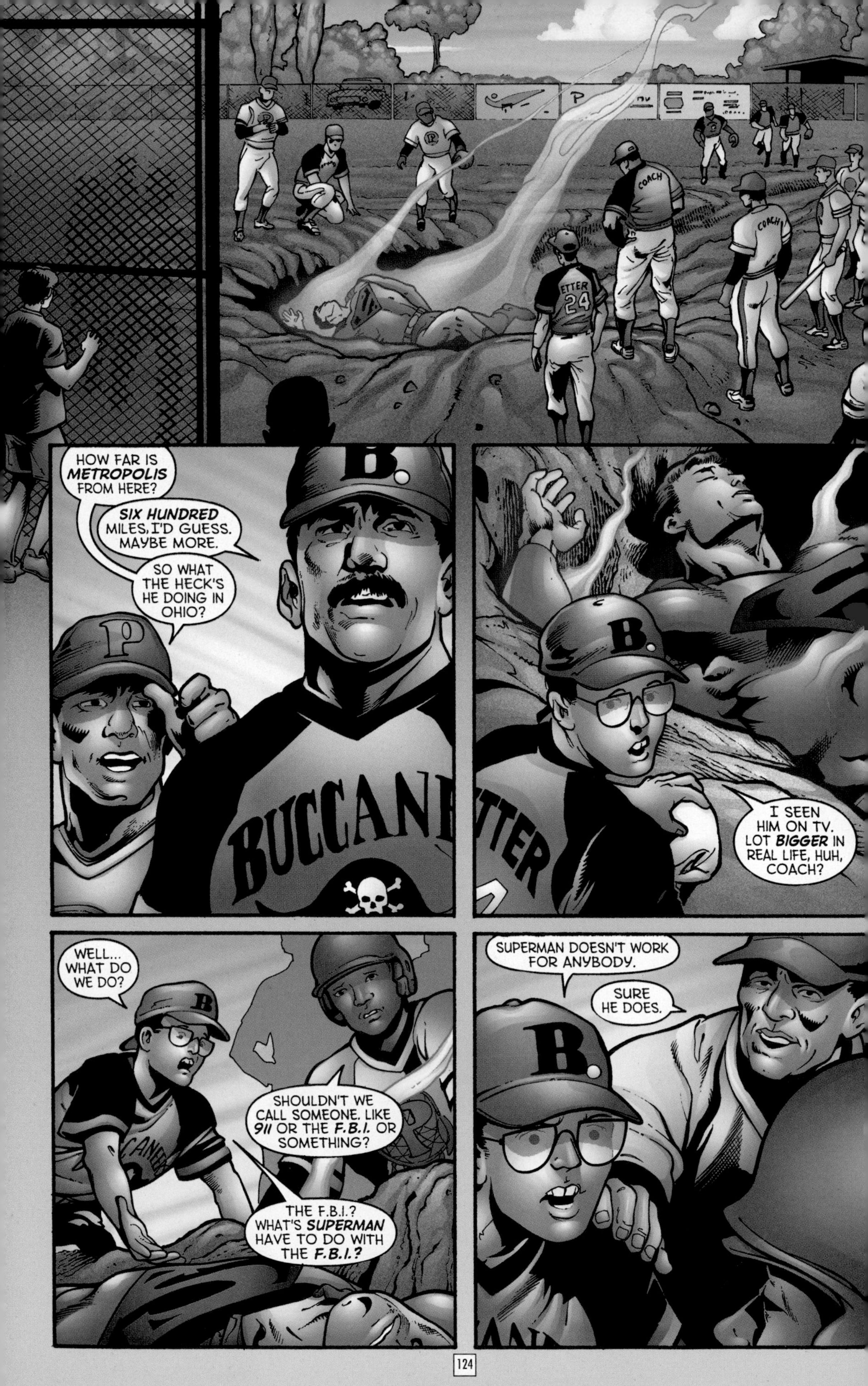
COACH
ETTER
24
COACH
HOW FAR IS METROPOLIS FROM HERE?
SIX HUNDRED MILES, I'D GUESS. MAYBE MORE.
SO WHAT THE HECK'S HE DOING IN OHIO?
BUCCANE
I SEEN HIM ON TV. LOT BIGGER IN REAL LIFE, HUH, COACH?
WELL... WHAT DO WE DO?
SHOULDN'T WE CALL SOMEONE. LIKE 911 OR THE F.B.I. OR SOMETHING?
THE F.B.I.? WHAT'S SUPERMAN HAVE TO DO WITH THE F.B.I.?
SUPERMAN DOESN'T WORK FOR ANYBODY.
SURE HE DOES.

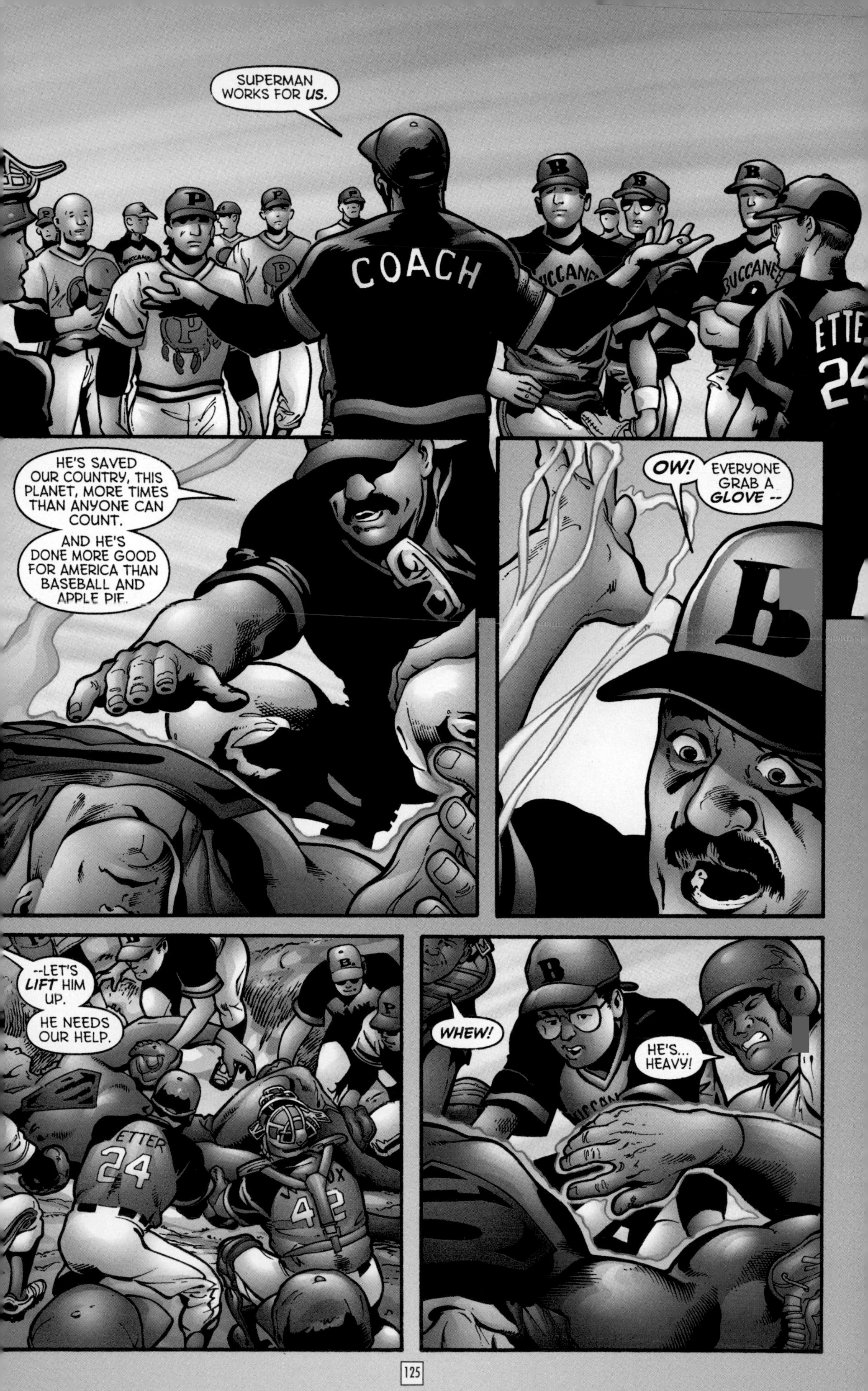
SUPERMAN WORKS FOR US.
COACH
ETTE 24
HE'S SAVED OUR COUNTRY, THIS PLANET, MORE TIMES THAN ANYONE CAN COUNT.
AND HE'S DONE MORE GOOD FOR AMERICA THAN BASEBALL AND APPLE PIE.
OW!
EVERYONE GRAB A GLOVE --
--LET'S LIFT HIM UP.
HE NEEDS OUR HELP.
ETTER 24
42
WHEW!
HE'S... HEAVY!

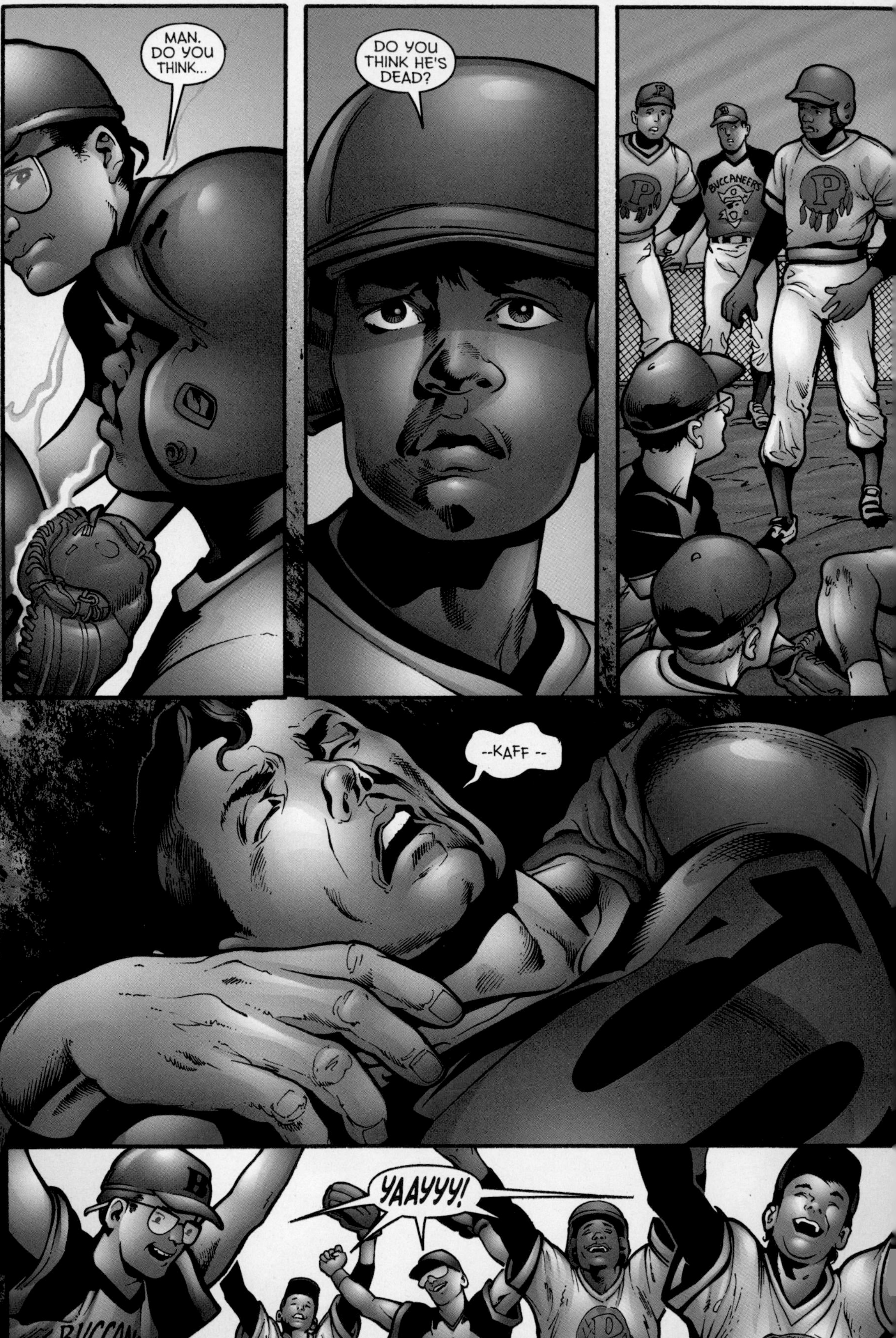
MAN. DO YOU THINK...
DO YOU THINK HE'S DEAD?
--KAFF --
YAAYYY!

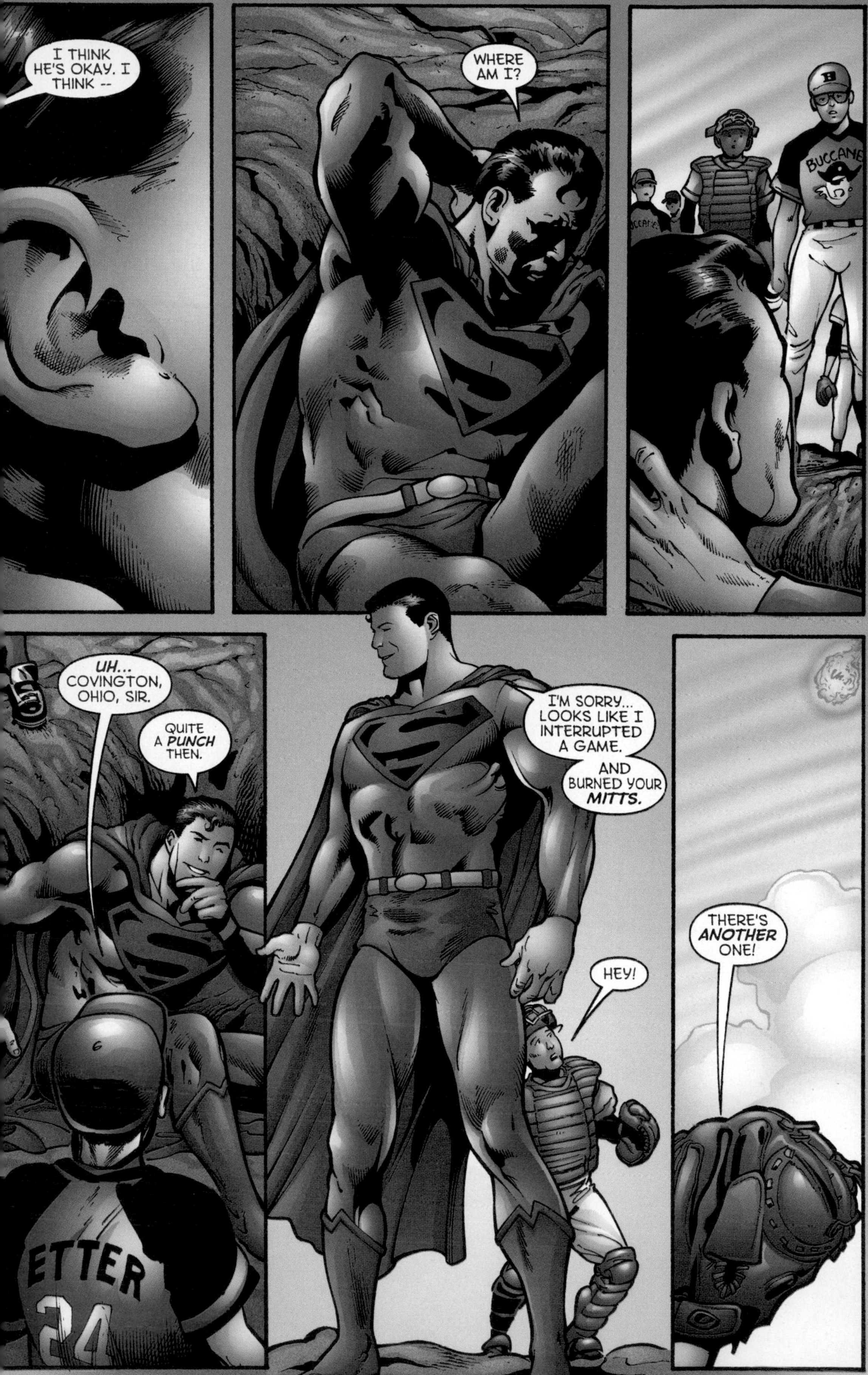
I THINK HE'S OKAY. I THINK --
WHERE AM I?
BUCCANE
UH... COVINGTON, OHIO, SIR.
QUITE A PUNCH THEN.
I'M SORRY... LOOKS LIKE I INTERRUPTED A GAME.
AND BURNED YOUR MITTS.
HEY!
THERE'S ANOTHER ONE!
ETTER
24

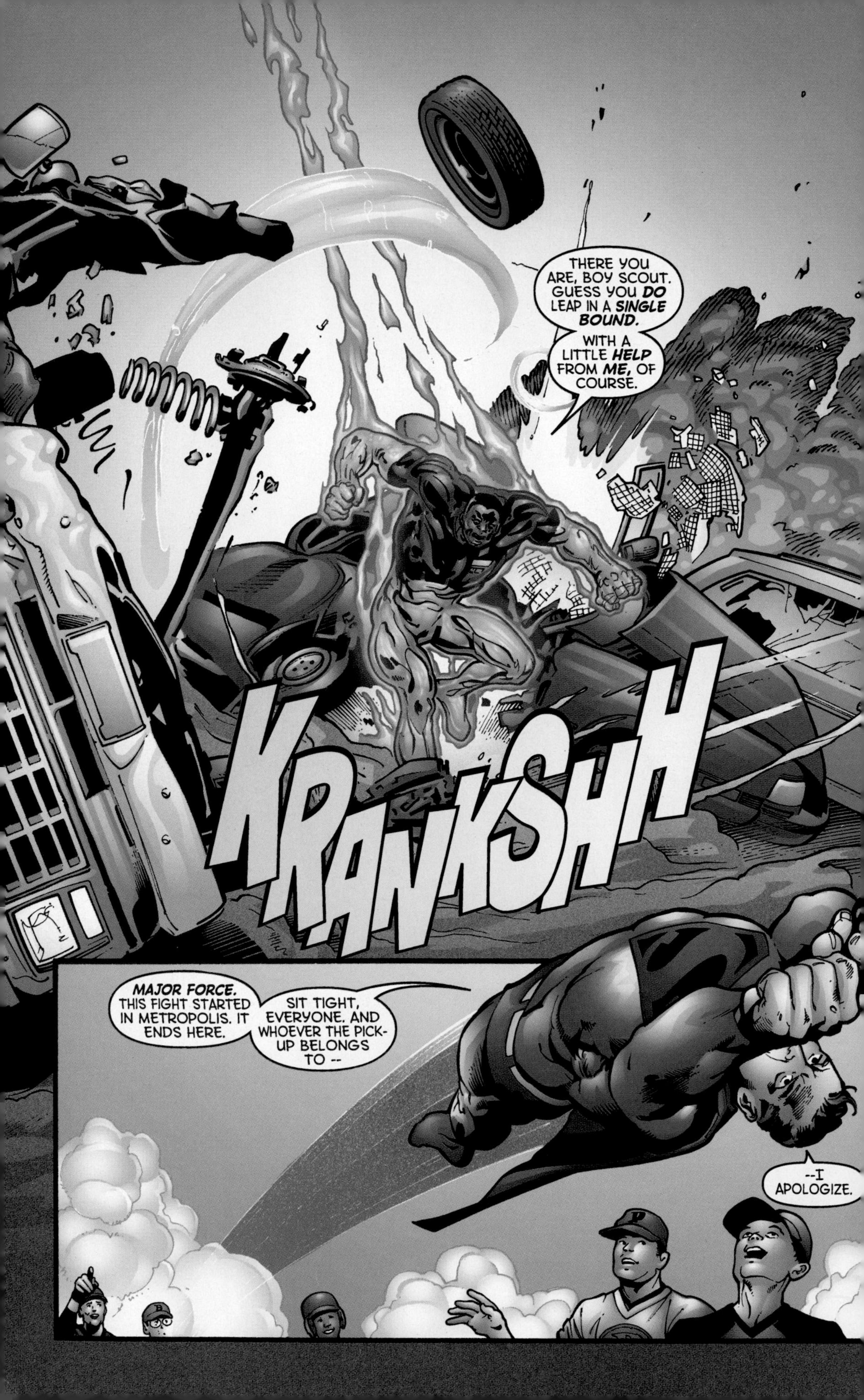
THERE YOU ARE, BOY SCOUT. GUESS YOU DO LEAP IN A SINGLE BOUND.
WITH A LITTLE HELP FROM ME, OF COURSE.
KRANKSHH
MAJOR FORCE. THIS FIGHT STARTED IN METROPOLIS. IT ENDS HERE.
SIT TIGHT, EVERYONE. AND WHOEVER THE PICK-UP BELONGS TO --
--I APOLOGIZE.

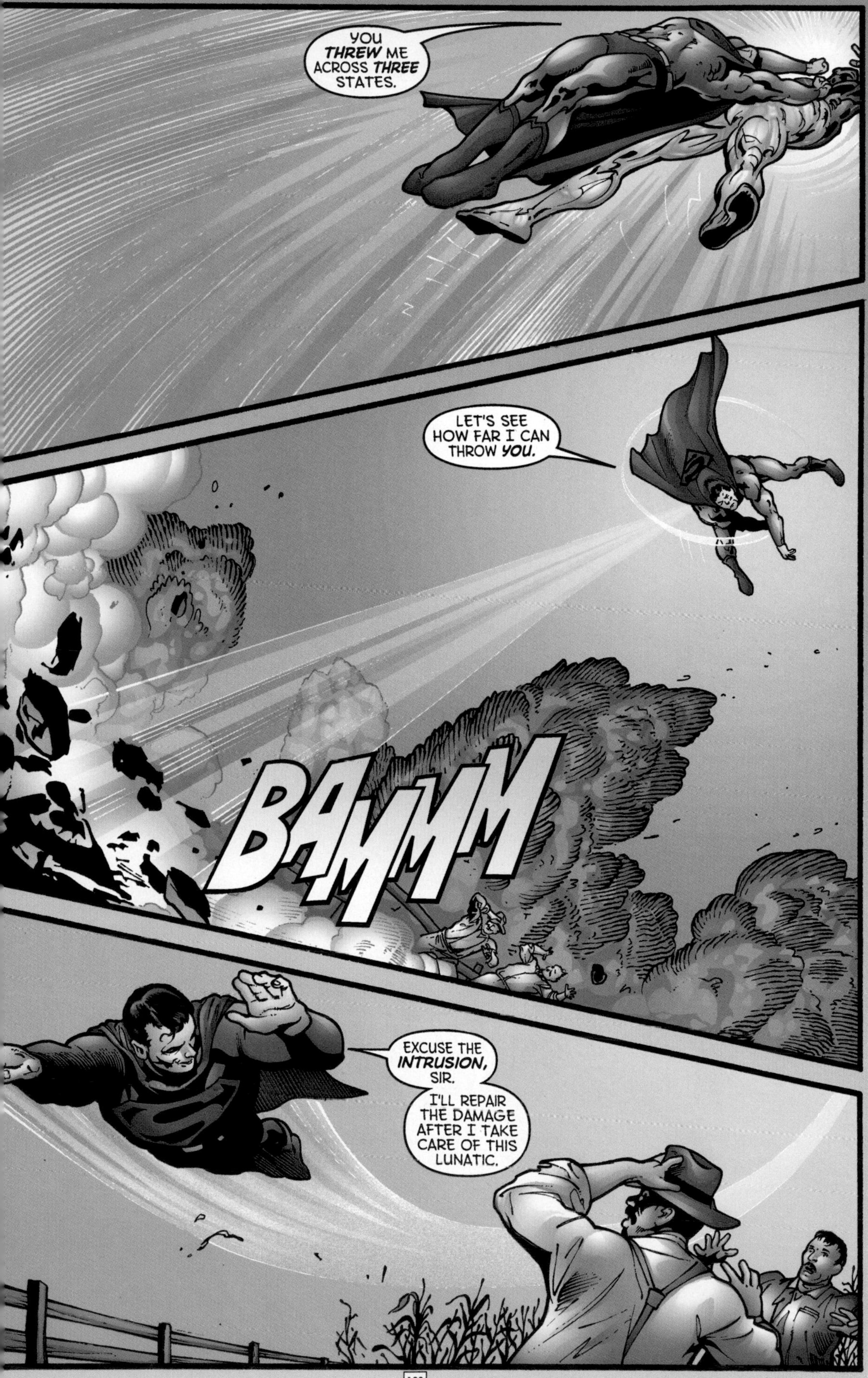
YOU THREW ME ACROSS THREE STATES.
LET'S SEE HOW FAR I CAN THROW YOU.
BAMMM
EXCUSE THE INTRUSION, SIR.
I'LL REPAIR THE DAMAGE AFTER I TAKE CARE OF THIS LUNATIC.

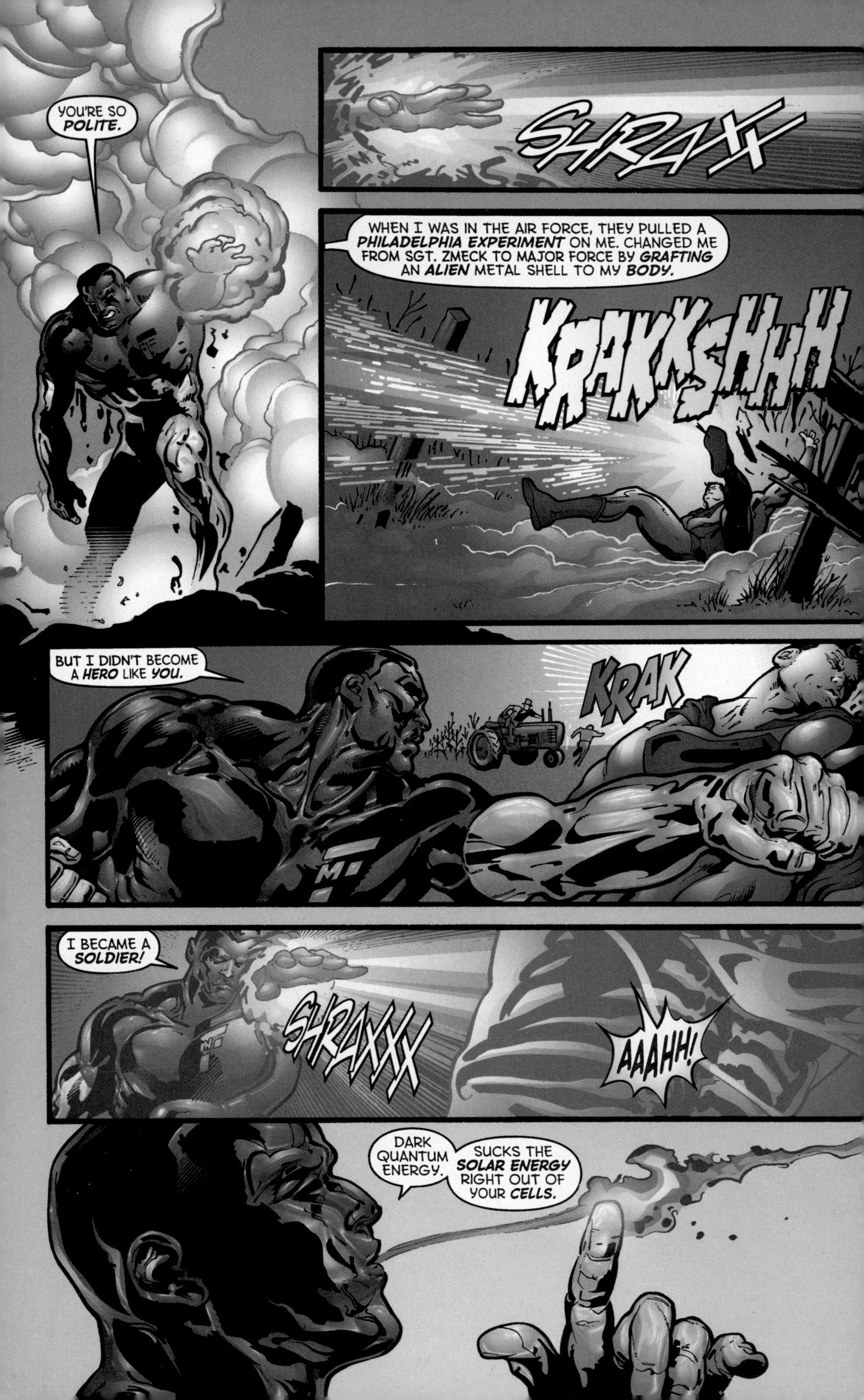
YOU'RE SO POLITE.
SHRAXX
WHEN I WAS IN THE AIR FORCE, THEY PULLED A PHILADELPHIA EXPERIMENT ON ME. CHANGED ME FROM SGT. ZMECK TO MAJOR FORCE BY GRAFTING AN ALIEN METAL SHELL TO MY BODY.
KRAKKSHHH
BUT I DIDN'T BECOME A HERO LIKE YOU.
KRAK
I BECAME A SOLDIER!
SHRAXXX
AAAHH!
DARK QUANTUM ENERGY.
SUCKS THE SOLAR ENERGY RIGHT OUT OF YOUR CELLS.

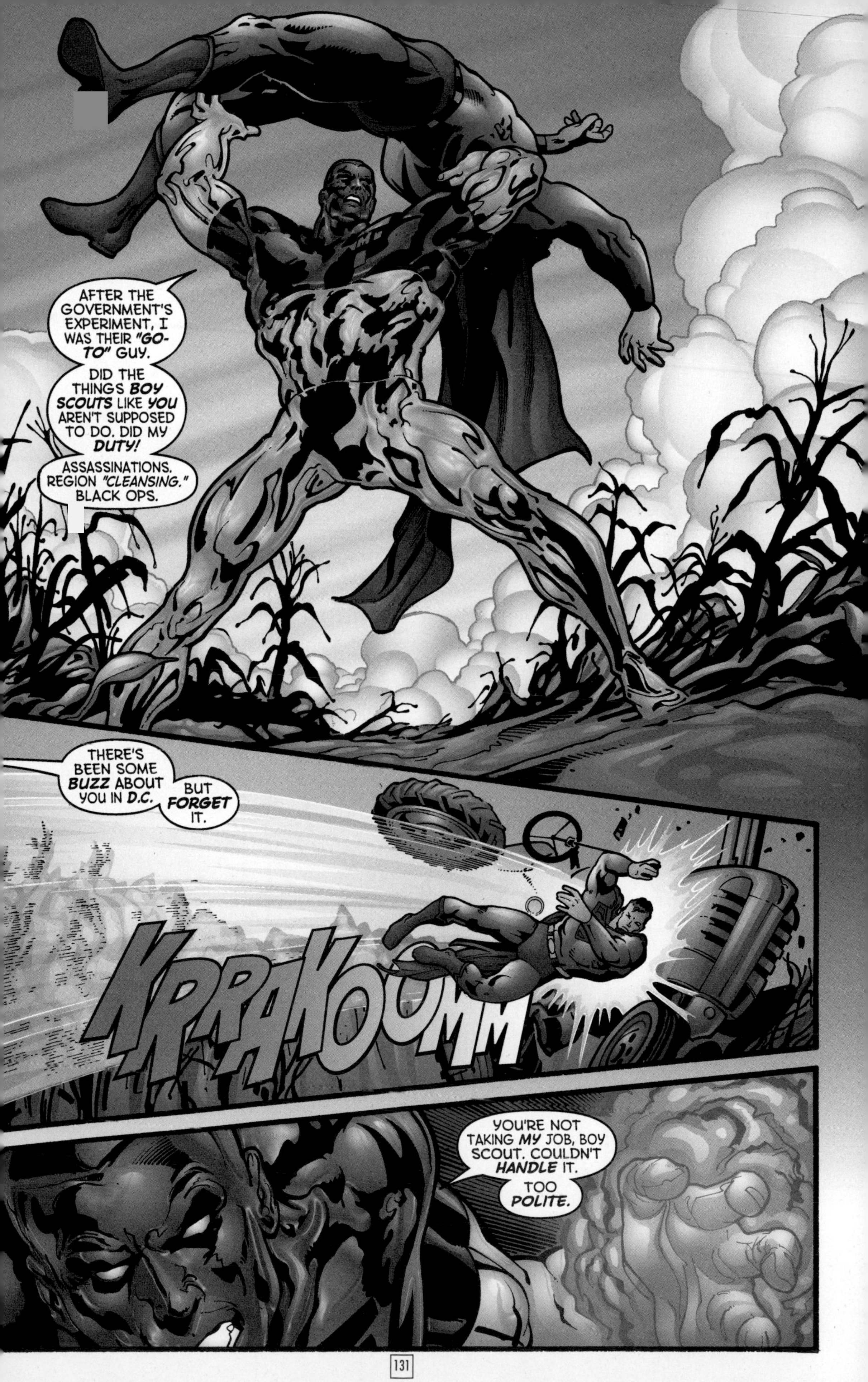
AFTER THE GOVERNMENT'S EXPERIMENT, I WAS THEIR "GO-TO" GUY.
DID THE THINGS BOY SCOUTS LIKE YOU AREN'T SUPPOSED TO DO. DID MY DUTY!
ASSASSINATIONS. REGION "CLEANSING." BLACK OPS.
THERE'S BEEN SOME BUZZ ABOUT YOU IN D.C.
BUT FORGET IT.
KRRAKOOMM
YOU'RE NOT TAKING MY JOB, BOY SCOUT. COULDN'T HANDLE IT.
TOO POLITE.

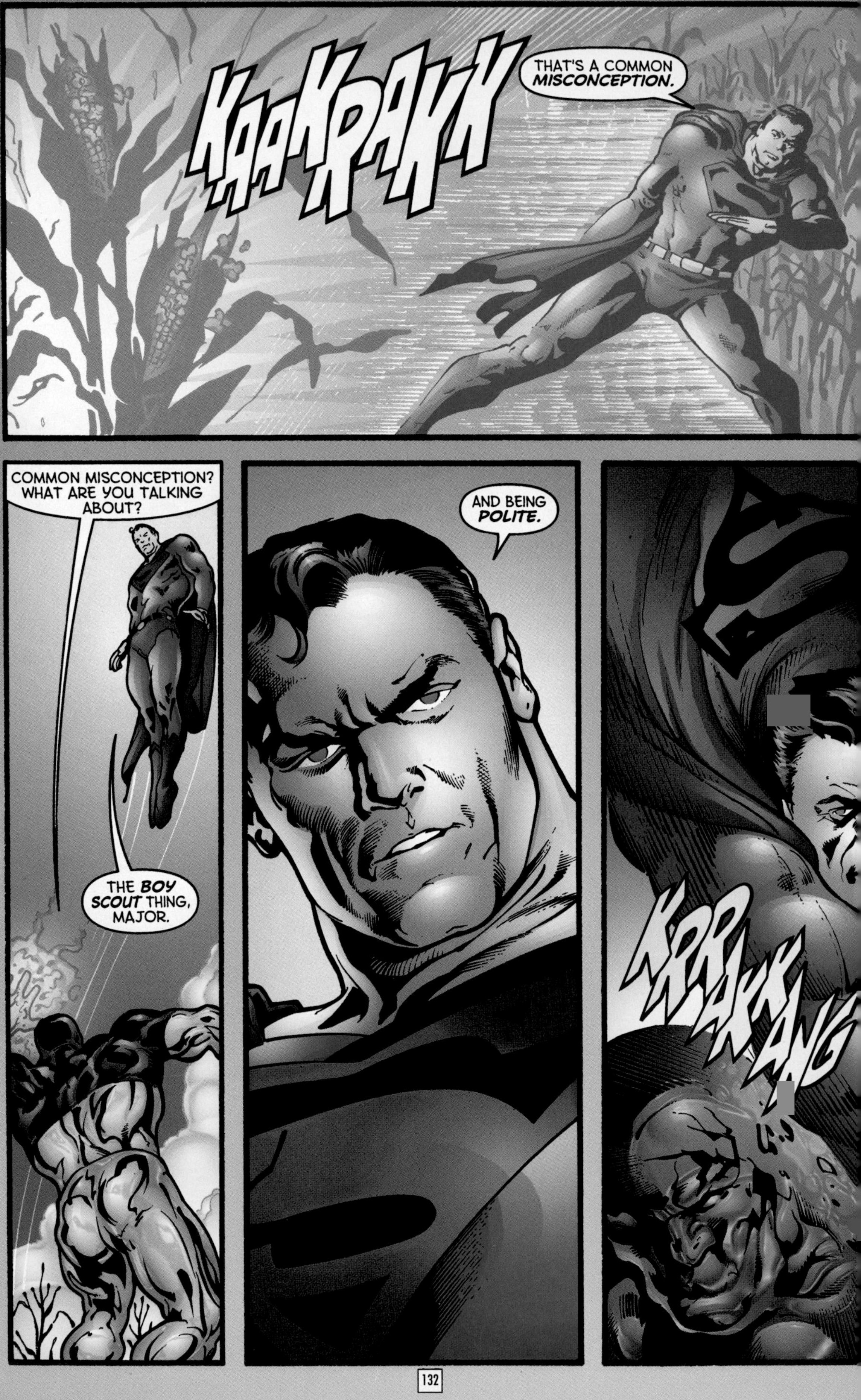
KAAKRAKK
THAT'S A COMMON MISCONCEPTION.
COMMON MISCONCEPTION? WHAT ARE YOU TALKING ABOUT?
THE BOY SCOUT THING, MAJOR.
AND BEING POLITE.
KRRAKKANG

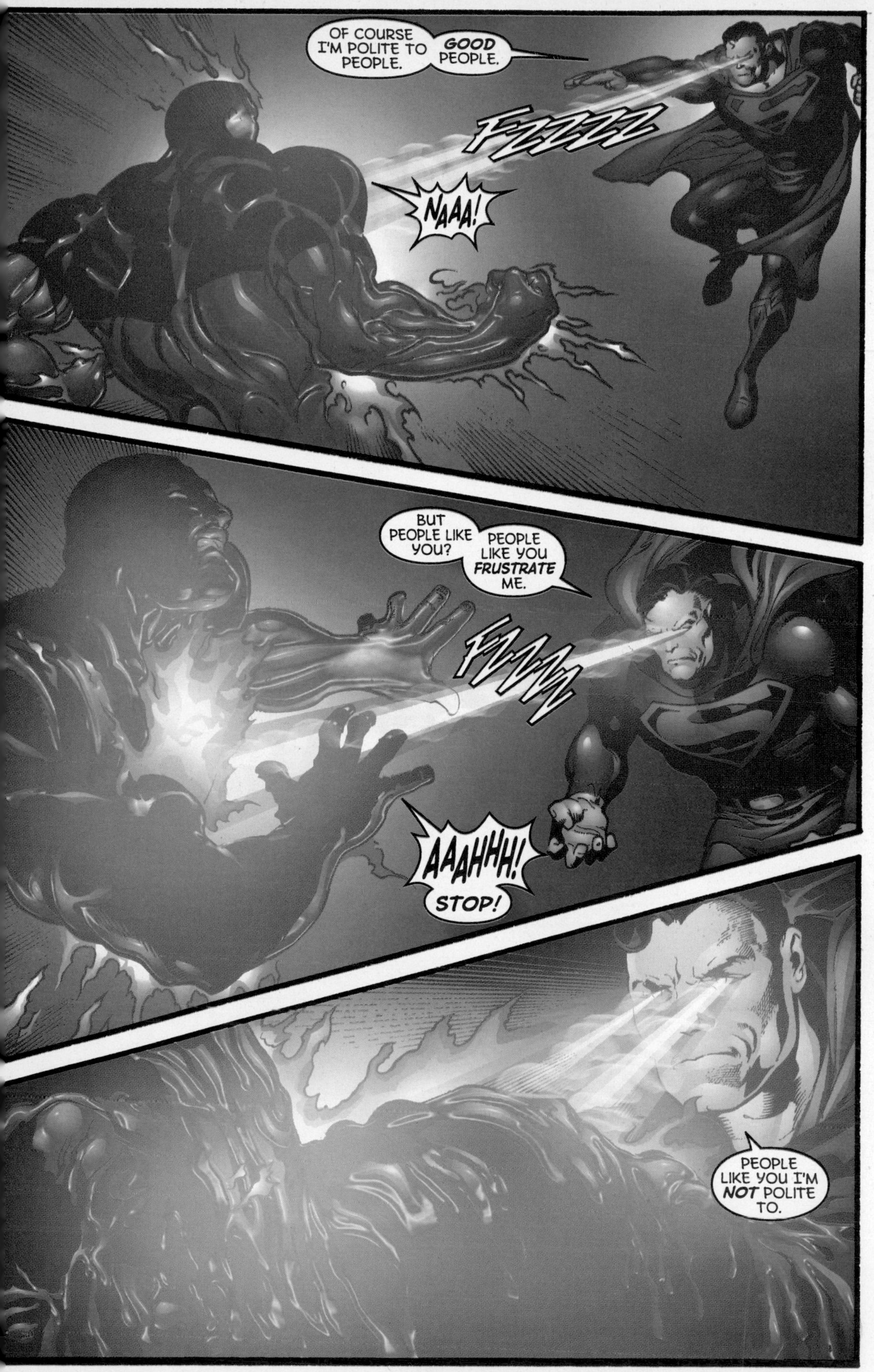
OF COURSE I'M POLITE TO PEOPLE.
GOOD PEOPLE.
FZZZZ
NAAA!
BUT PEOPLE LIKE YOU?
PEOPLE LIKE YOU FRUSTRATE ME.
FZZZZ
AAAHHH!
STOP!
PEOPLE LIKE YOU I'M NOT POLITE TO.

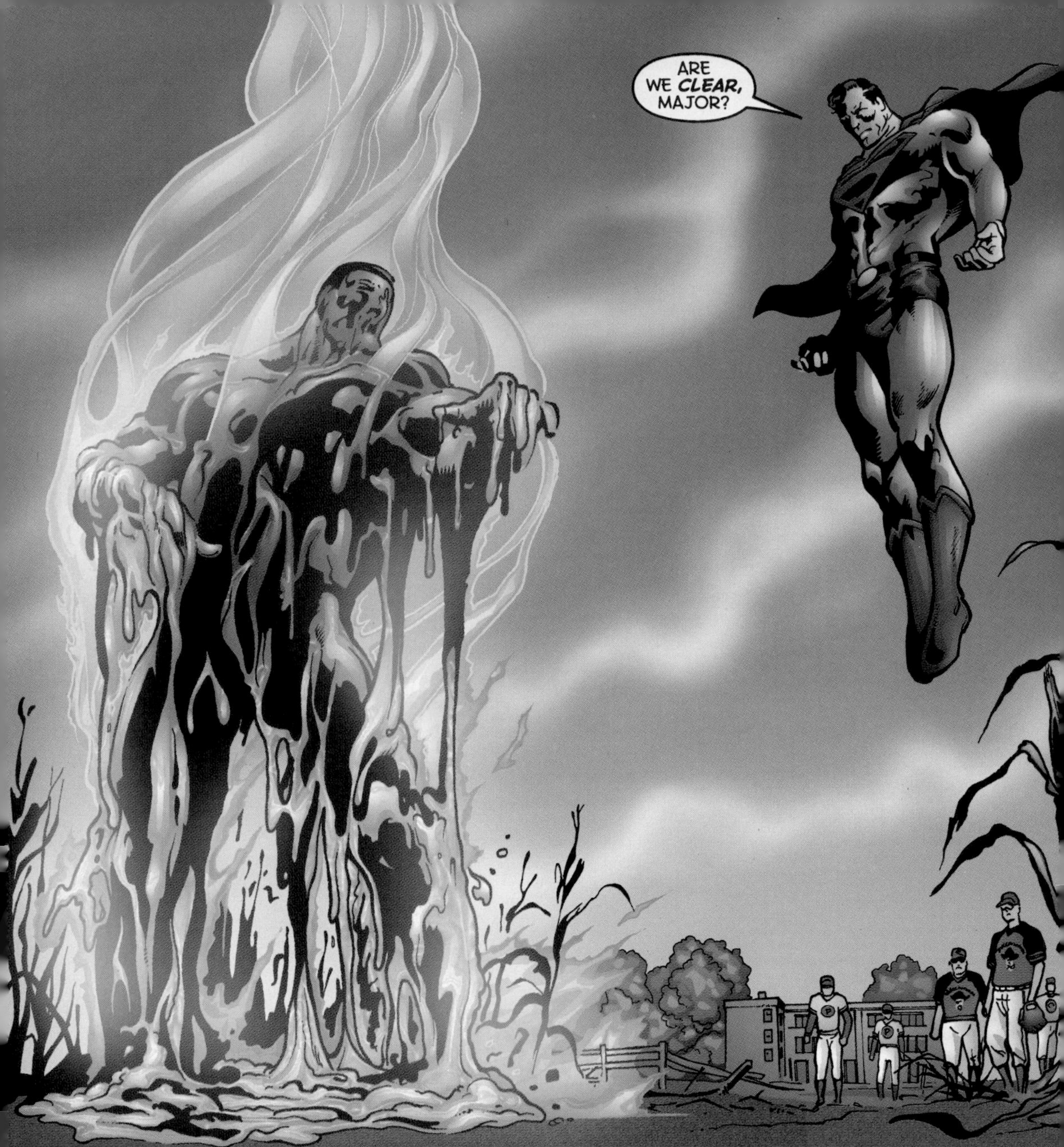
ARE WE CLEAR, MAJOR?

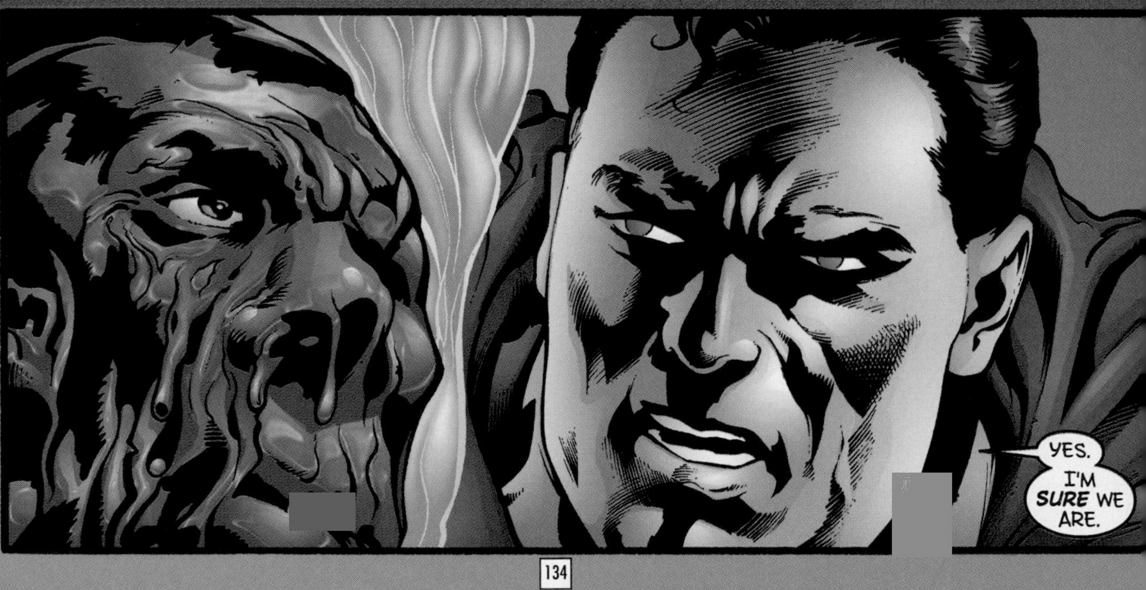
YES.
I'M SURE WE ARE.

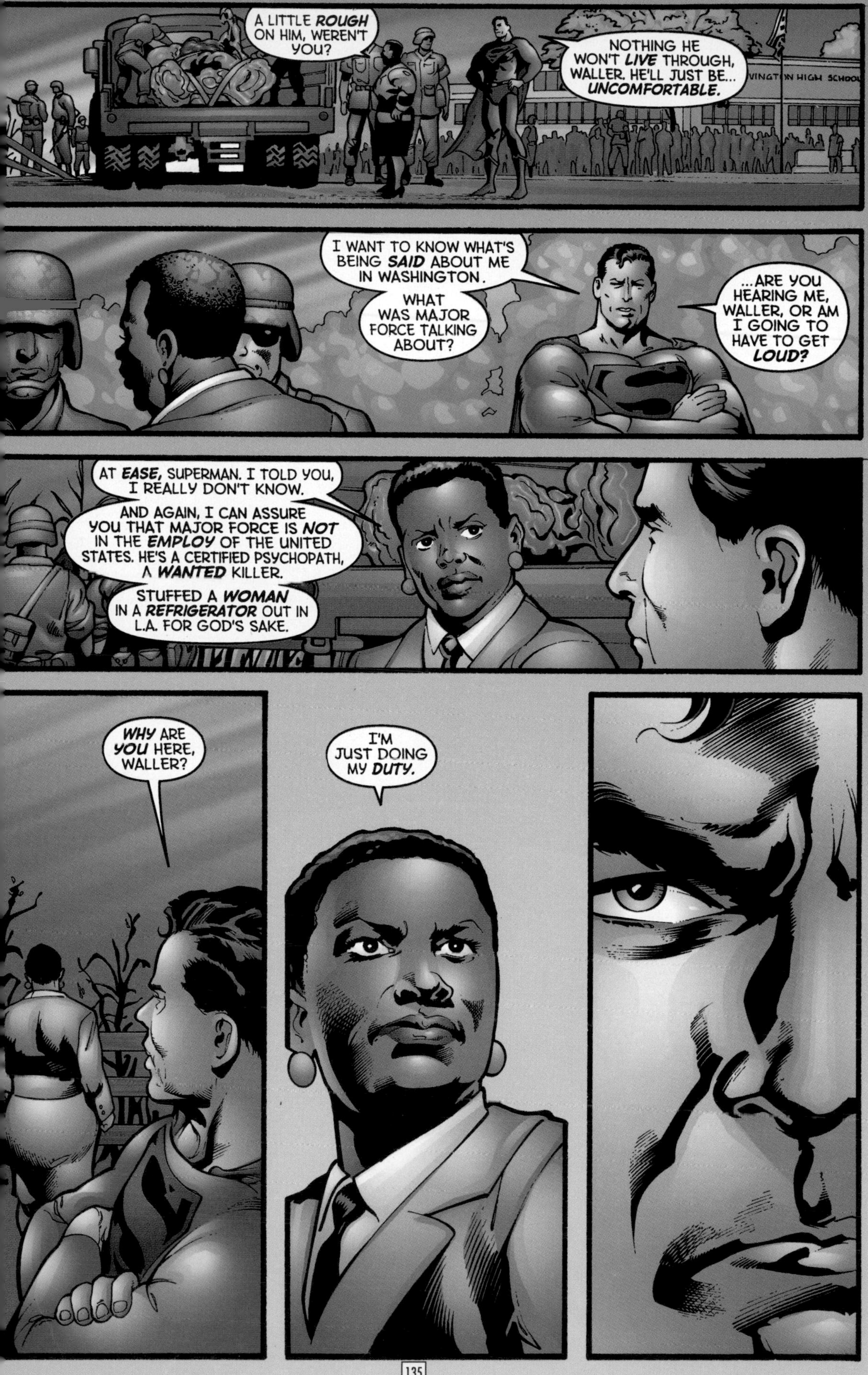
A LITTLE ROUGH ON HIM, WEREN'T YOU?
NOTHING HE WON'T LIVE THROUGH, WALLER. HE'LL JUST BE... UNCOMFORTABLE.
VINGTON HIGH SCHOOL
I WANT TO KNOW WHAT'S BEING SAID ABOUT ME IN WASHINGTON.
WHAT WAS MAJOR FORCE TALKING ABOUT?
...ARE YOU HEARING ME, WALLER, OR AM I GOING TO HAVE TO GET LOUD?
AT EASE, SUPERMAN. I TOLD YOU, I REALLY DON'T KNOW.
AND AGAIN, I CAN ASSURE YOU THAT MAJOR FORCE IS NOT IN THE EMPLOY OF THE UNITED STATES. HE'S A CERTIFIED PSYCHOPATH, A WANTED KILLER.
STUFFED A WOMAN IN A REFRIGERATOR OUT IN L.A. FOR GOD'S SAKE.
WHY ARE YOU HERE, WALLER?
I'M JUST DOING MY DUTY.

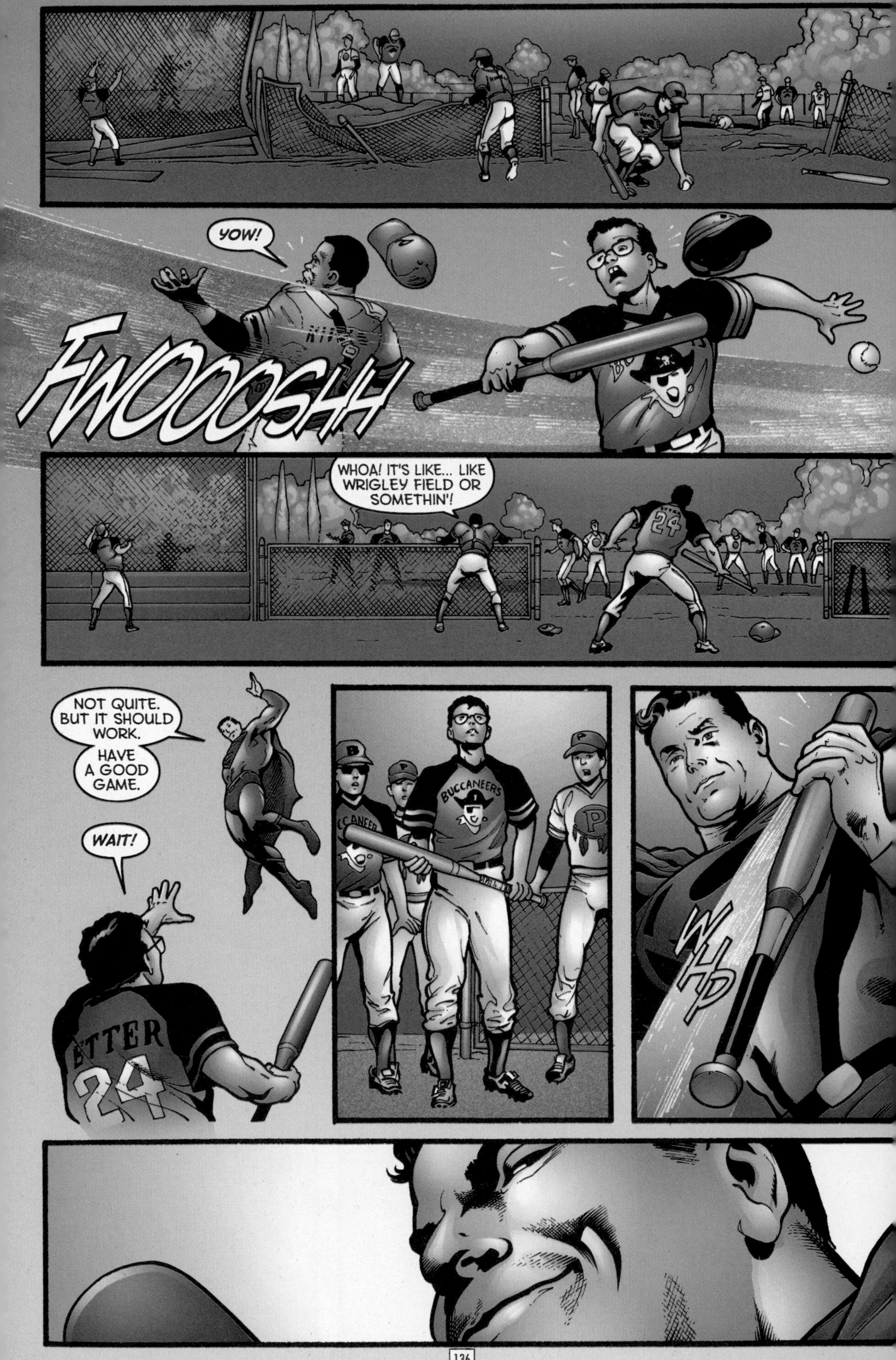
YOW!
FWOOOSHH
WHOA! IT'S LIKE... LIKE WRIGLEY FIELD OR SOMETHIN'!
NOT QUITE. BUT IT SHOULD WORK.
HAVE A GOOD GAME.
WAIT!
BUCCANEERS
ETTER
24
WHP

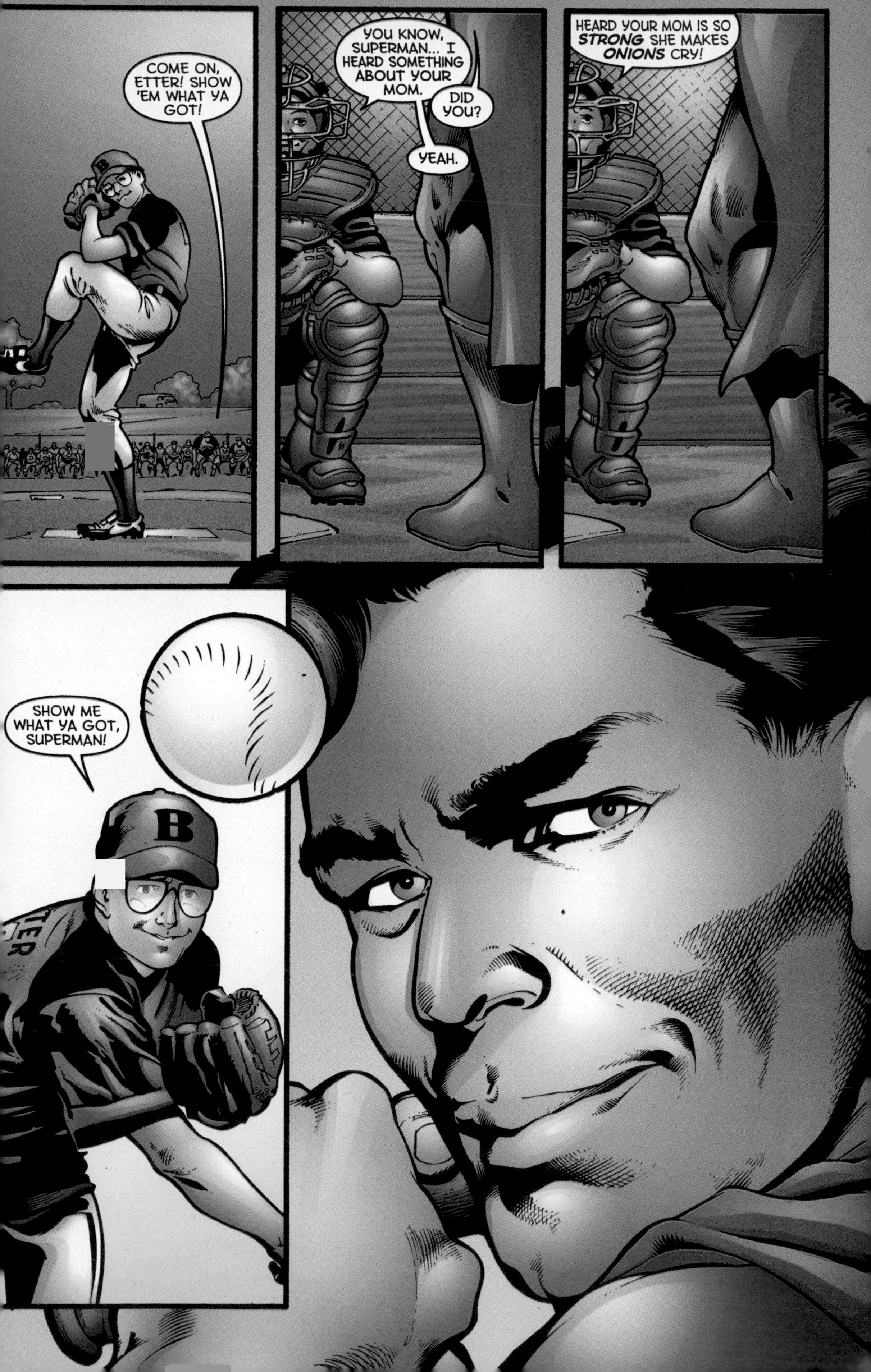
COME ON, ETTER! SHOW 'EM WHAT YA GOT!
YOU KNOW, SUPERMAN... I HEARD SOMETHING ABOUT YOUR MOM.
DID YOU?
YEAH.
HEARD YOUR MOM IS SO STRONG SHE MAKES ONIONS CRY!
SHOW ME WHAT YA GOT, SUPERMAN!

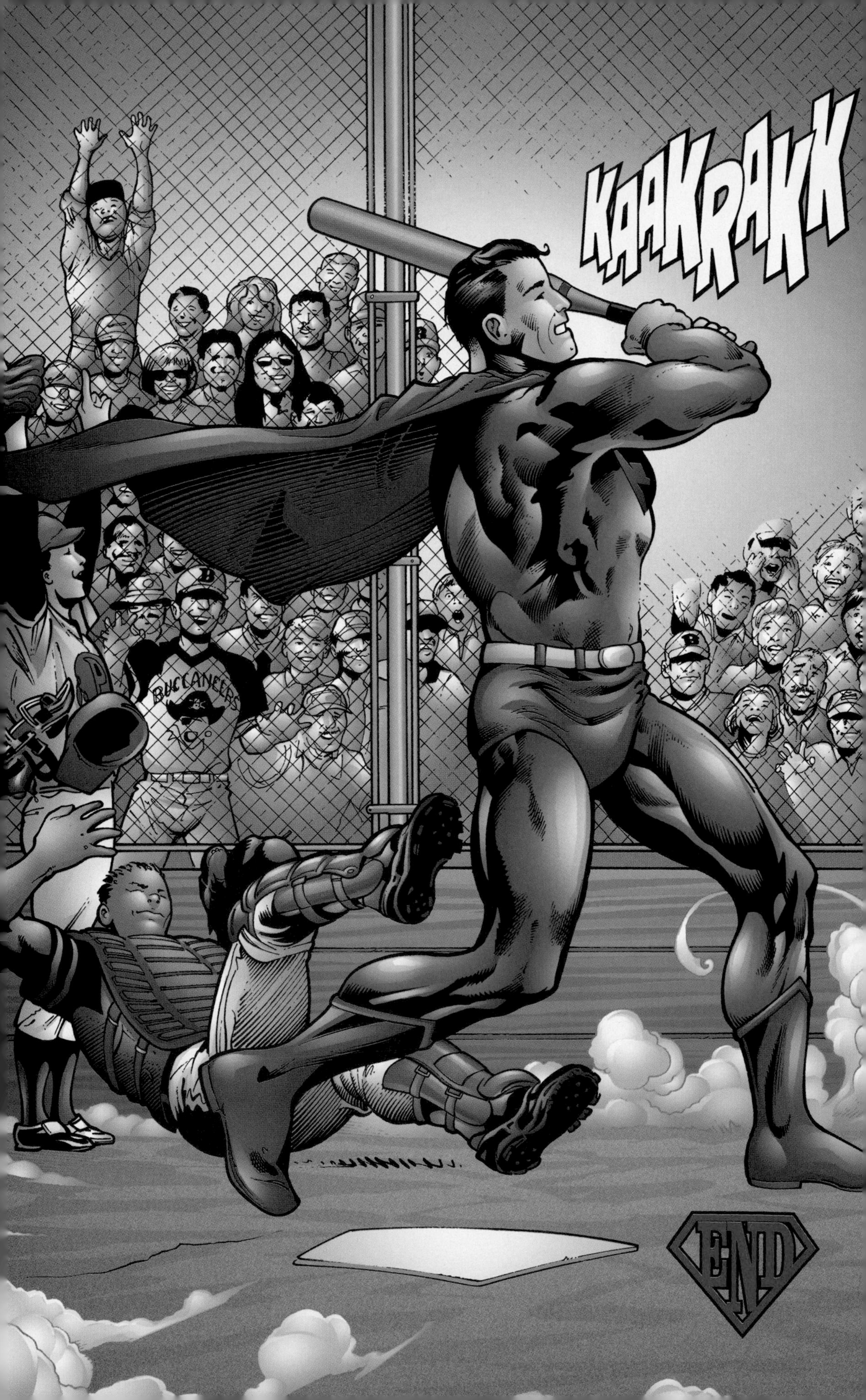
KAAKRAKK
BUCCANEERS
END

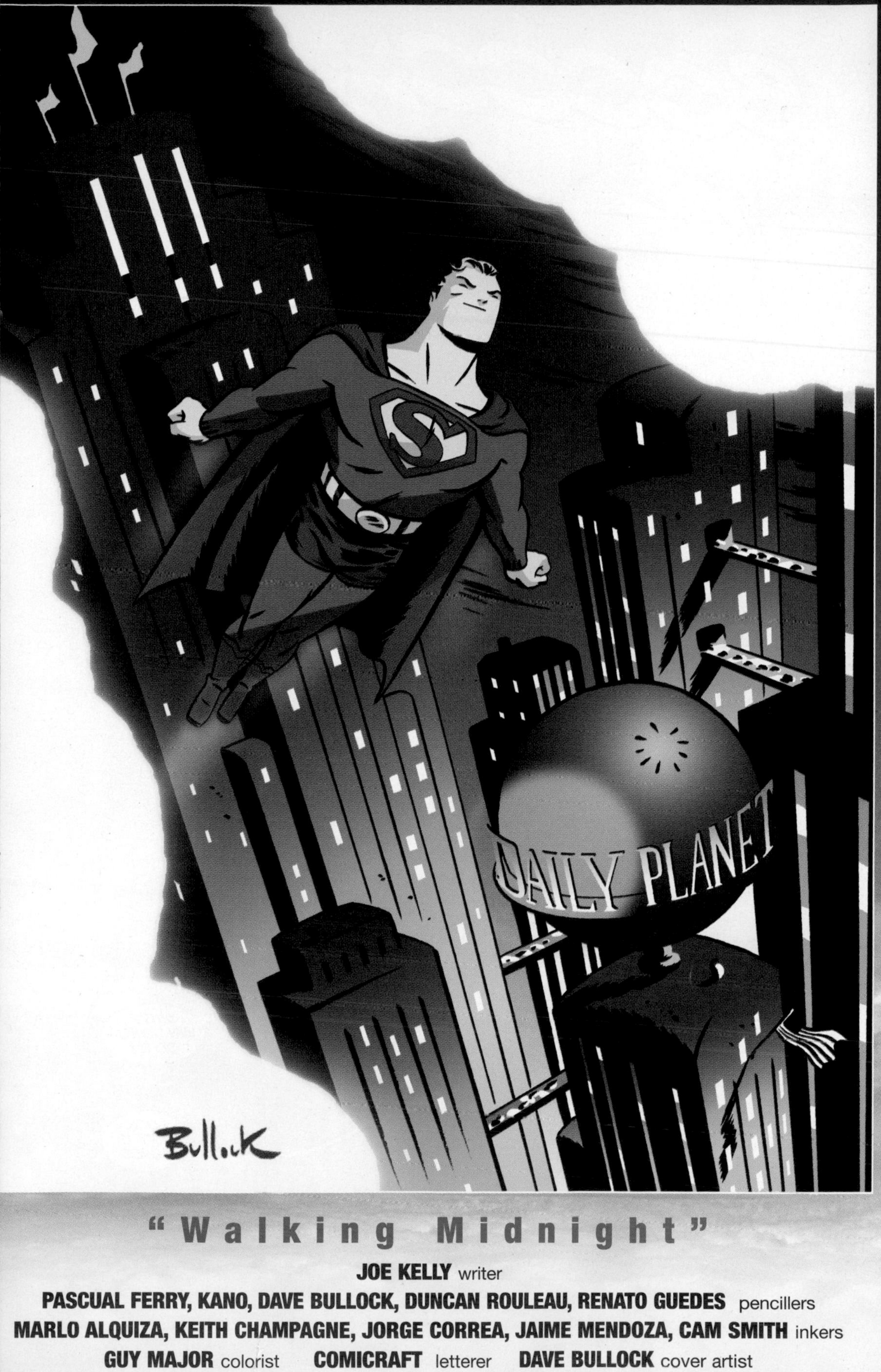
DAILY PLANET
Bullock

"Walking Midnight"

JOE KELLY writer

PASCUAL FERRY, KANO, DAVE BULLOCK, DUNCAN ROULEAU, RENATO GUEDES pencillers

MARLO ALQUIZA, KEITH CHAMPAGNE, JORGE CORREA, JAIME MENDOZA, CAM SMITH inkers

GUY MAJOR colorist **COMICRAFT** letterer **DAVE BULLOCK** cover artist

From the pages of one of DC's longest-running comics, and the debut title for Superman, comes this ACTION COMICS story showing how the Man of Steel spends New Year's Eve...

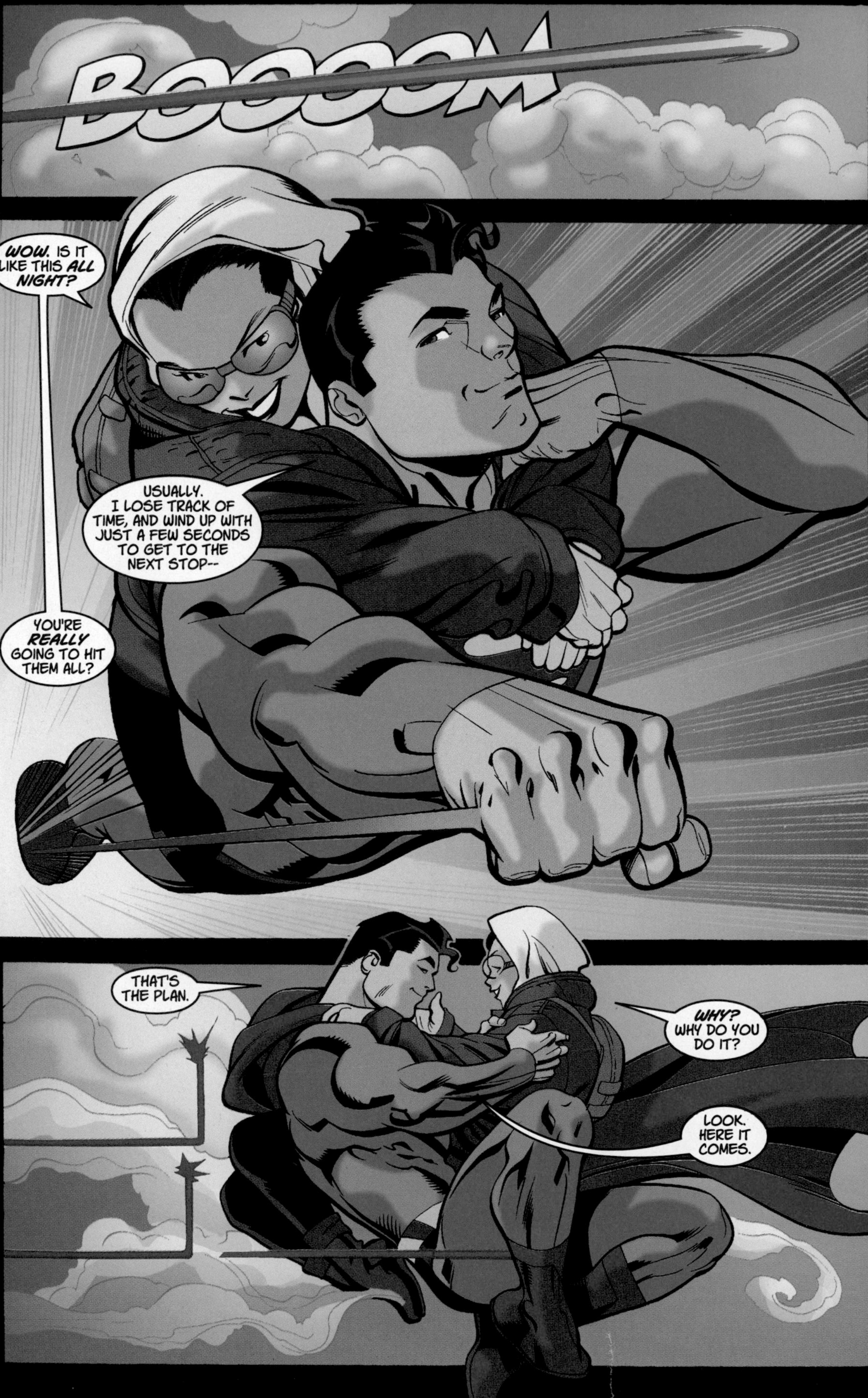
BOOOOOM
WOW. IS IT LIKE THIS ALL NIGHT?
USUALLY. I LOSE TRACK OF TIME, AND WIND UP WITH JUST A FEW SECONDS TO GET TO THE NEXT STOP--
YOU'RE REALLY GOING TO HIT THEM ALL?
THAT'S THE PLAN.
WHY? WHY DO YOU DO IT?
LOOK. HERE IT COMES.

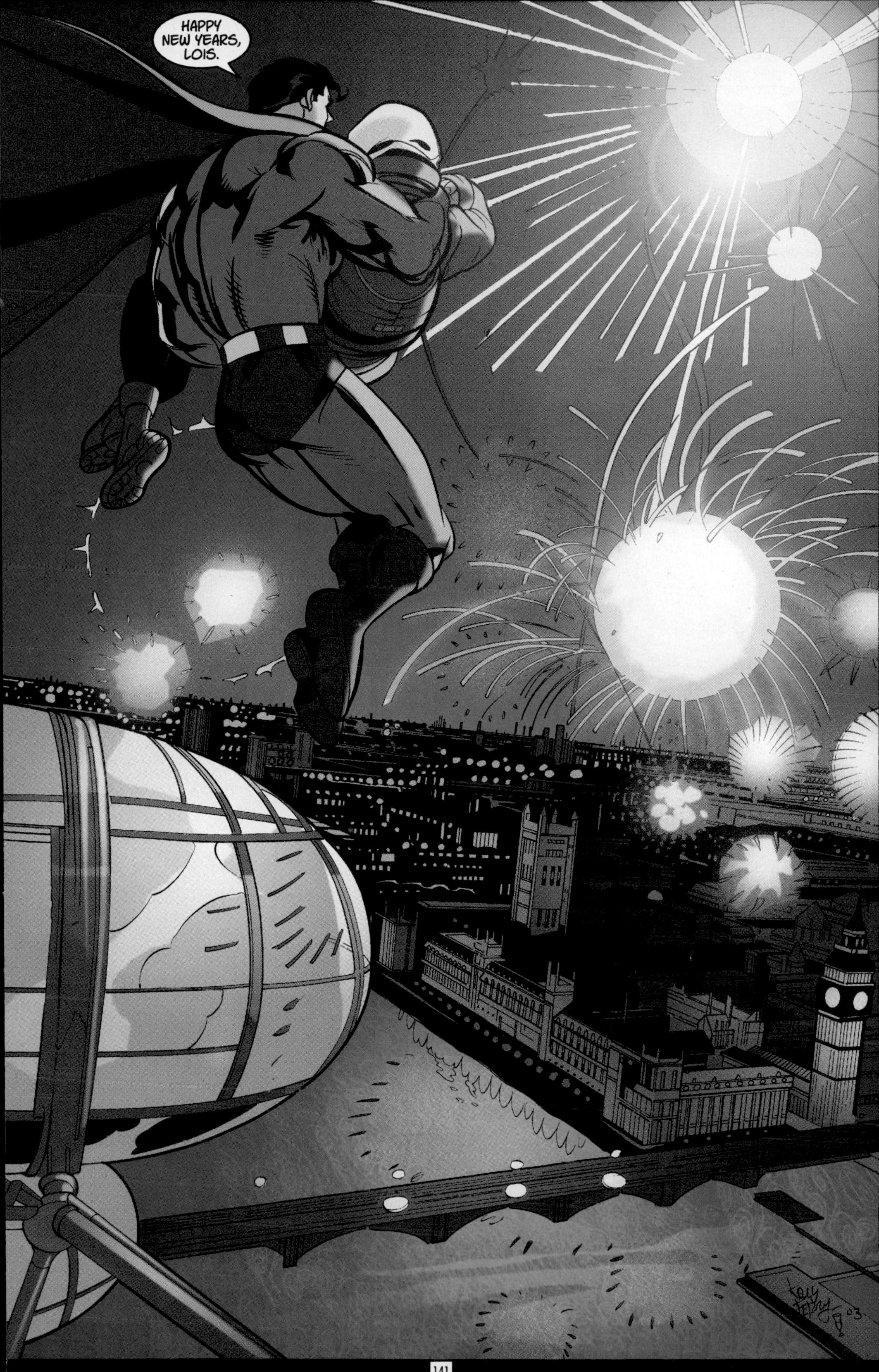
HAPPY NEW YEARS, LOIS.

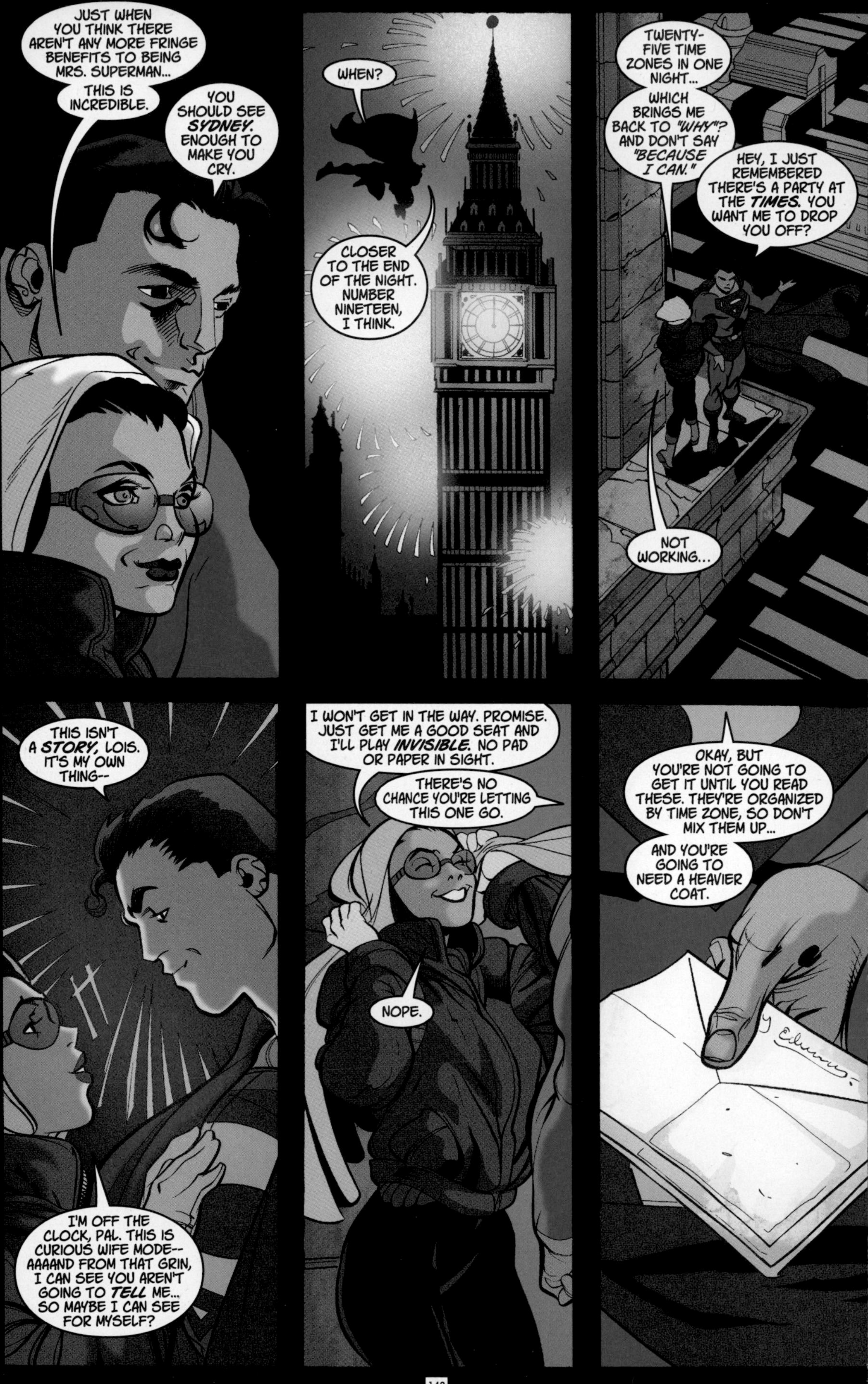
JUST WHEN YOU THINK THERE AREN'T ANY MORE FRINGE BENEFITS TO BEING MRS. SUPERMAN...
THIS IS INCREDIBLE.
YOU SHOULD SEE SYDNEY. ENOUGH TO MAKE YOU CRY.
WHEN?
CLOSER TO THE END OF THE NIGHT. NUMBER NINETEEN, I THINK.
TWENTY-FIVE TIME ZONES IN ONE NIGHT...
WHICH BRINGS ME BACK TO "WHY"? AND DON'T SAY "BECAUSE I CAN."
HEY, I JUST REMEMBERED THERE'S A PARTY AT THE TIMES. YOU WANT ME TO DROP YOU OFF?
NOT WORKING...
THIS ISN'T A STORY, LOIS. IT'S MY OWN THING--
I'M OFF THE CLOCK, PAL. THIS IS CURIOUS WIFE MODE-- AAAAND FROM THAT GRIN, I CAN SEE YOU AREN'T GOING TO TELL ME... SO MAYBE I CAN SEE FOR MYSELF?
I WON'T GET IN THE WAY. PROMISE. JUST GET ME A GOOD SEAT AND I'LL PLAY INVISIBLE. NO PAD OR PAPER IN SIGHT.
THERE'S NO CHANCE YOU'RE LETTING THIS ONE GO.
NOPE.
OKAY, BUT YOU'RE NOT GOING TO GET IT UNTIL YOU READ THESE. THEY'RE ORGANIZED BY TIME ZONE, SO DON'T MIX THEM UP...
AND YOU'RE GOING TO NEED A HEAVIER COAT.

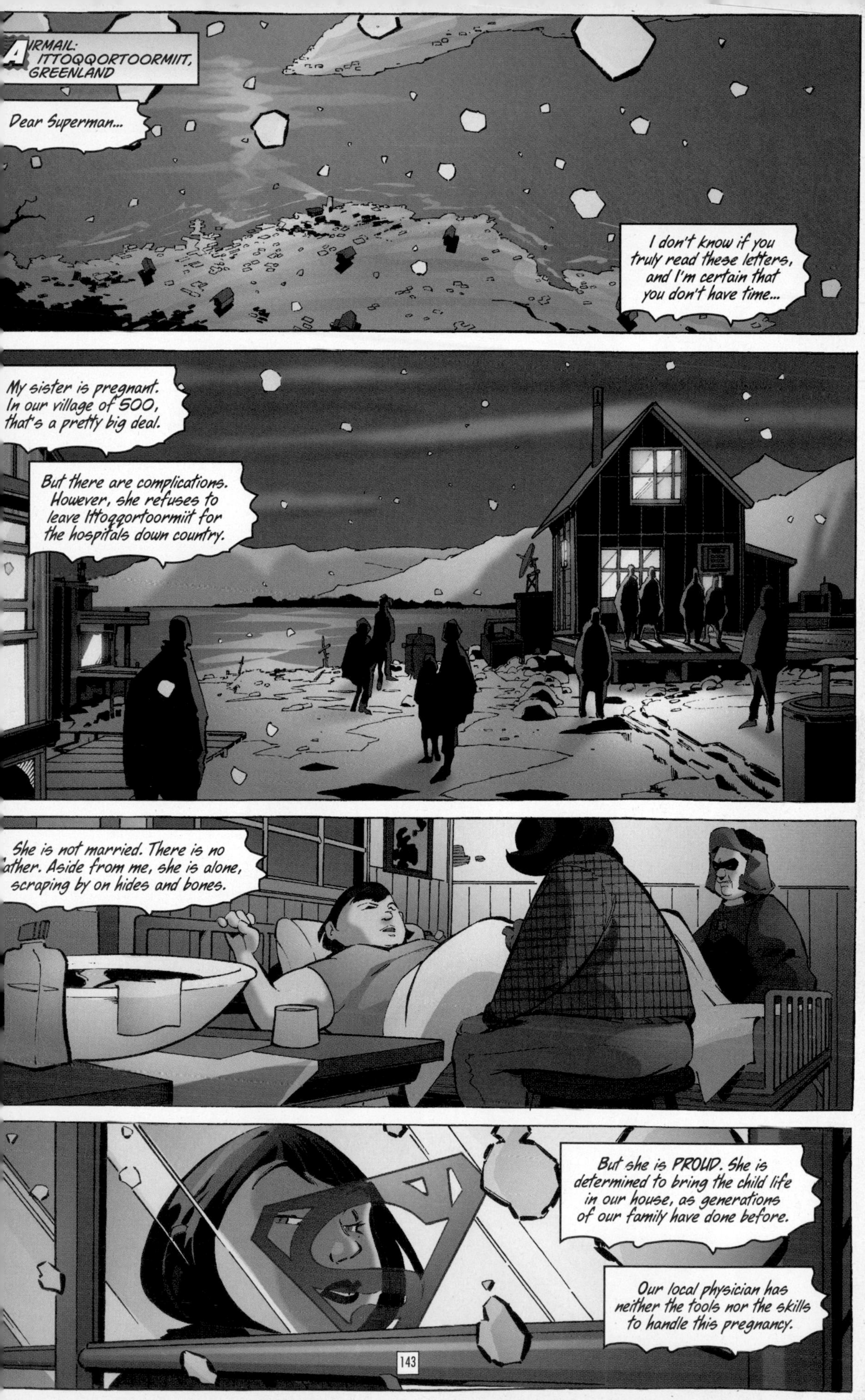
AIRMAIL: ITTOQQORTOORMIIT, GREENLAND
Dear Superman...
I don't know if you truly read these letters, and I'm certain that you don't have time...
My sister is pregnant. In our village of 500, that's a pretty big deal.
But there are complications. However, she refuses to leave Ittoqqortoormiit for the hospitals down country.
She is not married. There is no father. Aside from me, she is alone, scraping by on hides and bones.
But she is PROUD. She is determined to bring the child life in our house, as generations of our family have done before.
Our local physician has neither the tools nor the skills to handle this pregnancy.

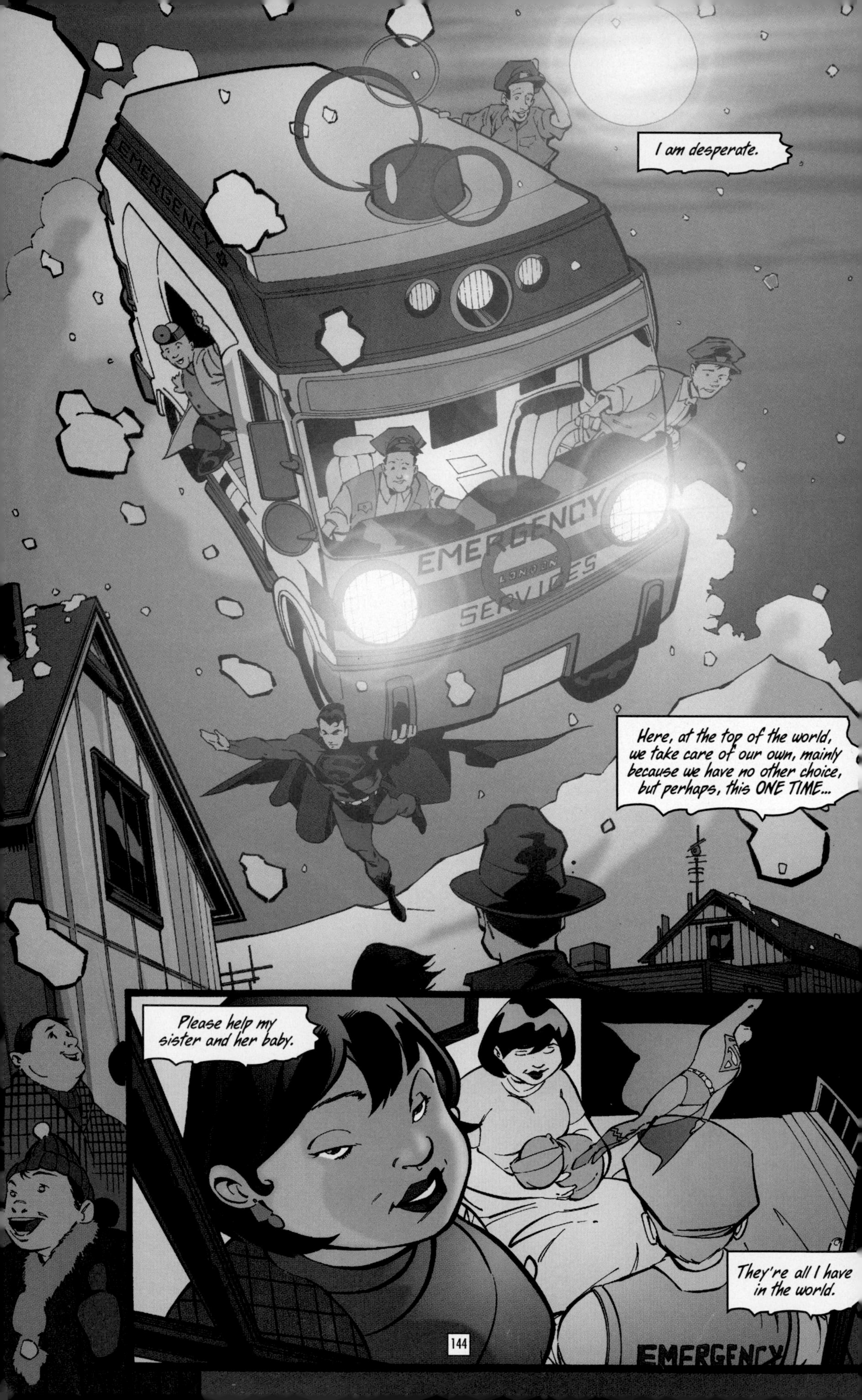
I am desperate.
EMERGENCY
EMERGENCY
LONDON
SERVICES
Here, at the top of the world, we take care of our own, mainly because we have no other choice, but perhaps, this ONE TIME...
Please help my sister and her baby.
They're all I have in the world.
EMERGENCY

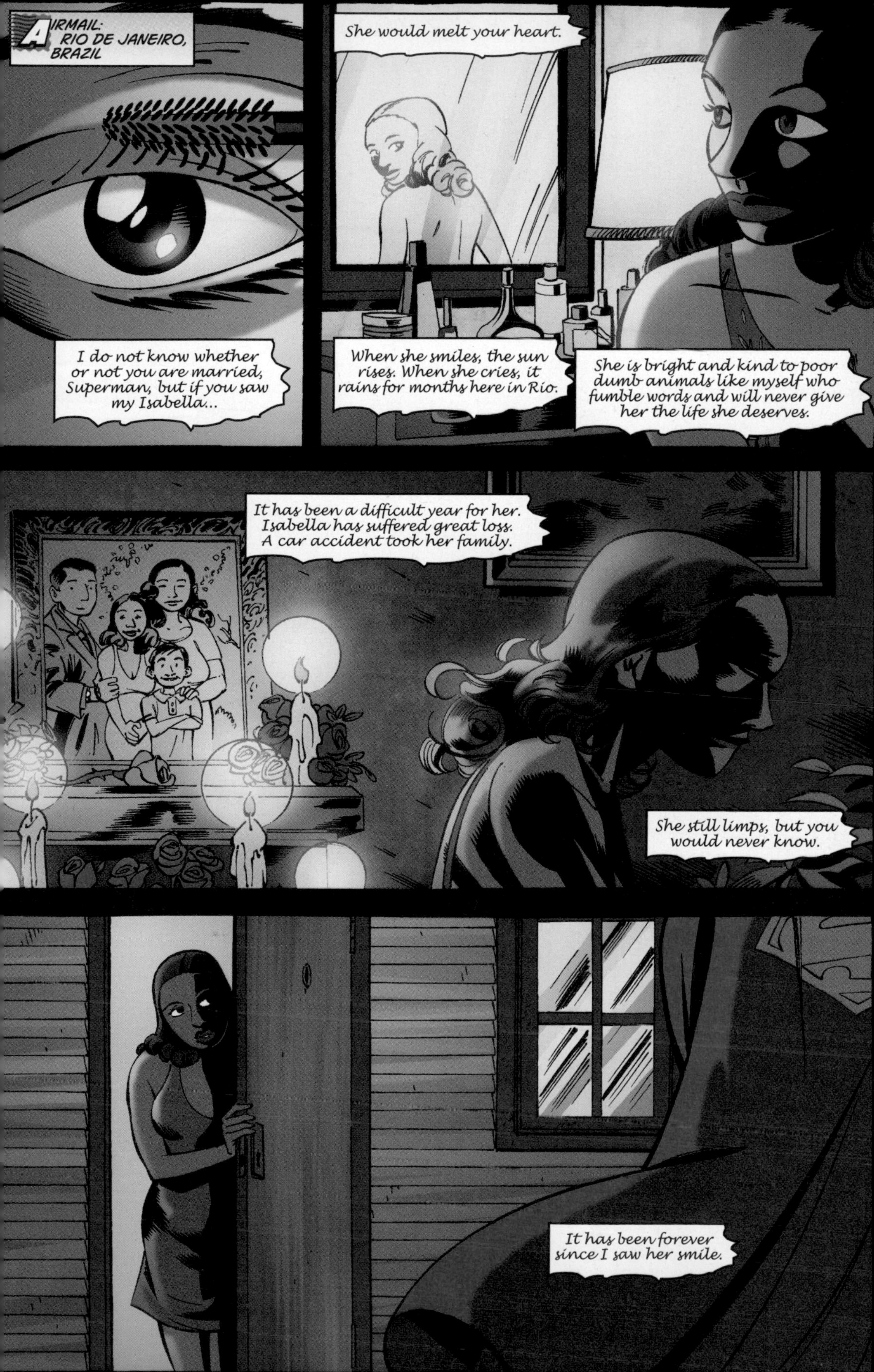
AIRMAIL: RIO DE JANEIRO, BRAZIL
I do not know whether or not you are married, Superman, but if you saw my Isabella...
She would melt your heart.
When she smiles, the sun rises. When she cries, it rains for months here in Rio.
She is bright and kind to poor dumb animals like myself who fumble words and will never give her the life she deserves.
It has been a difficult year for her. Isabella has suffered great loss. A car accident took her family.
She still limps, but you would never know.
It has been forever since I saw her smile.

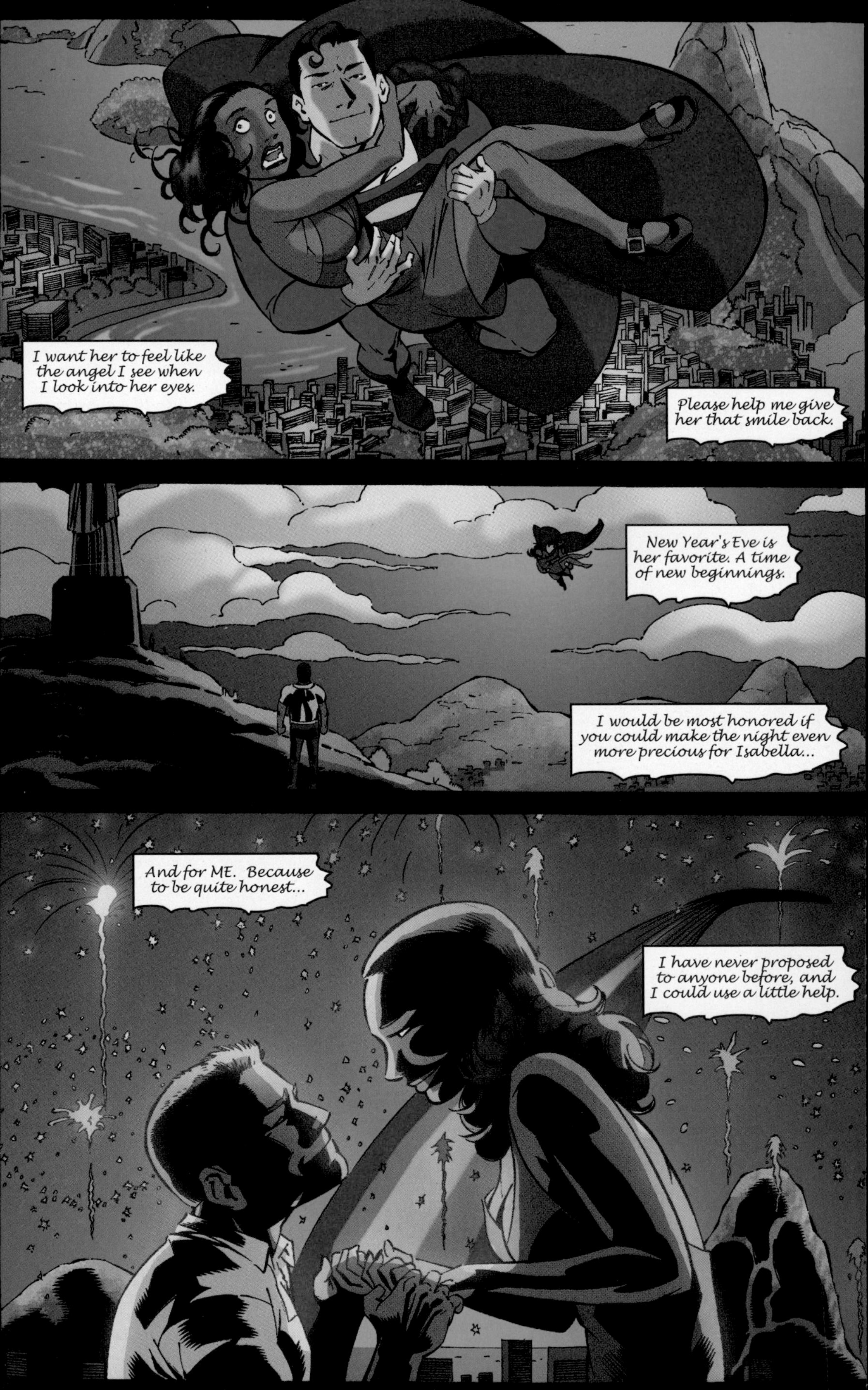
I want her to feel like the angel I see when I look into her eyes.
Please help me give her that smile back.
New Year's Eve is her favorite. A time of new beginnings.
I would be most honored if you could make the night even more precious for Isabella...
And for ME. Because to be quite honest...
I have never proposed to anyone before, and I could use a little help.

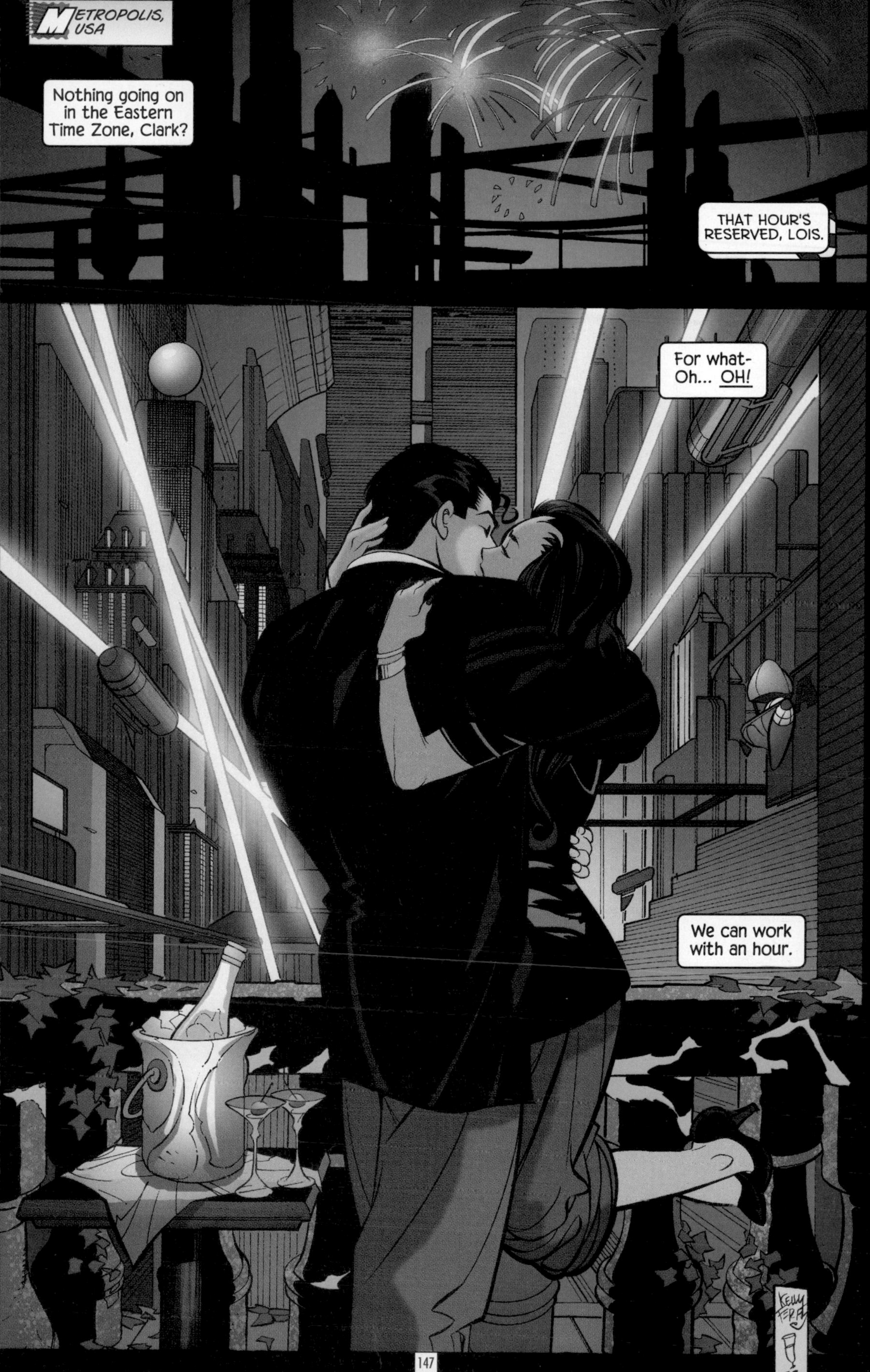
METROPOLIS, USA
Nothing going on in the Eastern Time Zone, Clark?
THAT HOUR'S RESERVED, LOIS.
For what-Oh... OH!
We can work with an hour.

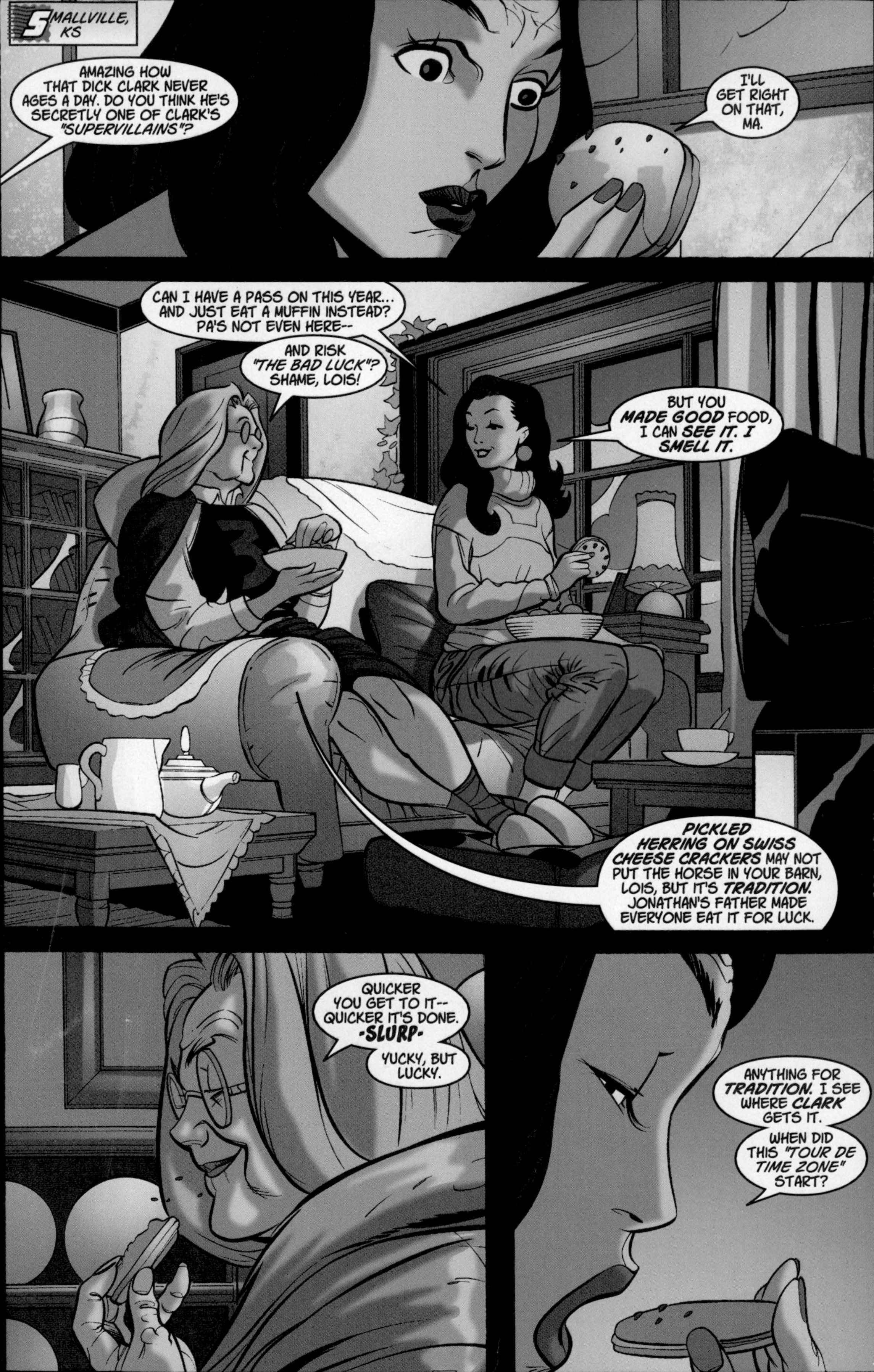
SMALLVILLE, KS
AMAZING HOW THAT DICK CLARK NEVER AGES A DAY. DO YOU THINK HE'S SECRETLY ONE OF CLARK'S "SUPERVILLAINS"?
I'LL GET RIGHT ON THAT, MA.
CAN I HAVE A PASS ON THIS YEAR... AND JUST EAT A MUFFIN INSTEAD? PA'S NOT EVEN HERE--
AND RISK "THE BAD LUCK"? SHAME, LOIS!
BUT YOU MADE GOOD FOOD, I CAN SEE IT. I SMELL IT.
PICKLED HERRING ON SWISS CHEESE CRACKERS MAY NOT PUT THE HORSE IN YOUR BARN, LOIS, BUT IT'S TRADITION. JONATHAN'S FATHER MADE EVERYONE EAT IT FOR LUCK.
QUICKER YOU GET TO IT-- QUICKER IT'S DONE.
-SLURP-
YUCKY, BUT LUCKY.
ANYTHING FOR TRADITION. I SEE WHERE CLARK GETS IT.
WHEN DID THIS "TOUR DE TIME ZONE" START?

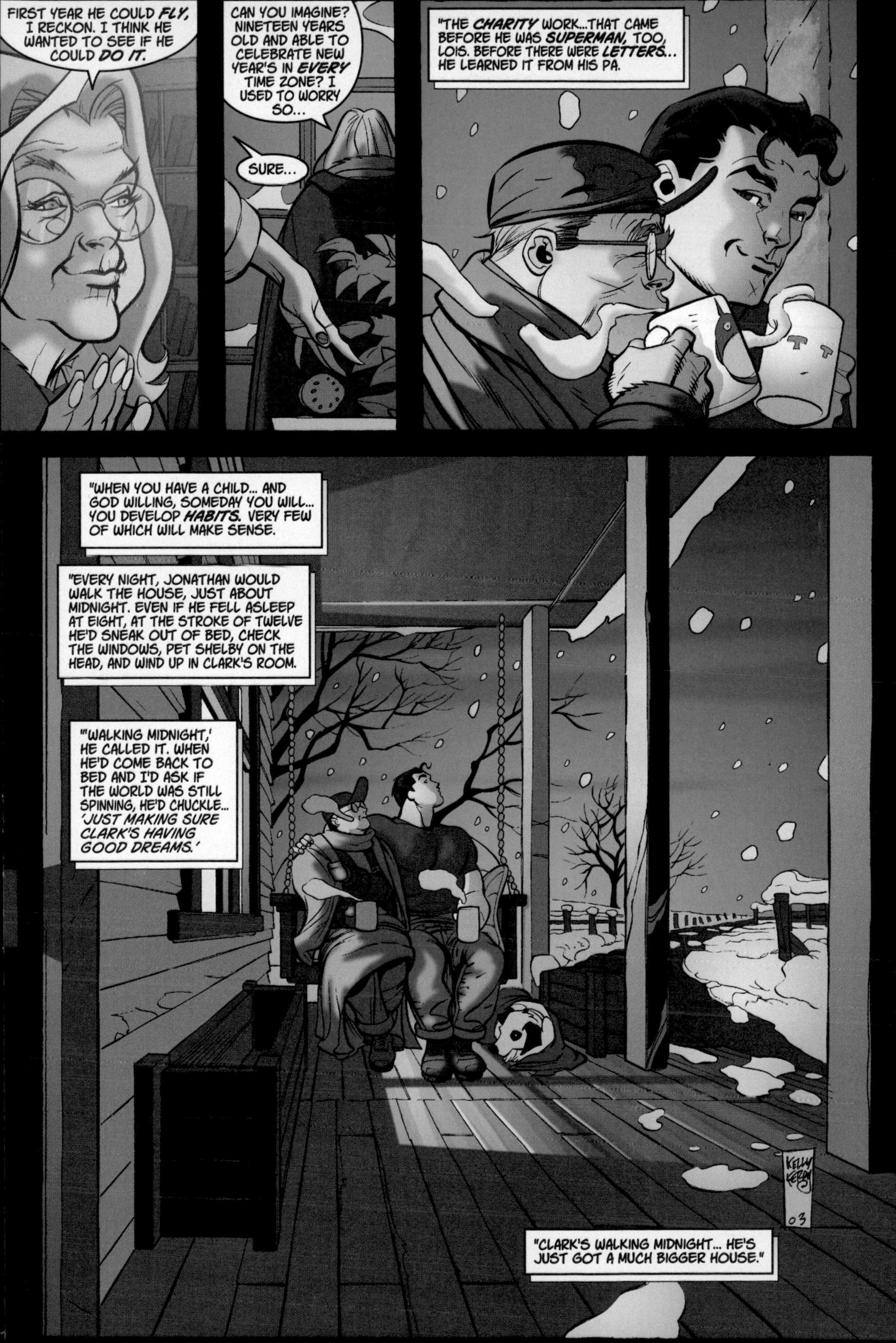
FIRST YEAR HE COULD FLY, I RECKON. I THINK HE WANTED TO SEE IF HE COULD DO IT.
CAN YOU IMAGINE? NINETEEN YEARS OLD AND ABLE TO CELEBRATE NEW YEAR'S IN EVERY TIME ZONE? I USED TO WORRY SO...
SURE...
"THE CHARITY WORK...THAT CAME BEFORE HE WAS SUPERMAN, TOO, LOIS. BEFORE THERE WERE LETTERS... HE LEARNED IT FROM HIS PA.
"WHEN YOU HAVE A CHILD... AND GOD WILLING, SOMEDAY YOU WILL... YOU DEVELOP HABITS. VERY FEW OF WHICH WILL MAKE SENSE.
"EVERY NIGHT, JONATHAN WOULD WALK THE HOUSE, JUST ABOUT MIDNIGHT. EVEN IF HE FELL ASLEEP AT EIGHT, AT THE STROKE OF TWELVE HE'D SNEAK OUT OF BED, CHECK THE WINDOWS, PET SHELBY ON THE HEAD, AND WIND UP IN CLARK'S ROOM.
"'WALKING MIDNIGHT,' HE CALLED IT. WHEN HE'D COME BACK TO BED AND I'D ASK IF THE WORLD WAS STILL SPINNING, HE'D CHUCKLE... 'JUST MAKING SURE CLARK'S HAVING GOOD DREAMS.'
KELLY KERSCHL 03
"CLARK'S WALKING MIDNIGHT... HE'S JUST GOT A MUCH BIGGER HOUSE."

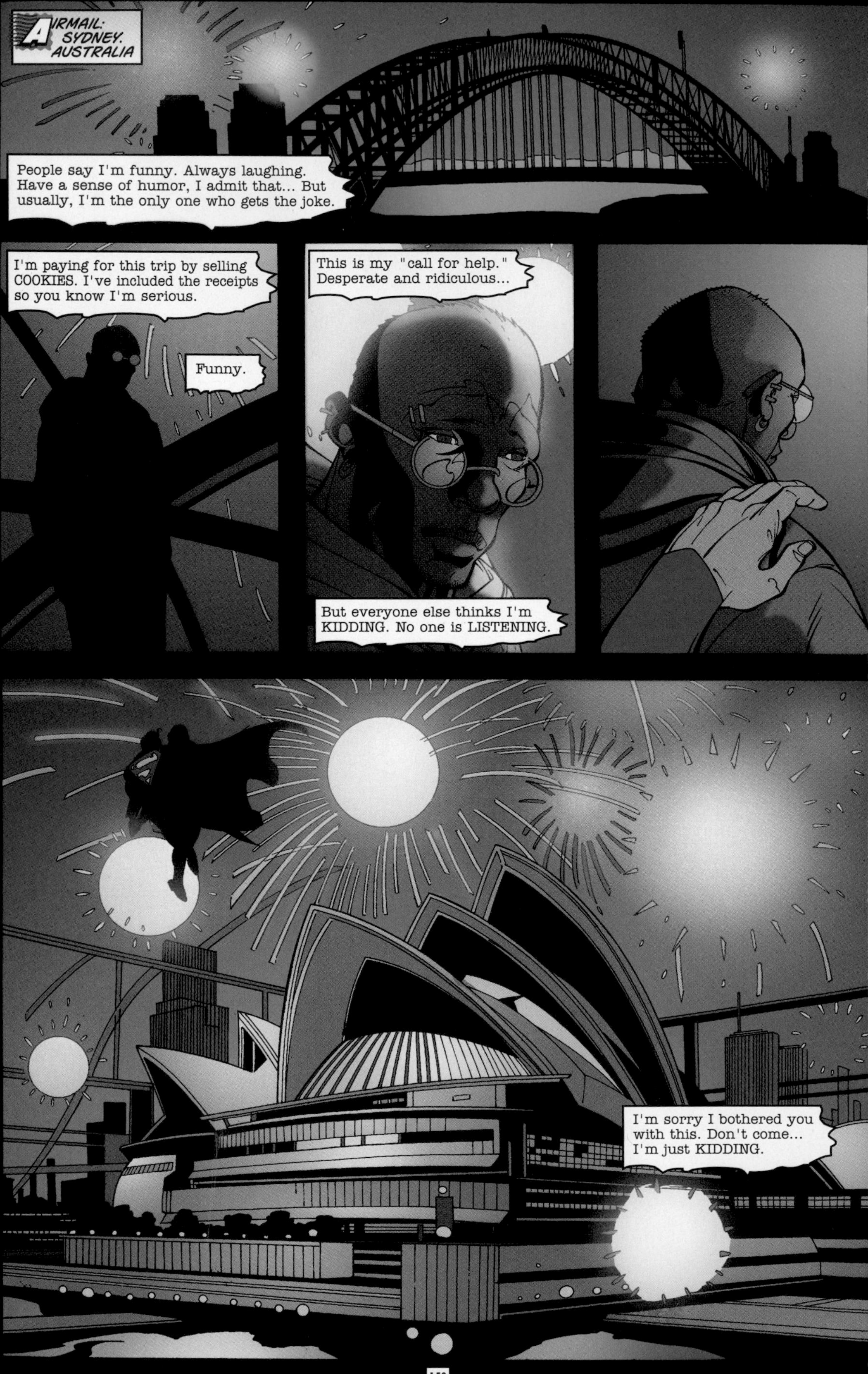
AIRMAIL: SYDNEY. AUSTRALIA
People say I'm funny. Always laughing. Have a sense of humor, I admit that... But usually, I'm the only one who gets the joke.
I'm paying for this trip by selling COOKIES. I've included the receipts so you know I'm serious.
Funny.
This is my "call for help." Desperate and ridiculous...
But everyone else thinks I'm KIDDING. No one is LISTENING.
I'm sorry I bothered you with this. Don't come... I'm just KIDDING.

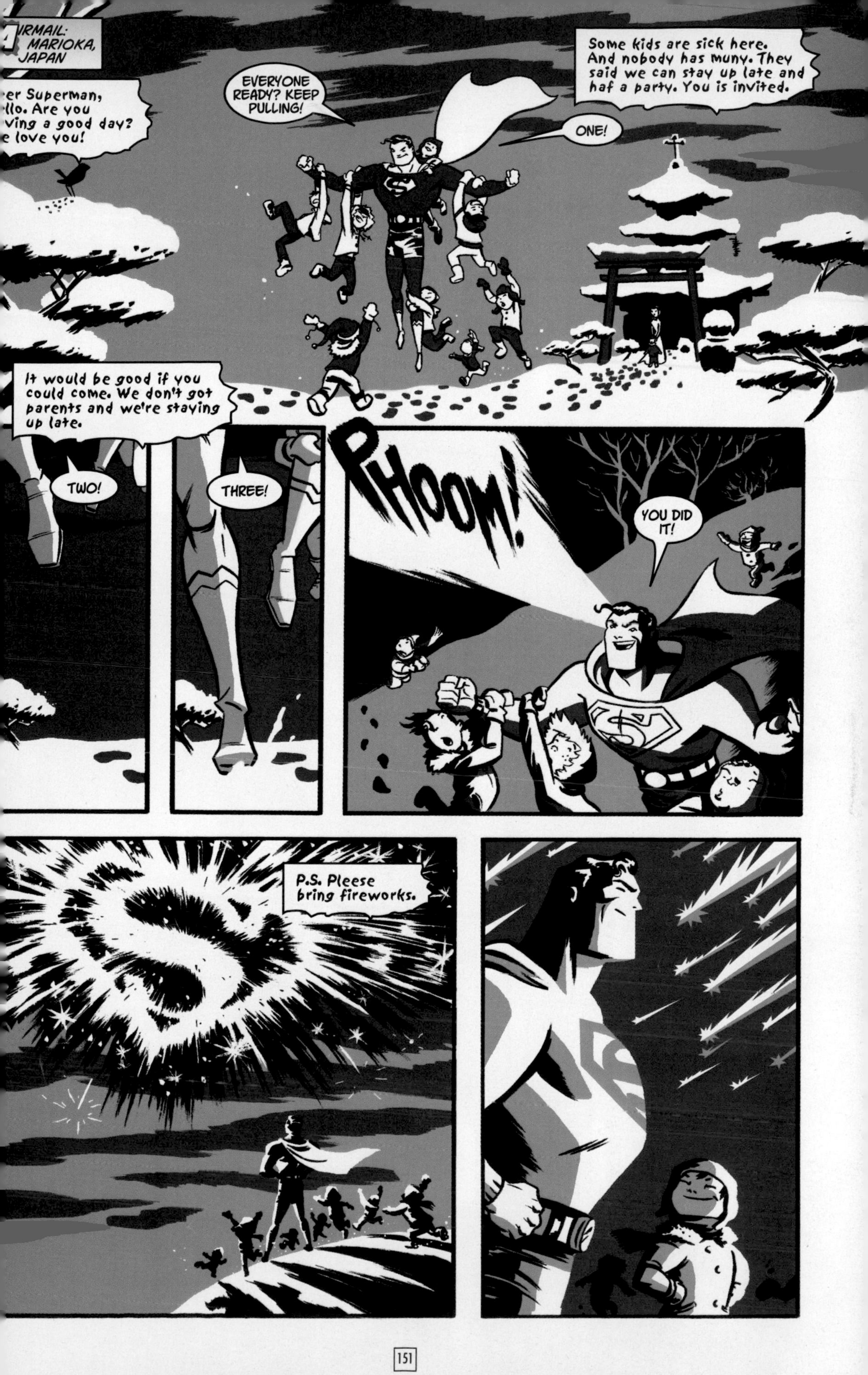
IRMAIL: MARIOKA, JAPAN
er Superman, ello. Are you ving a good day? e love you!
EVERYONE READY? KEEP PULLING!
Some kids are sick here. And nobody has muny. They said we can stay up late and haf a party. You is invited.
ONE!
It would be good if you could come. We don't got parents and we're staying up late.
TWO!
THREE!
PHOOM!
YOU DID IT!
P.S. Pleese bring fireworks.

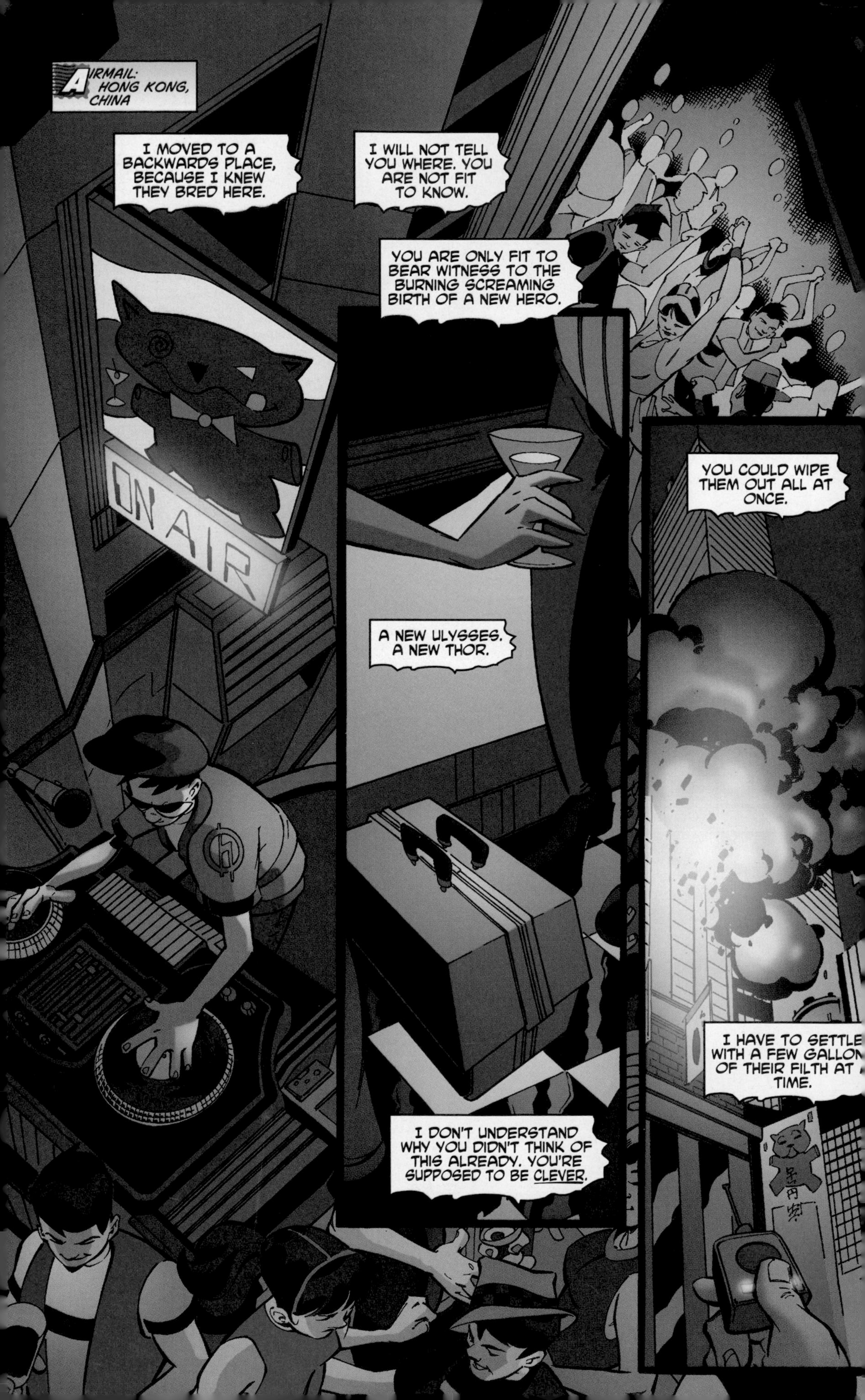
AIRMAIL: HONG KONG, CHINA
I MOVED TO A BACKWARDS PLACE, BECAUSE I KNEW THEY BRED HERE.
I WILL NOT TELL YOU WHERE. YOU ARE NOT FIT TO KNOW.
YOU ARE ONLY FIT TO BEAR WITNESS TO THE BURNING SCREAMING BIRTH OF A NEW HERO.
ON AIR
A NEW ULYSSES. A NEW THOR.
I DON'T UNDERSTAND WHY YOU DIDN'T THINK OF THIS ALREADY. YOU'RE SUPPOSED TO BE CLEVER.
YOU COULD WIPE THEM OUT ALL AT ONCE.
I HAVE TO SETTLE WITH A FEW GALLON OF THEIR FILTH AT TIME.

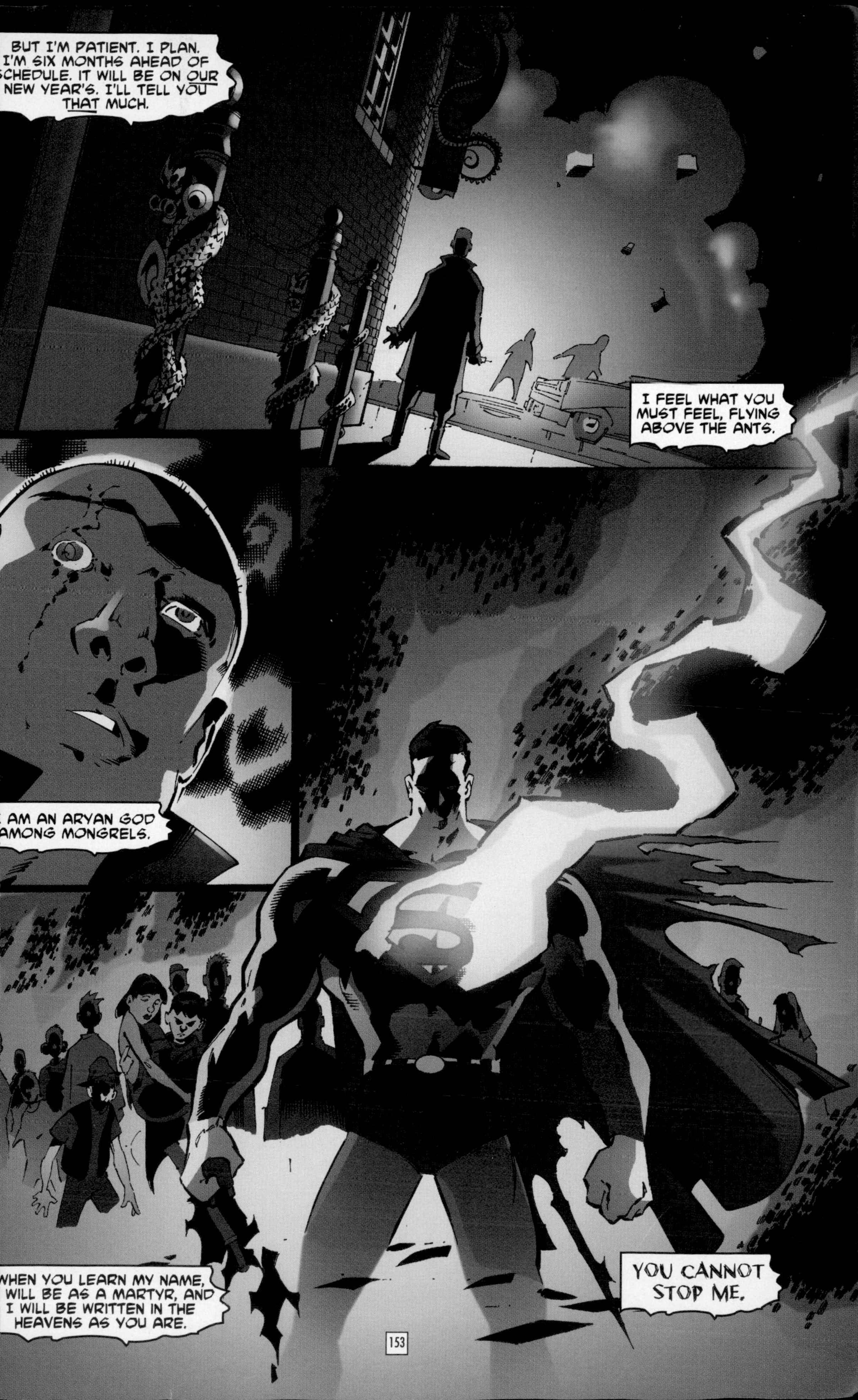

BUT I'M PATIENT. I PLAN. I'M SIX MONTHS AHEAD OF SCHEDULE. IT WILL BE ON OUR NEW YEAR'S. I'LL TELL YOU THAT MUCH.
I FEEL WHAT YOU MUST FEEL, FLYING ABOVE THE ANTS.
AM AN ARYAN GOD AMONG MONGRELS.
WHEN YOU LEARN MY NAME, WILL BE AS A MARTYR, AND I WILL BE WRITTEN IN THE HEAVENS AS YOU ARE.
YOU CANNOT STOP ME.

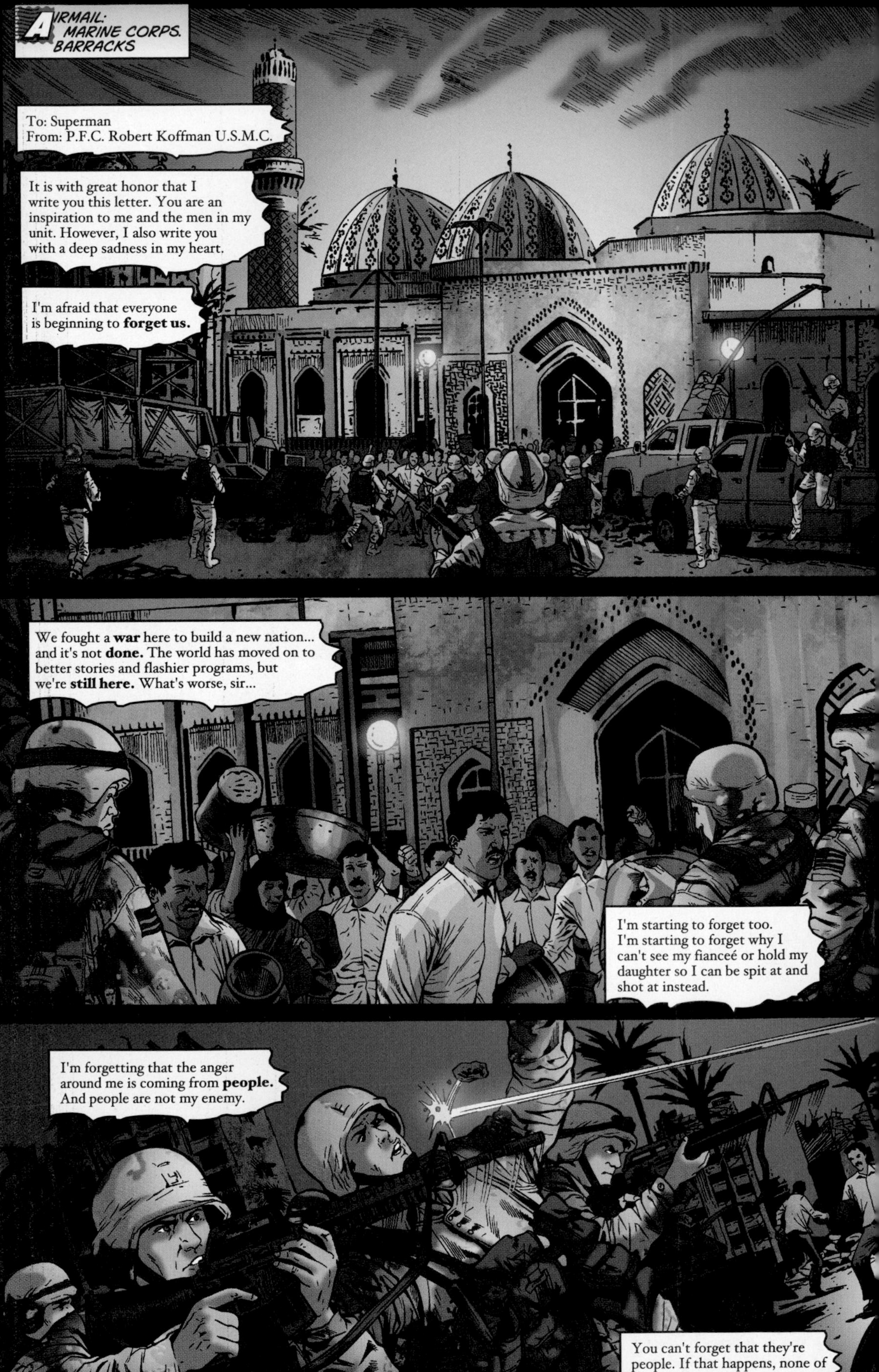
AIRMAIL: MARINE CORPS. BARRACKS
To: Superman
From: P.F.C. Robert Koffman U.S.M.C.
It is with great honor that I write you this letter. You are an inspiration to me and the men in my unit. However, I also write you with a deep sadness in my heart.
I'm afraid that everyone is beginning to **forget us.**
We fought a **war** here to build a new nation... and it's not **done.** The world has moved on to better stories and flashier programs, but we're **still here.** What's worse, sir...
I'm starting to forget too. I'm starting to forget why I can't see my fianceé or hold my daughter so I can be spit at and shot at instead.
I'm forgetting that the anger around me is coming from **people.** And people are not my enemy.
You can't forget that they're people. If that happens, none of this makes sense.

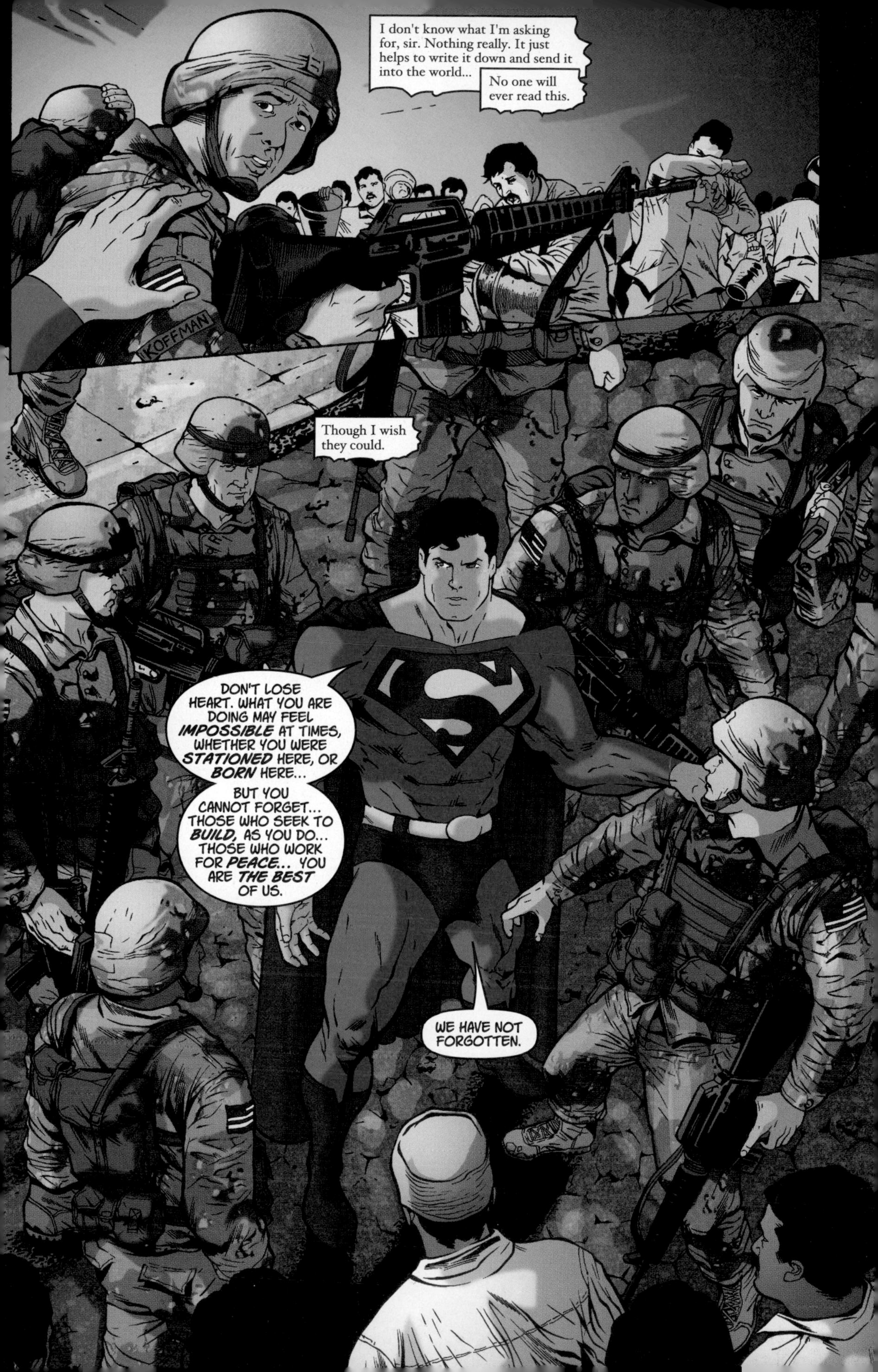
I don't know what I'm asking for, sir. Nothing really. It just helps to write it down and send it into the world...
No one will ever read this.
KOFFMAN
Though I wish they could.
DON'T LOSE HEART. WHAT YOU ARE DOING MAY FEEL *IMPOSSIBLE* AT TIMES, WHETHER YOU WERE *STATIONED* HERE, OR *BORN* HERE...
BUT YOU CANNOT FORGET... THOSE WHO SEEK TO *BUILD,* AS YOU DO... THOSE WHO WORK FOR *PEACE...* YOU ARE *THE BEST* OF US.
WE HAVE NOT FORGOTTEN.

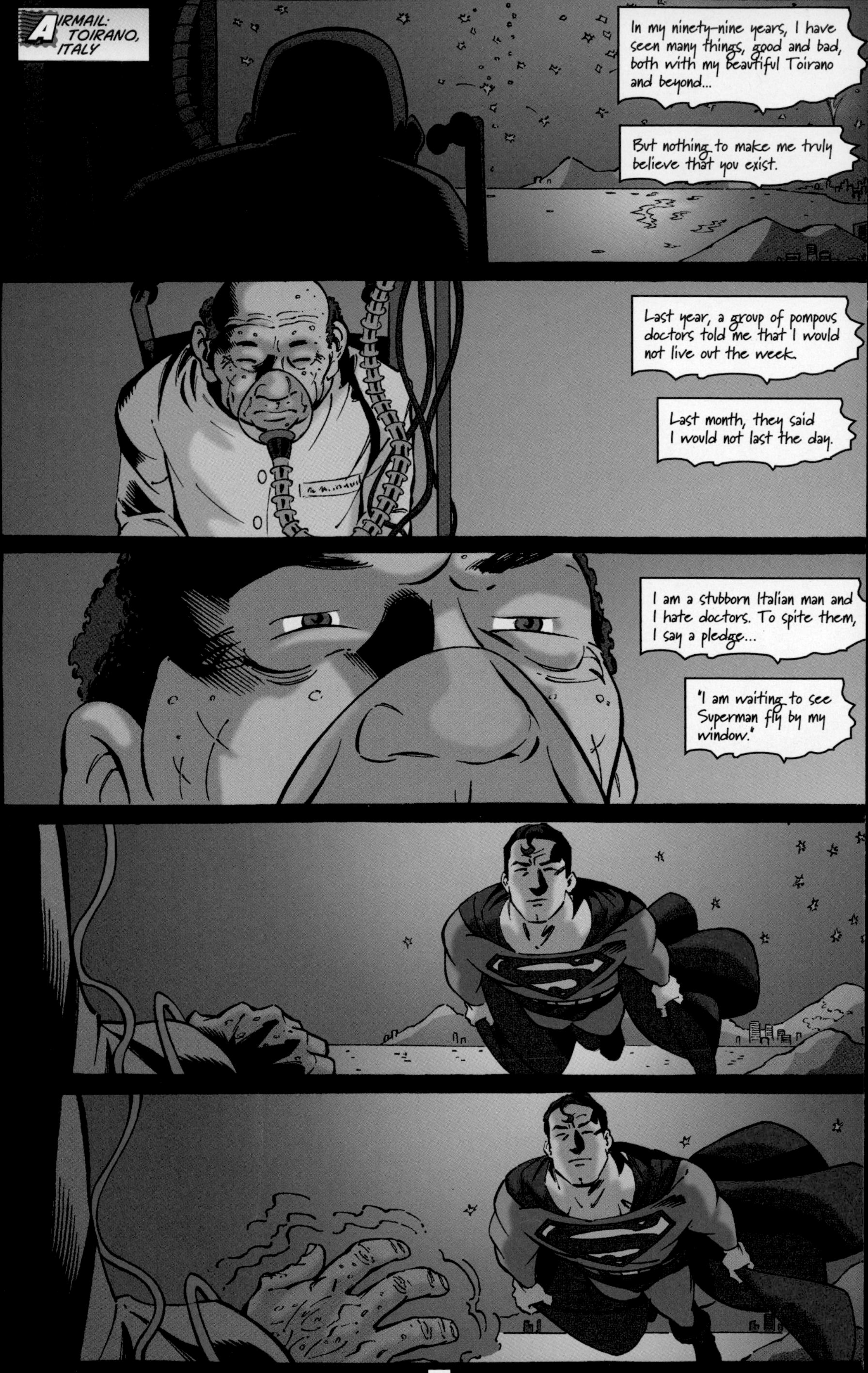
AIRMAIL: TOIRANO, ITALY
In my ninety-nine years, I have seen many things, good and bad, both with my beautiful Toirano and beyond...
But nothing to make me truly believe that you exist.
Last year, a group of pompous doctors told me that I would not live out the week.
Last month, they said I would not last the day.
I am a stubborn Italian man and I hate doctors. To spite them, I say a pledge...
"I am waiting to see Superman fly by my window."

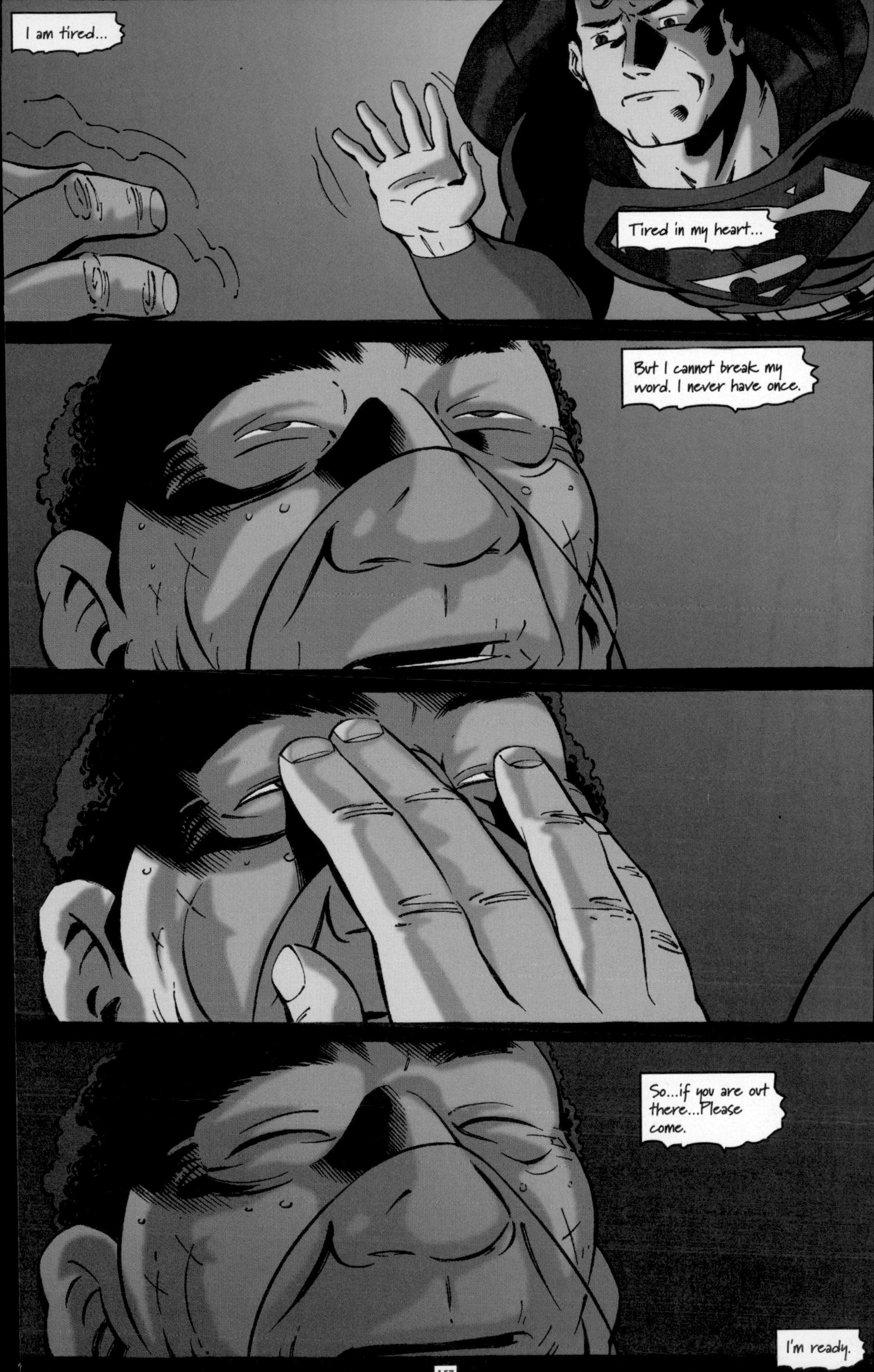
I am tired...
Tired in my heart...
But I cannot break my word. I never have once.
So...if you are out there...Please come.
I'm ready.

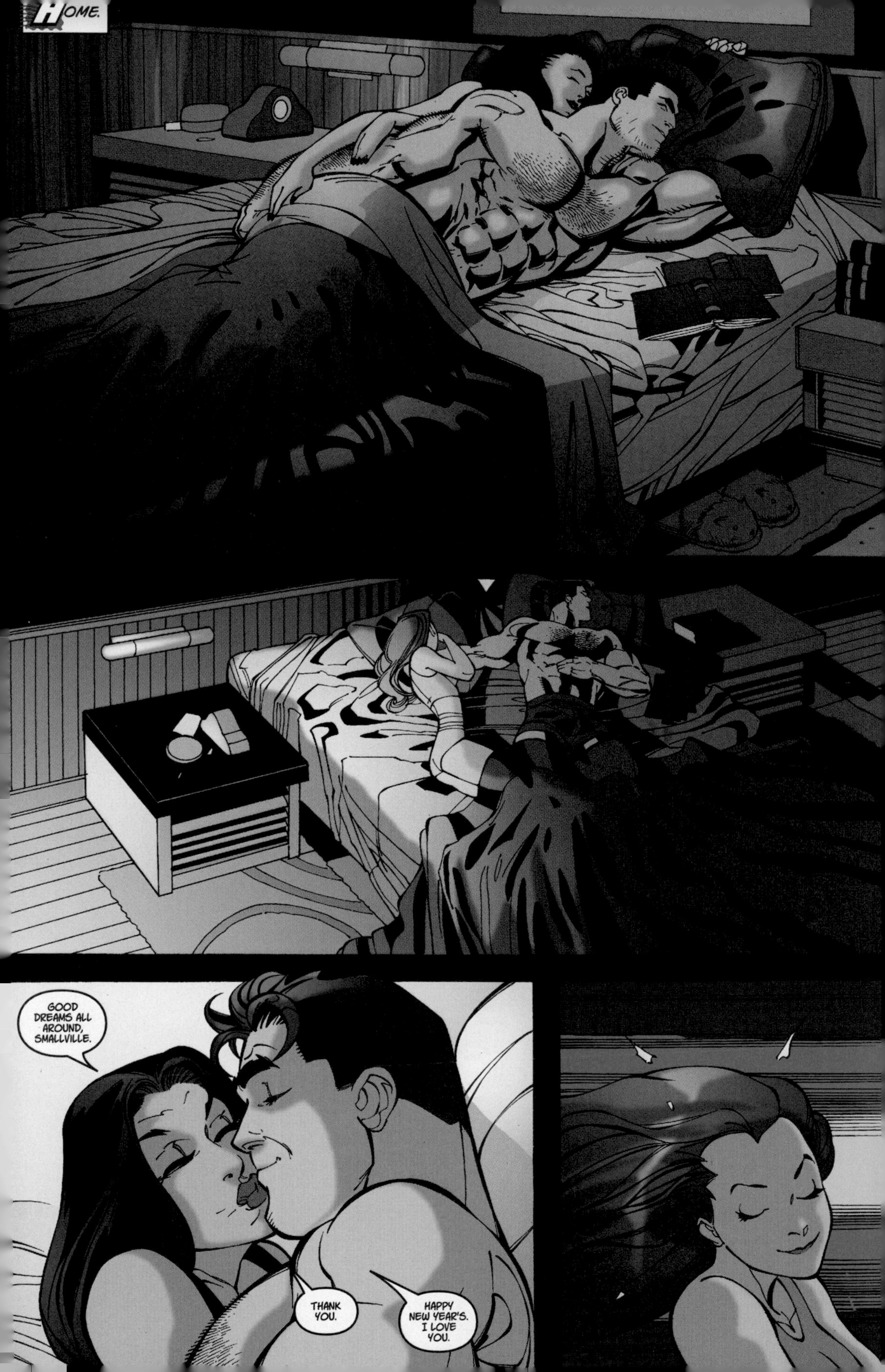
HOME.
GOOD DREAMS ALL AROUND, SMALLVILLE.
THANK YOU.
HAPPY NEW YEAR'S. I LOVE YOU.

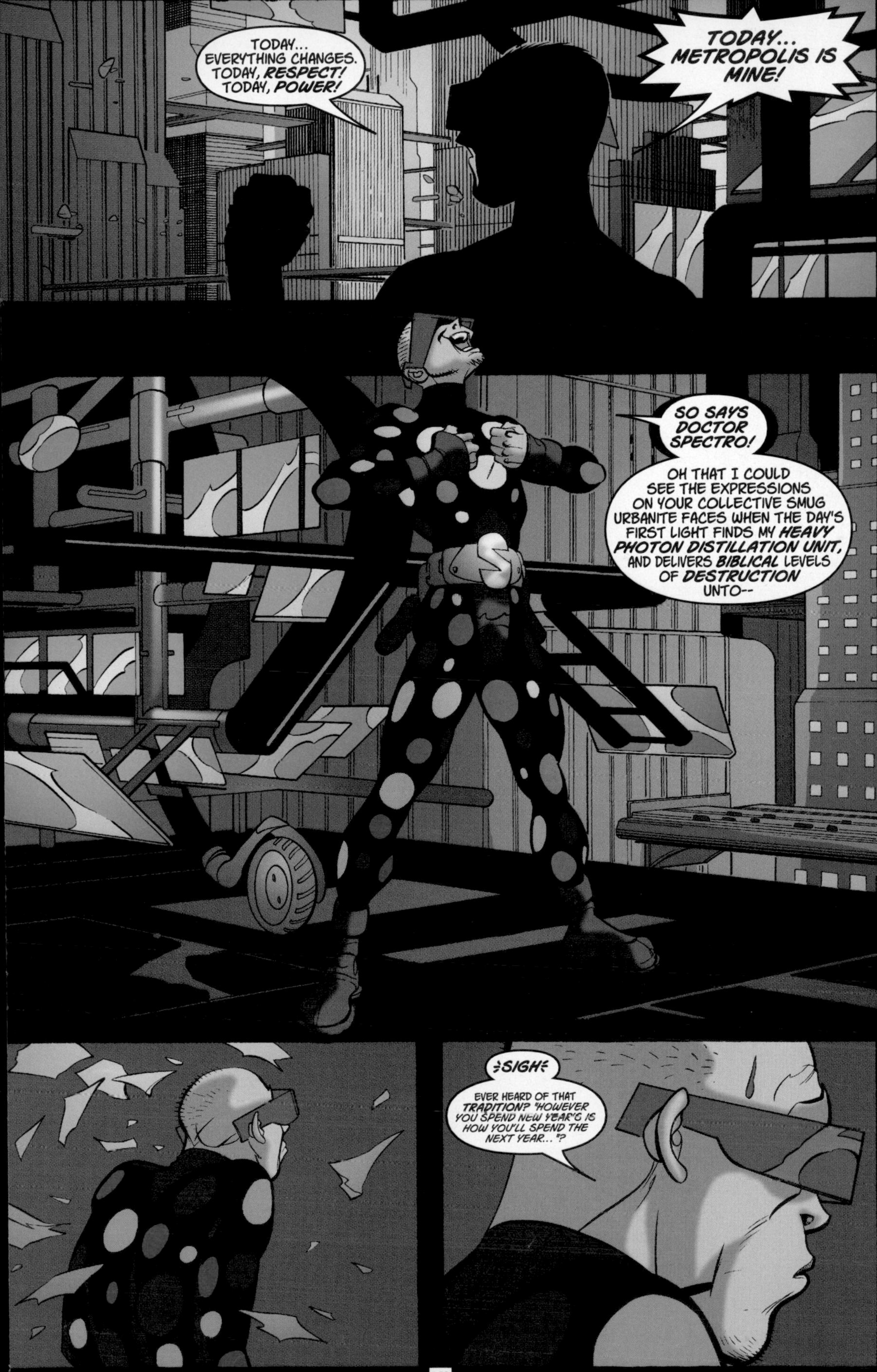

TODAY... EVERYTHING CHANGES. TODAY, RESPECT! TODAY, POWER!
TODAY... METROPOLIS IS MINE!
SO SAYS DOCTOR SPECTRO!
OH THAT I COULD SEE THE EXPRESSIONS ON YOUR COLLECTIVE SMUG URBANITE FACES WHEN THE DAY'S FIRST LIGHT FINDS MY HEAVY PHOTON DISTILLATION UNIT, AND DELIVERS BIBLICAL LEVELS OF DESTRUCTION UNTO--
SIGH
EVER HEARD OF THAT TRADITION? "HOWEVER YOU SPEND NEW YEAR'S IS HOW YOU'LL SPEND THE NEXT YEAR..."?

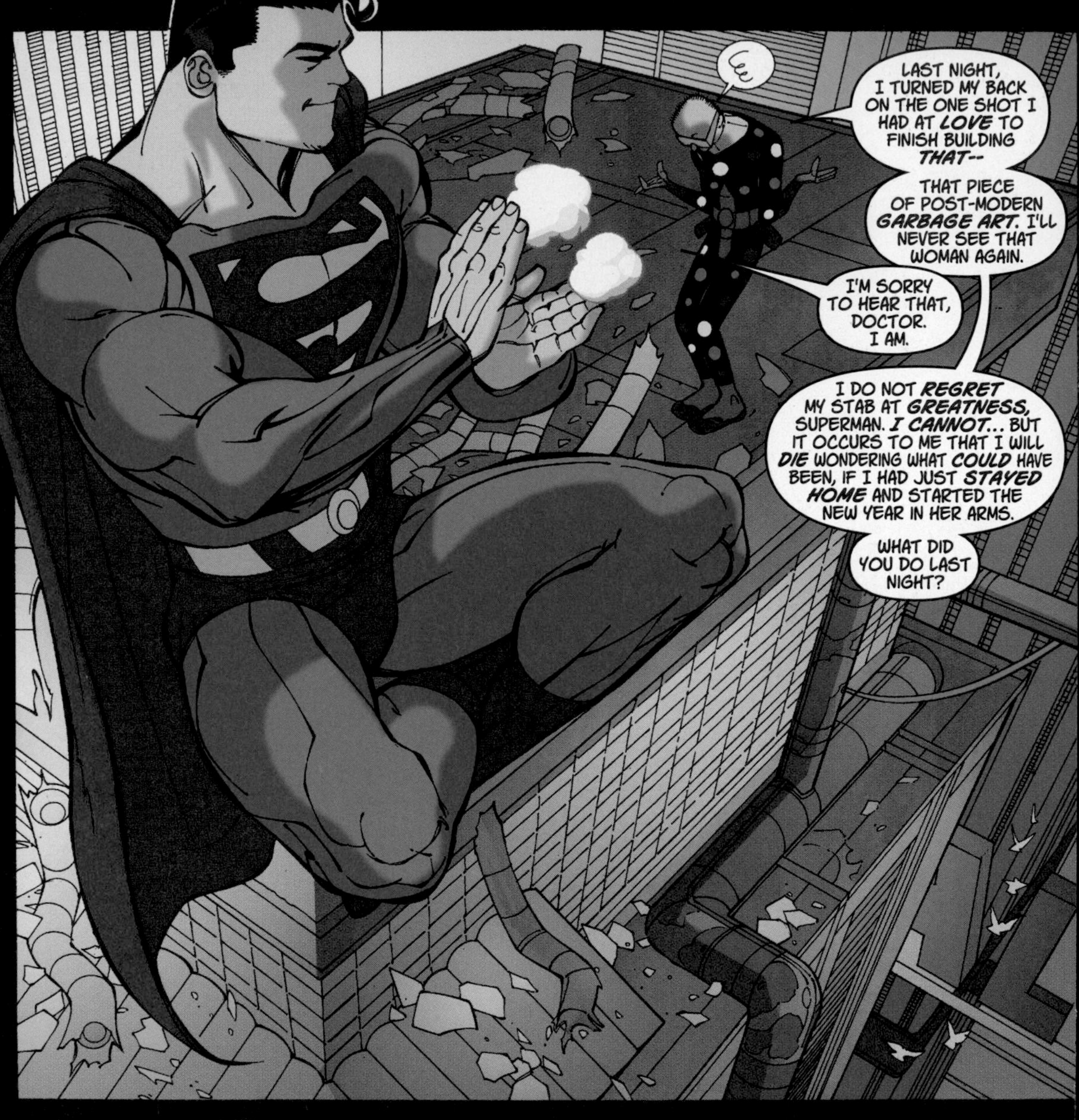
LAST NIGHT, I TURNED MY BACK ON THE ONE SHOT I HAD AT LOVE TO FINISH BUILDING THAT--
THAT PIECE OF POST-MODERN GARBAGE ART. I'LL NEVER SEE THAT WOMAN AGAIN.
I'M SORRY TO HEAR THAT, DOCTOR. I AM.
I DO NOT REGRET MY STAB AT GREATNESS, SUPERMAN. I CANNOT... BUT IT OCCURS TO ME THAT I WILL DIE WONDERING WHAT COULD HAVE BEEN, IF I HAD JUST STAYED HOME AND STARTED THE NEW YEAR IN HER ARMS.
WHAT DID YOU DO LAST NIGHT?

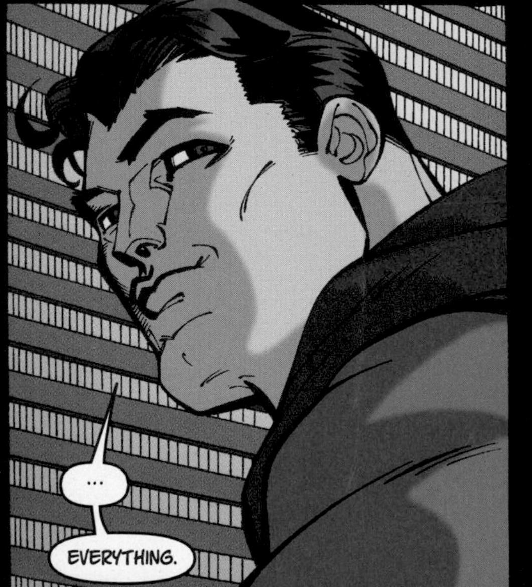
...
EVERYTHING.

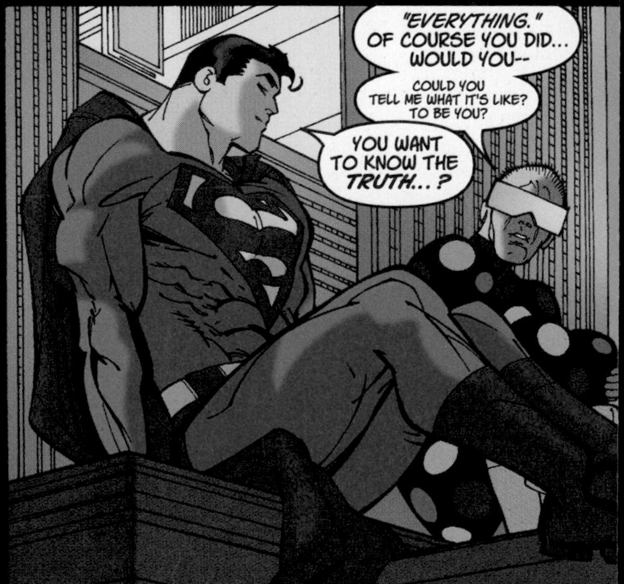
"EVERYTHING." OF COURSE YOU DID... WOULD YOU--
COULD YOU TELL ME WHAT IT'S LIKE? TO BE YOU?
YOU WANT TO KNOW THE TRUTH...?

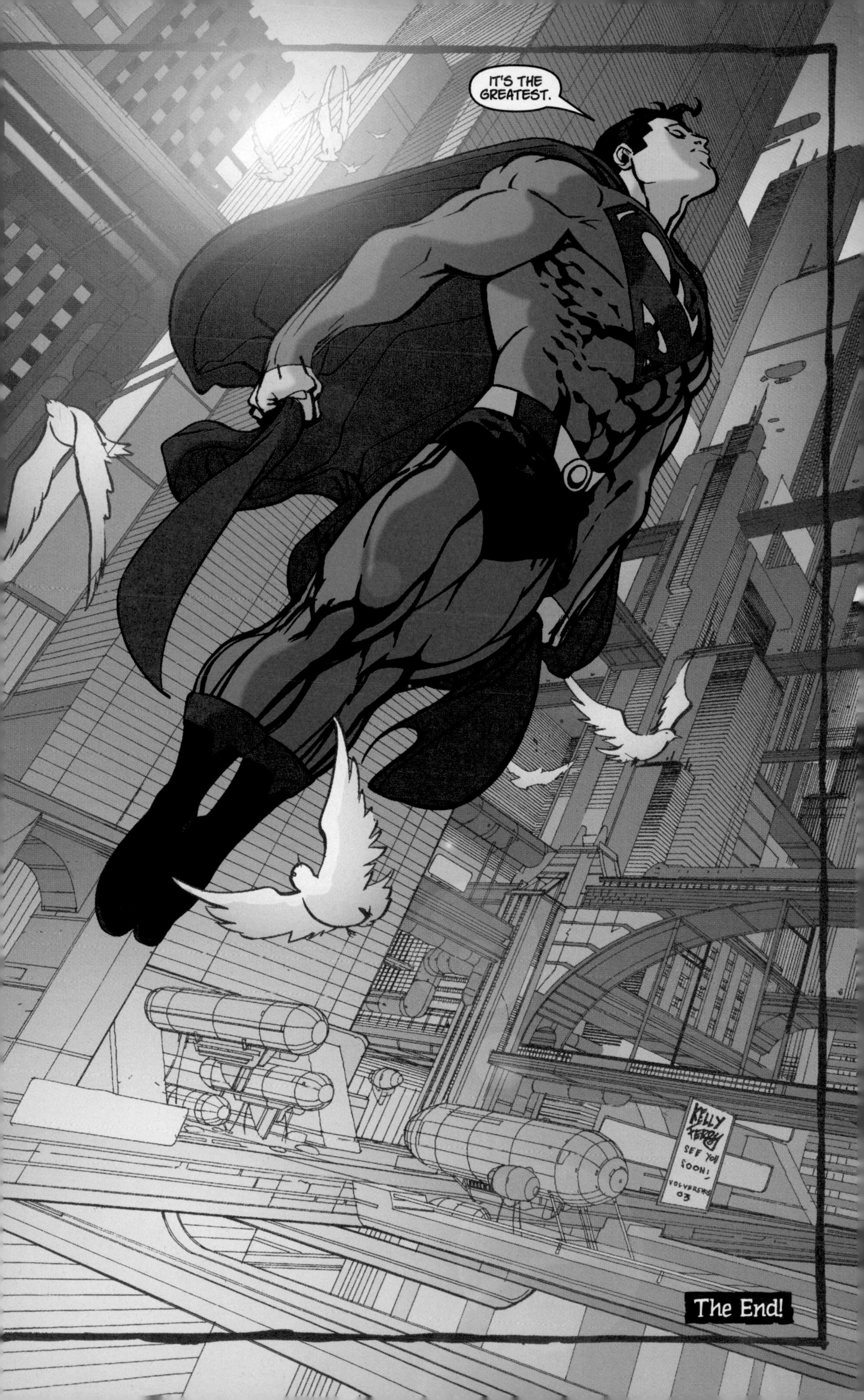
IT'S THE GREATEST.
KELLY FERRY
SEE YOU SOON!
The End!

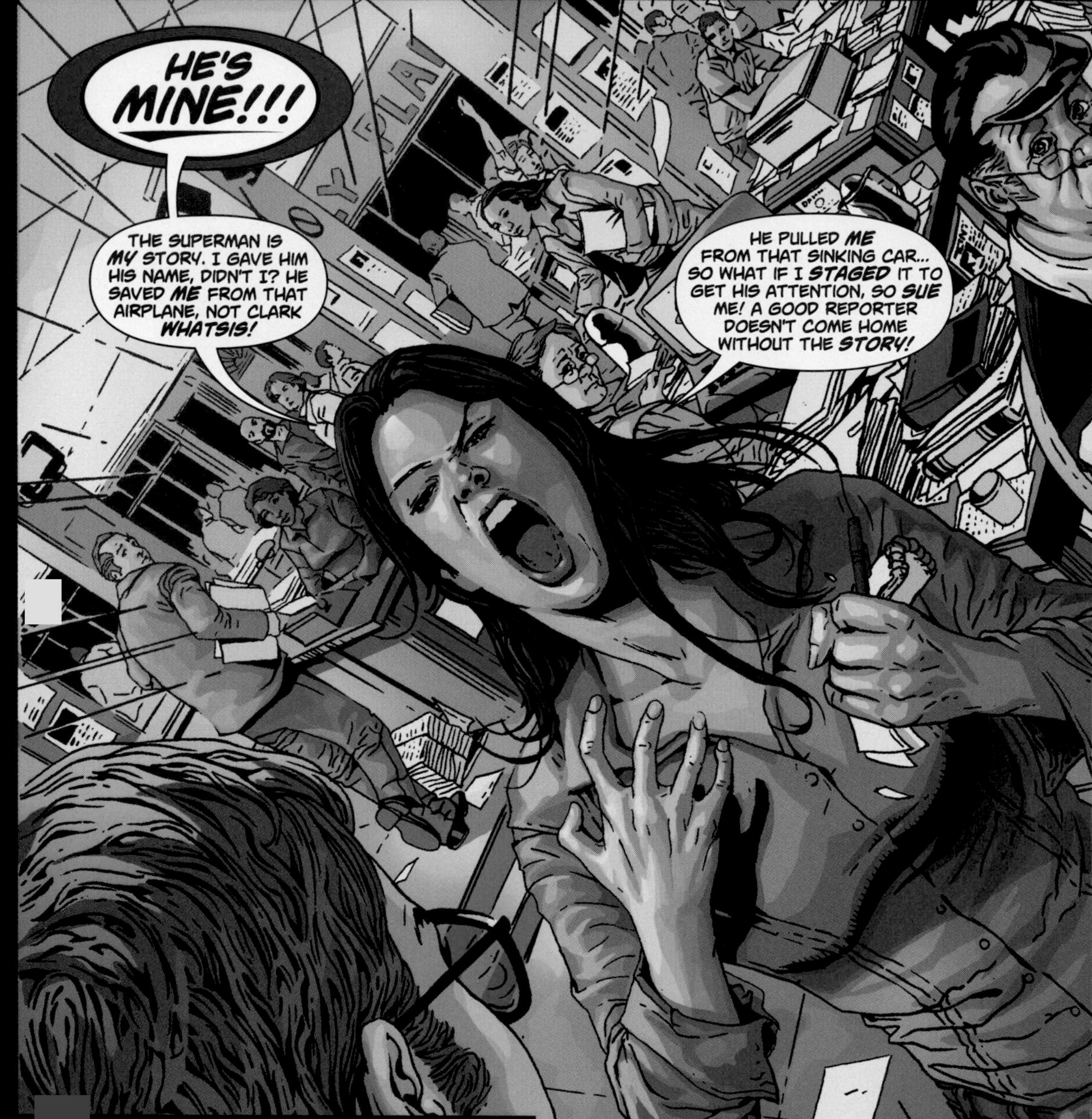
HE'S MINE!!!
THE SUPERMAN IS MY STORY. I GAVE HIM HIS NAME, DIDN'T I? HE SAVED ME FROM THAT AIRPLANE, NOT CLARK WHATSIS!
HE PULLED ME FROM THAT SINKING CAR... SO WHAT IF I STAGED IT TO GET HIS ATTENTION, SO SUE ME! A GOOD REPORTER DOESN'T COME HOME WITHOUT THE STORY!

“Lois & the Big One”

JAMI BERNARD writer **RENATO GUEDES** artist
NICK J. NAPOLITANO letterer

From SUPERMAN SECRET FILES comes this short story about Lois Lane's desire for the scoop on Superman...

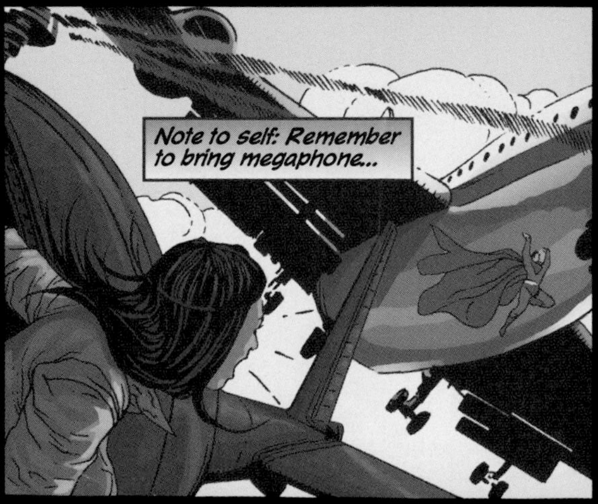
Note to self: Remember to bring megaphone...

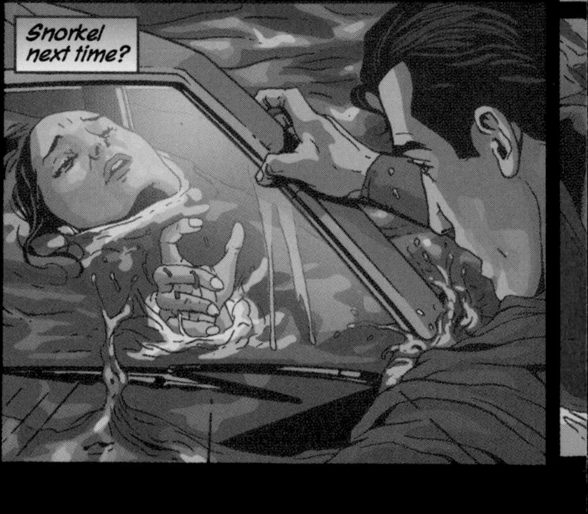
Snorkel next time?

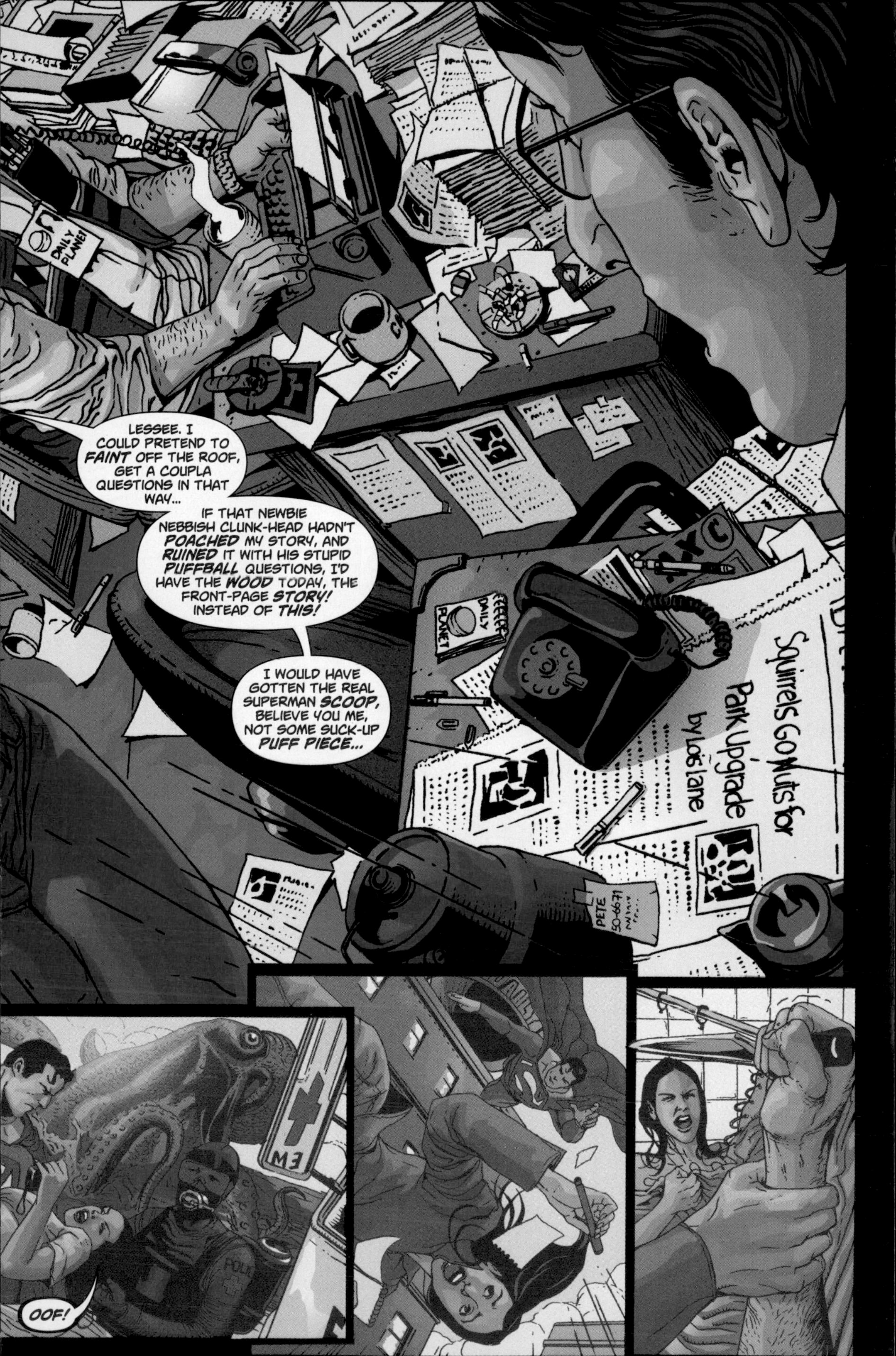
LESSEE. I COULD PRETEND TO FAINT OFF THE ROOF, GET A COUPLA QUESTIONS IN THAT WAY...
IF THAT NEWBIE NEBBISH CLUNK-HEAD HADN'T POACHED MY STORY, AND RUINED IT WITH HIS STUPID PUFFBALL QUESTIONS, I'D HAVE THE WOOD TODAY, THE FRONT-PAGE STORY! INSTEAD OF THIS!
I WOULD HAVE GOTTEN THE REAL SUPERMAN SCOOP, BELIEVE YOU ME, NOT SOME SUCK-UP PUFF PIECE...
DAILY PLANET
Squirrels Go Nuts for Park Upgrade
by Lois Lane
PETE
OOF!

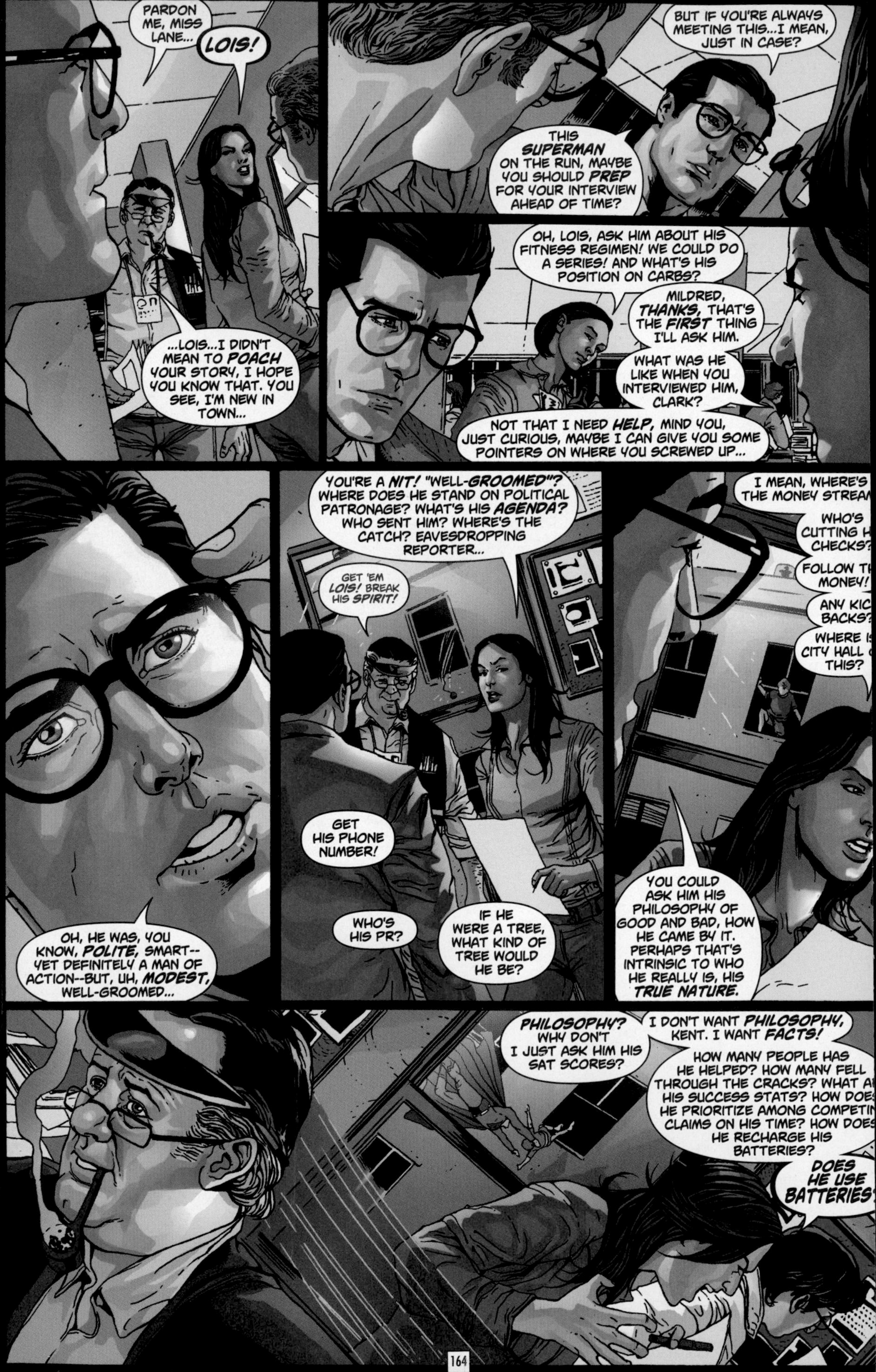
PARDON ME, MISS LANE...
LOIS!
...LOIS...I DIDN'T MEAN TO POACH YOUR STORY, I HOPE YOU KNOW THAT. YOU SEE, I'M NEW IN TOWN...
BUT IF YOU'RE ALWAYS MEETING THIS...I MEAN, JUST IN CASE?
THIS SUPERMAN ON THE RUN, MAYBE YOU SHOULD PREP FOR YOUR INTERVIEW AHEAD OF TIME?
OH, LOIS, ASK HIM ABOUT HIS FITNESS REGIMEN! WE COULD DO A SERIES! AND WHAT'S HIS POSITION ON CARBS?
MILDRED, THANKS, THAT'S THE FIRST THING I'LL ASK HIM.
WHAT WAS HE LIKE WHEN YOU INTERVIEWED HIM, CLARK?
NOT THAT I NEED HELP, MIND YOU, JUST CURIOUS, MAYBE I CAN GIVE YOU SOME POINTERS ON WHERE YOU SCREWED UP...
OH, HE WAS, YOU KNOW, POLITE, SMART--YET DEFINITELY A MAN OF ACTION--BUT, UH, MODEST, WELL-GROOMED...
YOU'RE A NIT! "WELL-GROOMED"? WHERE DOES HE STAND ON POLITICAL PATRONAGE? WHAT'S HIS AGENDA? WHO SENT HIM? WHERE'S THE CATCH? EAVESDROPPING REPORTER...
GET 'EM LOIS! BREAK HIS SPIRIT!
GET HIS PHONE NUMBER!
WHO'S HIS PR?
IF HE WERE A TREE, WHAT KIND OF TREE WOULD HE BE?
I MEAN, WHERE'S THE MONEY STREA
WHO'S CUTTING H CHECKS?
FOLLOW T MONEY!
ANY KIC BACKS?
WHERE I CITY HALL THIS?
YOU COULD ASK HIM HIS PHILOSOPHY OF GOOD AND BAD, HOW HE CAME BY IT. PERHAPS THAT'S INTRINSIC TO WHO HE REALLY IS, HIS TRUE NATURE.
PHILOSOPHY? WHY DON'T I JUST ASK HIM HIS SAT SCORES?
I DON'T WANT PHILOSOPHY, KENT. I WANT FACTS!
HOW MANY PEOPLE HAS HE HELPED? HOW MANY FELL THROUGH THE CRACKS? WHAT A HIS SUCCESS STATS? HOW DOES HE PRIORITIZE AMONG COMPETIN CLAIMS ON HIS TIME? HOW DOES HE RECHARGE HIS BATTERIES?
DOES HE USE BATTERIES

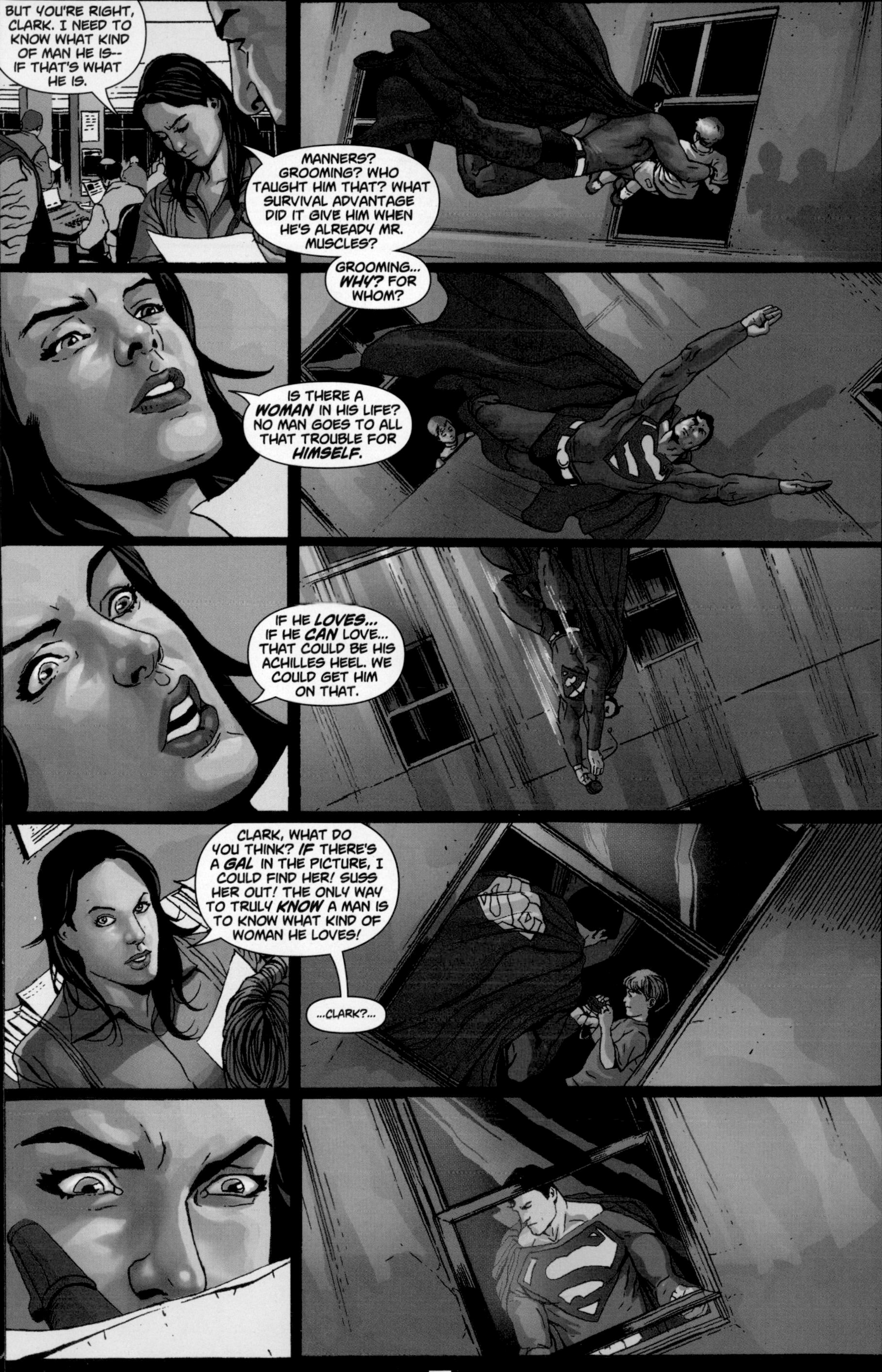
BUT YOU'RE RIGHT, CLARK. I NEED TO KNOW WHAT KIND OF MAN HE IS-- IF THAT'S WHAT HE IS.
MANNERS? GROOMING? WHO TAUGHT HIM THAT? WHAT SURVIVAL ADVANTAGE DID IT GIVE HIM WHEN HE'S ALREADY MR. MUSCLES?
GROOMING... WHY? FOR WHOM?
IS THERE A WOMAN IN HIS LIFE? NO MAN GOES TO ALL THAT TROUBLE FOR HIMSELF.
IF HE LOVES... IF HE CAN LOVE... THAT COULD BE HIS ACHILLES HEEL. WE COULD GET HIM ON THAT.
CLARK, WHAT DO YOU THINK? IF THERE'S A GAL IN THE PICTURE, I COULD FIND HER! SUSS HER OUT! THE ONLY WAY TO TRULY KNOW A MAN IS TO KNOW WHAT KIND OF WOMAN HE LOVES!
...CLARK?...

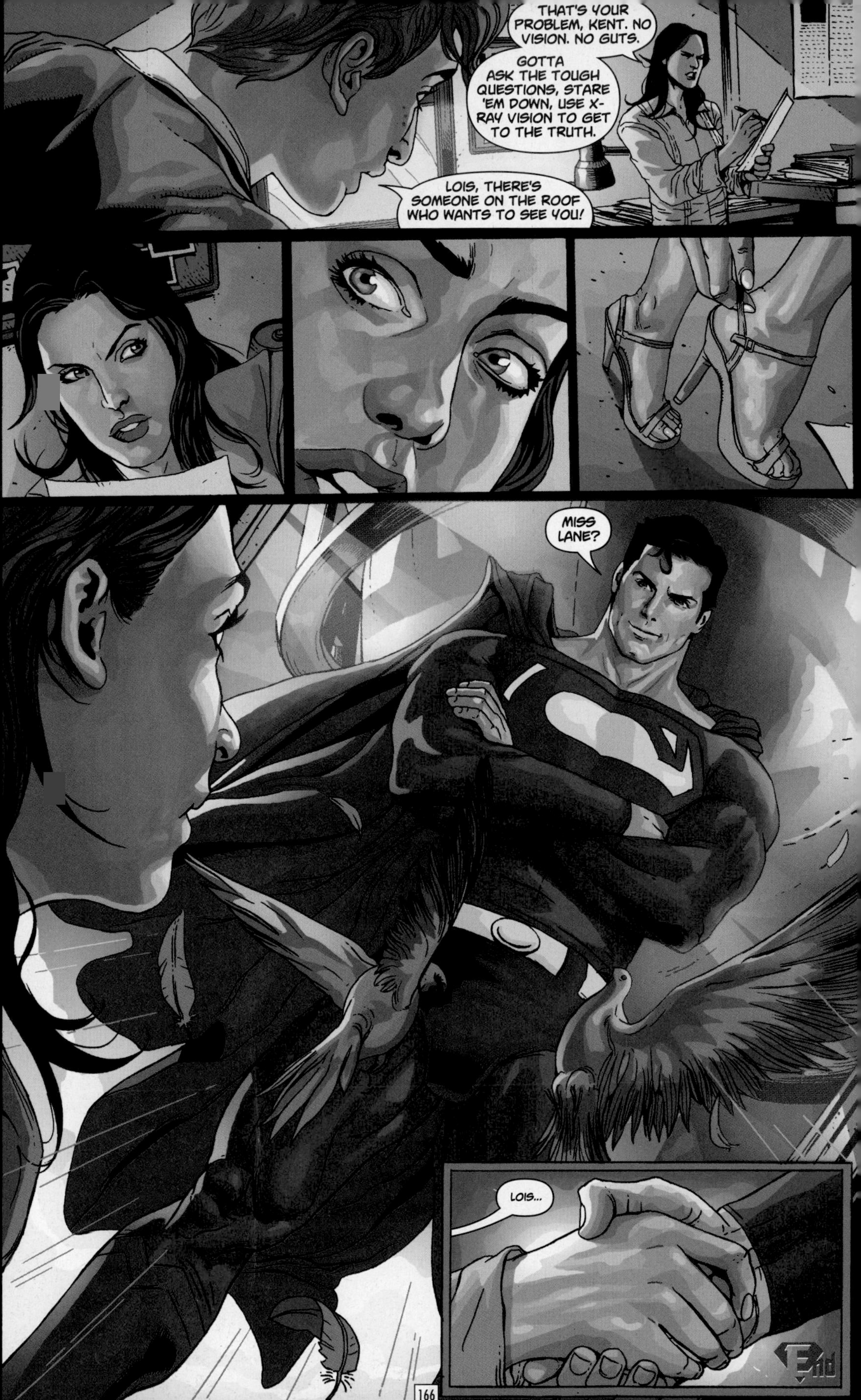
THAT'S YOUR PROBLEM, KENT. NO VISION. NO GUTS.
GOTTA ASK THE TOUGH QUESTIONS, STARE 'EM DOWN, USE X-RAY VISION TO GET TO THE TRUTH.
LOIS, THERE'S SOMEONE ON THE ROOF WHO WANTS TO SEE YOU!
MISS LANE?
LOIS...
End

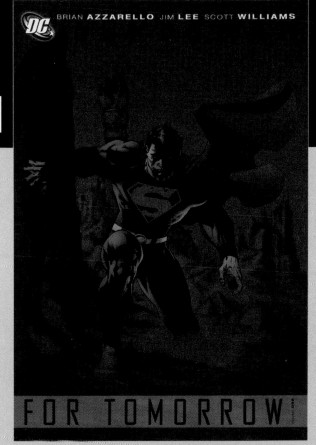
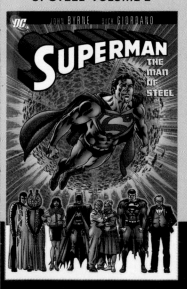

AND DON'T MISS THESE OTHER GREAT TITLES FEATURING **SUPERMAN!**

SUPERMAN: THE GREATEST STORIES EVER TOLD

**CURT SWAN
JOHN BYRNE
MIKE MIGNOLA**

SUPERMAN: SECRET IDENTITY

**KURT BUSIEK
STUART IMMONEN**

SUPERMAN: TRUE BRIT

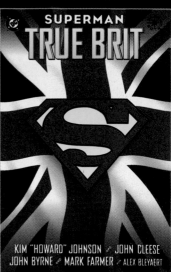

**KIM "HOWARD" JOHNSON
JOHN CLEESE
JOHN BYRNE**

SUPERMAN/BATMAN/ WONDER WOMAN: TRINITY

MATT WAGNER

SUPERMAN/BATMAN: PUBLIC ENEMIES

**JEPH LOEB
ED MCGUINNESS
DEXTER VINES**

SUPERMAN CHRONICLES VOL. 1

**JERRY SIEGEL
JOE SHUSTER**

SEARCH THE GRAPHIC NOVELS SECTION OF
WWW.TITANBOOKS.COM
FOR ART AND INFORMATION ON ALL OF OUR BOOKS!